THE SUN NEVER SETS...

Confronting the Network of Foreign U.S. Military Bases

Edited by Joseph Gerson and Bruce Birchard

A publication of the National Disarmament Program and the New England Regional Office of the American Friends Service Committee

South End Press
Boston, Massachusetts

Cover design by Nancy Adams
Cover photo by Kazuo Kuniyoshi, reprinted with permission from his
book, *Bases in Okinawa: Photographs* (Naha, Okinawa: Nirai Pub-
lishing, 1987)
Photo credits: Wolfgang Bartels, Fred Bronkema, Maria Socorro
Diokno, Melanie Friend, GABRIELA, Gensuikyo, Joseph Gerson, Eva
Gold, NARMIC, Erika Sulzer-Kleinmeier, UPI, and Reuters Photo
Libraries
Edited, designed, and produced by the South End Press collective
Manufactured in the U.S.A.

Library of Congress Cataloging-in-Publication Data
The sun never sets: confronting the network of foreign U.S. military
bases / edited by Joseph Gerson and Bruce Birchard.
p. cm.
Includes bibliographical references and index.
ISBN 0-89608-400-0: $40.00—ISBN 0-89608-399-3: $16.00
1. Military bases, American—Social aspects. 2. Militarism—United
States. I. Gerson, Joseph. II. Birchard, Bruce.
UA26.A2S86 1991
355.7'0973—dc 20

90-26605
CIP

South End Press, 116 Saint Botolph Street, Boston, MA 02115
99 98 97 96 95 94 93 92 91   1 2 3 4 5 6 7 8 9

THE SUN NEVER SETS...

Table of Contents

IV. THE MIDDLE EAST

V. CENTRAL AMERICA

VI. CONCLUSION

List of Tables

Acknowledgments

The Sun Never Sets could not have been written without the suggestions, support, and labor of countless people, many of whom are on the staff and committees of the American Friends Service Committee, and many of whom are political activists and researchers in the United States and in nations that suffer the presence of U.S. military bases. We are deeply indebted to far more people that we can mention here.

We must note our appreciation for the contributions of Roel Landingin and Christine Wing. Roel, an activist in the Philippine Anti-Bases Coalition, first proposed that we produce a book that would help to explain the meaning and impact of U.S. foreign military bases. Christine, who left AFSC for further studies in September 1989, served as co-director of AFSC's National Disarmament Program. In addition to writing the overview chapter on U.S. bases in the Pacific, Christine was our co-editor for more than a year. Christine played a critical role in conceptualizing and shaping this work; she deserves much of the credit and none of the blame for what the reader will find herein.

We want to thank the many analysts who contributed chapters to *The Sun Never Sets*. They endured and persevered through our editorial suggestions, and many went back to their word processors to revise their chapters as the dizzying pace of world events necessitated. Heartfelt thanks are due to Phyllis Cohen and Estella Smith who typed and retyped many of these chapters and attended to the daily details necessary to complete this work. Phyllis Cohen also made many helpful editorial suggestions. Karin Aguilar-San Juan, our editor at South End Press, was patient and understanding as we worked in needed revisions. Nora Lester gave a hand in our effort to meet final deadlines.

We also wish to thank Rob Leavitt, Randy Forsberg, and their colleagues at the Institute for Defense and Disarmament Studies, as well as Steve Kosiak and his colleagues at the Center for Defense Information for their help with research. Stephen G. Cary, Chairperson of the AFSC's Board of Directors, made substantial contributions to the concluding chapter. Gail Daneker, Saralee Hamilton, Corinne Johnson, Brenda Jones, Darryl Jordan, Michael Simmons, Joe Volk, and Warren Witte, all valued AFSC colleagues, made many substantial and helpful suggestions. For their work as translators, we thank Nancy Lukens and Tory Rhodin, as we do Jim O'Brien, who prepared the index.

Among the many people who made contributions to *The Sun Never Sets* we want to acknowledge here Feroz Ahmad, Angie Berryman, Phil Berryman, Courtney Cazden, Judy Claude, Pat Chilton, Tom Conrad, Rosemary Cubas, Burkhard Doempke, Brian Hall, Erich Schmidt-Eenboom, Dick Erstad, John Feffer, Roberta Foss, Nelson Foster, Humberto Garcia-Muniz, Brian Hall, Omer Karasapan, Michael Klare, Linda Love, Alfred Mechtersheimer, Everett Mendelsohn, Rajan Menon, Max Miller, Paula Rhodes, Joe Stork, Malcolm Spaven, John Sullivan, Gene Stoltzfus, Daniel Volman and Andreas Zumach.

Joseph Gerson wishes to express particular appreciation for the friendship, lessons, and visions shared by Vigfus Gierdal, of Iceland; Rieko Asato, Hiroshi Taka, and Shoji Niihara of Japan; and Maria Socorro Diokno and Charito Planas of the Philippines. Each of them led me to deeper understandings of foreign military bases, of national and human independence, of history, courage, and our common journey.

I should acknowledge the contributions of Senator Edward Kennedy (Democrat, MA) and Massachusetts Governor Michael Dukakis. Their failed attempt to transform Boston Harbor into a nuclear weapons base to homeport the battleship Iowa and its task force exposed our community to many of the lies, distortions, and dangers that come with military bases. Resistance to the homeporting proposal led us to understand what many people in "host" nations experience and to begin working in solidarity with them. I owe the deepest gratitude to Tony Palomba and others in the Boston area who opposed the homeporting proposal. Our struggle led to lessons, work, and unexpected and valuable friendships with people in the Pacific and the European nations of the North Atlantic.

This is a moment to remember and to be thankful for my father, Leon Gerson. In his all too brief life he helped raise my vision beyond the shores of the United States in the 1950s. His way of life was a quiet lesson in the pursuit of truth and justice. I must also thank Daniel Boone Schirmer and Wilfred Desan who helped prepare the way in different ways, and Mark Reader who has always encouraged *bon mots*. Roy Takumi's early appreciation of the importance of foreign military bases as a peace and justice issue was an important source of practical and moral support. More than appreciation is due to my wife, Lani Gerson, whose contributions to this book are many. My children, Leon and

Hannah, have not only patiently endured the process, but their lives have been enriched by the friendship of many of the people who made this book possible.

Joseph Gerson
Cambridge, MA

Bruce Birchard has a very special word of thanks to say to the women who participated in the AFSC "Voices of Hope and Anger" nationwide speaking tour in April 1989: Maria Socorro Diokno of the Philippines, Maria Isabel Fidalgo of Puerto Rico, Lilo Klug of the Federal Republic of Germany, Elzbieta Piwowarska of Poland, Marta Sandoval of Honduras, Aurora Camacho de Schmidt of Philadelphia, Fulani Sunni Ali of Atlanta, Suzuyo Takazato of Okinawa, Japan, and Yu Bok Nim of Korea. From my month with them, I learned much about the impact of foreign militaries on their peoples, and about the courage and commitment of women who struggle daily against violence and oppression.

So many colleagues, friends, and acquaintances in the AFSC, the Religious Society of Friends, and peace and justice movements in the United States, India, the Philippines, and Europe have contributed to whatever understanding I have of these issues. I would like to express particular appreciation to two who got me started, David McAllester and George Lakey, and to my AFSC colleague for five years, Christine Wing.

My wife, Dr. Demie Kurz, has been working on my political education for 21 years; for this and for constant support I thank her always. Julie Forsythe, Tom Hoskins, and Stephanie Judson all helped keep me going when the times got rough. Along with them my children, Ethan and Joshua, my parents, "June" and Bea, and my brother Rob have provided the love I need to keep working for peace and justice.

Bruce Birchard
Philadelphia, PA

October 1990

Preface

The Sun Never Sets: Confronting the Global Network of Foreign U.S. Military Bases has been a project of the American Friends Service Committee's National Disarmament Program and the AFSC's New England Peace Education Program. The experience and observations of many AFSC staff and programs in the United States and abroad, as well as those of many people outside the AFSC, led the editors and their committees to the decision to prepare this book. The American Friends Service Committee is indebted to the editors: Joseph Gerson, Peace Education Secretary of AFSC's New England Regional Office, who initially suggested the project, and Bruce Birchard, National Coordinator of the AFSC's Disarmament Program.

The AFSC wants to stimulate public discussion about U.S. foreign military bases, installations, and deployments in the hope that such discussion will eventually lead to better policies and greater security for all people. The book is not an official pronouncement of the AFSC, but it does follow a series of AFSC studies that have challenged the commonly accepted assumptions that peace and justice can be won with military threats.

This series of AFSC books began in 1949 with the publication of *The United States and the Soviet Union*. The series was continued in 1951 with *Steps to Peace*, and in 1952 with *Toward Security through Disarmament*. *Speak Truth to Power: a Quaker Search for an Alternative to Violence* was published in 1955, and was followed by a series of booklets entitled "Beyond Deterrence..." Our challenge to containment and anti-communism was put forth in 1969 in *Anatomy of Anti-Communism*. In 1970, we looked especially at the Israeli-Palestinian conflict in our study *Search for Peace in the Middle East*. We put forward a call to U.S. citizens to practice active nonviolence with the publication of James Bristol's *Nonviolence: Not First for Export* in 1972. In 1989, we took another look at the Middle East in *A Compassionate Peace: A Future for Israel, Palestine, and the Middle East*, and we analyzed the dramatic changes in East-West relations in *Beyond Detente: Soviet Foreign Policy and U.S. Options* in 1990.

Present historical events validate AFSC's basic analysis. Still, there has been no change in the consciousness of U.S. power holders. The same misunderstanding of the world and its common future continues to influence U.S. foreign policy, especially in the Third World. In 1955, Stephen G. Cary, chairperson of the *Speak Truth to Power* working group wrote:

> ...There is now almost no place in our great universities, few lines in the budgets of our great foundations, and little space in scholarly journals, for thought and experimentation that begin with the unconditional rejection of organized mass violence and seek to think through the concrete problems of present international relations in new terms. It is time there was...

In 1990, in the United States, we are watching a government and a military establishment search frantically for new enemies to replace the enemies lost when nonviolent, popular revolutions deposed communist regimes in Eastern Europe and the "Soviet threat" evaporated. Instead of redefining our national purpose and converting our national resources to peace and civilian needs, our policy makers appear bent on redirecting military force, not de-militarizing policy and de-mobilizing troops.

Drug traffickers, third world terrorists, dark-robed mullahs, Marxist-Leninist revolutionaries, and certain Arab despots (but not others) compose the new class of enemies. If we begin to disarm along the East-West axis, U.S. strategic policy planners tell us, we must be prepared to deter, destroy, and replace these newly developing threats from the South. This new doctrine is called discriminate deterrence, and it uses a war of attrition method called low-intensity conflict or "LIC"—bringing low-intensity effects for people living in the United States, but high-intensity suffering, death, and destruction to the people of developing countries where LIC is used.

As Albert Camus remarked in *Neither Victim Nor Executioner,* the seventeenth century will be remembered as the century of the mathematical sciences, the eighteenth as the century of the physical sciences, the nineteenth as the century of the biological sciences, and the twentieth as the century of war, when all the sciences and technologies were put together to cause and threaten mass destruction. Recent events throughout Eastern Europe and the Soviet Union suggest that the end of the twentieth century may be remembered as the century of democracy and the renunciation of armed struggle—a century of people power. Current U.S. policy, as described in *The Sun Never Sets,* seems determined to prove Camus right.

As in AFSC's Board statement on Central America, "Breaking with a Bitter Past," we appeal to the U.S. government and to all U.S. citizens to give up the claim to a "Manifest Destiny," the "God-given" duty to make things "right" throughout the world, and especially in U.S. "spheres of influence." It is not too late to join other nations of the world in developing non-military arrangements for common security and equitable sharing of the world's resources.

Joe Volk
National Secretary for Peace Education
American Friends Service Committee

February 8, 1990

"We stand by the Philippines. We stand by you, sir. We love your adherence to democratic principles and to the democratic process, and we will not leave you in isolation."

—Toast by Vice President George Bush to
Ferdinand Marcos in Manila, 1981

"Why do I want to sell the country?" said the Prime Minister. "Because my conscience tells me to...What is Iceland for the Icelanders? Nothing. Only the West matters for the North. We live for the West; we die for the West; one West. Small nation?—dirt. The East shall be wiped out. The dollar shall stand."

—Halldor Laxness, Icelandic Recipient of the Nobel Prize
for Literature, from the novel The Atom Station

"Even the toughest truth expressed publicly...suddenly becomes liberating."

—Vaclav Havel, Disturbing the Peace

Part I: Introduction

Chapter 1

The Sun Never Sets

Joseph Gerson

> Providing for the defense of other countries is a source of American influence and regional stability. It affects the way Western Europe and Japan respond to U.S. interests in the economic as well as the military and political areas.[1]
>
> —*Joseph Nye*

> If anything, the global conditions that led us to make these uses of force (in Korea, Vietnam, and Grenada) are likely to be even more important in the future...*Glasnost* does not change the fact that there has been an average of more than 25 civil and international conflicts in the developing world every year since the end of World War II...[2]
>
> —*Senator John McCain*

As the Berlin Wall collapsed, so did the ideological underpinnings of the Cold War. The U.S. government's 45-year-old rationale for the deployment of more than half a million troops around the world, with their arsenals of conventional and nuclear weapons on 375 major foreign military bases and installations lay in ruins. Hope rose that their toll on the U.S. economy and values, and on the sovereignty, self-determination, human rights, and cultures of host nations would be lifted. But, as economic and political pressures forced reductions in U.S. military spending, and significant reductions of U.S. forces in Europe were planned, political and military leaders sought new enemies to justify the forward deployment of U.S. military forces. They hoped to ensure that the United States would remain a European power, an Asian power, and the dominant power in the Third World.

Seven months later, when Saddam Hussein invaded Kuwait, George Bush seized upon the event to assert the United States' post-Cold War role: policeman and enforcer of the world order. One-quarter of all U.S. military forces and more than half of its combat strength were deployed to the Middle East, including half of the Navy's aircraft carriers and battle ships, three-quar-

3

ters of all Marine combat forces, and two-thirds of the Army's most modern heavy battle tank units. Bases in Europe were used as transit points, as armories, and as hospitals, to support "out-of-area" operations in the Middle East and Persian Gulf. Bases and facilities in Japan and the Philippines disgorged Marines and the nuclear-armed aircraft carrier task forces. Bases built and assembled in Saudi Arabia, Bahrain, Oman, and Egypt to support the Rapid Deployment Force (RDF) and Central Command served an armada of aircraft that landed every 10 minutes with U.S. troops and equipment.

In truth, the United States began building its foreign military bases long before the beginning of the Cold War. In 1898, Teddy Roosevelt and his Rough Riders "liberated" Cuba from Spain, and in the same year Admiral Dewey sailed into Manila Bay and destroyed the Spanish fleet. Five years later, and only months after the United States had completed its brutal war against Filipino nationalists, President Roosevelt "bought" Panama from Colombia and began integrating Panama into the U.S. infrastructure. Hundreds of thousands of people died as U.S. soldiers brought "American values," if not the U.S. "way of life," with their bayonets so that the United States could build strategically important foreign military bases. These bases, in turn, were constructed to make the United States a maritime power and to give U.S. corporations privileged access to regional markets, natural resources, and cheap labor.[3]

Even before the United States unilaterally used its global basing structure to airlift 400,000 troops to Saudi Arabia, the United Arab Emirates, and the Persian Gulf in late 1990, the Bush Administration had signalled that the collapse of the Cold War would mean continuity as well as change. In December 1989, as pieces of the Berlin Wall were being sold in U.S. suburban shopping centers, the hangar of a U.S. base in Panama was used to swear in Guillermo Endara as President of Panama moments before 35,000 U.S. soldiers, sailors, and marines invaded the country to install the new government. In a battle that was ostensibly fought as a skirmish in the "War on Drugs," the Bush Administration ensured continued U.S. access to bases in Panama and its domination of the Panama Canal. That same month, the Bush Administration also displayed its military muscles in the Philippines. According to *Jane's Defence Weekly,* 20,000 U.S. troops were secretly moved to U.S. bases in the Philippines in anticipation of a military coup. During the attempted coup, an additional 12,000 troops in Hawaii were placed on alert for possible deployment to Manila in the event that "persuasion" flights over the capital failed to guarantee the survival of the Aquino government— Washington's best bet for preserving access to its strategically important bases in the Philippines.[4] Heartened by the quick victories in Panama and the Philippines, and by the outcome of the 10-year "low-intensity" *contra* war against the Sandinistas in Nicaragua, the Bush Administration had also turned its attention to Cuba. In the early months of 1990, the naval base at Guantanamo served as the focal point for increasingly aggressive naval exercises designed to increase pressure on the isolated Cuban government.[5]

As they turned their attention to Europe, President Bush and his strategic planners worked to create new doctrines that would allow the United States to remain a continental power. "Uncertainty and instability" replaced the ideology of a Soviet threat, and in the fog of public debate it became unclear whether the U.S. forces sought to contain German or Soviet power in Europe. Political leaders and planners described how U.S. and Soviet troops, based in Germany and other European countries, could influence German reunification. They sought to develop a "less military, more political NATO" in order to retain a dominant role for the United States in an increasingly independent Europe. Little was said, however, about scenarios for U.S. forces based in Europe to participate in "out-of-area" operations in North Africa or the Middle East which would soon be implemented.

With international concern riveted on Europe as the Soviet Empire collapsed and Germany reunited, little public attention in the United States was focused on the future of the massive U.S. basing structure in the Pacific and on the periphery of Asia. Behind closed doors, minor modifications of the structures of U.S. power in the Pacific were planned. Token force reductions were announced by the Pentagon to pacify the Congressional pursuit of a "peace dividend" and to hedge against the possible loss of bases in the Philippines. President Bush, Defense Secretary Cheney, and their deputies spoke in unequivocal terms that the United States would remain, "eternally," an Asian power.

On the same day that Iraq invaded Kuwait, the Pentagon's plans for the post-Cold War era were leaked to the press in the form of a confidential report presented to President Bush, Secretary Cheney, and General Colin Powell, the chair of the Joint Chiefs-of-Staff. While the plan called for the gradual reduction of U.S. forces from 2.1 million to 1.6 million troops, it relied on foreign deployments, rapid deployment of U.S. forces based in the United States, and the use of reserve Army divisions to bring the military up to "full strength" in time of war. The blueprint sought to organize the U.S. military into four integrated components: 1) an Atlantic Force that would preserve U.S. interests in Europe and respond to threats to U.S. dominance of the Persian Gulf; 2) a Pacific Force that would "emphasize naval and tactical air units" to retain U.S. power in Asia and the Pacific; 3) a "Contingency Force" for rapid deployment in the Third World and to serve as "the leading edge in major American military intervention;" and 4) the "Strategic Force" of long-range nuclear weapons.[6]

Critical Juncture for U.S. Foreign Military Bases

The global infrastructure of U.S. overseas bases, assembled over a century of expansion, conquest, and intervention, has arrived at a critical juncture. Demands for major reductions of U.S. forces based abroad are being voiced by people in Europe, the Pacific, many third world nations, and the United States. These pressures are compounded by the fact that many U.S. basing agreements with countries such as Portugal, Morocco, the Philippines, Kenya, Oman, and Turkey are scheduled to expire between 1990 and 1994. With the U.S. economy less competitive internationally than in the past, pressures for reduced military security have been reinforced by an electorate that understands that economic security can be more important than military spending. People in the United States, and in nations that "host" U.S. bases, have thus been presented an historic opportunity to dismantle the global infrastructure of foreign military bases and installations that has necessitated and reinforced foreign military intervention, and that has made possible planning for fighting and "winning" nuclear war. In the 1990s we are in a unique position to construct new structures of security based on interdependence, democratic values, and respect for self-determination that allow for our economic well-being and the environmental survival of the planet.

Since toppling Hawaii's Queen Liliuokalani in 1893—an event that marked Hawaii's first stage of transformation from a Pacific paradise to a forward military base—the United States has assembled a global basing structure to support foreign military intervention, and since 1945, nuclear war. By the end of World War II, the United States had constructed a worldwide network of foreign military bases and installations. In 1989, more than 525,000 U.S. military personnel were deployed at bases and installations around the world. Nearly half (230,000) were based in the Federal Republic of Germany, with another 125,000 deployed elsewhere in Europe. There were 48,000 forces in Japan, 44,000 in South Korea, and approximately 50,000 elsewhere in Asia, the Pacific, Africa, the Middle East, Latin America, and the Caribbean.

Defining Terms

Because there is no clear agreement on the distinctions between military bases, installations, and facilities, we ask our readers' patience to allow us to define our terms. Robert Harkavy, in his recent book *Bases Abroad*, makes the useful distinction between "bases," in which "the user nation has unrestricted access and freedom to operate," and "facilities," in which the host nation exerts ultimate sovereignty. While this is a helpful distinction, there is no clear dividing line between the two.

U.S. Military Bases Worldwide

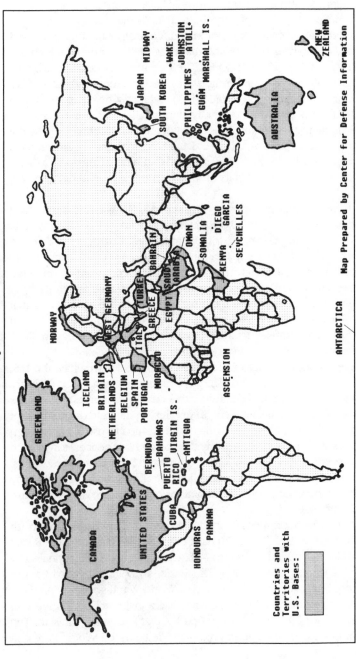

U.S. Military Bases Worldwide. Reprinted with the permission of the Center for Defense Information.

Readers will also discover that foreign military bases differ greatly in size and function. For example, the United States maintains an enormous network of military facilities for "command, control, communication, and intelligence," known in military shorthand as "C3I," many of which are operated by only a few U.S. personnel. The Department of Defense's lists of U.S. foreign military bases and installations do not mention these smaller facilities, nor do they mention facilities in Honduras, where between 1,000 and 6,000 U.S. troops were constantly deployed during the *contra* war against Nicaragua. Department of Defense documents also omit the growing U.S. military presence in Peru, where U.S. military "advisers" are directing the "anti-drug war" against Peruvian peasants and the Shining Path guerillas. Also omitted are "Saudi Arabian" military bases which are, in everything but name, U.S. bases.

To further complicate matters, most large U.S. military bases include several separate facilities, each with different functions. For the large U.S. Army base in Stuttgart, Germany, for example, the Department of Defense lists 16 installations in different locations in Stuttgart and five surrounding towns, yet they are all listed as one base. With these complications in mind, we find the Center for Defense Information's conservative estimate of 375 U.S. foreign military bases to be the most functional.[7] We note as well that William Arkin and Richard Fieldhouse, in an exhaustive study of the United States' global nuclear infrastructure, list more than 1,500 U.S. foreign military facilities involved in preparations for nuclear war.

These numbers do not include ports and airfields to which the U.S. military has regular access. The U.S. government has negotiated "military access agreements" with many countries that enable U.S. forces to use these facilities for refueling, replenishment of supplies, repairs, and operations. For example, Liberia has allowed U.S. aircraft and ships to use a port and an airfield for landing and refueling at any time on 24-hour notice. However, in Pentagon parlance, this does not constitute a base. Such access agreements, in which the host nation retains sovereign control over the facilities used by U.S. forces, are becoming common as nations become increasingly sensitive to sovereignty issues.

Though this book focuses on U.S. foreign military bases, it is worth bearing in mind that, as Bruce Birchard describes in Chapter 3, the Soviet Union has also assembled a powerful—if disintegrating—international infrastructure of foreign military bases. The Soviet army that liberated Eastern Europe from Nazi occupation at the end of World War II stayed to impose a Stalinist order. For many years, the Soviets had a major military presence in Mongolia, and for 10 years Soviet troops were at war in Afghanistan. The Soviet Union also acquired access rights in Vietnam, the Middle East, and

Africa. The presence of a 3,000-man Soviet "combat brigade" in Cuba served, in 1979, as President Jimmy Carter's rationale for suspending efforts to ratify the second Strategic Arms Limitation Treaty. But the present reality is that the Soviet foreign military presence is being sharply reduced due to the revolutionary changes in Eastern Europe and pressures from within the Soviet Union.

When it announced troop reductions in 1989, the Soviet Union had 627,000 troops deployed in 19 nations.[8] More than half (380,000) were based in the German Democratic Republic. Nearly a quarter (185,000) were deployed in Hungary, Poland, and Czechoslovakia. Nearly all of these forces are slated for repatriation to the Soviet Union within the next four years. The remaining 62,000 troops were in third world nations.

Other countries, including France, the United Kingdom, India, and Pakistan, also have military forces in other nations. However, while these foreign military deployments also undermine democracy, self-determination, and security, the number of troops they deploy abroad does not begin to compare with those of the United States and the Soviet Union.

Numbers, however, fail to communicate the deeper meanings of foreign military bases, and they are not the primary focus of *The Sun Never Sets*. Bases bring insecurity; the loss of self-determination, human rights, and sovereignty; as well as the degradation of the culture, values, health, and environment of host nations. Foreign military bases are designed to integrate host nations into U.S. military strategies and structures. The people of Okinawa, Guam, the Philippines, and Korea thus became deeply engaged in the U.S. war in Indochina. Communities in countries such as Britain, Germany, Iceland, Italy, and Turkey have been transformed and endangered as the United States prepared to launch nuclear war from their soil. As the rhetoric of the "Cold War" grew stale, and as ancient patterns of gunboat diplomacy became transparent, people in many host countries increasingly understood the vital connections between their work against militarism and foreign bases and their struggles for democracy, freedom, self-determination, and real security. Raul Landingan, a young Filipino anti-bases activist, initially suggested that the American Friends Service Committee write *The Sun Never Sets*. It was his hope that if the people of the United States learned what is being done in their name, they would work for the withdrawal of foreign military forces and for the democratic values that we have so long espoused.

While the toll of U.S. bases on the people and societies of host nations is more immediately visible than its toll on the people of the United States, there are many similarities. Military bases corrupt what remains of our national commitment to democratic values, and they alienate us from people with whom we share the planet. Military forces endanger our lives by increasing the likelihood that conflicts will escalate into wars, and they drain our national economic, ecological, and spiritual resources. Simply on the level of economic security, forward-deployed U.S. forces and U.S.-based forces for foreign intervention cost the United States more than $200 billion per year—a staggering *two-thirds* of the total military budget. This money could be used for investment in housing, education, health care, infrastructure repairs, and for the research and development needed to boost the competitiveness of U.S. industries. Paradoxically, the pursuit of security through conquest and global militarization has made the United States less secure and less independent.

Historical Background

Opposition among the people of the United States to foreign military bases has deep roots in U.S. history. In pre-Revolutionary times, people in England's North American colonies were angered by the presence of British and mercenary troops in their midst. When tensions between the colonies and England intensified after the imposition of the Quebec Act in 1763, the presence of British troops and bases became a focal point of the colonists' anger. The struggle was particularly bitter in New York, where the colonial assembly refused to make provisions for housing British soldiers as required under British law. In response, the English Crown suspended the New York Assembly until it bowed to British demands four years later. In the words of historian Charles Beard, "the necessity of housing and supplying British soldiers stirred up wrath among the residents of the colony."[9]

In New England tensions between colonists and British soldiers led to the Boston Massacre in 1770, and to the burning of a British naval vessel in Narragansett Bay by Rhode Island colonists in 1772. When the British Parliament enacted new laws to suppress colonial uprisings such as the Boston Tea Party, it explicitly demanded that Massachusetts towns host British troops. When the final break between the colonies and England came, the Declaration of Independence cited the fact that King George had "kept among us, in times of peace, Standing Armies" as one of the "abuses and usurpations" that justified the Revolutionary War.

The lesson was not long remembered, and the once colonized became colonizers. Alfred Thayer Mahan, a naval officer, historian, and friend of President Theodore Roosevelt, is widely recognized as the intellectual father of the United States' global network of bases. Mahan argued that, with the United States' continental empire established, its "manifest destiny" would lead it to Asia and Europe.[10] Mahan's reading of history, particularly of the rise of commercial trading powers such as Venice, Holland, and Britain, led him to conclude that the United States could become an "island power." This would require that the United States exercise control over the world's oceans. This, in turn, necessitated the construction of a powerful navy and a network of foreign military bases that could provide fuel, supplies, and repairs.

Between 1890 and the beginning of World War II, the United States gradually fulfilled Mahan's vision while competing with European colonial powers and Japan. As Christine Wing recounts in her overview of U.S. bases in the Pacific (Chapter 7), Hawaii was the United States' first such major acquisition. U.S. settlers overthrew Queen Liliuokalani, established a "republic," negotiated two annexation treaties with the U.S. government, and by 1900 had led the way for Hawaii to became a formal territory of the United States. But fears that "Japan and the European powers were going to divide China among themselves"[11] spurred the McKinley Administration to move beyond Hawaii. Spanish repression in Cuba, sensationalized through William Randolph Hearst's "yellow journals," and the sinking of the battleship Maine in Havana harbor, provided the rationale for McKinley to launch a war to gain Spain's strategically located colonies. The Philippines (with its exceptional port at Subic Bay), Guam, Puerto Rico, and Cuba thus became U.S. dominions, though it took another five years, and the deaths of an estimated 616,000 Filipinos, to subdue nationalist forces in the Philippines.[12]

Slowly, other bases on the Galapagos Islands, the Azores, and Liberia became links in the imperial chain. The United States assumed control of British bases in the North Atlantic and Caribbean in 1940-41. The transfer was legitimized through the Destroyer-Base and the Lend Lease agreements between Washington and London.

The second phase in the development of the United States' global military network came with the era of *Pax Americana,* from the end of World War II to the U.S. defeat in Indochina. These bases reinforced what Richard Barnett has described as the "four pillars" of U.S. foreign policy.[13] The first pillar was "nuclear deterrence." This involved the manufacture and deployment of more than 12,000 deterrent and first-strike nuclear weapons. The United States repeatedly threatened to use this nuclear arsenal in response to a Soviet attack on Europe *and* to prevent the Soviet Union from countering U.S. military interventions—particularly in the Third World.[14] The second pillar was the organization of a "global coalition," maintained by political and military alliances, and ostensibly designed to "contain" the Soviet Union. The third pillar was the commitment to intervene if necessary to maintain U.S. hegemony in the Third World. The fourth pillar was the liberal international economic order based on "free trade" and dominated by the United States.

Even before the defeat of Germany and Japan, the United States began consolidating control over what it described as "the Grand Area," a "global system that the United States would dominate and within which U.S. business interests would thrive...subordinated to the needs of the U.S. economy."[15] Perhaps the largest imperial domain in history, "the Grand Area" was conceived to include the entire globe, excepting only the Soviet Union, Eastern Europe, and later China.

With the creation of the North Atlantic Treaty Organization, the Central Treaty Organization, the Southeast Asia Treaty Organization, the ANZUS Pact, and bilateral treaties with Japan, South Korea, and Taiwan, the United States consolidated its political and military power through coalitions and reconfirmed access to many bases built during the war or secured through war-time victories. By one count, 70 nations hosted U.S. bases and installations immediately following World War II.[16] These alliances provided the United States with an unprecedented basing structure that could be used across the entire spectrum of conventional and strategic nuclear warfare. The Soviet Union was thus encircled by U.S. and allied forces, by U.S. nuclear weapons, and by the world's most sophisticated command, control, communications, and intelligence infrastructure. While U.S.-Soviet conflicts in this period were limited to nuclear threats and proxy wars, the global network of U.S. foreign military bases was employed to support *more than 200* U.S. military interventions in the Third World by the United States: Vietnam, Cambodia, Lebanon, Libya, Zaire, Dominican Republic, the Islamic Republic of Iran, Cuba, and Guatemala to name but a few.[17]

The post-war consolidation of the war-time network of bases was not universally supported by the United States' Western allies. Iceland, a small nation with no military of its own, joined NATO reluctantly and only on the condition that there would be no military troops based in the country during peacetime. Even this compromise, which Icelandic nationalists knew would leave Keflavik airbase in U.S. hands, sparked a bloody conflict outside the parliament. Within two years "peacetime" ended for Iceland. Though this small Nordic nation was thousands of miles from Korea, the United States used the pretext of the Korean war to reintroduce U.S. troops into Iceland.[18] The people of Iceland were not the only ones to resist their consolidation into the U.S. military structure. As described in the chapters that follow, farmers in Okinawa, Guam, and Puerto Rico have refused to sign contracts ceding their land to the United States for military bases.

The third phase in the development of the United States' basing network came with the decline of the Cold War. A process described as "decoupling" began when the interests of U.S. elites diverged increasingly from those in economically reconstructed Europe and Japan, the "newly industrialized countries," and the no longer "newly independent" nations. Governments in host nations began to insist upon more restrictive terms for access to bases in their countries. In some cases, U.S. bases were formally returned to host nations, ostensibly becoming NATO, Philippine, or Japanese bases, to ease growing nationalistic pressures. In Turkey, the Philippines, Greece, and Portugal, where U.S. bases were once welcomed free of charge, the United States found itself paying rent in the form of hundreds of millions of dollars of foreign and military aid.

In the late 1970s, shortly after the Soviet Union found itself struggling to compensate for lost access to bases in Albania, Egypt, and Somalia, "national security" planners in Washington were seeking alternative sites for U.S. installations and bases. After the Shah of Iran was overthrown in 1978, as Denis Doyon describes in Chapter 13, the Carter and Reagan Administrations redoubled efforts to build or maintain intelligence installations in Turkey, China, Pakistan, and Norway for espionage against the Soviet Union. New U.S. bases were built in Oman, Bahrain, Somalia, and Kenya, and new access agreements were negotiated with Egypt and Israel to support the Rapid Deployment Force (later renamed the Central Command). When New Zealand banned nuclear-armed and nuclear-powered ships from its ports, the Reagan Administration retaliated by ousting the former ally from the ANZUS pact and by denying it vital naval intelligence lest the "Kiwi disease" become contagious. In the late 1980s, as opposition to U.S. bases in the Philippines mounted, contingency plans were developed to reassign the forces and missions based at Subic Bay and Clark Air Field to bases in Palau (also known as Belau), Guam, Japan, Singapore, and Brunei.

Missions

It has long been argued that U.S. overseas bases serve four principal missions.[19] They have been used to project "conventional" military power, to prepare for and to launch nuclear war, to serve as tripwires guaranteeing a U.S. military response to attack (as in the cases of Germany and Korea), and to serve as symbols of U.S. power, influence, and ambitions. They serve other purposes as well.

In the post-war era, U.S. bases have played a critical role in maintaining U.S. dominance in much of the Third World. Bases such as Torrejón in Spain, Palmerola in Honduras, Al Jufair in Bahrain, and Camp Courtney in Okinawa are primarily designed to support U.S. power projection and non-nuclear military intervention in third world countries. These bases played key roles in the United States' war in Indochina, the *contra* war against Nicaragua, the 1987 U.S. intervention in the Iran-Iraq war, and the 1990-91 U.S. intervention in the Gulf.

More than 1,500 U.S. foreign military installations are part of the U.S. nuclear warfighting infrastructure. U.S. nuclear weapons are based in seven

NATO countries and in Korea, and they pass through many other countries aboard U.S. ships and aircraft. As many chapters in this book illustrate, elements of this far-flung nuclear warfare infrastructure include C3I facilities, storage depots, and launch pads for intermediate range and tactical nuclear weapons and for nuclear testing and training ranges.

While some U.S. bases are designed for nuclear warfighting, and others support intervention and "low-intensity conflicts" in the Third World, still others are designed to serve as tripwires. U.S. forces stationed in South Korea and in West Germany were deployed there partly to insure that an attack by the Soviet Union (or North Korea) would "inevitably result in U.S. involvement."[20]

The fourth, and symbolic, purpose is served by bases such as the Navy's outpost in Guantanamo, Cuba. Initially designed to dominate the Caribbean and to support sea lines of communication, Guatanamo now stands primarily as a symbol of continued U.S. power and determination in the Caribbean.[21]

Two related missions, closely linked to classical imperialism, are also served by foreign military bases. Admiral Mahan was clear that if the United States were to dominate trade with China, it required foreign military bases to support an interventionist Navy. Since that time, U.S. bases in the Asia/Pacific region, Central America, the Middle East, and elsewhere in the Third World have ensured that U.S. economic interests have privileged access to the resources, labor, and markets of these regions. Finally, U.S. forces abroad are used to influence and limit the political, diplomatic, and economic initiatives of host nations. Thus, U.S. military bases in Panama and the Philippines were used in December 1989 to overthrow one national leader (Noriega in Panama) and to protect another (Aquino in the Philippines.) This mission is also evident in Germany, where U.S. forces were used to influence the process of German reunification. (Moscow also used its troops in the former German Democratic Republic in the same manner.)

Bases, Sovereignty, and Independence

Sovereignty and independence are complex and elusive concepts in an increasingly interdependent world, yet they lie at the heart of popular resentment against foreign military installations. People in many countries "hosting" U.S., Soviet, and other foreign military forces rightly ask: "Who exercises supreme authority, our government or the foreign power?" It was easy for people in the United States to support Czech, Polish, and German resistance to Soviet domination of their countries. Our colonial origins also helped us to identify with the resistance of Tahitian and other Pacific island nations to French military bases and nuclear testing in their midst. Yet, because so many people in the United States want to believe that U.S. troops and bases have been deployed around the world to do good, it has been more difficult to understand why our allies and the people we "protect" oppose U.S. bases in their countries.

Puerto Rico and Guam, the sites of strategically important U.S. bases, and Palau—which has been discussed as a fall-back site for U.S. bases in the Philippines—are U.S. colonies in everything but name. In these nations, islands have been depopulated, farmland and fishing waters have been seized, and, in the case of Palau, referenda rejecting the use of scarce land for U.S. military bases have been repeatedly ignored by the U.S. authorities. Elsewhere, colonies of U.S. allies, such as Greenland and Diego Garcia, also have been incorporated within the U.S. global military system.

Though most U.S. forces in Greenland are outside the NATO command, the creation of NATO was used to legitimize the U.S. presence in this Danish colony. To this day, Greenland remains strategically important in U.S. efforts to remain the militarily dominant power in the North Atlantic and Arctic regions, yet Greenland's people are not accorded the respect one would expect to be shown to allies. Instead, as one report put it, "Greenlanders are declared incompetent, and even Copenhagen can have no influence on what is happening militarily since most of the bases in Greenland come under the U.S. North American Defense Command, not NATO."[22] The people of Diego Garcia, a British colony in the Indian Ocean, have paid close to the ultimate price. All the people of Diego Garcia were permanently removed from the island to make way for airfields and a naval base built to support U.S. intervention in the Middle East.

While popular opposition to the presence of U.S. foreign military bases and forces is clearly linked to broader movements for independence and sovereignty, the analysis grows somewhat more complex when we turn our attention to former colonies and protectorates. As Walden Bello and Mary Day Kent describe in Chapters 8 and 15, the Philippines and Panama are countries that were "awarded" their independence in exchange for the right of the United States to maintain bases in the host country over the long term. As the U.S. "persuasion flights" over Manila and the invasion of Panama in December 1989 underscored, the United States has frequently acted to ensure that governments supportive of U.S. bases remain in, or come to, power, though less overt means often are employed. It should come as no surprise that the Anti-Bases Coalition in the Philippines is deeply rooted in a Filipino nationalism that views the Military Bases Agreement with the United States as "a colonial document forced upon us by a colonial aggressor."[23]

Similarly in Panama, despite his government's well known corruption, General Noriega was long able to maintain a semblance of legitimacy through appeals to nationalism and resistance to U.S. imperialism. The 1989 U.S. invasion and the subsequent occupation led many Panamanian intellectuals to accuse the United States of "treating their nation like a former colony," with some saying the intervention was "another manifestation of...U.S. imperialism."[24]

Interventions and destabilization efforts are not limited to former colonies, protectorates, or even to third world nations. In 1971, when the Labour Government of Australia was threatening to close the then-secret satellite intelligence base at Pine Gap, the government of Gough Whitlam was toppled with assistance from the CIA.[25] As Yarrow Cleaves and I describe in our chapters about U.S. bases in Germany and Japan, still more subtle debates about sovereignty arise in these countries which host the largest concentrations of U.S. overseas bases. Though Germany has once again emerged as the most powerful European nation, for 40 years its sovereignty was formally limited by conventions and treaties that provided the victors of World War II with the right to station military forces in Germany, much as they did during their formal occupations. In Japan, the United States demanded the negotiation of the 1951 U.S.-Japan Mutual Security Treaty, which legitimizes the continued presence of U.S. troops and bases in Japan to this day as a condition for ending the war-time occupation. Germans and Japanese both endure "extra-territoriality" under which U.S. forces are, in large measure, governed by U.S.—not German or Japanese—law. To the horror of many Japanese, their country's peace constitution and national policies which ban the presence and introduction of nuclear weapons into Japan are violated when U.S. warships from the Seventh and Third Fleets regularly carry nuclear weapons into Japanese ports.

Even in a more conventional alliance, such as that between the United States and Britain, the question of sovereignty remains a focus of tension. Britain "hosts" 104 U.S. bases and smaller installations.[26] It was the first country to host Strategic Air Command nuclear bombers and is today the only foreign country to host U.S. strategic nuclear-powered ballistic missile submarines. Duncan Campbell put the problem succinctly in his book, *The Unsinkable Aircraft Carrier: American Military Power in Britain:*

> Whether the bases eventually stay or go, only the most pusillanimous of public officials could accept the inadequacies of the present relationship as they affect British political control of the use of foreign military bases, the legal status of 'visiting' military forces, or the lack of information provided in Britain about the development and use of U.S. bases and facilities...Where the risks for and restraints on British independence created by the presence of foreign military bases on our soil are concerned, British sovereignty is regarded both as negotiable and almost irrelevant.[27]

Campbell's analysis was re-confirmed when British Defence Minister Hasel-tine threatened the lives of British people who protested the cruise missiles deployed at Greenham Common and other U.S. bases in England, and when U.S. bombers based in Britain led the aerial bombardment of Tripoli, Libya in 1986.

Human Rights

Respect for human rights has always played second fiddle to the quest for strategically important bases in U.S. policy. Whether the goals were to ensure that "the trade of the world must and shall be ours," as Senator Albert J. Beveridge said in 1897,[28] or to contain Russian, German, or Japanese ambitions, policy makers in Washington have accorded greater value to strategic considerations than to a country's democratic ideals and commit-ments.

The histories of Turkey, Somalia, Saudi Arabia, Honduras, and the nations of NATO's Southern Flank, recounted in Chapters 12, 13, and 14, describe how the United States has repeatedly supported the repression of human rights to maintain access to foreign military bases and installations. The Philippines, however, remains the classic case of U.S. violation of human rights in pursuit of strategic outposts. Subic Bay Naval Base in the Philippines is the oldest U.S. foreign military base and the U.S. Navy's largest foreign base. It was obtained through a brutal conquest that tragically demonstrates that disregard for the human rights of the people of host nations has been linked to the quest for foreign bases since the beginning. Since the United States officially granted the Philippines its independence on July 4, 1946—in exchange for the (since modified) right to maintain bases in the Philippines rent-free for 99 years—a wealthy elite has controlled the country with little or no regard for human rights and with the active support of the U.S. government.

So deep was the U.S. commitment to retaining these bases that when Marcos was re-elected President in the Philippines "by unprecedented violence and widespread payoffs and fraud" in 1969,[29] Senator J. William Fulbright, then Chairman of the Senate Foreign Relations committee, re-marked, "We will always resist any serious change in the political and social structure of the Philippine government, which is very likely to be, in the long run, a detriment to the people of the Philippines."[30] Fulbright was not far off the mark. In 1972, *after* consulting with President Nixon, President Marcos declared martial law, suspending all democratic institutions. For the next 14 years, he ruled by decree and through a "series of rigged and manipulated referenda."[31] He jailed thousands of opponents, closed down the Congress, took over the media, and, according to Amnesty International, resorted to "widespread abuses of human rights, including the systematic use of torture against political prisoners."[32]

Unfortunately, Philippine repression of human rights did not end with the coup and the "People's Power Revolution" that finally ousted Marcos in 1986. Though the United States forced the coup's leaders (Generals Ramos and Enrile) to accept Corazon Aquino as head of state and to allow the creation of some "democratic space," the Philippines did not become democratic. After a brief period of calm, critics of the Aquino government, including human rights attorneys and anti-bases activists, were "salvaged" (disappeared), and peaceful protests were frequently dispersed by truncheon-wielding police. In the provinces, beyond the view of the international press, extra-judicial killings and torture by military and para-military forces have been much worse. When Vice President Dan Quayle visited the Philippines in 1989, 165 people were arrested in one day—before any rally was held—signalling that "as the debate on the bases heat[ed] up, so too [would] police action against anti-bases activists."[33]

As in many host countries, U.S. forces in the Philippines also exact a tragic toll from poor women. The enormous bases at Subic Bay and Clark Air Field also serve as "rest and recreation" centers for U.S. forces stationed throughout the Asia/Pacific region. In the cities of Olongapo and Angeles which adjoin the bases, thousands of women and many children work as prostitutes. Drug trafficking flourishes, and AIDS, brought to the Philippines by U.S. sailors and airmen, is now a growing problem. As Aurora Camacho de Schmidt and Cynthia Enloe explain in Chapters 4 and 5, Pentagon policies have systematized and institutionalized the exploitation of women in many countries.

In Europe, the United States negotiated basing agreements with the Franco and Salazar dictatorships in Spain and Portugal until their demise in the late 1970s. In the 1960s and early 1970s, the United States supported military dictatorships in Greece and Turkey—a legacy which continues to undermine the legitimacy of U.S. bases in these strategically located Mediterranean countries.

In Africa and the Middle East, strategic considerations have also superseded U.S. commitments to human rights. To gain access to a naval base at Berbera in Somalia as part of the basing structure to support the Rapid Deployment Force, the United States allied itself in 1979 with Mohamed Siad Barre. Barre was later described by the *New York Times* as "the most ruthless and cunning despot" in the nation's history.[34] Siad Barre has ruled Somalia for 20 years through military councils, emergency laws, arrests, and execution of his political enemies. According to a report commissioned by the U.S. State

Department, the Somali Army murdered at least 5,000 unarmed civilians in 1988–89 to repress opposition to Siad Barre's rule. Africa Watch estimated the number at between 50,000 and 60,000.[35] Similarly, in the Middle East, Bahrain, Oman, Saudi Arabia, and the other Middle East member states of the Gulf Cooperation Council are absolute monarchies with severe restrictions on civil liberties and human rights. In most of these nations, women enjoy few of the rights exercised by women in the West, citizenship is denied not only to foreign workers, but even to those foreign workers' children who are born in these countries, and there is nothing resembling a free press.

The situation is much the same in Central America. In Honduras, U.S. bases were used in 1954 when the United States toppled the Arbenz government in Guatemala. In the 1980s, it was from bases in Honduras that the United States directed and supported wars in Central America in its efforts to reinforce the Salvadoran oligarchy and to topple the Sandinista government in Nicaragua.

As we celebrate the ouster of Stalinist dictatorships in Eastern Europe, the deadly connection between U.S. foreign military bases and the repression of human rights in many countries is barely noticed in the United States.

Land and Ecology

The impact of the U.S. bases is not limited to traditional political categories of sovereignty and human rights. Even for people who are not inclined to political activism, there is no escaping the consequences of the foreign military presence. Representatives of Guam's Land Owner's Association explain their predicament by drawing maps of the island. On the first map they shade in locations of the best farmland, fishing areas, and drinking water. On a second map they indicate the location of the U.S. bases. The two maps are identical.

As decribed in Chapter 9, in Japan, where the United States already has 105 bases and installations,[36] the construction of new facilities is exacting a heavy environmental and spiritual toll on urban and rural people. When the Navy ran out of room to house its sailors and their dependents in Yokohama, the Japanese and U.S. governments chose the suburban community of Zushi as the site for a new military housing project. Against the will of Zushi's voters, its mayor, and its town council, Ikego Forest—one of the few remaining areas of greenery in the Tokyo-Yokohama megalopolis—was targeted for "development," making it one of the most contested pieces of real estate in Japan.

Further from Tokyo, Miyakejima Island has also been targeted for devastation. Known as "Bird Island" for its vast variety of bird species, Miyakejima has traditionally been a conservative community, a home to farmers, fishermen, and a small tourist trade. The island's forests, coral reefs, and bird sanctuaries were long protected by the Japanese Environmental Agency. This life is now threatened by the proposed construction of a 2,000-meter runway for "night-landing exercises" for pilots based on U.S. aircraft carriers deployed at U.S. bases in Japan.

The people of Guam and Japan are not the only ones to suffer the environmental impact of U.S. military bases. As Yarrow Cleaves describes in Chapter 11, frequent military exercises have destroyed farmland and forests in Germany. In communities such as Heilbronn, troops have bivouacked in people's yards, and tank crews have been known to drag farm machinery from barns to make room for their tanks during war games.

Sixty-eight thousand hours of low-altitude flying practice each year have also traumatized thousands of West Germans. The *New York Times* has described jets "screaming" over Landau "near the giant American air base at Ramstein, almost half the days of the year, often 100 times in a single day."[37] In one case, U.S. pilots picked a school bus filled with children as a "target of opportunity." The bus and its young passengers suffered "repeated passes during which one plane's wings almost scraped the vehicle. Children inside screamed in panic. A nearby school was also attacked with one witness saying 'the planes almost flew into the classrooms.' "[38]

Because scientists in host nations have extremely limited access to U.S. bases, it has been difficult to monitor the environmental destruction they cause. However, with the U.S. military generating more than 400,000 tons of hazardous waste in the United States (much of it illegally), it should come as no surprise that U.S. overseas bases are heavy polluters. One major study has used Defense Department data about toxic wastes generated on bases within the United States to extrapolate the environmental impact of U.S. bases in the Philippines. Acids, ammunition wastes, organic solvents, chemical warfare agents, industrial sludge, and PCBs are released into the environment surrounding U.S. bases. These wastes "migrate," contaminating aquifers, poisoning soil, and threatening human and animal life.[39]

The environmental threat is not limited to "conventional" pollutants. One of the best known nuclear weapons accidents, called "broken arrows" by the military, occurred over Palomares, Spain in 1966. Four hydrogen bombs smashed into the countryside and the Mediterranean Sea when a B-52 bomber collided with an aerial tanker. Two bombs were so damaged that they released radiation. A third bomb was missing for months before it was finally found at sea.[40] In 1968, a hydrogen bomb was lost over the side of the USS Ticonderoga as the ship passed within 40 miles of Okinawa. The details of that accident, and the fact that the pressure of the ocean probably destroyed the bomb's casing and dispersed its radioactive plutonium, were kept a state secret for more than 20 years. Thule, a remote U.S. Air Force base in Greenland, was the site of one of the Air Force's most notorious and destructive "broken arrows." It was there that a nuclear armed B-52 bomber crashed and burned in 1969, scattering radioactive plutonium over acres of glacial ice.

For the Future

The collapse of the Soviet Union's Eastern European empire, the economic reconstruction of Japan and Western Europe, and the end of the Cold War have transformed the Cold War Order. With its massive and essentially unilateral military intervention into the Persian Gulf, the Bush Administration has relied on a global network of foreign military bases and installations and the new military doctrine of "discriminate deterrence" to stanch the relative decline of U.S. power and to consolidate U.S. control over its Trilateral allies and competitors and third world nations valued for their resources and markets.

Even before the collapse of the Berlin Wall in 1989, the weight of history and financial pressures were leading "national security planners" in Washington to reconsider the scope and missions of the United States' global network of military bases. Congress, anxious to reduce the cost of the country's foreign military commitments, pressed burdensharing on European and Asian allies while ignoring the burdens they already bore. As the post-war era came to an end, some were concluding that more than discriminating strategies and "burdensharing" were needed. As Robert E. Harkavy noted, "The present diplomatic epoch is characterized by a lessened overall propensity by most nations to engage in formal security pacts."[41] NATO allies, Japan, and more than a few third world countries had begun to impose stricter conditions on U.S. access to bases and other facilities in their countries.

The 1988 Pentagon study prepared by some of the most senior figures of the U.S. national security elite, *Discriminate Deterrence: Report of the Commission on Integrated Long-Term Strategy,* is referred to in several chapters of this book. It was among the most important governmental responses to the changing international environment. The working party included Zbigniew Brzezinski, Henry Kissinger, Samuel Huntington, General Andrew Goodpastor and General John Vessey. While never formally adopted as U.S. policy, the report has deeply influenced Washington. Its recommendations called for a redefinition of U.S. strategic interests, insisting that if the United States was to remain *the* global power for the "long haul" it must continue to control the Persian Gulf, the Pacific, and the Mediterranean Sea. Anticipating difficult economic choices for military planners as the

Pentagon's budget constricted, it recommend increased preparations for wars of intervention in the Third World. It called for increased spending for airlift and sealift capabilities and for greater spending for research and development for advanced technology that could be used in conventional, as well as nuclear, warfare. These strategic and planning priorities clearly played a role in President Bush's decision to respond to Iraq's 1990 invasion of Kuwait with the largest U.S. military intervention since the Vietnam War.

Discriminate Deterrence addressed the question of foreign military bases, underlining that "uncertainty about allies and friends granting us access to bases and overflight rights" would contribute to an undermining of U.S. power.[42] However, the report's authors argued that "in many contexts…bases will continue to be critically important." Bases for intervention in the Persian Gulf, they noted, "will increase our ability to concentrate tactical air forces in addition to those which could be provided from our aircraft carriers." The report stressed that U.S. success in "low-intensity conflicts" in the Third World would need to be augmented by increased attention to airlift and sealift capabilities and the development of "light" mobile forces.[43]

The House of Representatives' "Defense Burdensharing Panel," chaired by Patricia Schroeder (D, CO), released its report within months of the publication of *Discriminate Deterrence*. With less concern about nuance, and with apparently equal appreciation for the power U.S. bases have allowed the United States to exercise over its allies, the panel's report stated four conclusions and raised one caveat for future reference.

The report was clear that "forward deployment of U.S. troops should remain the cornerstone of U.S. military strategy in the near-term," but, bowing to economic reality, it noted that "force levels should be continually reassessed." The panel's second recommendation was that the costs of U.S. "forward deployment" should be trimmed by ending "the linkage between foreign aid and U.S. base rights…as base agreements come up for renegotiation." Bases, it boldly stated, were either necessary to preserve U.S. interests, or they weren't, implying that a number of bases would be closed. In making its third recommendation, however, the committee was unable to hold to its principles and logic. "Despite the previous recommendations," the committee recommended, "it is the responsibility of all allied industrialized nations to assist less-well-off allies with their economic and military needs." Anticipating the Philippines Aid Plan initiated by the Reagan Administration with the assistance of Japan, and the Bush Administration's efforts to assemble an Arab Alliance against Saddam Hussein, the Panel recommended that "one or more new common funds be created…so that the industrial world may pool its resources and target them to strategically important countries of mutual interest. The Panel's final recommendation, for which it was best known, was for burdensharing. It argued in essence that if U.S. allies wanted U.S. troops and bases in their countries, they should "share or pay for all of the additional costs incurred by the United States in stationing its forces overseas,"[44] a message that President Bush bore in mind as he mobilized support for his massive 1990-91 Middle East intervention.

Though the Panel's final recommendation played well in the press, its authors recognized that, as Western Europe and Japan assumed greater financial responsibility for U.S. forces, critics might argue that this would transform U.S. troops based abroad into "mercenaries."[45] Unfortunately neither the panel nor the press explored the implications of this caveat.

Discriminate Deterrence and the "Burdensharing Report" have undoubtedly affected the design, scope, and function of the United States' global military infrastructure in the post-Cold War era. The collapse of the Soviet Union's Eastern European empire and U.S. efforts to contain and control dynamic developments in Europe and the western Pacific have also played their roles.

Before Berlin's Brandenberg Gate reopened, the restructuring of the U.S. and Soviet "forward deployed" forces had already begun. Both superpowers saw their troops and bases in Europe as levers to influence the future shape of Germany, to limit German military options, and to ensure that the emerging political and military structures of Europe would leave both the United States and the Union of Soviet Socialist Republics as "European" powers. The United States has sought to legitimize its continued military presence in Europe through the maintenance and transformation of NATO, making it— rather than the European Community (EC) or the Conference for Security and Cooperation in Europe (CSCE)—the dominant international institution on the continent. In the months that preceded German reunification, using active diplomacy, testimony before Congress, and leaks to the press, Washington attempted to avoid being overtaken by events and to demonstrate its flexibility as it moved to define the outlines of the new European military order. Even as President Bush elevated Germany over Britain as the United States' primary European partner, he sought to contain emerging German power through a series of agreements with his NATO allies and the Soviet Union. Throughout the diplomatic maneuvering, U.S. troops and bases in Europe gave the Bush Administration leverage to ensure that the United States would remain a "European" power in the post-Cold War era.

Through all of this, there has been little public discussion about the role U.S. and NATO troops based in Europe are likely to play in "out-of-area" operations—intervention in North Africa and the Middle East. However, even before the August 1990 intervention in the Gulf, the Army made it clear in the budget battles on Capitol Hill that it was becoming a "fast-reaction force" oriented to such hot spots as the Persian Gulf, Latin America, and the Middle East.[46]

In the wake of the Cold War, little public attention has been accorded to Asia and the Pacific. Despite Gorbachev's proposals to demilitarize Asian and Pacific politics, the United States led "PACEX '89," the largest post-war military exercise ever conducted in the Pacific, in the fall of 1989. Designed to reassert U.S. leadership and power in the region, "PACEX '89" sought to more fully integrate the Japanese, Philippine, and Korean militaries into the U.S. structure. In response to proposals from critics that the size and commitments of the U.S. Navy be reduced, Chief of Naval Operations C.A.H. Trost threw down a gauntlet. He said that "we want to remain a superpower,"[47] in his reassertion that the United States is a maritime nation. "We are," he said, "dependent on the seas for our economic health, and we have critical alliances across both oceans."[48] Admiral Trost had the support of senior Japanese officials who argued against any reductions in the United States' military presence in the Asia-Pacific region. Even as Japanese and Soviet diplomats explored the possible basis for their post-Cold War relations, one senior Japanese official remarked, "the situation in Europe is one thing, and the situation in Asia is another."[49]

In its effort to re-consolidate U.S. power in Latin America and the Caribbean, the Bush Administration has returned to the "War on Drugs" to generate bipartisan support for its military budget and for the forces essential for military intervention into the region. When the Colombian government complained that the Defense Department was "using the fight against drug trafficking as a ruse for installing a radar system on a Colombian island in the Caribbean to monitor activities in Nicaragua," Senator John Kerry responded that for too long "the war on drugs has been secondary to other foreign policy interests."[50] Six months later came the first reports about the construction of a U.S. base in Santa Lucia, Peru. The heart of Peru's coca growing district had become a base for operations against the rebel *Sendero Luminoso* (Shining Path) army.[51] In December 1989, as Mary Day Kent describes in Chapter 15, the war against "narco-terrorism" paid enormous domestic dividends when President Bush used U.S. forces based in Panama and in the United States to oust Manuel Noriega from power and to reassert U.S. influence in Panama. Hardly a word protesting this invasion was voiced in the Congress or the U.S. press.

A Democratic Opposition

Drug wars, trade wars, and Iraq's invasion of Kuwait notwithstanding, a foreign policy consensus that supports the nuclear arms race and wars of foreign military intervention will not be easily reconstructed. Following the excesses of the Reagan era, people in the United States have become increasingly concerned about the deteriorating economic health and fiber of the nation. Repeated polls have found that the majority of U.S. people believe the United States should devote more attention to the country's economic problems and less to its military forces, and that "economic power is *more* important than military power in determining a country's influence."[52] Increasingly, analysts are turning to history and asking if, like Portugal, Spain, Holland, and Britain, there does not come a time when the United States and the Soviet Union should "have to ask, as their predecessors were compelled to, are these bases quite so necessary?"[53] Thoughtful members of Congress have concluded that in the long term, the United States will have to adjust to having fewer foreign bases and facilities; Congressman Lee Hamilton has noted that "this need not be a negative development."

This changing environment provides people committed to democracy, justice, and peace a unique opportunity to redefine the national interests and the vision of the United States. The maintenance of the global system of bases and facilities for military intervention and nuclear war has no place in this vision. As the people of the United State know, our interests lie in using our limited financial resources to reconstruct the nation's economic infrastructure, for education and training, for housing and accessible medical care, and for research and development to make important industries economically competitive. The nation's security, and that of future generations of people in the United States, lies in thoughtful stewardship of our resources and in relations of mutual respect with other nations.

Fortunately, people in other nations who share these values and a new vision of global security have long been engaged in an alternative form of burdensharing, a struggle for justice and peace that is in many ways more advanced than ours in the United States. People in New Zealand led their government to ban port calls by nuclear-powered and nuclear-armed ships nearly a decade ago. The city council in Kobe, Japan, in response to popular pressure, has successfully banned visits by all ships that do not clearly affirm that they are nuclear free. Popular movements in the nations of the North Atlantic Network (Britain, Ireland, Norway, Sweden, Denmark, Iceland, Greenland, the Faroe Islands, and Canada) are following these examples. In the Philippines, where a nationalist spirit has blossomed since the fall of the Marcos dictatorship, anti-bases activists and organizations maintain that there

Laura Richardson climbs over the fence during a civil disobedience action at the Greenham Common base for U.S. cruise missiles in Britain. Photo by Melanie Friend.

will be no real sovereignty or democracy until the U.S. bases are ousted. They have forced at least symbolic concessions from their government and the United States in the renegotiation of a new bases treaty.

The presence of limited financial resources and competing visions of its future have led the Soviet Union to withdraw all of its troops from Afghanistan and most from Mongolia. It has negotiated agreements for the withdrawal of all its forces from Germany, Hungary, and Czechoslovakia. Nationalist demands from the peoples of Eastern Europe and the Republics of the Soviet Union and Moscow's own desperate economic problems are likely to force still deeper cuts in the Soviet Union's foreign military presence in the coming years. Similar pressures from people in nations that host U.S. bases, the stagnation of the U.S. economy, alternative visions of U.S. national interests, and pressures from U.S. justice and peace movements to close military bases and demobilize troops could also lead to significant reductions in U.S. foreign military deployments and in the number of U.S. military bases and installations abroad.

About This Book

The Sun Never Sets has been organized to provide readers with a concise but comprehensive background about U.S. foreign military bases and installations. Following initial chapters which describe planning for future forward deployment, Soviet foreign bases and intervention, and the impact of bases on women and on individual communities, the book is organized on a geographic basis and explores the missions and long-term impact of U.S. bases on individual countries and regions. It is our hope that this approach makes the book accessible and useful for readers seeking an introduction and an overview, and for others who need more specialized information. In addition to describing the many missions of the bases under consideration, there are other consistent threads that reappear within this work. Though there are considerable differences between U.S. bases in countries such as Germany, the Philippines, Honduras, and Saudi Arabia, the importance of the issues of sovereignty, independence, human and social rights, social, cultural, and environmental impacts in almost every country is undeniable.

Our decision not to assemble a book of encyclopedic proportions means that there is no detailed discussion of French or British foreign military bases, nor of the foreign military presence of other lesser powers. We have included one chapter on the foreign military presence of the Soviet Union, both because its foreign military deployments have equalled those of the United States in total numbers in the past (mostly in Eastern Europe and two other countries along its borders), and because "Soviet expansionism" was long cited as the reason for the global U.S. military presence. The major reductions in Soviet forces abroad are analyzed in light of the history of post-war Soviet foreign policy. Chapters by Paul Walker, Denis Doyon, Eduardo Gonzalez, and our concluding chapter describe the variety of alternatives for the future being considered by the national security establishment, by people in host nations, and by the American Friends Service Committee.

This book has been written to help stimulate and inform public debate about U.S. military bases and forces abroad. It explores the missions, human and environmental impacts, and political consequences of these bases and installations. Unfortunately, consideration of the missions and impacts of military bases *within* the United States lies beyond the scope of this book. In the future, work exploring the similarities between U.S. foreign and domestic military bases will be an important contribution to the struggle for justice, peace, and security. It is also important to note that as this book goes to press, the United States has deployed over 400,000 troops, a naval armada, and aircraft to Saudi Arabia and the Persian Gulf in what may well prove to become an inexorable mobilization for war. Such a war would, obviously, have deep implications for the future of U.S. interventions and its network of foreign military bases.

As the imperative for a public debate grows, there are too few resources to which people can turn for information and analysis. We recommend two reference books to interested readers: *Bases Abroad: The Global Foreign Military Presence* by Robert E. Harkavy of the Stockholm International Peace Research Institute, and *Nuclear Battlefields: Global Links in the Arms Race* by William M. Arkin and Richard Fieldhouse. Other useful books, which focus on particular countries and regions, are listed in our abbreviated bibliography.

Foreign Deployments of U.S. Military Personnel:
1980, 1988, and 1990

Region and Nation	1980	1988	1990
Europe Western and Southern			
Federal Republic of Germany	249,256	249,411	239,894
United Kingdom	23,969	28,497	26,441
Italy	12,031	14,829	15,631
Spain	8,832	8,724	7,277
Turkey	4,911	5,034	4,780
Iceland	2,819	3,234	3,240
Greece	4,480	3,284	2,895
Netherlands	2,645	2,872	2,766
Belgium	2,143	3,317	2,281
Portugal	1,385	1,664	1,634
Norway	199	1,674	226
Greenland	319	202	165
France	82	86	92
Denmark	44	67	68
Afloat	23,162	33,199	15,584
Other	148	157	150
Total Western and Southern Europe	**336,425**	**356,251**	**323,124**[1]
East Asia and Pacific			
Japan (including Okinawa)	46,121	49,680	47,386
Republic of Korea	39,795	45,501	40,673
Philippines	13,714	16,655	12,982
Guam (U.S. Territory)	8,980	8,519	7,497
Australia	660	753	732
Thailand	101	110	208
Johnston Atoll (U.S. Territory)	114	136	178
New Zealand	766	59	53
Marshall Islands (U.S. Territory)	15	42	50
Indonesia	73	42	35
Midway Islands (U.S. Territory)	515	13	12
Afloat	23,828	28,056	23,835
Other foreign countries	99	111	131
Other U.S. Territories	20	59	58
Total East Asia and Pacific	**134,801**	**149,736**	**133,830**
Africa, Near East and South Asia			
Saudi Arabia	485	421	322,000[2]
British Indian Ocean Territory (Diego Garcia)	1,253	1,001	983
Egypt	370	1,468	607
Bahrain	63	153	182
Israel	99	73	71
Morocco	54	48	43
Somalia	8	53	15
Afloat	12,723	14,512	108,000[2]
Other	469	644	634
Total Africa, Near East and South Asia	**15,524**	**18,373**	**432,535**

Western Hemisphere and Antarctica			
Panama	9,313	11,100	14,870[3]
Puerto Rico (U.S. Territory)	3,653	3,361	3,179
Cuba Guantanamo	2,165	2,337	2,635
Bermuda	1,342	1,844	1,616
Honduras	46	1,573	1,604
Canada	685	533	562
El Salvador	27	78	86
Antigua	122	70	75
Antarctica	74	141	60
Brazil	45	50	50
Costa Rica	11	97	18
Bahamas	42	59	30
Afloat	934	6,375	2,319
Other foreign countries	303	380	473
Other U.S. Territories	11	13	6
Total Western Hemisphere and Antarctica	**18,773**	**28,011**	**27,583**
Total in Other (Non-U.S.) Areas	**2,491**	**360**	**818**
Total Deployments of U.S. Military Forces in Foreign Countries and U.S. Territories	**508,014**	**552,731**	**817,890[2]**
Total Active Duty Personnel in U.S. Armed Forces	**2,036,287**	**2,138,213**	**2,132,406[4]**

1. The number of U.S. troops deployed in Europe declined in late 1990 as approximately 100,000 were sent to the Persian Gulf. Therefore, by early 1991, the actual number was approximately 223,000. Under terms of the 1990 Treaty on Conventional Forces in Europe, the U.S. will reduce its forces in Europe to 195,000 or lower.

2. Following the Iraqi invasion of Kuwait, the United States began deploying large numbers of troops to Saudi Arabia and the Persian Gulf. Precise numbers are not available, but the Associated Press reported (11/30/90) that there were 230,000 troops in the region with another 200,000 expected by January, 1991. Of these 430,000, most are in Saudi Arabia or on ships in the region, though it is likely that the numbers of troops in other countries in the region (e.g. Egypt, Diego Garcia, Bahrain) have been increased somewhat. No breakdown of how many of these 430,000 troops are deployed on land and how many are deployed at sea is available. Our best estimate is that one quarter of the forces may be at sea, so we have estimated 322,000 troops in Saudi Arabia and 108,000 at sea in the region. Finally it is known that some—perhaps half—of the additional 200,000 troops which the President announced on November 9 would soon be sent to the Gulf are being transferred from Europe and (in smaller numbers) other foreign bases. We have not adjusted the figures for U.S. troops in Europe to reflect this decrease; but we have adjusted the final total for all foreign deployments of U.S. forces so as not to count them twice.

3. At the height of the occupation of Panama (which began with the U.S. invasion on December 20, 1989), approximately 24,000 U.S. troops were in Panama. By June 30, 1990, this number had declined to 14,870, approximately 3,000 above the pre-invasion level.

4. This figure of 2,132,406 active duty U.S. military personnel includes an estimated 80,000 reservists who were mobilized for Operation Desert Shield in the last 5 months of 1990.

Figures from U.S. Department of Defense "Fact Sheet on Military Strength—Worldwide, June 30, 1980," "September 30, 1988," and "June 30, 1990," except for 1990 figures on Saudi Arabia and "Near East, Afloat."

U.S. Naval Access to Foreign Bases and Ports in 1988

Host Nation and Base	Brief Description
Guam Apra Harbor	Major naval base: repairs, fuels, munitions, communications; naval air station; patrol boats.
Japan Yokosuka	The primary U.S. naval base in NW Pacific. Homeport for ten ships of the U.S. 7th Fleet, including the carrier Midway. Huge logistics, repair, and drydock facilities; forward port for nuclear attack subs; munitions maintenance; naval hospital.
Sasebo	Base used jointly with Japanese Navy. Large fuel and munitions storage, drydock and repair facilities. Homeport for nuclear attack submarine.
White Beach (Okinawa)	7th Fleet forward port, occasional use by submarines.
Philippines Subic Bay	Major US Navy base for the SW Pacific and Indian Ocean. Naval air station; base for nuclear-armed surface ships. Major ship repair center for all but the largest aircraft carriers; support and munitions storage. Marine training, bombing and gunnery practice ground.
Australia Cockburn Sound	Australian base for 4 subs and 4 destroyers, possibly to be expanded for carriers; a potential homeport for a U.S. destroyer. Pine Gap and Nurrungar are communications and intelligence facilities.
Thailand Sattahip	Military port constructed by U.S.A.; heavy use during U.S. war in Indochina.
Singapore Sembawang	Some repairs and supplies for U.S. ships, potential for expanded use.
Diego Garcia	U.S. Naval support facilities; Central Command's material storage ships based here; naval air station. Expansion for use by a carrier battle group underway.
Oman Muscat (Mina Qaboos)	Restricted use by Indian Ocean task force, contingent use by Central Command in a Persian Gulf crisis.
Bahrain Al Jufair	Homeport for 4-destroyer Mideast Force; communications, storage, co-use of adjacent airfield; re-supply base for Indian Ocean Task Force; potential for greater use in a crisis.
Somalia Berbera	Port used by Indian Ocean Task Force, with possible storage of material for Central Command.
Mogadiscio	Port visits and possible storage of equipment and supplies for Central Command.
Djibouti	Refuelling and reprovisioning port for Indian Ocean Task Force.

Kenya Mombasa	Port visits, possible pre-positioning of material for use in Middle East.
Greece Souda Bay (Crete)	NATO naval base, with anchorage large enough to accommodate entire U.S. 6th Fleet, including nuclear-armed surface ships. Large underground storage for fuel & munitions.
Athens/Piraeus	A major base for 6th Fleet, with pier and shipyard facilities. Linked to Hellenikon Air Base. U.S. may be forced to leave by government of Greece.
Italy Naples	Major support complex for U.S. 6th Fleet, and homeport for attack submarines, destroyer tender.
Gaeta	Important naval base, headquarters for U.S. 6th Fleet, including homeport for aircraft carrier.
La Maddalena (Sardinia)	Base for U.S. nuclear-powered attack submarines on patrol in Mediterranean, and a submarine tender.
Spain Rota	A main base for U.S. naval operations in Western Mediterranean, primarily as an intelligence and communications center, along with major repair facilities, fuel depot, and air base.
Portugal Ponte Delgada (Azores)	Communications, intelligence, and transport facility in Atlantic Ocean.
United Kingdom Holy Loch (Scotland)	Homeport for 10 Poseidon subs, with permanent berthing of submarine tender and a large floating dry dock.
Cuba Guantanamo Bay	Port visits, training and exercises, dry dock and naval air station.
Panama Rodman Naval Station	Fleet support, logistics, small craft training facility.

This table is based principally upon Table 5, "Main and secondary surface-ship and submarine operating bases of the US Navy," in Robert Harkavy, *Bases Abroad*, 1989: 45-47. Additional information came from Simon Duke, *United States Military Forces and Installations in Europe*, 1989; Peter Hayes, Lyuba Zarsky and Walden Bello, *American Lake*, 1986; and International Institute for Strategic Studies, *The Military Balance: 1989-1990*, 1989.

Notes

1. Joseph S. Nye, Jr., "Understanding U.S. Strength," *Foreign Policy,* #72, Fall 1988, 115-116.

2. Michael T. Klare, "Policing The Gulf —And The World," *The Nation,* 15 October 1990.

3. William Appleman Williams, *The Tragedy of American Diplomacy* (New York: Delta Books, 1959), 24-37; George Kennan, *American Diplomacy 1900-1950* (New York: The New American Library, 1951), 9-23.

4. *Philippine Daily Inquirer,* 8 May 1990.

5. "US Plays Dangerous Games with Cuba," *Granma Weekly Review International Edition,* Havana, 22 April 1990.

6. *New York Times,* 2 August 1990.

7. "The Global Network of United States Military Bases," *The Defense Monitor,* Center for Defense Information, Vol. XVIII, N. 2, 1989.

8. Associated Press, *Boston Globe,* 16 December 1989.

9. Charles A. and Mary R. Beard, *The Beards' Basic History of the United States* (New York: Doubleday, Doran & Co., 1944), 100.

10. Ibid., 339.

11. Williams, 35.

12. Daniel Boone Schirmer, *Republic or Empire: American Resistance to the Philippines War* (Cambridge: Schenkman, 1972).

13. Richard Barnett, "The Four Pillars," *The New Yorker,* 17 November 1987.

14. Joseph Gerson, *The Deadly Connection* (Philadelphia: New Society Publishers, 1986), 13-16; Barry M. Blechman and Stephen S. Kaplan, *Force Without War: U.S. Armed Forces as a Political Instrument* (Washington, D.C.: The Brookings Institution, 1978).

15. Noam Chomsky, *Necessary Illusions: Thought Control in Democratic Societies* (Boston: South End Press, 1989), 25.

16. Jeff Stein, United Press International, *New Hampshire Sunday News,* 2 October 1988.

17. Gerson, 10-13; Blechman and Kaplan, 53.

18. *The North Atlantic Network: The Alternative Alliance* (London: CND, 1984), 36-37.

19. *The Defense Monitor.*

20. Ibid.

21. Ibid.

22. Ibid., 34.

23. Roland G. Simbulan, *A Guide to Nuclear Philippines* (Manila: Ibon Databank, 1989), 16.

24. *Boston Globe,* 1 January 1990.

25. *Boston Globe,* 25 January 1988; Robert Lindsey, *Falcon and the Snowman* (New York: Simon and Schuster, 1979).

26. Simon Duke, *United States Military Forces and Installations in Europe* (London: SIPRI, Oxford University Press, 1989), 314-323.

27. Duncan Campbell, *The Unsinkable Aircraft Carrier: American Military Power in Britain* (London: Michael Joseph Ltd., 1984), 297, 299.

28. Williams, 17.

29. Daniel B. Schirmer and Stephen Rosskamm Shalom, *The Philippines Reader: A History of Colonialism, Neocolonialism, Dictatorship and Resistance* (Boston: South End Press, 1987), 163.

30. U.S. Senate Hearings, as quoted in "U.S. Bases in the Philippines: In Whose Interest?," *Third World Reports,* 1989, 8.

31. Schirmer and Shalom, 27.

32. Ibid.

33. Personal communication from Maria Socorro Diokno.

34. *New York Times,* 9 September 1989.

35. *Manchester Guardian Weekly,* 28 January 1990.

36. Japan Council Against Atomic & Hydrogen Bombs, *Proceedings of 1986 Okinawa International Conference for Prevention of Nuclear War, Elimination of Nuclear Weapons and Nuclear-Free Pacific* (Tokyo: JCAAHB, 78).

37. *New York Times,* 10 August 1988.

38. Bob Aldridge, "U.S. Military Exercises in West Germany," *The Monthly Planet*, March 1989.

39. Jorge Emmanuel, "Environmental Destruction Caused by U.S. Military Bases and the Serious Implications for the Philippines," a talk presented at Crossroads 1991: Towards a Nuclear Free, Bases Free Philippines, An International Conference, May 14-16, 1990, Manila, Philippines.

40. Tad Szulc, *The Bombs of Palomares* (New York: Viking Press, 1967).

41. Robert E. Harkavy, *Bases Abroad: The Global Foreign Military Presence* (London: SIPRI, Oxford University Press, 1989), 321.

42. *Discriminate Deterrence: Report of the Commission on Integrated Long-Term Strategy* (Washington, D.C.: U.S. Government Printing Office), 11 January 1988.

43. Ibid., 3.

44. "Interim Report of the Defense Burdensharing Panel of the Committee on Armed Services," House of Representatives, One Hundredth Congress, Second Session, August 1988, 6-7.

45. Ibid., 7.

46. *New York Times*, 12 December 1989; 9 January 1990; 2 August 1990.

47. Klare.

48. *New York Times*, 1 January 1990.

49. *New York Times*, 31 January 1990.

50. *New York Times*, 5 April 1989.

51. *New York Times*, 21 June 1990.

52. "Americans Talk Security," Winchester, MA, April 1989.

53. Jonathan Power, *Philadelphia Inquirer*, 9 November 1989.

Chapter 2

U.S. Military Power Projection Abroad

Paul Walker

On May 17, 1987, the USS Stark, a modern, hi-tech U.S. Navy frigate, was patrolling the waters of the Persian Gulf when it was suddenly struck by two sea-skimming anti-ship missiles. The French-built Exocet cruise missiles, only one of which successfully detonated after launch by an Iraqi Mirage aircraft, killed 37 U.S. sailors, wounded another 21, and heavily damaged the warship. A Congressional report subsequently emphasized the seriousness of the Mideast incident in describing efforts to prevent the Stark from sinking as "nothing short of heroic."[1]

Military observers, not to mention the Stark's crew, were surprised by both the Iraqi attack and its deadly results. The $325 million Stark guided missile frigate was in the Gulf as part of the U.S. Middle East Force (MEF), a flotilla of U.S. warships intended to protect U.S.-flagged merchant ships during the long Iran-Iraq war. Since the start of the war in September 1980, over 300 ships, primarily oil tankers, had been attacked by both warring nations. The United States had maintained a naval presence in the Gulf since 1949 for the stated purpose of "naval diplomacy, regional deterrence, and limited crisis response," but expanded its role in the mid-1980s, effectively joining the Arab alliance fighting Iran, as the tanker war began to intensify At the time of the Stark attack, and two months after the U.S. had agreed to escort 11 Kuwaiti tankers flying the U.S. flag, the MEF included seven modern warships in the Gulf, supported by at least twice that number of ships as part of an aircraft carrier battlegroup outside the Strait of Hormuz in the Arabian Sea.[2]

The Stark disaster should be understood in its historical context. Just five years earlier, during the Falklands War in the South Atlantic, the British destroyer, Sheffield, was destroyed by a similar Exocet cruise missile launched by an Argentine jet. The Sheffield was a modern destroyer, yet it was caught by surprise when it was struck amidships by the "smart" homing missile.

In both these cases, a heavily armed, modern warship of a first world power was embarrassingly defeated by a much smaller third world nation. These tragedies and others, such as the 1989 U.S. invasion of Panama and the 1990 U.S. and allied intervention in the Iraq-Kuwait war, illustrate that superpowers continue to project power far from their shores through foreign bases and deployments and that "there are inherent risks whenever a nation sends its armed forces abroad."[3] Unfortunately, there is also a strong tendency among first world governments and military establishments to dismiss such incidents as "accidents"…human and technical failures…and to ignore the implications of the end of the Cold War.

Changing U.S. Military Strategy

Since World War II, U.S. military strategy has been based on four primary goals: 1) nuclear war-fighting strategies and deterrence of nuclear attack through "mutual assured destruction" (MAD); 2) deterrence of a major conventional (non-nuclear) war in Europe; and 3) the ability to engage in or intervene in smaller wars anywhere around the globe. The first goal has propelled an ever-spiraling nuclear arms race with the Soviets for the past four decades. Although more than a dozen nuclear arms control treaties have been signed by the United States, the Soviets, and others, the nuclear arms competition continues unabated with more countries seeking to join the nuclear club every year. Both Soviet and U.S. strategic nuclear arsenals have expanded from a few hundred weapons some 25 years ago to over 12,000 each in 1990. Though both superpowers have agreed to sizeable reductions of their strategic arsenals within the START (Strategic Arms Reduction Talks), a glance at current nuclear "modernization" plans shows that this commitment has not yet affected military plans to enlarge nuclear arsenals by several thousand warheads.[4]

Prior to former President Richard Nixon's rapprochement with China in the early 1970s, the Defense Department planned for a second major war contingency in Korea. Thus, military planning was defined for two decades after the Korean War as a "two-and-one-half war" strategy. The "half war" has always been defined as a much smaller contingency in the Third World—such as the Middle East, Cuba, or Southeast Asia. Given the unlikelihood of major war in Asia, this "two-and-one-half war" strategy was modified in the mid-1970s to become a "one-and-one-half war" plan, retaining the European contingency along with the smaller war option. Interestingly, the size of standing U.S. military forces remained constant, raising serious doubt as to how relevant strategy actually is to force structure.[5] Senator Sam Nunn and others commented on similar planning discrepancies between strategy and forces after studying President George Bush's "post-Cold War" 1990-1991 military budgets.

Regardless of how many wars the Pentagon has planned to fight in the post-World War II period, the major contingency was Europe and the ostensible containment of the Soviet Union. The U.S. military commitment to the North Atlantic Treaty Organization (NAT0), formed in 1949, and to other U.S. forces in Western Europe has accounted for at least $150 billion of annual military spending. This accounts for half the military budget. These funds have supported 341,000 U.S. troops stationed in and around Europe, much of current airlift and sealift capabilities, and large numbers of additional troops, primarily heavy army divisions, trained for European reinforcement from the United States in the event of war.[6]

Between $60 and $90 billion (20-30 percent of the Pentagon's budget) has gone to maintaining foreign bases, ships, aircraft, and troops abroad outside the European continent. The United States stations 510,000 troops abroad, with 169,000 of these located along the Pacific Rim in South Korea, Japan, and elsewhere throughout the globe. These numbers reflect an increase since the immediate post-Vietnam period when 43,000 fewer troops were deployed abroad. Over the past decade, U.S. forces overseas have remained concentrated in Europe, but numbers in Korea, Japan, Latin America, and elsewhere in the Third World—most recently in the Middle East—have risen. The greatest percentage increase between 1976 and 1989 came in the basing of U.S. forces in Latin America and the Caribbean. This figure remains small, just over 4 percent of the 1989 total, but it has expanded by 91 percent in absolute terms and also doubled as a percent of total forces overseas in the last year, largely as a result of the December 1989 invasion of Panama. This indicates both the massive worldwide deployment of U.S. forces, including expansion of the U.S. Navy under recent administrations, and the recent concentration on Central and Latin America. 1990 saw a sudden deployment of over 400,000 U.S. troops to Saudi Arabia and the Persian Gulf region; this will likely portend larger, longer-term U.S. forces in the Mideast than in recent years. Proposed troop cuts in Europe will leave the majority of U.S. forward deployed forces prepared for interventions in the Asia/Pacific region and the Third World.

Former defense secretary Frank C. Carlucci, in his last two annual statements to Congress, reflected the still current Washington consensus when he reviewed the threats to U.S. power in Western Europe, the Middle East, and Latin America. He prescribed a policy of "flexible response for deterrence and defense." According to the Defense Secretary, the United States must:

> instill in potential adversaries a measure of both certainty and uncertainty. They must be certain of our strength, and our resolve to use it. Thus we must have—and our adversaries must perceive that we have—the means and the will to respond to aggression and resist coercion. We also deter potential adversaries by the uncertainty that arises when we avoid specifying the exact means, location, timing, and scope of our response to aggression.[8]

Such a broad and dire perception of threat and counter-threat drives the need for a large standing army, navy, and air force.

The policies of "forward deployment" and "power projection," recently reaffirmed by both the Bush Administration and the House of Representatives' Burdensharing Committee, have been essential to "flexible response."[9] Ostensibly this has been an effort to engage military enemies as far away from U.S. shores as possible, thus limiting damage to the continental United States and providing the earliest feasible opportunity to defeat opponents. Forward deployment strategies have also represented an effort to promote coordinated use of allies' forces and bases, thereby theoretically minimizing U.S. commitments while maximizing those of U.S. allies. The 1990 U.S. deployment in the Mideast, although undertaken in coordination with the United Nations and allied forces, remained largely a unilateral rather than a multilateral operation, however. Forward deployment strategies have been re-emphasized with the discussion of "low-intensity conflict" or LIC. The Pentagon defines LIC as "protracted struggles of competing principles and ideologies ranging from subversion to the use of armed force. It is waged by a combination of means employing political, economic, informational and military instruments. Low-intensity conflicts are often localized, generally in the Third World, but contain regional and global security implications."[10]

A recent Air Force publication, for example, states that LIC "represents an arena of conflict for today and for tomorrow...Low-intensity conflict appears in the guise of proxy warfare, religious extremism, ethnic and racial rivalries, and on the heels of failed development projects. All these events threaten our friends, our allies and ourselves." It also places LIC in Cold War terms: "The Soviet Union and its proxies have come to the conclusion that the global system is vulnerable to low-intensity conflict. We can therefore expect more of it. Only when the United States has developed a flexible capacity to deal with its root causes around the world can we better secure our own interests and suppress Soviet efforts in this domain."[11]

Though the Defense Department initially defined LIC in East-West conflict terms, citing "the revolutionary warfare strategems of communist insurgency movements," its practices have been focussed in third world nations: El Salvador, Nicaragua, Panama, Afghanistan, Cambodia, and the Philippines. The U.S. invasion of Grenada in 1983 is treated as a case where U.S. forces undertook a "rescue operation" to restore democracy and oppose destabilizing "communist subversion."[12] Similarly, the 1989 U.S. invasion of Panama by 25,000 troops to "save American lives" and to end General Manuel Noriega's role in drug trafficking has reinforced the movement of LIC as a growth area of Defense Department planning. The latest larger-scale, 1990 intervention in the Mideast has been defined as "America's stand against aggression." President George Bush, invoking "memories of Normandy, Khe Sanh, [and] Pork Chop Hill," described the U.S. role as one "to stop aggression, help our friends, and protect our own interests and the peace and stability of countries around the globe...America stands where it always has—against aggression, against those who would use force to replace the rule of law."[13]

In an effort to meet the perceived demand for more low-intensity conflict capability, the Defense Department has been increasing its Special Operations Forces (SOF). The annual budget is now over $3 billion, funding Army special forces, rangers, psychological operation battalions, Navy SEAL teams, Air Force special forces, and others at some five dozen bases in the U.S. and abroad. Major special forces units abroad are based in Germany, Britain, Panama, Puerto Rico, the Philippines, and Japan.

In January 1988, a Pentagon special committee, the Commission on Integrated Long-Term Strategy, issued a report, *Discriminate Deterrence*, which argued that flexible response capabilities for both low-intensity and apocalyptic contingencies should remain the basis for U.S. strategy. Chaired by defense consultants Fred C. Ikle and Albert Wohlstetter, and including former national security advisors Zbigniew Brzezinski and Henry Kissinger, the Commission argued for maintaining the basic U.S. strategy of deterrence against nuclear attack, but more importantly "to take account of contemporary realities and guide long-term defense plans" for a "far more complicated environment" in which a "world with three or four major, global military powers would confront American strategic planners."[14] *Discriminate Deterrence* promotes the use of U.S. forces outside the direct U.S.-Soviet context. Indeed, it sees the relaxation of East-West tensions during a period of *glasnost* and *perestroika* as a unique opportunity to refocus military force elsewhere. The Commission argues, for example, that third world conflicts are "obviously less threatening than any Soviet-American war would be," yet such conflicts are increasingly important because "they have had and will have an adverse cumulative effect on U.S. access to critical regions, on American credibility among allies and friends, and on American self-confidence."[15]

Low-intensity conflict, it is argued, must therefore become a permanent addition to the range of important defense planning in order to support anti-communist insurgencies through special and/or covert operations.

The Commission, along with other current military planners within the Bush Administration, foresaw the need to expand military intervention options, looking beyond traditional all-or-nothing scenarios of East-West confrontation. Wars thus become more likely in the Third World and may not require the commitment of major U.S. ground forces. Instead, proxy or "cooperative" forces are to be developed, in coordination with third world allies; advanced intelligence gathering technologies (satellites) are to be utilized; and naval alternatives to overseas bases (aircraft carriers and task forces, including barge depots such as those utilized in the Persian Gulf) are to be established, maintained, and expanded. The Commission went so far as to suggest that merchant container ships could be used in covert interventionary operations with innocent-looking crates holding self-contained military troops and/or equipment.

A Time to Reconsider Power Projection

The Defense Department does recognize many of the current changes taking place in international security: the fall of the Berlin Wall and the lessening of East-West tensions; the rising importance of economic competition abroad; the restructuring of Soviet and Warsaw Pact forces along smaller, more defensive lines; the expanding complexity of regional warfare and ethnic unrest; and the proliferation of sophisticated weapons technologies, including nuclear warheads and ballistic missiles.[16]

There is, however, a nagging reluctance to interpret these events in other than a traditional way. *Discriminate Deterrence,* for example, described the contemporary world as an expanding powder keg in need of greater United States military attention. Commission members decried the lack of cohesion within NATO, for example, and castigated Spain and Portugal for showing "little concern for their role in reinforcing Turkey or allied forces in the [Persian] Gulf." They criticized European advocates of "non-offensive defense" for eschewing all offensive weapons and argued that such policies "would not prevent enemy attack, but...would prevent [NATO] counterattacking." They advocated the need "to consider a wider range of more plausible, important contingencies" for the application of U.S. force abroad, to expand the U.S. military budget further, to utilize "surgical-strike" conventional and nuclear weapons, to escalate conventional war to the nuclear level if necessary, and to be prepared to unilaterally protect U.S. interests should allies decline to participate. The Commission also pointed to the importance of maintaining U.S. military bases abroad, particularly in Korea and Japan, "because it is also of great importance in increasing our capability to deal in a timely way with threats elsewhere."[17]

The Defense Department has been following these suggestions in a variety of ways in recent force structure planning. The Army has been developing more mobile and flexible military units capable of moving faster over longer distances; more emphasis is being placed on so-called light army divisions which do not rely on 50-ton main battle tanks, but are instead capable of airborne and light ground-assault operations. A variety of airlift and attack aircraft and helicopters are being developed and produced which are flexible (capable of takeoff and landing at limited facilities, and of night-time and poor weather flying) and are difficult to detect, identify, or destroy. Naval construction includes a variety of smaller and faster ships for deploying troops and equipment in constricted and shallow waters, up rivers, and across beaches. And C3I (communications, command, control, and intelligence) operations are being developed to provide more flexibility, redundancy, and decentralization for interventionary operations in third world regions.

The Navy, in fact, sank about $75 billion into its shipbuilding program during the Reagan era, "largely to make its fleet more mobile and less dependent on specific bases."[18] Moreover, lessons in mobile basing have been available from the experience of the "Near-Term Prepositioned Force" that is continuously stationed at the harbor in the small Diego Garcia atoll. Geared to support a heavily mechanized Marine Amphibious Brigade, this unit is made up of 17 fully loaded vessels, including six enormous roll-on/roll-off (roro) cargo ships which are "packed with all the supplies needed for a Middle East invasion, already loaded into trucks. Everything—right down to water tankers, for the thirsty troops."[19] These plans have now been put to use in the major Mideast operation, "Desert Shield," perhaps portending much larger U.S. presence in third world areas, should the Defense Department have its way.

The dramatic changes, in the Soviet Union also point to the need for restructuring U.S. military policies much more along smaller, more defensively oriented lines. With the demise of Brezhnev, Andropov, and Chernenko and the rise of Mikhail Gorbachev as party chair in March 1985, the Soviet Union has presented a very different reality to the West and, indeed, to all its neighbors. The changes, designed to allow the Soviet Union to address its domestic agenda, led to the renunciation of the Brezhnev Doctrine and the collapse of the Soviet Union's Eastern Empire. These changing priorities and commitments were initially reflected in the 1985 unilateral moratorium on nuclear testing, which lasted 19 months, as well as the INF Treaty, which followed in December 1987. In 1986, Gorbachev put forth a plan to abolish nuclear weapons by the turn of the century and introduced the concept of "reasonable sufficiency" when he addressed the Twenty-seventh Communist Party Congress in Moscow. And, at the United Nations in December 1988, he announced the unilateral withdrawal of 50,000 Soviet troops, 5,000 main battle tanks, and other equipment from Central Europe. Since the New York speech, Hungary, the German Democratic Republic, Czechoslovakia, and Bulgaria all followed suit in announcing unilateral troop and equipment withdrawals. Hungary, Germany, and Czechoslovakia have pressed the Soviet Union to make still deeper cuts in Soviet troops based in their countries, and it now appears highly likely that all Soviet troops will be withdrawn from both Hungary and Czechoslovakia by the end of 1990.

Financial factors reinforce the changing strategic environment for military planners and set limits on military expansion. The U.S. military budget, after undergoing the largest growth in post-war history for the first half of the 1980s, peaked in fiscal year 1985 and has declined slightly since then. Funding requests for major weapons programs such as the Strategic Defense Initiative, the Midgetman, and MX ballistic missile programs have been annually reduced. Dozens of domestic military bases will undoubtedly close in coming years. Furthermore, projected costs for large programs, such as the B-2 Stealth bomber and the Arleigh Burke naval destroyer, are drawing increasing public scrutiny. Even Defense Secretary Richard Cheney has recently proposed major reductions in the B-2 and other weapons programs, and a bipartisan concensus has developed for major military budget reductions. Fiscal constraints have also been exacerbated by the billions of dollars committed to operation "Desert Shield." The gap between a level U.S. military budget and the sums required in the early 1990s simply to maintain current forces and field weapon systems now in the pipeline will be at least $250 billion.

Related to budgetary constraints is the issue of burdensharing. The U.S. House of Representatives established a panel in 1988, chaired by Representative Patricia Schroeder, to investigate how equitably the security burden is divided amongst allies. After 13 hearings, meetings with European parliamentarians, and fact-finding missions to Europe and Japan, the panel questioned whether the U.S. should continue bearing such a large share of military spending for the "defense" of Western Europe and Japan. The United States, the panel reported, commits some 60 percent of its annual military spending to the NATO contingency, a sum which surpasses the combined spending of the other 15 NATO allies. The United States, it noted, commits 6 percent of its annual Gross National Product to military spending, while Japan spends about 1 percent. United States' troops in Korea cost $5-6 billion, but the United States runs large annual trade deficits with South Korea.

The panel concluded, among other things, that "U.S. diplomacy has failed over the years to bring about more equitable burdensharing."[20] Such arguments will influence future inter-alliance negotiations and planning in coming years, and Congressional support for future U.S. military interventions, as has been the case with the "multinational" operation "Desert Shield." Some military planners would like U.S. allies to draw the conclusion that they should "pick up more of the burden" as the United States strives to reduce its own. A more likely and more productive scenario is that alliances will reassess the threat in order to reduce—rather than shift—burdens across the board. The burdensharing debate is likely to encourage either the withdrawal of U.S. troops and bases from foreign soil or increase allied financing of such deployments by "host" countries.

Significantly, a recent high-level Pentagon study has claimed that the United States can afford to shut down its bases in the Philippines and withdraw most of its troops from Korea and still successfully deal with "'any non-Soviet' war contingency." The study asserts that "a much smaller array of land, sea, and air units based in the western Pacific would save money, without abandoning the concept of "forward deployment" that U.S. forces have maintained there since World War II.[21]

A final but equally important factor in reconsideration of forward basing of U.S. forces is growing local concern and opposition to continued hosting of foreign troops in many nations around the globe. Visible political opposition has been building in diverse nations such as the Philippines, Korea, Japan, Germany, Panama, and Saudi Arabia. The reasons are many: diminishing local concern about the likelihood of enemy invasion, particularly in Europe; rising nationalism, demanding greater independence from the United States; frustration with negative domestic social impacts of foreign troops (for example, in the Philippines, where women have organized groups to oppose their exploitation, or in Saudi Arabia, where the open presence of female troops has offended local citizens); disagreement among allies about mutual responsibilities for "out-of-area" operations or military strategies (for example, Saudi Arabia, where the U.S. commanding officer and the Saudi Defense Minister have disagreed over "offensive" versus "defensive" operations); research and actions by public interest groups such as "Greenpeace" pointing to environmental and other negative impacts of military bases; and a spreading anti-nuclear sentiment, most evident in the Pacific from Japan to New Zealand, where people are understandably wary of the danger of radiation.

All these factors—politics, economics, and technology—argue strongly that the time is now ripe for a serious and thorough reevaluation of the need, cost, and practicality of maintaining large numbers of troops and equipment at foreign bases overseas.

The 1990s present, in light of these many interrelated political, economic, and military issues, a unique and opportune moment for a fundamental re-evaluation of U.S. foreign and military policies, of which the military basing structure must be a central feature. The United States now commits more dollars annually (in real terms) to militarism than at any prior time in the twentieth century with the exception of during World War II. The warming of East-West relations, the spread of deadly and sophisticated technology, the ineffectiveness of superpower involvement in regional conflicts, and competing fiscal priorities all indicate that international security relations are shifting ahead of military policies. The need for reassessing U.S. interests, redefining security so as to include non-military issues such as environment and health, determining priorities anew, relating these with national and international economic goals, and only then devising military force structures to meet these needs, is more clear than ever before in the post-war period.[22]

Notes

1. George C. Wilson. "Panel Faults Officers of USS Stark," *Washington Post,* 14 June 1987.

2. For additional detail on naval presence in the Gulf, see E.C. Collier, et al. "The Persian Gulf and the U.S. Naval Presence: Issues for Congress," *Congressional Research Service Issue Brief IB87145,* 15 June 1987; also C.R. Mark, "The Persian Gulf, 1987: A Chronology of Events," Congressional Research Service Report 88-129F, 10 February 1988; and Caspar W. Weinberger, "A Report to the Congress on Security Arrangements in the Persian Gulf," U.S. Department of Defense, 15 June 1987. For discussion of hi-tech naval warfare, see Paul F. Walker. "Smart Weapons in Naval Warfare," *Scientific American* 248:5 (May 1983) 53-61.

3. U.S. Department of State, "U.S. Policy in the Persian Gulf," Special Report No. 166 (Washington, DC: U.S. Government Printing Office, July 1987), 5.

4. See, for example, Paul F. Walker, "Did Anyone Tell the Pentagon?" *The Bulletin of the Atomic Scientists* 45:8 (October 1989), 12 and 40.

5. For a fuller discussion of war strategies, see Alain Enthoven and K. Wayne Smith, *How Much Is Enough? Shaping the Defense Program 1961-1969* (New York: Harper & Row, 1971).

6. U.S. Department of Defense, *Annual Report to the President and the Congress* (Washington, DC: U.S. Government Printing Office, 1990), 74. For a recent report on NATO, see *New Directions for NATO: Adapting the Atlantic Alliance to the Needs of the 1990s,* A Joint Report of the Institute for Resource and Security Studies and the Institute for Peace and International Security, Cambridge, MA, December 1988.

7. U.S. Department of Defense, Annual Report to the Congress, Fiscal Year 1990 (Washington, DC: U.S. Government Printing Office, 1989), 227; and Annual Report to the President, 74.

8. *Annual Report to Congress,* Ibid., 34.

9. U.S. House of Representatives, Committee on Armed Services, *Report of the Defense Burdensharing Panel* (Washington, DC: U.S. Government Printing Office, August 1988).

10. Ibid., 43.

11. Colonel Sidney J. Wise, in Lewis B. Ware, et al., *Low-Intensity Conflict in the Third World* (Maxwell Air Force Base, Alabama: Air University Press, 1988).

12. *Annual Report to Congress FY90,* 43-44.

13. Speech before the Veterans of Foreign Wars, Baltimore, MD, 20 August 1990; U.S. Department of State Current Policy #1294.

14. *Discriminate Deterrence: Report of the Commission on Integrated Long-Term Strategy* (Washington, DC: U.S. Government Printing Office, 11 January 1988), 5-7.

15. Ibid., 13.

16. See, for example, Paul F. Walker, "High-tech killing power," and Janne E. Nolan, "Missile mania: some rules for the game," *The Bulletin of the Atomic Scientists* 46:4 (May 1990), 23-29.

17. See, for example, the concluding section, "Connecting the Elements of the Strategy," in *Discriminate Deterrence,* 63-69.

18. James Fallows, "The Bases Dilemna," *The Atlantic,* February 1988, 27

19. Owen Wilkes and Marie Leadbeater, "The Asia-Pacific Situation," Paper presented at Asia-Pacific People's Conference on Peace and Development, January 1989, 6

20. Report of the Defense Burdensharing Panel, 70.

21. Patrick Tyler, "Cheney, Powell Are Told: U.S. Can Cut Korea Forces, Give Up Philippine Bases," *Washington Post,* 20 December 1989, A9.

22. The House Burdensharing Panel has recommended a "zero-based study of U.S. military commitments and bases overseas." Report of the Defense Burdensharing Panel, 52. The Committee on Common Security (CCS) has also recommended a "zero-based military budget" and a joint House-Senate hearing on threat reassessment. See George W. Rathgens, "The New Security Agenda for the 1990s," CCS Policy Paper #1, January 1990.

Chapter 3

The Rise and Decline of the Second Superpower

*Soviet Foreign Policy and
Foreign Military Presence*

Bruce Birchard

For the first time in many years, not a single Soviet soldier is participating—nor, I'm sure, will participate—in military actions anywhere in the world. We have now put forth the initiative of curtailing all of our military bases abroad as well as our military presence there by the year 2000. We are prepared to head toward the dissolution of the military-political blocs in Europe on a mutual basis.

> —*former Soviet Foreign Minister Eduard Shevardnadze*
> *in a speech to the Supreme Soviet*
> *October 24, 1989*

Revolutionary changes have swept the Soviet Union and Eastern Europe. Soviet troops deployed in foreign countries, which numbered 760,000 in 1988, are being withdrawn and demobilized by the hundreds of thousands. Radically new thinking dominates Soviet foreign policy, apparently stemming from both a major reassessment of international relations and military threats and from domestic economic and political needs. The 45-year-old Cold War is over. The Warsaw Pact is dead. A new era has begun.

While *The Sun Never Sets* is primarily concerned with foreign U.S. military forces and bases, it would not be complete without examining "the other side." This is a complex task. On the one hand, the "Soviet threat" has been enormously exaggerated and exploited by forces within the United States in order to justify a militarized and imperialist system. On the other hand, those who have resisted U.S. wars and militarism have at times ignored

Soviet military domination and intervention, or apologized for it as merely a reaction to U.S. or Western aggression.

Our analysis must therefore be "nuanced." The Soviet Union clearly maintained communist governments in several Eastern European countries with its occupying armies and the use of, or threatened use of, military force. Moscow also expanded its military presence in the Third World and on the oceans, as well as its ability to project military force into much of Asia from its own territory. However, the Soviet Union never developed large military bases in the Third World that could rival those of the United States, and Moscow is now reducing the military, political, and economic support it has given to sympathetic third world regimes and movements.

Because public knowledge of Soviet foreign policy in the United States is limited, and because it has been so distorted by decades of Cold War rhetoric, we need to place the issue of foreign Soviet military bases and presence in the larger context of Soviet foreign policy. This can only be understood in an historical context. An examination of Soviet foreign and military policy since World War II enables one to appreciate the magnitude of the changes which have recently swept the Soviet Union and the world. It will be helpful first to consider Soviet foreign and military policy toward the Eastern European nations, where the great majority of its foreign bases have been. Then we will look at the Third World, and finally examine the "new thinking" which has so changed Soviet foreign policy.

This focus makes sense because of the 760,000 Soviet troops deployed outside Soviet borders in 1988, the great majority—565,000—were in Eastern Europe. It appears that most of these will be pulled out within two or three years. Another 116,000 were in Afghanistan; they were all removed by February 15, 1989. Of 55,000 Soviet troops in Mongolia in 1988, 37,000 remained in mid-1990, of which 27,000 were soon to be withdrawn. (See Table on page 72.)[1]

Outside of these nations, Moscow maintained no combat ground forces, with the possible exception of the alleged "combat brigade" of 3,000 men in Cuba. Other Soviet deployments were limited to military advisers, technicians, air-defense forces, and support personnel. Unlike the United States, the Soviet Union has rarely used its own military force for coercive military intervention or the preservation of military access outside of the countries along its immediate border. Moscow has frequently helped friendly regimes defend themselves, for example, by providing air-defense systems and advisers to Egypt and Syria, and by providing military assistance to Ethiopia when it was attacked by Somalia. It has supported insurgencies with arms and training as well. But when told to leave, as in Egypt in 1972 and 1975 and Somalia in 1977, the Soviets packed up and got out.

The Soviet Military in Eastern Europe

Eight days before German troops swept into Poland on September 1, 1939, the Soviet leadership shocked the world by signing a non-aggression treaty with Nazi Germany. In two secret protocols, Hitler and Stalin agreed to divide northeastern Europe into spheres of influence. After the Nazi invasion of Poland, the Soviet Army moved into Estonia, Latvia, Lithuania and eastern Poland. In July 1940, questionably elected parliaments of what had been, since the end of World War I, the three independent Baltic states voted to seek admission to the Soviet Union.

Hitler broke his agreement with Stalin and invaded the Soviet Union on June 22, 1941. After losing 20 million lives and suffering incalculable destruction, the Soviet Union emerged from World War II determined to prevent such an invasion from ever happening again. The Red Army had pushed the Nazis out of Poland, Czechoslovakia, Hungary, Romania, and Bulgaria and had reached the Elbe in Germany. At Yalta, Roosevelt and Churchill recognized Stalin's *fait accompli:* an Eastern European sphere of Soviet influence. Moscow incorporated Poland's three Eastern provinces plus parts of Czechoslovakia, Romania, Finland, and East Prussia (formerly part of Germany), within its own borders.

By 1948, the Soviets had established compliant communist regimes in all of the Eastern European nations, including the Soviet-controlled part of Germany. Indigenous Eastern European communist parties were brought under the control of Moscow; when necessary, they and the Russians rigged elections, intimidated, arrested, and executed political leaders who opposed Soviet control. In tightening his grip on Eastern Europe, Stalin, admittedly a ruthless dictator, was in part responding to hostile post-war initiatives taken by the United States.

Following the experience of Hitler and the Nazis, Stalin's imposition of control over Eastern Europe contributed to the popular picture in the West of an expansionist Soviet Union intent upon sending the Red Army into surrounding nations in an effort to take over the world. This view was reinforced by the Soviet Army's brutal suppression of the Hungarian uprising in 1956, the Soviet occupation of Czechoslovakia in August 1968, and the Soviet military intervention in Afghanistan from 1979 to 1989. Messianic Soviet rhetoric trumpeting the inevitability of the triumph of socialism over capitalism lent credence to this view.

Until recently, control of Eastern Europe was seen as essential by Moscow. With the establishment of communist regimes in Poland, the German Democratic Republic (GDR, or "East Germany"), Czechoslovakia, Hungary, Romania, Bulgaria, Yugoslavia, and Albania, the Soviets finally had a buffer between themselves and the Western European nations which had launched such devastating invasions of Russia in the past. As the Cold War hardened, so did the Soviet grip on most of these countries.

The Warsaw Treaty Organization

In 1949, the United States, Canada, Iceland, Britain, Norway, Denmark, the Netherlands, Belgium, Luxembourg, France, Italy, and Portugal established the North Atlantic Treaty Organization (NATO), a military alliance aimed at "containing" the Soviet Union. Six years passed before the Soviets responded with the establishment of their own military alliance, the Warsaw Treaty Organization (WTO, often referred to as the "Warsaw Pact"). Moscow, fearful of German militarism, had advocated a plan for a neutral, demilitarized, and permanently divided Germany. But the Western powers refused and, on May 9, 1955, the Federal Republic of Germany was incorporated into NATO. Five days later at a meeting in Warsaw, government representatives from Albania, Bulgaria, Czechoslovakia, the German Democratic Republic, Hungary, Poland, Romania, and the USSR signed the Warsaw Treaty. (Yugoslavia refused to join, and Albania left the Pact in 1968.)

The Warsaw Treaty committed its signatories to several steps, including: 1) consultation should the security of any of the signatories be threatened, with the commitment to assist one another in the event of an armed attack in Europe on any one of them; 2) establishment of a joint command for their armed forces, as well as a political consultative committee which put the communist parties in control of the militaries; 3) cooperation in economic and cultural relations, but with an explicit commitment not to interfere in one another's internal affairs. The Warsaw Treaty also legitimized the presence of Soviet troops in Eastern Europe. Status-of-forces agreements were concluded with Hungary, Romania, the GDR, and Poland, which provided for a continuation of the Soviet military presence in those countries and the right to carry out exercises.[2] Romania, while never formally withdrawing from the Warsaw Pact, forced Moscow to remove its troops in 1958 and developed an independent military force capable of resisting Soviet military intervention.

In addition to strengthening the Soviet Union's ability to defend against an attack from Western Europe, the Warsaw Pact provided (until 1989) a means of assuring the "stability" and continuation of compliant communist regimes in most member states. The presence and active intervention of Soviet troops prevented Eastern European peoples from forming other governments or breaking with the Soviet Union. Domination of the armed forces of Poland, Czechoslovakia, Hungary, and the GDR by the Soviet military command precluded the possibility that these forces might oppose

Soviet forces in the event of a popular revolt. By controlling the size, armament, training, and to some extent the command of Eastern European armies, and by requiring all higher Eastern European officers in these armies to study in Soviet military academies, Soviet leaders prevented the evolution of independent Eastern European military forces which conceivably could resist Soviet military intervention in a crisis.[3]

Soviet Military Intervention in Eastern Europe

During the Cold War period, Soviet troops engaged in direct military intervention in the GDR, Hungary, and Czechoslovakia, and twice threatened military intervention in Poland. In each case, Moscow was responding to serious threats to the communist regimes or to the continued leading role of the Communist Party. Without Soviet intervention or the clear threat of intervention, the communist governments in each of these nations would probably have been ousted or the power of the communist parties greatly weakened.

The first direct military intervention occurred in the GDR in June, 1953, when Soviet troops already stationed there moved quickly to put down spontaneous strikes and protests initiated by East German workers.[4] The bloodiest case of direct Soviet military intervention in Eastern Europe came in 1956 with the suppression of the Hungarian revolt. Rebelling Hungarians sought wide-ranging political and economic reforms and a greater degree of sovereignty in their relationship with the Soviet Union. The revolt was initially directed against the Hungarian Communist Party and the political police, but the introduction of a few thousand Soviet troops into the streets of Budapest generated increased resistance and gave a strongly anti-Soviet character to the fighting.

Eventually, 200,000 Soviet troops and 2,000 tanks were used to crush the Hungarian uprising. Several thousand Hungarians were killed. Newly appointed reform leader and Prime Minister Imre Nagy was arrested and executed. The Hungarian Army, elements of which had fought Soviet troops, was virtually disbanded and never again allowed to reach even half its 1956 size. The Hungarians had to agree to the "temporary stationing" of Soviet troops in their country; in 1988, these numbered some 65,000.[5]

Immediately prior to the Hungarian revolt, the Soviets also threatened military intervention to stem a crisis in Poland. To forestall direct intervention, the leader of the reformist wing of the Polish Party, Wladislaw Gomulka, threatened to call on the Polish people to fight Soviet troops if Moscow intervened directly. Polish troops were deployed around Warsaw to stop advancing Soviets, and Polish forces actually fired upon a Soviet regiment trying to enter Poland from the GDR. At the same time, Gomulka assured

Soviet General Secretary Khrushchev of his desire to bring the situation in Poland under control. Khrushchev decided to call off plans for military action to see what Gomulka would do. He was soon rewarded as Gomulka brought the crisis under control and announced that Soviet troops would remain in Poland, stating that this was "in accordance with our highest state interests."[6]

In 1968, Soviet troops invaded and occupied Czechoslovakia. As in Hungary, and Poland, Moscow was alarmed by political developments threatening socialist orthodoxy and the relationship with the Union of Soviet Socialist Republics. Unlike Hungary, however, this revolution was directed by the Communist Party. Alexander Dubcek and other Czech Communist Party reformers assumed power in January, 1968, seeking to develop "socialism with a human face." Czech citizens responded enthusiastically. There were no riots or disturbances to justify Soviet military action, and the Soviets had no troops stationed within the country.[7]

As demands for reforms in Czechoslovakia grew and Soviet pressure proved ineffective, Moscow became deeply alarmed. On July 14, leaders of the Soviet Union, East Germany, Poland, Hungary, and Bulgaria met in Warsaw and addressed a stern letter to the Czech leadership:

> This is no longer your concern alone...We shall never consent to the endangering of these historic achievements of socialism...The danger to the basis of socialism in Czechoslovakia threatens also the common interests of other socialist countries...[8]

This was the first statement of what came to be known as the "Brezhnev Doctrine." It established the basis for direct military intervention in the affairs of allied socialist states if and when the rule of a compliant Communist Party was threatened.

Dubcek, however, continued on the reform path, and on August 20, 1968, 400,000 Soviet and allied troops entered and occupied Czechoslovakia. These included 100,000 troops from four non-Soviet Warsaw Pact nations: Poland, Hungary, the GDR, and Bulgaria. Though most of these were withdrawn within a few days, the implied political support was important. Soviet forces arrested Dubcek and several other key reform leaders. Though no military resistance was offered, the Czechs surprised the Soviets with a spontaneous, sustained campaign of nonviolent civilian resistance. The resistance was so strong that the Soviets could not get rid of Dubcek until April 1969, when he finally was forced to step down in favor of the pro-Soviet Gustav Husak as Party Secretary. Eventually, Soviet troops were reduced to 80,000, a level which remained fairly constant through 1989.

The final major threat of direct Soviet military intervention in Eastern Europe came in 1980-81 in response to the movement led by Solidarity, the powerful independent Polish trade union. The rise of Solidarity began with a strike by workers in the huge Lenin Shipyard in Gdansk on August 14, 1980. Solidarity soon mounted the most serious challenge to Soviet hegemony in Eastern Europe since the war. Workers and intellectuals led the movement, and most of Polish society united behind them. This was a mass popular revolt, which—nine years later—finally took over the government and ended the "leading role" of the Communist Party in Poland.[9]

Moscow immediately appreciated the magnitude of this threat to communist rule. However, Soviet leaders wanted to avoid direct military intervention if possible. Were Soviet forces to invade, they could expect massive, violent popular resistance and direct attacks by some elements of the Polish armed forces. Even after crushing most resistance, a long and costly occupation would be necessary. The spectre of Afghanistan, where the Soviet military was deeply bogged down, must have had a sobering influence. Western European governments, which had not made a big issue over Afghanistan, could not be expected to ignore bloodshed in Poland. As Poland and other Eastern European nations had developed important economic relations with Western Europe, a serious setback to East-West detente would be a serious problem for Warsaw and Moscow, even though NATO would almost certainly have refrained from using military force. In short, the growing interdependence of all European nations helped to restrain Moscow from direct military invasion of another Eastern European country.

In the end, Brezhnev and the moderate Polish Party leadership played a waiting game for 15 months before acting decisively. By December 1981, splits within Solidarity had deepened and economic problems troubled many Poles. General Jaruzelski then declared martial law, replaced the civilian government with a Military Council of National Salvation, ended the legal status of Solidarity and arrested hundreds of its leaders. Moscow must have been relieved, but its troubles in Poland were by no means over.

Recent Political and Military Developments in Eastern Europe

In the latter half of 1989, a tidal wave of change inundated Eastern Europe. In September, Solidarity formed the first non-communist government in Eastern Europe in over 40 years. Within four months, movements for democracy in all of the Warsaw Treaty countries, finding massive public support, swept existing Communist Party leaders from power. These movements forced the communist parties of Poland, Hungary, East Germany, Czechoslovakia, Bulgaria, and Romania to renounce their constitutionally guaranteed "leading roles" and to promise free elections. By the spring of 1990, non-communists governed Czechoslovakia, the German Democratic Republic, and Hungary, as well as Poland. The German Democratic Republic reunified with—or was assimilated by—the Federal Republic of Germany on October 3, 1990. Only in Romania and Bulgaria did people elect socialist governments in the spring of 1990.

Most of the rigid communist parties of Eastern Europe had long exhausted whatever popular support they once enjoyed. Only the threat of Soviet intervention kept them in power for so long. When Gorbachev renounced the Brezhnev Doctrine, their fate was sealed. Gorbachev's first statement on this came in February 1986, when he proclaimed "unconditional respect" for each socialist nation's right "to choose the paths and forms of its development." Gorbachev stated this still more clearly in a speech to the European Parliament in Strasbourg in July 1989, pledging that people had the right not only to choose, but to change their social system without interference from any outside force.

In October 1989, as the East German party was tottering, Soviet Foreign Minister Eduard Shevardnadze reminded the Supreme Soviet, "[In the Warsaw Pact] there have been historic, qualitative changes. We are building our relations with [our allies] on the basis of sovereign equality, the impermissibility of any intervention and the recognition of each country's absolute freedom of choice."[10] Early in October, during his visit to East Berlin, it is widely assumed that Gorbachev told Honecker that he would receive no help from Soviet troops in his attempts to retain power. The Kremlin also sent clear signals to hard-line Czech Party leaders that they should make way for change.

There are many reasons that Moscow gave up its "right" to intervene in Eastern Europe. First of all, Gorbachev's own program of *perestroika, glasnost,* and democratization would have been aborted if Soviet troops fought in Eastern Europe. Secondly, mass public support for change in these countries was so deep and so highly mobilized that the Soviets had to expect massive resistance from many elements of the national armed forces and from entire populations if Moscow tried military intervention. Thirdly, the Cold War—apparently dead, or at least moribund—would have been born again, with serious economic, military, and political consequences for the Soviet Union. Fourthly, the fact of increased communication and stronger economic ties between Eastern and Western European nations and the rest of the world made it very difficult for Moscow to ignore the likely reactions to military intervention from other nations and peoples. Finally, Moscow had its hands full at home with independence-minded nationalities and desperate economic problems. Soviet leaders appeared to appreciate that the forces of history, on top of which they long had claimed to ride, made resistance to the tide of change in Eastern Europe futile. In fact, *glasnost* and *perestroika* in the Soviet Union had been a major stimulus to revolution in Eastern Europe.

During the revolutions of 1989, Soviet leaders initially insisted upon one bottom line: the integrity of the Warsaw Pact. In forming a government, Solidarity allowed the Polish Communist Party to retain the Ministries of Defense and of Internal Affairs (which oversees the police and internal security), and assured the Soviets that they would not leave the Warsaw Pact. A Soviet Deputy Foreign Minister warned the Poles against "attempts to exploit the process of forming a government for the purpose of destabilizing the situation in the country and inflicting damage on its obligations as an ally."[11] For a brief time, Moscow appeared to have Washington's support in this matter. Even U.S. leaders hoped Gorbachev could "manage" a relatively smooth transition in Eastern Europe through the Warsaw Pact structure. Washington also recognized how difficult it would be to retain its own troops (and influence) in Europe without the Warsaw Pact.

By early 1990, however, it became apparent that most Soviet troops would be withdrawn from Eastern Europe and that the Warsaw Pact was finished as a military alliance. Moscow agreed to remove all Soviet troops from Czechoslovakia and Hungary by July 1, 1991, and the old mutual assistance treaties with these two countries were scrapped. The 360,000 Soviet troops in the German Democratic Republic will all be withdrawn by the end of 1994, four years after the reunification of Germany. The German government agreed to provide substantial financial aid to the USSR to help construct housing for these soldiers and their families. Only the Polish government has evinced any interest in retaining a temporary Soviet military presence, giving it leverage to assure German adherence to the post-war German/Polish border. In June 1990, ministers of the Warsaw Pact nations met for the last time as leaders of a military alliance.

These developments have outstripped the pace of the negotiations on Conventional Forces in Europe (CFE), in which the United States and the Soviet Union agreed that each be allowed to maintain 195,000 troops in Central Europe (plus another 30,000 in Britain, Italy, and Turkey for the United States). With almost all Soviet troops now forced to leave Eastern Europe, questions are focussed on the size and goals of U.S. force deployments in Europe and the overall relationships of Washington and Moscow to the "new Europe" of the 1990s. Proposals from independent experts and Senator Sam Nunn are calling for reductions in U.S. forces in Europe to a range of 70,000 to 100,000.

In the meantime, all of the former Eastern European Warsaw Pact allies are unilaterally reducing their own military forces, developing independent defense policies which clearly conflict with Soviet-Warsaw Pact policies, and seeking closer ties with the European Community and even NATO. A historic opportunity exists to establish an entirely new collective security system for

Europe with sharply reduced levels of military forces deployed in largely defensive modes. The Conference for Security and Cooperation in Europe (CSCE) provides an important forum for discussing such a new system; the Soviets and many Europeans are interested, but the United States is dragging its feet. Instead, Washington used the "2 plus 4" talks (West and East Germany plus the United States, Britain, France and the Soviet Union) on German reunification as the primary forum for establishing a European security system which will continue to be dominated by the United States.

Soviet Foreign Military Presence in Areas of the Third World

The Soviet Union never had a global basing structure as extensive as that which the United States developed after World War II. Outside of Eastern Europe, the only large deployments of Soviet forces have been in Mongolia (1936 to 1956 and 1966 to the present), and in Afghanistan (1979 to 1989). Beyond its border areas, Soviet access to foreign military bases and support facilities grew slowly after 1953. Even with its increasing military access to foreign facilities, however, Moscow always maintained a much smaller military presence in the Third World than did the United States.

Soviet foreign policy toward the Third World has generally been cautious, particularly regarding the possibility of open military conflict with the United States. At least since the early 1970s, Soviet leaders have believed that the United States would risk nuclear war to protect its "vital interests" in the Third World, and particularly in the Middle East.[12] This belief was confirmed when the United States placed its nuclear forces on a high state of alert during the 1973 Arab-Israeli war, and when President Carter proclaimed in 1980 (in response to the Soviet invasion of Afghanistan) that the United States would use "any means necessary" to defend access to Persian Gulf oil.

Like the United States, the Soviet Union has had its share of failures in the Third World, as in China, Indonesia, Egypt, Somalia, and Afghanistan. Both superpowers have had to contend with growing nationalism in third world nations. But Moscow now faces a larger problem—a growing conviction that socialism does not work. The Soviet Union came to be seen as a one-dimensional power, its superpower status resting almost solely upon its military might and arms sales. The United States, on the other hand, remains an economic as well as military superpower, and its influence is correspondingly larger. Now Japan and Western Europe have become economic superpowers—and their military capabilities are increasing as well. In terms of priority, relations with most of the Third World always ranked below other concerns for the Soviet Union. Relationships with the United States, Europe,

China, and Japan; maintenance of a nuclear and conventional military balance; and avoidance of a major war with these nations all weighed more heavily for Soviet leaders than power in the Third World. Until recently, maintaining Soviet hegemony in Eastern Europe also ranked as a top foreign policy priority for Moscow. Compared with these concerns, Soviet interests in Africa, Latin America, and the Pacific were much less important.[13] Moscow engaged in large-scale military action only in those countries within its "national security zone" along its own borders. Outside of this zone, Moscow's interests were much more limited than those of Washington.

Stages of Soviet Policy toward the Third World

The history of post-war Soviet foreign and military policies toward the Third World can be divided into four phases. Until the death of Stalin in 1953 there was very little Soviet activity in this area. This stemmed from the need to recover from the massive destruction of the war and the preoccupation with Eastern Europe, where Stalin sought to consolidate Soviet power.

In the second phase between 1954 and 1969, Khrushchev, then Brezhnev and Kosygin, pursued a more active, global foreign policy. They were able to capitalize upon goodwill in nations emerging from centuries of colonial domination by the capitalist West. Leaders of many of these countries were developing third world variants of Marxist-Leninist policies. The rapid industrialization of the Soviet Union under a highly centralized system was encouraging to them. Many third world leaders wanted weapons with which to defend their regimes, and the Soviets were prepared to supply them—$4 billion dollars worth between 1954 and 1969, plus $2 billion in economic aid. However, during this period, Moscow was limited in its ability to project military power in support of third world friends. Soviet weakness was evident during the 1956 Suez war, when they provided little direct help to Nasser as Egypt was attacked by Britain, France, and Israel; and in the 1960 Congo crisis, when Patrice Lumumba's requests for help went for nought. This pattern was repeated in the June 1967 Middle East war, when Soviet clients Egypt and Syria lost the Sinai Peninsula, the Gaza Strip, and the Golan Heights to Israel, and Jordan lost the West Bank.[14] The third phase of Soviet policy toward the Third World began in 1970. This marked the beginning of major Soviet military assistance to third world nations. The value of Soviet arms exports to third world nations in the decade 1970 to 1980, while somewhat lower than that of the United States, totalled over $30 billion. With its ally Cuba, the Soviets intervened with decisive military assistance to bring about favorable outcomes in the Angolan civil war and in Ethiopia's war with Somalia, and with less success aided Ethiopia's war against Eritrean rebels.

In December 1979, the Soviets launched a major invasion of Afghanistan.[15] In the wake of the U.S. defeat in Indochina, the "correlation of forces" seemed to the Soviets to be shifting in their favor.

During the period of 1970 to 1983, the Soviet Union gave considerable support to socialist nations and "states of socialist orientation," including Vietnam, Kampuchea, Afghanistan, South Yemen, Syria, Ethiopia, Mozambique, Angola, Cuba, and Nicaragua. This support included weapons, training of military and security personnel (the latter often by East Germans), and provision of Soviet military advisors. In return, they were able to gain access to military bases and support facilities in most of these countries (though not in Nicaragua). By 1983, however, Soviet leaders recognized major problems with this policy. First, the United States had adopted more aggressive and militarized policies toward these nations and toward the Soviet Union. Under the "Reagan Doctrine," the United States created and/or supported counter-revolutionary armed struggles in Kampuchea, Afghanistan, Angola, Mozambique, and Nicaragua, and intervened in the tiny island of Grenada to overthrow a Marxist regime. Even before Reagan's election, Soviet military intervention in Afghanistan dealt the death blow to what remained of detente—and the SALT II Treaty.

In addition, it was obvious to Moscow that its clients were among the economically weakest states in the Third World. Most represented a net loss for an already ailing Soviet economy. In many, the nationalization of industries and collectivization of agriculture seemed to aggravate existing economic problems—particularly in the context of a world economy dominated by capitalists. Meanwhile, the growing third world powers were pursuing capitalism with a vengeance, and few (with the exception of India) were aligned with the Soviet Union.

Under Mikhail Gorbachev and the new reform leadership, Soviet foreign policy toward the Third World entered a fourth phase marked by pragmatism and retrenchment. Soviet leaders began reducing assistance to the struggling "states of socialist orientation" and seeking stronger ties with "newly industrializing countries" and regional third world powers such as Brazil, Argentina, Mexico, Egypt, Saudi Arabia, Oman, the United Arab Emirates, Kuwait, even Israel; the ASEAN states of Indonesia, Malaysia, and Thailand; and India. Such a course is consistent with Moscow's desire to become more fully integrated into the (capitalist) world economy. It has also meant that Moscow had to reduce its military presence in many areas of the world.

The Far East and the Pacific

Since the late 1970s, the United States has decried a massive Soviet military buildup in East Asia and the Pacific. In 1983, the Joint Chiefs of Staff cited growth in the Soviet Pacific fleet ("now the largest"), naval aviation threatening sea lines of communication, strengthened air and ground units in the eastern U.S.S.R., and use of "important air and naval bases" in Vietnam.[16] In a 15-year period, the Soviet Pacific fleet more than doubled its tonnage.[17]

Ground and air forces deployed against China were also doubled, totalling nearly 500,000 troops in 1987. In 1966, the Soviet Union introduced troops into Mongolia; they numbered 55,000 in 1988. In 1969, Sino-Soviet tensions came to a head with heavy fighting along parts of their common border in incidents spanning a six-month period. At one point the Kremlin warned Beijing that it was courting the risk of nuclear war if Chinese troops continued to attack.[18] Nuclear weapons in the Soviet Far East, both strategic and theater, were increased. By the mid-1980s, these weapons included SS-20 intermediate range nuclear missiles, air-launched cruise missiles on bombers, as well as sea-launched cruise missiles on submarines and ICBMs. In 1978 and 1979, the Soviets sent more than 20 warships to patrol the southern Chinese coast as a warning to China to limit its military actions against Vietnam.[19] In addition to these China-oriented deployments, 10,000 Soviet troops and 40 MiG-23s were deployed in the Kurile Islands, just north of Hokkaido, which the Soviet Union took from Japan at the end of World War II, and which Japan wants returned. Soviet forces also began practicing amphibious landings in these islands in 1978 and increased naval and military aircraft activities around the main Japanese islands.[20]

The East Asian region boasts the only real foreign Soviet base in the Third World—the former U.S. naval port at Cam Ranh Bay in Vietnam. As of 1988, the Soviets had 2,500 military personnel in Vietnam, most at Cam Ranh Bay. The Soviets maintained a substantial force there, including two or three submarines, three or four surface combatants, a squadron of medium-range bombers, another squadron of 14 fighter planes, and a few propeller- driven long-range bombers.[21] In 1988, the Pentagon expressed its fears:

> Access to Cam Ranh Bay has enabled the Soviets to establish a continuous naval presence in the South China Sea and to support naval operations in the Indian Ocean more efficiently. Cam Ranh Bay also extends the Soviets war-time reach over East Asia's sea lines of communication in the South China Sea and poses a challenge as well to the U.S. military presence in the Philippines.[22]

Compared with U.S. bases in the Philippines, with 17,000 military personnel and 13,000 civilians at Subic Bay Naval Base and Clark Air Field, the Soviet presence in Vietnam paled in significance. Outside of Vietnam,

Soviet military access in the region was extremely limited. In fact, Soviet naval vessels tended to use offshore anchorages for mooring (for example, near the Philippines, and south of Singapore) because of the unavailability of ports in other countries.[23] By early 1990, even the Soviet presence at Cam Ranh Bay was being reduced, as they withdrew their squadron of MiG-23 fighter planes and TU-16 bombers.[24]

The Soviet Pacific buildup also cost Moscow dearly in terms of relations in the region. Writing in 1988, one analyst stressed:

> In overall terms Soviet policies toward East Asia must be assessed as a spectacular failure. Indochina excepted, it has earned the hostility and enmity of all its Asian neighbors, Socialist and non-Socialist alike. The two main Soviet efforts to contain China, and to weaken the American alliance system, have both failed. Instead, China has moved into alignment with the United States and Japan. The United States, on friendly terms with both China and Japan, has never had better relations with East Asia in the twentieth century, while the USSR's relations are almost universally poor.[25]

Mikhail Gorbachev responded to this "spectacular failure" with major peace initiatives in the East Asian and Pacific region, hoping to enable the Soviet Union to participate in the booming Pacific Rim economy. The INF agreement to destroy nuclear-armed SS-20 missiles in Asia, visits by Soviet Foreign Minister Shevardnadze to Japan and the ASEAN nations of Thailand, Malaysia, and Indonesia, and endorsement of the South Pacific nuclear-free zone treaty all improved Moscow's standing.[26] In 1988, Moscow proposed a mutual pullout of Soviet and U.S. forces from their bases in Vietnam and the Philippines, pressured Vietnam to get its troops out of Cambodia, dropped claims and reduced tensions along the Chinese border, and promised to cut 200,000 of the roughly 450,000 Soviet troops in the Soviet Far East. Most of the 55,000 Soviet troops in Mongolia are being withdrawn; they should number no more than 10,000 by the end of 1991 and be reduced to zero by the end of 1992. Soviet naval and air forces in the Pacific have been cut by 15 to 25 percent, and warships are spending less time at sea.[27] With these initiatives, plus the withdrawal from Afghanistan, Gorbachev was able to get a summit meeting in Beijing. Sino-Soviet political and economic relations are warming. In June 1990, Gorbachev became the first Soviet leader to meet with a head of state of South Korea. He also affirmed his desire for a summit meeting in Tokyo, which will probably occur in 1991, and began indicating flexibility on the disputed Kurile Islands. Moscow thus continues to work for detente in the Pacific and an entree into the booming East Asian/Pacific economy.

Afghanistan and South Asia

Soviet military intervention in Afghanistan was the final blow to U.S.-Soviet detente in the 1970s. The introduction of 115,000 Soviet troops, beginning in December of 1979, convinced most Americans of the aggressive intentions of the Soviet Union. This helped pave the way for the election of Ronald Reagan and a massive U.S. military buildup. Alarmists saw in the Soviet move proof of the "historic Russian drive for warm-water ports," and President Carter announced that the United States would use "any means necessary" (that is, nuclear weapons) to protect "vital interests" in the Persian Gulf. Most of the world condemned the Soviet action throughout the years of war; Islamic states were particularly vehement in their denunciations.

Finally, on February 15, 1989, the last Soviet soldier left Afghanistan. More than one million Afghans are believed to have been killed (on both sides). Five million refugees (of a total population of 15 million) fled Afghanistan for the relative safety of Pakistan and Iran. The Soviets suffered 13,310 soldiers killed and 35,478 wounded.[28] A comparison with the U.S. war in Indochina is instructive: U.S. troops in Vietnam numbered 540,000 in 1969; by war's end, 58,000 U.S. soldiers had been killed and 153,000 wounded. More then 2.2 million Indochinese are estimated to have been killed during the U.S. war in Indochina.

Afghanistan had been within the Soviet sphere of influence throughout the post-war period, accommodating its foreign policy to Soviet wishes while allowing traditional Afghan political institutions to operate within the country. In 1978, Afghan Marxists toppled a pro-Soviet but non-communist government. By late 1979, they were losing control as their leaders fought each other, and armed resistance to their reforms grew. Alarmed at the prospect of a hostile rebel government in Kabul, Soviet troops entered Afghanistan in force on December 27, 1979. The current party leader was murdered, and Babrak Karmal, another Afghan Marxist preferred by the Soviets, was brought in to rule.[29]

There is no evidence to support the theory that the invasion of Afghanistan was viewed by Soviet leaders as a prelude to further aggression in the region. At most, the Brezhnev Doctrine was being applied to an Asian neighbor. After years of bitter fighting and a marked escalation of U.S. and Chinese military aid to the Mujahideen, Moscow installed a new leader, Najibullah, and began negotiating for an end to the war.

Having left Afghanistan, Soviet military access in South Asia is extremely limited. Despite their long-standing relationship with India, the Indian government has always refused to provide basing rights to the Soviet military. Soviet ships occasionally call at ports in southern India for refuelling, but nothing more.[30] During the 1980s, the Soviet Navy's Indian Ocean

Squadron averaged 20 to 25 ships, including surface combatants and submarines. This force depended primarily upon naval support facilities on Dahlak Island in the Red Sea (Ethiopia) and ports in and off the coast of South Yemen.[31]

The Middle East and North Africa

The potential for superpower military conflict in the Middle East was, for a long time, much higher than in any other part of the world. This is a region of many deep and violent conflicts. The West—and particularly the United States—claims vital interests in this oil-rich area, all of which lies within a few hundred miles of the Soviet border. Beginning with Khrushchev, Soviet leaders sought to build influence and compete with the United States for strategic position on their southern flank.

The extent of the enormous changes in U.S.-Soviet relations by mid-1990 might best be measured by the remarkable degree of cooperation between Washington and Moscow in condemning the Iraqi invasion of Kuwait and supporting an economic blockade of Iraq. It is unlikely that any previous U.S. president would have dared to deploy such a huge contingent of U.S. military forces into this region so close to the Soviet border, for the risk of war, and a nuclear exchange, with the Soviet Union would have been too great. While Moscow appeared to try to restrain Washington to some extent, Soviet leaders supported the U.S.-led anti-Iraq alliance, turning their backs on their former ally. They even acceded to the presence of more than 350,000 U.S. troops in the Persian Gulf, just a few hundred miles from their border.

Despite major Soviet investments in the region in the 1950s, 1960s, and 1970s, Moscow has little to show in terms of influence and military access. One of its most spectacular foreign policy failures in the Third World was in Egypt. For nearly two decades (1955-1972), the Soviet Union provided Cairo with more arms and military advisors than it did for any other third world country.[32] By 1972, 21,000 Soviet military personnel were in Egypt, most manning an air-defense system against Israeli air attacks. In return, the Soviet Navy enjoyed the use of extensive port facilities on the Mediterranean, and they began to build a new base at Mersa Matruh. But Egyptian President Anwar Sadat became angry with Moscow, in part over its refusal to meet certain requests for arms. By the end of 1972, he expelled the Soviet air-defense operators and advisors, took over the uncompleted Soviet naval base at Mersa Matruh, and ordered Soviet naval reconnaissance, antisubmarine, and offensive aircraft out of Egypt.[33]

Moscow continued to supply Egypt and Syria with weapons, and in October 1973, Sadat launched attacks against Israeli troops who had been occupying the Sinai. Within a few weeks, the Soviet government delivered tens of thousands of tons of war materiel to Egypt and Syria, increased its naval presence in the Mediterranean to 96 ships and submarines, and threatened to insert its own troops into the fighting if Israel proceeded to destroy a huge contingent of Egyptian forces which had already surrendered. In response, President Nixon leaned on Israel, put U.S. nuclear forces on a heightened state of alert, and a truce was soon achieved.[34] Believing that the United States was the real kingpin in the region, Sadat expelled all remaining Soviet military personnel in 1976, terminated the 1971 Soviet-Egyptian Treaty of Friendship and Cooperation, and made his historic turn toward Camp David and the United States. All of Moscow's arms and assistance had been for nought.

Since the loss of Egypt, Moscow's most powerful ally in the region has been Syria. Syria's war in Lebanon and its efforts to create "strategic parity" with Israel created a strong need for a continuous flow of arms. Beginning in the late 1970s, Syria found itself increasingly isolated as tensions with its Arab neighbors Iraq and Jordan grew. Feeling itself in need of support from a superpower, Damascus moved closer to Moscow, signing a Treaty of Friendship and Cooperation with the U.S.S.R. in 1980.[35] After the Israeli invasion of Lebanon in 1982, the Soviets delivered a sophisticated air-defense system of SAM-5 missiles to Syria to enable it to defend against Israeli air attacks. With the missiles came 5,000 Soviet troops and technicians to operate them. Reflecting Soviet distrust of its Syrian ally, Soviet soldiers appeared to maintain complete control over the missile system.[36] The U.S.S.R. also re-equipped Syria's military, providing $8.9 billion worth of arms between 1983 and 1987.[37] In 1990, 2,000 Soviet troops were stationed in Syria.

In return for Soviet arms and assistance, Syria provided facilities which supported the Soviet military presence in the Mediterranean. Soviet naval reconnaissance aircraft frequently used airfields in Syria, and port facilities at Latakia have been used for refueling and supplying surface ships.[38] By 1990, however, Soviet military and diplomatic support for Damascus was decreasing as Moscow sought to cut its expenses and seek better relations with moderate Arab regimes and with Israel.

Moscow's most dependable ally in the Middle East was the Marxist state of South Yemen, situated at the tip of the Arabian Peninsula along the strategic Bab el Mandab Strait between the Red Sea and the Indian Ocean. The Soviets assisted anti-Royalist forces with military advisors there in 1967, and Soviet pilots allegedly flew combat missions.[39] In return, the Soviet military enjoyed extensive use of a naval base at Aden (capital of South Yemen), as well as a few other ports, anchorages, and airfields. The naval base at Aden has been particularly important for the small Soviet Indian

Ocean fleet.[40] In 1990, Soviet forces in South Yemen numbered 1,000. With the unification of North and South Yemen in May 1990, however, continued Soviet access to military facilities in Yemen is uncertain.

In Libya, the Soviet Union maintained 2,000 military personnel and has had regular access to port facilities at Tripoli and Benghazi and to Okba ben Nafi air base. Libyan airfields were used by Soviet transport planes during the 1975 airlift to Angola. Soviet forces in Libya include advisors and technicians who help maintain Soviet fighter planes, bombers, transport planes, and helicopters in the Libyan air force.[41] Libya has an enormous supply of arms and advanced weapon systems, half of which have come from the Soviet Union. Early in 1989, Washington expressed alarm when it learned of a transfer of six sophisticated SU-24D Soviet bombers to Libya.[42] The Soviet Union also has 1,000 military personnel in Algeria and had 600 in Iraq. Soviet ships have made port calls in both of these countries for many years.

Mikhail Gorbachev has wrought important changes in Soviet policies toward the Middle East and North Africa. The Soviet stress on avoiding major regional wars has become even stronger; in 1987, Gorbachev told Syrian President Assad that "the reliance on military force has completely lost its credibility as a way of solving Middle East conflict."[43] This complements the new Soviet concern to cultivate closer relations with all states in the region, including pro-Western ones. Moscow established full diplomatic relations with Oman and the United Arab Emirates in 1985, arranged contacts with prominent Saudi diplomats, promptly responded to Kuwait's request for protection of its ships during the the Iraq-Iran "tanker war" of 1987, and strongly opposed Iraq's invasion of Kuwait in 1990.[44] By agreeing to reschedule Egypts's $3 billion debt, Moscow improved relations with Cairo. The Soviet Union is also developing ties with Iran: an oil pipeline from Iran to the Black Sea is planned, and a multibillion dollar arms deal may be in the works.[45]

With the collapse of Eastern Europe and further Soviet retrenchment, radical Arab regimes and the Palestinian Liberation Organization have become acutely aware of the loss of Soviet support. Former Soviet Foreign Minister Shevardnadze met with Prime Minister Peres of Israel as the Kremlin edged toward resumption of diplomatic relations, and Moscow pressured the PLO to make a clear statement on Israel's right to exist.[46] PLO cadres no longer get military training in the Soviet Union and Eastern Europe; the supply of weapons, and even scholarships for Palestinian students to study in Eastern European universities, has evaporated.

As for Syria, intelligence sources report a "dramatic drawdown of Soviet advisors and technicians" as well as cuts in the supply of sophisticated weaponry. The Kremlin is also asking Damascus to repay $15 billion in military debts. Soviet leaders reduced supplies of arms and cut-rate oil to Marxist South Yemen and pressed it to seek unification with non-Marxist North Yemen. Reflecting on the changes in the Middle East, Iraqi President Saddam Hussein declared, "After the dramatic and big change which has occurred, the Soviet Union has retreated in order to deal with its internal problems... The Soviet Union has shifted from its position of counterbalancing America."[47] After Iraq's August 1990 invasion of Kuwait, these words proved prophetic as Washington and Moscow united in condemning the invasion and supporting a United Nations boycott of trade with Iraq.

Africa

Soviet military assistance to Black African states grew substantially between the mid-1970s and the mid-1980s. Arms deliveries to the region in the years 1976 to 1983 totalled $7 billion—10 times more than those of the United States.[48] Soviet arms sales to the area reached $12.6 billion in the 1983-1987 period, during which time U.S. deliveries were under $1 billion. Eighty percent of these arms went to Angola and Ethiopia.[49] Washington viewed with alarm the new ability of the Soviet Union to provide meaningful military support to Marxist governments in Africa, thousands of miles from Soviet territory. The Pentagon also made much of Soviet military facilities in this huge continent.

Soviet military support to Somalia, Ethiopia, and Angola was particularly significant, and led to Soviet use of naval facilities in all three countries. Moscow began by supporting Somalia with arms, signing a friendship treaty in 1972, and gaining access to the port of Berbera. But when Somalian General Siad Barre used Soviet arms to attack the new Marxist government of Ethiopia in 1977, Moscow switched sides, delivering $1 billion in arms and assisting the transport of 10,000 Cuban troops to Ethiopia. Somalia immediately abrogated its friendship treaty with the Soviet Union and expelled Soviet advisors.[50] Within two years, former Soviet military facilities in Somalia were being used by the United States.

Meanwhile, Soviet military support for the Ethiopian regime continued. Ethiopian and Cuban forces, with assistance from Soviet officers, defeated Somalian troops. Moscow and Havana also continued to supply arms (worth over $6 billion in the period 1978 to 1987) and troops as the Ethiopian regime prosecuted a war with rebels in the provinces of Eritrea and Tigre. In return, the Soviet Navy enjoyed the use of Dahlak Archipelago as a major anchorage for its Indian Ocean squadron. Its ships also called at Assab, where a floating drydock was moored.[51] But in 1989, Moscow cut its massive arms transfers to Ethiopia's military regime and began pushing the government to negotiate with the Eritrean and Tigre rebels. In the spring of 1990, Ethiopia's military government appeared to be losing the battle with rebel troops, yet Moscow refused to allow the Ethiopian army to use Soviet aircraft in Addis Ababa to transport troops to the war zones. Soviet officials have stated that their military assistance program to the Ethiopian government will not be renewed after 1990.[52]

Soviet and Cuban military assistance was also decisive in the victory of the MPLA in Angola over rival liberation movements, the FNLA and UNITA. When Portugal granted independence to Angola in January 1975, fighting broke out among these three movements. The MPLA had been receiving Soviet aid for its liberation struggle against Portugal since 1958; the FNLA and UNITA received U.S. and Chinese aid. In June 1975, South African forces entered southern Angola on the side of the FNLA and UNITA and began pushing deep into the country. In response, Moscow and Havana increased their level of aid dramatically. The Soviets airlifted and sealifted $600 million in arms, and the Cubans sent 10,000 troops. The Soviet Navy sent a few ships to stand off the Angolan coast to discourage attacks on ports at which Soviet arms were being offloaded. Soviet military personnel in Angola were limited to 200 advisors. The U.S. public, remembering the lessons of Vietnam, would not condone massive aid to the other side. By March 1976, the MPLA had won a clear victory and recognition by the Organization of African Unity.[53]

Fighting in Angola continued after the MPLA's victory. U.S. assistance to UNITA was eventually increased, and South African support continued. Moscow sent $950 million in military aid during the 1978-1982 period, and $5.8 billion from 1983 to 1987.[54] Angola received a Soviet anti-aircraft missile defense system, Soviet fighter planes, and helicopters. In 1990, 1,000 Soviet and 500 East German military advisors remained in Angola. The Soviet Navy used Luanda as its principal naval base on the West African coast. A guided-missile destroyer and accompanying ships operated from this base, and an 8,500-ton floating drydock was used for ship repairs.[55] In addition, Moscow had 700 military personnel in Mozambique and 750 in other sub-Saharan African countries in 1990.

By the late 1980s, the Soviet relationship to many Black African states was changing. In Angola, Moscow urged the MPLA government and the Cubans to reach a compromise agreement with UNITA to halt the fighting. The Soviet Union promised major cuts in military assistance to Mozambique and reportedly will withdraw all its military advisers.[56] Moscow also began pressing the African National Congress to seek a negotiated solution in South Africa. Former Soviet allies in Eastern Europe no longer provide support for African liberation struggles; Hungary even welcomed a South African trade mission.[57]

Latin America

For years, alarms have been raised in the United States about the Soviet-Cuban threat to Central American and Caribbean nations and even to South America. Citing risks to Caribbean Basin nations and to "sea lines of communication," the Joint Chiefs-of-Staff, in their 1983 annual report to Congress, stated:

> Cuba and the Soviet Union constitute the greatest threat to U.S. security in the Caribbean Basin. Armed and supported economically by the Soviet Union, Cuba serves as a springboard for efforts to spread insurgency and revolution, as well as a base from which to project Soviet power into the Western Hemisphere in wartime... Threats to regional stability are further compounded by increased Soviet-Cuban ties to Nicaragua and combined efforts to instigate and support violence in Central America.[58]

Cuba has been a major point for East-West confrontation since the success of the Cuban revolution in 1959. The Cuban missile crisis of October 1962 possibly brought the world as close as it has ever come to the brink of nuclear war. Soviet General Secretary Nikita Khrushchev had secretly shipped 24 medium-range missiles to Cuba and was arming them with nuclear warheads when they were discovered by U.S. intelligence. After several tense days, President Kennedy secretly offered to withdraw obsolete U.S. nuclear missiles from Turkey and never to invade Cuba if Khrushchev would get his missiles out of Cuba. This offer, plus a selective U.S. Navy blockade of Cuba, the possibility of a U.S. invasion of the island, and the terrifying threat of nuclear war, convinced Khrushchev to withdraw Soviet missiles, and the crisis abated.[59]

Beginning in the 1960s, Moscow provided Havana with arms and economic aid. Between 1961 and 1975, Soviet military aid to Cuba was estimated at $4.5 billion. During the 1983 to 1987 period, this aid reached $7 billion.[60] As of 1990, the International Institute for Strategic Studies reported a Soviet combat brigade of approximately 2,800 men, another 1,200 Soviet military advisors, and some 2,100 Soviet military technicians in Cuba. Many of the latter operate a major intelligence and communications facility at Lourdes.[61] Soviet economic assistance to Cuba has been massive, reaching $5 to $8 billion per year by 1988.[62] The economic aid and arms help support 180,000 Cuban active-duty armed forces; in Latin America, only Brazil's armed forces are larger. But Soviet aid to Cuba is expected to decrease as Moscow seeks to ease the drain on its floundering economy and to further ease tensions with the United States.

The U.S. government saw the Nicaraguan revolution, the leftist insurgency in El Salvador, and the New Jewel Movement in Grenada as manifestations of the Soviet-Cuban threat. This threat was used to justify the *contra* war against the Sandinistas in Nicaragua; massive military and economic aid to the government of El Salvador; a major military presence, including new military bases in Honduras; and, ultimately, the invasion of Grenada. In fact, the Soviets have always been loathe to support armed struggle in Latin America, coming to the support of revolutionary Cuba and Nicaragua well after the success of each revolution—and after U.S. hostility to each new government was clearly manifested. Moscow failed to save the elected socialist government in Chile in 1973, and even Cuba has given little military aid to rebels in El Salvador. The roots of revolution in Latin America clearly lie in the soil of gross injustice and exploitation, not in the Soviet Union.[63]

Soviet 'New Thinking' in Foreign and Military Policy

Throughout the post-World War II period, the Soviet Union engaged in direct military intervention in countries removed from its borders far less often than did the United States. It used its enormous military forces primarily to maintain its control of Eastern Europe, to try to control Afghanistan, and in its conflict with a hostile China through massive deployments along the Sino-Soviet border and in Mongolia. Though its ability to provide direct support to third world governments in distant parts of the world grew in the 1970s and 1980s, Soviet leaders were generally careful not to provoke a direct military confrontation with the United States. The Cuban missile crisis was the exception which established the rule.

Though Moscow's ability to project military power over great distances grew, Soviet global reach—in terms of military presence, power projection capabilities, and access to bases, ports, airfields, communications and intelligence facilities—always paled beside that of its superpower rival. Moreover, Moscow—like Washington—suffered serious setbacks in its attempts to win favor and exert control in both the First and Third World. Nationalism, the strongest force in twentieth century international politics, led nations to resist any infringement on their sovereignty. Soviet leaders have had to face this force in China, Egypt, Afghanistan, Eastern Europe, and even within the Union of Soviet Socialist Republics.

During the latter half of the 1980s, a process of change in Soviet foreign and military policies (as well as domestic policies) began under General Secretary Mikhail Gorbachev and other Soviet reformers. This process accelerated as grass-roots opposition movements in Eastern Europe (and within many parts of the Soviet Union) exploded, catalyzing enormous popular protests which succeeded in overthrowing entrenched communist governments in matters of months or even weeks. While the outlines of a new

Europe and a new world order are not yet clear, and the possibility of domestic or inter-state violence in the Soviet Union and Eastern Europe cannot be ruled out, world leaders have proclaimed, "The Cold War is over."

What was the "new thinking" on foreign and military policy all about, and how did it contribute to the sweeping changes of 1989-1990? In his speech to the Twenty-seventh Congress of the Communist Party of the Soviet Union on February 26, 1986, Mikhail Gorbachev made a startling pronouncement on national security:

> The character of present-day weapons leaves any country no hope of safeguarding itself solely with military and technical means, for example, by building up a defense system, even the most powerful one. The task of ensuring security is increasingly seen as a political problem, and it can only be resolved by political means...Security cannot be built endlessly on fear of retaliation...or "deterrence."
>
> In the context of the relations between the U.S.S.R. and the U.S.A., security can only be mutual, and if we take international relations as a whole it can only be universal...It is vital that all should feel equally secure, for the fears and anxieties of the nuclear age generate unpredictability in politics and concrete actions.[64]

Departing from a fundamental tenet of Marxist-Leninist thought, Gorbachev insisted that the central imperative for Soviet foreign policy must be common human values and the need for peace, not a class analysis and the struggle between capitalism and socialism.[65]

Such "new thinking" led Soviet leaders to reverse long-held views and advocate startling new policies. They began by elevating the prevention of war far above any goal of winning a war. Though no rational leader would deliberately initiate a nuclear strike, they feared that a crisis could spiral out of control, creating an atmosphere of tension in which nuclear war could be initiated. If this were so, the pre-eminence of political measures for security, measures which ease tensions, prevent crises, and build peace and cooperation, are indeed more important than new weapon systems. This is also the basis for the assertion that security, especially among the major powers, can only be mutual. The more threatened Chinese or U.S. leaders feel by Soviet military forces, the more likely they are to panic in a crisis and launch an attack.

These premises led Soviet military analysts—particularly those outside the military itself—to the doctrine of "reasonable sufficiency." They argued that the Soviet Union did not need to match the United States missile for missile, but only to have reasonably sufficient forces to deter or defend against an attack. Thus, Gorbachev assured his people that the Soviet Union would respond to the threat of the Strategic Defense Initiative not by an equally costly program of space-based missile defense, but by developing far less costly countermeasures to the evolving U.S. system.[66] It was this understanding of "reasonable sufficiency" which led Mikhail Gorbachev to confound the experts and his own military leaders by promising unilaterally to reduce Soviet armed forces by half a million men, eliminating 50,000 troops and 5,000 tanks from Eastern Europe, in his dramatic speech to the United Nations on December 7, 1988.

This unilateral reduction is also an example of the most radical departure from long-standing Soviet military doctrine, namely, the concept of "non-offensive defense." While Soviet leaders have always described their military doctrine as "defensive," insisting that they would only resort to military force to defend against an attack on socialism, their actual strategy for such a defense was offensive. Soviet forces were designed and trained to carry war into the territory of the enemy. Gorbachev, however, called for "a force posture and military strategy sufficient to repel a conventional attack, but incapable of conducting a surprise attack with massive offensive operations against the territory of the other side."[67] Though Soviet military leaders resisted this revolutionary notion, Gorbachev initiated a restructuring of Soviet forces which would make it nearly impossible for them to launch a surprise attack in Europe. This restructuring began with the unilateral reductions promised in his speech to the United Nations, continued with the signing of the Treaty on conventional forces in Europe, and will culminate with the withdrawal of almost all Soviet forces from Eastern Europe and the dissolution of the Warsaw Pact.

How does new Soviet thinking about security affect Soviet foreign policy and its military presence beyond its borders? The most dramatic changes are clearly in the areas in which the Soviet military presence has been largest: the withdrawal of troops from Eastern Europe and the end of the Warsaw Pact, the withdrawal of all Soviet troops from Afghanistan, and major reductions of Soviet forces in Mongolia and along the Soviet border with China. In the Third World, Moscow has sharply reduced support for many Marxist regimes, liberation movements, and "states of socialist orientation," many of which were economically weak and constantly seeking Soviet aid. Soviet leaders have reduced material and military support to most former allies and clients in Asia, the Middle East, Africa, and the Caribbean Basin.

While turning away from many former third world allies and clients, Moscow has been seeking improved relations with regional powers such as Brazil, Argentina, Israel, Saudi Arabia, Iran, Japan, the "newly industrializing countries" of East Asia, and even South Africa. Responding to the need to conserve funds for domestic economic needs as well as the dictates of their new foreign policy, the Kremlin has also reduced its deep-water naval presence and withdrawn some forces from Cam Ranh Bay.[68] In early 1989, Gorbachev told Western visitors that Soviet military spending would soon be reduced by 14 percent, troop strength by 12 percent, and arms production by 19 percent.[69] In May 1990, a Soviet government spokesperson announced that the 1990 military budget was 8 percent lower than the 1989 budget and would be cut an additional 14 percent in the next two years.[70] Though development of advanced conventional munitions and the reorganization of Soviet forces may strengthen the Soviet military in certain respects, analysts agree that Moscow's capacity for surprise attack is greatly diminished.

How confident can the world be that these changes in Soviet military doctrine, military forces, and foreign policy are permanent? Since he became General Secretary, Gorbachev has insisted that Soviet foreign and military policy would be driven by domestic needs, and specifically by the requirements of *perestroika*. The burden of military spending has been enormous for the Soviet Union, amounting to at least 15 to 17 percent of gross domestic product (GDP) by the mid-1980s, and perhaps as high as 30 percent. U.S. military spending has amounted to 6.5 percent of GDP; for other NATO countries, the burden has been 2 to 5 percent. Military industry has drawn the best scientists and engineers, material resources, and the most funds from those sectors of the civilian economy which must be modernized for *perestroika* to succeed.[71] Thus, new Soviet military thinking is consistent with urgent economic needs.

Radically new Soviet foreign and military policies thus are based both in a new assessment of geostrategic realities and in economic necessity. Political and economic problems facing Soviet leaders will require their full attention for a long time. While the Soviet Union will certainly continue to play a major role in world affairs, maintain large armed forces, and probably export large quantities of arms, Moscow is not likely to employ direct military force in pursuit of its foreign policy goals any time soon. Indeed, the desperate economic situation and nationalist revolts within the Soviet Union are undermining Soviet power in a fundamental way. Some assert that the Soviet Union can no longer claim superpower status. Some even question the very ability of the Soviet state to survive. There are reasons to fear possible outcomes of growing instability within the Soviet Union and Eastern Europe, for the potential for violent conflict within the region is considerable, but it is hard to imagine Moscow expanding its military presence or engaging in military intervention again in Europe, Asia, or other parts of the world in the foreseeable future.

Foreign Deployments of Soviet Military Personnel:
1982, 1988, and 1990

Region and Nation	1982	1988	1990
Eastern Europe			
German Democratic Republic	380,000	380,000	364,000[1]
Czechoslovakia	80,000	80,000	50,000[1]
Hungary	65,000	65,000	40,000[1]
Poland	40,000	40,000	56,000[1]
Total Eastern Europe	**565,000**	**565,000**	**510,000[1]**
East and South Asia			
Afghanistan	95,000	116,000	advisers
Mongolia	55,000	55,000	37,000[2]
Vietnam	5,000	2,500	2,800
Laos	500	500	500
India		200	500
Kampuchea (Cambodia)	300	200	500
Total East and South Asia	**155,800**	**174,400**	**41,300**
Middle East and North Africa			
Syria	2,500	4,000	2,000
Libya	1,800	2,000	1,500
Algeria	1,000	1,000	700
South Yemen	1,500	1,000	1,000
Iraq	1,200	600	200
Other	500		
Total Middle East/North Africa	**8,500**	**8,600**	**5,400**
Sub-Saharan Africa			
Ethiopia	1,350	1,700	600
Angola	200	1,200	1,000
Mozambique	500	850	700
Mali	200	200	75
Congo	250	100	75
Other	200	900	600
Total Sub-Saharan Africa	**2,700**	**4,950**	**3,050**
Western Hemisphere			
Cuba	2,800	8,000	6,000
Nicaragua		250	100
Peru		115	50
Total Latin America	**2,800**	**8,365**	**6,150**

Total Third World (excluding Afghanistan) and Mongolia	19,800	25,000	18,900
Total Third World (including Afghanistan and Mongolia)	169,800	196,000	55,900
Total Foreign Deployments	734,800	761,315	565,900

1. Of the 510,000 Soviet troops in Eastern Europe in mid-1990, all troops in Czechoslovakia (50,000) and Hungary (40,000) are scheduled to be withdrawn by July, 1991. All of the 364,000 Soviet troops in Germany are scheduled to be withdrawn by the end of 1994, or possibly sooner. This leaves only the 56,000 Soviet troops in Poland for which no withdrawal has yet been announced.

2. Of the 37,000 Soviet troops estimated to be in Mongolia in 1990, 27,000 are scheduled to be withdrawn in 1990 and 1991, and all Soviet troops are to be out by the end of 1992.

Figures from the International Institute for Strategic Studies, *The Military Balance 1982-1983, 1988-1989*, and *1989-1990*. All figures are approximate; the numbers shown for Mongolia and Cuba are specifically acknowledged by IISC to be estimates.

Soviet Naval Access to Foreign Bases and Ports in 1988[1]

Host Nation and Base	Brief Description
Vietnam Cam Ranh Bay	Largest Soviet base in Third World outside of Mongolia, principal Soviet naval base in East Asia outside of Soviet territory. Guided missile cruisers, frigates, minesweepers based here, also attack submarines. Average deployment: 4 attack submarines, 2-4 combat ships, 10 auxilliaries.
Syria Latakia	Main base for Soviet Mediterranean squadron: fuel, supplies.
Tartus	Regular access, maintenance facility for attack submarines, oiler, tender. Rumors of development of much larger Soviet base here appear unfounded.
Libya Tripoli	Regular access for Soviet Mediterranean squadron.
Benghazi	Regular access for Soviet Mediterranean squadron.
Algeria Annaba	Soviet repair ships deployed; submarine repair facilities reported.
Romania Mangalia	Reported Soviet submarine base on Black Sea.
Yugoslavia Tivat	Repair of Soviet ships and submarines.
South Yemen Aden	Main base for Indian Ocean operations: fuel tanks, supplies, reports of submarine pens alongside berths for major surface ships.
Socotra Island	Anchorage used by Soviet ships, possible shore facilities.
Ethiopia Dahlak Archipelago	Large anchorage for Indian Ocean naval squadron.
Assab	Important Soviet naval facility, floating dry dock moored here.
Angola Luanda	Main Soviet naval base on West African coast; guided-missile destroyer and several accompanying ships based here.
Cuba Cienfuegos	Replenishment base for Soviet attack submarines.
Nipe Bay	Port calls, submarines, intelligence collectors.

1. In addition, in 1988 the Soviet Navy had access to as many as 28 additional ports in 18 nations, including five of the nations listed above. Overall, the Soviet Navy has access at most to 47 foreign ports and base facilities.

All data in this table come from Table 6, "Main and secondary surface-ship operating bases of the Soviet Navy," in Robert Harkavy, *Bases Abroad*, 1989: 52-54.

Notes

1. International Institute for Strategic Studies (IISS), *The Military Balance 1988-1989*, 1988, 39-44, and IISS, *The Military Balance 1990-1991*, 1990, 43. Unless otherwise noted, all figures on numbers of troops or weapon systems deployed in different countries or regions are taken from this series of IISS publications.

2. Gerard Holden, "The Warsaw Treaty Organization: Soviet Security Policy and the Alliance Division of Labor," University of Sussex, 1987, unpublished manuscript, 11-15.

3. Malcolm Mackintosh, "The Warsaw Treaty Organization: A History"; and Christopher Jones, "National Armies and National Sovereignty," in David Holloway and Jane M.O. Sharp, eds., *The Warsaw Pact: Alliance in Transition* (Ithaca: Cornell University Press, 1984), 43-45 and 87.

4. Stephen S. Kaplan, *Diplomacy of Power: Soviet Armed Forces as a Political Instrument* (Washington: Brookings, 1981), 72-73.

5. This brief account of the Hungarian uprising is taken from F. Stephen Larrabee, "Soviet Crisis Management in Eastern Europe," in Holloway and Sharp, 112-113.

6. Michel Tatu, "Intervention in Eastern Europe," in Kaplan, 239-242.

7. This account is drawn from Tatu, 223-239 and 249-259; and Larrabee, 120-125.

8. Tatu, 225.

9. This account is drawn from Larrabee, 128-132, and a 1987 interview with former Polish Colonel Ryszard Kuklinski which was translated and published as "The Crushing of Solidarity," in *Orbis*, Winter 1988, 7-31.

10. *New York Times*, 25 October 1989, A12.

11. Keller, *New York Times*, 21 August 1989, A6.

12. Michael McGwire, *Military Objectives in Soviet Policy* (Washington, DC: Brookings, 1987), 217-218.

13. Rajan Menon, *Soviet Power in the Third World* (New Haven: Yale University Press, 1986), 97-99.

14. Ibid., 4-8.

15. Ibid., 8-12.

16. *United States Military Posture for FY 1983* (Washington: The Organization of the Joint Chiefs of Staff, 1983), 10.

17. Joseph G. Whelan and Michael J. Dixon, *The Soviet Union in the Third World* (New York: Pergamon-Brassey's, 1986), 64.

18. Kaplan, 140-142.

19. Peter Hayes, Lyuba Zarsky, and Walden Bello, *American Lake* (New York: Viking-Penguin, 1986), 317.

20. Georges Tan Eng Bok, *The U.S.S.R. in East Asia* (Paris: The Atlantic Insitute for International Affairs, 1986), 40-51; and Robert A. Manning, "Moscow's Pacific Future," *World Policy Journal*, Winter 1987-88, 58.

21. Captain William H. Manthorpe, Jr., "The Soviet Navy," *Proceedings, U.S. Naval Institute*, May 1989, 230; see also U.S. Department of Defense, *Soviet Military Power*, 1988, 29.

22. U.S. Department of Defense, 28.

23. Robert Harkavy, *Bases Abroad* (Stockholm: Stockholm International Peace Research Institute, 1989), 52-57.

24. *New York Times*, 19 January 1990.

25. Bok, 19.

26. Manning, 60-69.

27. Gerald Segal, "Informal Arms Control: The Asian Road to Conventional Reductions," *Arms Control Today*, May 1989, 16-18.

28. *Los Angeles Times*, 27 May 1988, 20.

29. This account drawn from Eqbal Ahmad and Richard Barnet, "Bloody Games," *New Yorker*, 11 April 1988, 44-59.

30. Harkavy, 53.

31. Whelan and Dixon, 207.

32. Menon, 216-217.

33. Kaplan, 167-172.

34. Ibid., 185-187.

35. Karen Dawisha, "The Correlation of Forces and Soviet Policy in the Middle East," in Robin F. Laird and Erik P. Hoffman, eds., *Soviet Foreign Policy in a Changing World* (Hawthorne, NY: Aldine Publishers, 1986), 771-772.

36. Whelan and Dixon, 178-181.

37. U.S. Arms Control and Disarmament Agency, *World Military Expenditures and Arms Transfers, 1988* (Washington, DC: 1989), 114.

38. Harkavy, 54.

39. Fred Halliday, "Gorbachev and the Arab Syndrome," *World Policy Journal*, Summer 1987, 421; and Kaplan, 170.

40. Harkavy, 53 and 91.

41. Ibid., 54, 91, and 97.

42. E.A. Wayne, "U.S. Gauging Soviet Intent After Bomber Sales to Libya," *Christian Science Monitor*, 12 April 1989, 8.

43. Galia Golan, "Gorbachev's Middle East Strategy," *Foreign Affairs*, Fall 1987, 51.

44. Francis Fukuyama, "Gorbachev's New Politics: Soviet Third World Policy," *Current*, June 1988, 21-22.

45. Michael Dobbs, "Soviet Says U.S. Becoming a 'Partner,'" *Washington Post*, 12 June 1989, A1-2.

46. Everett Mendelsohn, *A Compassionate Peace* (NY: Farrar, Straus and Giroux, 1989), 209-213.

47. "Soviet's Mideast Retreat Alters Power Equation," *Boston Globe*, 3 April 1990.

48. Whelan and Dixon, 222.

49. Arms Control and Disarmament Agency, 111.

50. Menon, 138-144.

51. Harkavy, 53.

52. E.A. Wayne, "Ethiopia Regime Looks West for Helping Hand," *Christian Science Monitor*, 8 May 1989, 1-2; Robert M. Press, "Ethiopia Edges Toward Peace Talks," *Christian Science Monitor*, 10 August 1989, 1-2; and "Ethiopian Government Seen as Fighting to Survive," *New York Times*, 17 April 1990, A5.

53. Menon, 132-138.

54. Arms Control and Disarmament Agency, 1983 and 1989.

55. Harkavy, 52-55 and 92.

56. E.A. Wayne, "US Seeks End to Mozambique War," *Christian Science Monitor*, 12 July 1989, 8.

57. *In These Times*, 7-13 February 1990, 8.

58. Joint Chiefs of Staff, *United States Military Posture for FY 1983*, 12-13.

59. Walter Pincus, "Standing at the Brink of Nuclear War," *Washington Post*, 25 July 1985, A1 and A10.

60. Arms Control and Disarmament Agency, 113.

61. Whelan and Dixon, 311-312.

62. Linda Feldman, "Sweet Smiles, Tough Talk When Gorbachev Visits Castro," *Christian Science Monitor*, 31 March 1989, 8.

63. John Lamperti, *What Are We Afraid Of?* (Philadelphia: NARMIC, AFSC, 1986).

64. Mikhail Gorbachev, *Political Report of the CPSU Central Committee to the 27th Party Congress* (Moscow: Novosti, 1986), 81-82.

65. Francis Fukuyama, *Gorbachev and the New Soviet Agenda in the Third World* (Santa Monica, RAND Corporation, 1989), 11.

66. Stephen M. Meyer, "The Sources and Prospects of Gorbachev's New Political Thinking on Security," *International Security*, Fall 1988, 144-150.

67. Ibid., 150.

68. Manthorpe, 226-227.

69. "Gorbachev Announces 14% Cut in Defense Spending," *Baltimore Sun*, 14 January 1989, 2.

70. Colonel General Nikolai Chervov, "We'd Like to Cut Our Forces More…," *New York Times*, 29 May 1990, A23.

71. Christopher Wilkinson, "Soviet Defence Expenditure: Past Trends and Prospects," *NATO Review*, April 1989, 20.

Chapter 4

The Corruption of a Community's Economic and Political Life

The Cruise Missile Base in Comiso

Laura Simich[*]

In 1979, the North Atlantic Treaty Organization (NATO) decided to deploy cruise and Pershing missiles in England, Germany, the Netherlands, Belgium, and Italy as a response to the modernization of Soviet medium-range nuclear forces. A popular international movement against this deployment swept across Europe, including the Sicilian town of Comiso, the projected deployment site for Italy's missiles.

Construction of the Comiso base began in 1982. In 1983, U.S. military personnel began to arrive, in small groups of 30 to 40 in order to keep a low profile in the community. At the same time, thousands of anti-nuclear activists descended on Comiso to establish huge international summer peace camps. In spite of their protests, the missile deployment began by 1984. Only with hindsight is it now clear that the protests were effective, contributing as they did to public pressure which led to the 1988 superpower agreement to destroy all U.S. and Soviet intermediate-range nuclear missiles in Europe and the Soviet Union.

* This chapter is based on the author's 15 months in residence in Comiso as an anthropologist. She gratefully acknowledges the financial support of a 1984-85 Fulbright-Hayes Grant for Dissertation Research, awarded by the Commission on Cultural Exchange between Italy and the United States, and a 1987-88 MacArthur Fellowship in International Peace and Security Studies, awarded by Columbia University in New York.

But the withdrawal of the nuclear weapons has not ended the problems in Comiso, where the military base remains. In 1981, news reports led the people of Comiso (Comisani) to believe that construction of the base would pump $100 million into the local economy. The real effects of the military base have been quite different. The base brought few jobs and little spending in the local community. Instead, short-term housing shortages, land speculation, and a rise in crime coincided with its construction. As the base grew, Comisani saw their local government undermined and their hopes of economic revitalization destroyed. The anticipated "Cruise dollars" never appeared.

Comiso is a town of 28,000 in the province of Ragusa at the southern tip of Sicily. One enters the town on a steep, narrow highway winding down the mountain side, through vineyards, citrus groves, old stone walls, and abandoned olive trees. Greenhouses spread toward the sea, 12 miles away. By night modest street lamps bathe Comiso in a light suited to the quiet lives its citizens lead. But at night one now also sees a jarring sight—the military base: an immense, glaring concentration of modern floodlights rising from the deeply black countryside just outside the town, "like a piece of Los Angeles," as the young people say.

The decision to choose Comiso as a cruise missile site was made by Italy's top government leaders. The deployment of these missiles in Europe was meant to provide concrete assurance to Europeans of the U.S. intention to stand with them in the event of war or the threat of war from the East. European NATO leaders feared the "decoupling" of the United States and Europe in the face of a nuclear threat: would Washington really risk New York to "save" Bonn and Paris?[1]

The presence of U.S.-owned and -operated nuclear missiles at the "front lines" in Europe was supposed to constitute an affirmative answer. But the 1979 NATO decision to proceed with deployment of cruise and Pershing II missiles backfired, as mass opposition to new nuclear weapons—in a period of rising East-West tensions—put European governments on the defensive. As millions demonstrated across Europe, the U.S. government insisted on keeping its allies in line, pushing forward with preparations for deployment.[2] The Italian government, one of Washington's most obedient allies, used delaying tactics in Parliament until construction of the Comiso base was already underway. In doing so, Rome violated a statute which gives the president of the Sicilian Regional Assembly the right to vote on matters concerning Sicily in the national Council of Ministers.

The people of Comiso were as surprised as any when the site of the new missile base was announced on August 7, 1981, during Parliament's summer recess. With the concurrence of the Italian Defense Ministry, NATO chose to build the base in an area authorities considered "deserted," on the site of an abandoned military airport originally built by Mussolini. U.S. engineers had surveyed the site in January 1981, and construction began in April 1982. One day after unprecedented mass protests, bulldozers began demolishing the old buildings on the site. Because this was a completely new NATO facility, rather than an expansion of an old one, construction costs were high. With funds appropriated by the U.S. Congress, plus "host support" (land, access roads, and utilities provided by the Italian government), construction of the missile base proceeded while the peace movement continued its struggle.

Now complete, Comiso Air Base covers 379 acres amidst vineyards less than two miles north of Comiso. Technically a NATO base, it is run by United States Air Force personnel. A contingent of 200 Italian soldiers reinforces perimeter security, but they have nothing to do with operation of the base or the cruise missiles. Military authorities refer to the Comiso Air Base as a NATO or an Italian installation, but local people think of it as a U.S. base.

A new military base is like a small city. In 1985, 1,278 U.S. servicemen and women were assigned to Comiso, with several hundred more scheduled to arrive. To allay local fears of disruptive behavior by unmarried servicemen, Comisani had been told that U.S. military personnel would bring their families. The town asked for reassurance that they would live off-base to benefit the local economy. Although the estimated 3,000–4,000 dependents had not appeared by 1985, housing, schools, churches, and extensive facilities for shopping, banking, repair, and recreation had been built in preparation for their arrival. The U.S. military community would be largely self-sufficient.[3]

Comisani reacted to the nearly complete segregation of the military with resentment. The promised economic benefits from the base were to be severely limited. Mafia-controlled firms from outside the region soon won most contracts for the construction of the base, and Comisani understood that base construction was not effectively under the jurisdiction of Italian law.

Comisani were thus understandably ambivalent about the military base. In a 1983 poll, 70 percent opposed the military base, but most also felt they could do nothing about it since that was "up to the superpowers."[4] The majority of active base opponents were affiliated with left-wing parties, primarily the Communists and Socialists, but some were Christian Democrats. Most locals who opposed the base adopted a "wait-and-see" attitude. In 1983, some still hoped to benefit financially from the base. This hope was encouraged by opportunistic local politicians who promised that the base would bring much new money to Comiso's citizens. Some years later the disadvantages of hosting a missile base became clearer to townspeople. Many have expressed feeling uneasy co-existing with U.S. military personnel whom they describe (generously) as "misbehaving guests." Many felt that they were being subtly exploited by a military occupation, however "friendly" it has been. Also disturbing to Comisani is their sense that they have less control over their lives than they did before the base was established.

To understand the impact of the missile base (as well as how it might have been more successfully opposed) it is important to know the traditions that have shaped political life in Comiso. Frustrated by apparent Comisani political apathy, peace organizers and political analysts foreign to the region characterized Comisani as morally or ideologically "backward." In fact, they misunderstood Comiso and its people, most of whom doubted that much could be done to change the situation, and most of whom also found foreign peace activists to be strange and insensitive.

Comiso's political history contains many paradoxes. The town is in a province which, compared to the rest of Sicily, has been unusually prosperous and Mafia-free. Very few large estates, the traditional breeding-ground of the Mafia, ever existed in Comiso. Middle-class and small land holders prevailed, and Socialist Farmers' Leagues evolved as early as the 1890s. Since the early 1950s the town has also been a Communist stronghold, unusual in Sicily. During the 1960s and 1970s the Communist Party regularly captured 40-45 percent of Comiso's vote; the Christian Democrats (dominant elsewhere in Italy) won about 25 percent; and the Socialists gained 10-15 percent, with the remainder going to smaller parties.

In the late 1970s and early 1980s, two developments particularly affected the debate over the missile base. First, the mainstay of the provincial economy, greenhouse agriculture, sank into a recession because of an unfavorable European market and rising production costs. In Comiso, profits declined and unemployment rose. Second, the Italian Socialist Party under Prime Minister Bettino Craxi became a conservative force and a crucial governing coalition partner with the Christian Democrats. Both Socialist and Christian Democratic parties supported the deployment decision. The Italian Communist Party, becoming increasingly moderate though still in the opposition, supported NATO but not cruise missiles.

Following suit on the local level, a coalition of conservative Socialists and Christian Democrats in Comiso under the leadership of Socialist Mayor Salvatore Catalano, first elected in 1978, crippled the long-dominant Communist Party. When two Communist councillors joined the center-left coalition in the early 1980s (allegedly bribed by Mayor Catalano to do so), the mayor's reelection was assured. The local government now solidly supported the establishment of the military base. When construction of the missile base was announced in 1981, Comisani were already facing an uncertain economic future. The promises of economic revitalization made by Socialist Defense Minister Lelio Lagorio and Mayor Catalano sounded good. People were assured that construction of the base would alleviate local unemployment because the $100 million in construction funds would be used to pay local labor.[5] Local merchants were encouraged to believe their business would increase with the entry of up to 15,000 U.S. nationals with "pockets full of dollars."[6] Defense Minister Lagorio promised that the military base would be made available for commercial air transport of local agricultural produce, a use of the old airport farmers had long requested of the government to no avail.[7] Lagorio went so far as to suggest that housing and offices would be built on the base so that they could be "recycled" for civilian use should arms negotiations succeed.[8] Comisani recognize these elusive promises were "smoke in our eyes," now that the missiles are to be withdrawn, and the future of the base remains uncertain.

The Opposition

As rumors about the coming missile base spread through Comiso in August 1981, a popular petition campaign opposing the base was immediately organized by local young people. Sicilian regional deputies, whose constitutional rights had been violated by the top-down deployment decision, signed a letter of protest. Mayor Catalano visited Minister Lagorio in Rome with a delegation of provincial mayors and union representatives. But after a private phone conversation with Lagorio, Catalano reversed his position and announced that the decision was "irrevocable."[9] Local party leaders, in all parties, obediently aligned themselves with the central government, but the majority of the population remained opposed.

Townspeople worried about side-effects of the military base, including a rise in the cost of living, land expropriations, Mafia involvement, drugs, and prostitution. The Mafia and Mafia-related crime were largely foreign to the experience of Comisani, who are known all over Sicily as law-abiding. In addition, most local people were skeptical about the need for the new missiles. Situated close to North Africa and the Middle East, the missiles seemed more provocative than protective. Concerned local people joined other Sicilians in an October 1981 rally opposing the cruise missile base. Thirty thousand people, an extraordinary number for a town Comiso's size, came to the rally. A local "United Committee for Disarmament and Peace" (CUDIP) was formed by Giacomo Cagnes, the former Communist mayor. He was a formidable and charismatic elder statesman with popular support— though he also had many political rivals. About half the townspeople who joined him in protest were also Communists, while most of the remainder were independent of any political party.

Fear of the base's repercussions spread through the town. Many assumed that the Mafia would take advantage of opportunities in construction, land speculation, drugs, and prostitution. Local anxieties were expressed by Pio La Torre, a leading member of the Italian parliamentary Anti-Mafia Commission. Speaking at the first protest in Comiso, La Torre prophetically linked spreading Mafia influence and militarization:

> In recent years grave events have occurred in Sicily. Mafia power
> has raised its head and we have witnessed a dramatic sequence of
> political homicides...the State shows itself ever more impotent
> before criminal and Mafia violence which each day sows terror and
> death. And why isn't it obvious that this alarming degeneration is
> pushed to its extreme by the transformation of Sicily into a giant
> base for war?[10]

La Torre, a well-loved national Communist leader who had long supported progressive forces in Sicily, then asked the Sicilian parliament to support a popular referendum on the deployment of nuclear missiles in Comiso— which they declined to do.

In some of the most Mafia-ridden towns in Sicily, including Palermo, Partinico, and Corleone, labor unions boldly collected signatures to oppose the missile base in Comiso. By the end of April 1982, over one million signatures of voting adults (of a total Sicilian population of five million) had been collected on the petition asking suspension of construction of the missile base. In Comiso alone, 13,000 signatures were gathered. Six courageous local hunger strikers gradually won the moral support of the population.

Then the international peace movement moved in. In April 1982, more than 60,000 demonstrators from Northern Italy and the rest of Europe converged on Comiso. Most were young people proudly unconventional in their dress and mores. They wore torn clothes, washed in the main fountain, and embraced in the streets. They set up summer peace camps, demonstrated in the main piazza, and carried out direct nonviolent protest actions at the site of the military base.

La Torre repeatedly denounced Mafia infiltration of the construction work at the military base in Comiso. Then, on April 29, 1982, Pio La Torre and his bodyguard were assassinated by the Mafia in Palermo. It was the first time in history that the Mafia had dared to murder a member of the Italian parliament. La Torre had been scheduled to speak in support of the peace movement on May 1. The loss of La Torre demoralized the local opposition.

The international peace activists carried on the struggle, but they failed to gain local support. Local peace activists distanced themselves from their foreign counterparts' frequently arrogant behavior and radical actions. Sensitive to accusations of involvement with "terrorism," the Communist Party opposed civil disobedience. Many local Communists, some veterans of other militant political struggles who might have been expected to oppose the military base, were ambivalent about publicly joining protesters. Having a strong sense of propriety, most townspeople were offended by the appearance and behavior of foreign demonstrators. Although Comisani wanted "peace," the extraordinary culture of the larger movement was too alien and, in the context of small-town mores, too dangerous to share.

While outside activists unwittingly erected barriers to solidarity with local people, secular and sacred authorities effectively took advantage of respected social institutions to persuade Comisani to accept the missile base. Local Catholic priests inveighed against the demonstrators from their pulpits. In public ceremonies, the provincial bishop officiated at the first marriage of a U.S. military officer and a local woman while the press trumpeted the "love story in the shadow of the missiles." The bishop also prayed ceremoniously over the foundation of the multi-million dollar "Christ our Peace" Catholic Church inside the base. The Sicilian writer, Leonardo Sciascia, remarked, "As usual, the Church is blessing the banners of war."

The authorities displayed their power more bluntly during the mass protests of August 6-9, 1983. Members of the national police force seriously injured and hospitalized protesters who had blockaded the gates of the base, leaving local people afraid to join further protests. A U.S. consular official in Palermo later shrugged and confessed with a smile, "The police got a little out of hand."

The police brutality marked the beginning of the decline of the mass protests. Through 1984 and 1985, a core group of local CUDIP activists—primarily teachers, businesspeople, and young blue-collar workers and professionals—persisted in holding peace vigils and publishing written protests against the militarization of the town. But their actions were colored by resignation, not hope.

The accomplishments of these local activists should be evaluated in light of the real obstacles they faced on the local political scene. At the core lay a tradition of Sicilian patronage politics. The hope of winning military contracts corrupted local politics to an extreme, offering tempting profits to unscrupulous local party leaders. National party leaders also became involved, dictating the outcome of local political struggles. As the international peace movement's presence waned, Comiso's internal politics were quietly and permanently altered by the existence of the missile base. Political maneuvering over the base effectively paralyzed Comiso. Comiso's town council was deadlocked for almost a year after inconclusive elections in 1984, leaving the community effectively without local government. At the root of the crisis were promises made by the military base to rival conservative Socialists and Christian Democrats for lucrative service and construction contracts at the base. With such contracts, the politicians controlled few (but badly needed) jobs which they exaggerated in number and then manipulated in *quid pro quo* exchanges for individual voters' support. Fighting over the division of the military pie, the quibbling right-wing politicians were unable to cooperate in forming a municipal administration.

After several months of waiting out their rivals, Communist city councillors attempted to take control of city hall. National politicians, normally oblivious to the small Sicilian town, suddenly took a great interest in the composition of Comiso's government. Socialist and Christian Democratic party leaders—and allegedly U.S. officials—intervened in negotiations to prevent the Communists from returning to power. Rome had been informed that the U.S. officials were uncomfortable with the image of a Communist administration in "the city of missiles."

The crisis was resolved in 1985 with a second election. Comisani ousted from the council all "middlemen" who personally benefitted from the military base. Communists and moderate Socialists more interested in community welfare, but still circumspect in challenging the military base, resumed leadership of Comiso.

Economic Benefits: Jobs, Construction, and Local Spending

Comisani took the international political implications of the missile base seriously, but more immediate were their expectations of the military base's impact on their local economy. In spite of hopes and promises that the base would bring economic revitalization, their experience was disappointing. In one area after another—jobs, construction, housing, and spending—hopes of widespread economic benefits were disappointed.

Local benefits were temporary and limited. Fewer than half a dozen local people received long-term jobs at the base; those few involved short-term carpentry work and menial jobs in the cafeteria. Most jobs were in construction, and these went to outsiders. No more than a dozen local people, most with the right party or family connections, received contracts for services and maintenance. Renting apartments and houses to military personnel profited some people, but only until the construction of permanent military housing on the base was completed. The North Americans' spending on local food and retail items was so paltry it became a joke. In short, local economic benefits from the military base were a mirage. Only 31 Italians—of whom few were from Comiso—worked full-time at the base in 1985. This did not include a few hundred temporary construction workers, most from Mafia-controlled firms of western Sicily, and Italian military personnel, primarily from northern Italy.

Expectations of employment at the military base had been raised by Mayor Catalano, who used pledges of jobs to buy votes. During the campaign in 1983, the base employment office in the heart of Comiso collected over 10,000 job applications for jobs at the base.[11] The next year, when a new office opened, the North American woman in charge explained, "We don't give out applications anymore. We have too many already." The local labor office affiliated with the large Communist trade union organization tried to monitor employment conditions at the base. The labor office director intimated that the provincial work inspector was "persuaded" by contractors to make infrequent visits to the construction site. "The employment office has no control over the contractors that don't comply," he said.

The way military personnel secured and built housing in Comiso also shows how selective economic benefits were for the local population. Although many people in Comiso hoped to benefit from the air base, some—for example, those with Socialist party connections—were in a better position to profit than others. One local contractor, by the name of Occhipinti, joined the Socialist Party and quickly became part of an exclusive group of decision makers within it. He soon acquired land in a suburban zone of Comiso where he hurriedly built a residential complex and a "clubhouse" for North Americans. It was generally believed in Comiso that military authorities agreed to lodge base personnel in the complex because of the contractor's party connections.

Party connections appear to have been more important than quality of work in securing construction contracts for the base itself. Under pressure from NATO to speed construction, Defense Minister Lagorio personally chose 13 firms to compete for construction contracts.[12] The U.S. Embassy in Rome (which in 1982 controlled the closed bidding process for major contracts at the base) awarded Occhipinti the first contract for demolition work at the base, worth approximately $400,000, just a few days after he created his company.[13] Multi-million dollar contracts repeatedly went to firms with Socialist connections, generally based in Northern Italy. These firms subcontracted to Sicilian firms, some of which had ties to criminal networks in Palermo.[14] Half of all local temporary construction workers were hired without contracts through an "irregular" process by brokers, which included kickbacks of 10-20 percent from paychecks averaging $12 for a nine-hour day.[15]

With construction of military housing going slowly, the first North American personnel to arrive in Comiso were temporarily housed off-base. In 1982, apartments in Comiso and three small resort hotels on the coast were made available—evidently through sympathetic Socialist contacts—and rented at twice the normal rate. U.S. military representatives combed Comiso and surrounding towns for suitable housing. This raised hopes that Americans would continue to live off-base as tenants of local families, who in turn withheld their rental property from others, creating a housing shortage for local people and inflating rents.

By 1985, the need for military housing had become urgent.[16] U.S. personnel lingering in the seaside resorts were satisfied with their situation, but the hotel owners and merchants who depended on the tourist trade were not. Free-spending tourists had to be turned away because military guests overstayed their welcome waiting for housing to be built. Military authorities searched frantically for ways around the problem.

The military's procedures to secure more housing created misunderstandings locally, and speculators stood ready to profit from the confusion. Provincial building firms cut deals with local landowners. Strings were pulled in the provincial capital to authorize residential construction in areas zoned for agriculture.

Rumors of lucrative plans for off-base housing flourished in this expectant atmosphere. Word spread that a village of 422 family dwellings for the military would be built near the coast. Once news of this housing project got around, the Italian Defense Ministry, NATO authorities, and the U.S. Consulate in Palermo were forced to deny the plan to build housing outside the base. The controversy was never satisfactorily resolved. Five months later the local newspaper announced that additional housing would be constructed inside the military base only. Adding insult to injury, Comisani were told that the contracts would go, not to local construction firms, but to firms based in Northern Italy.

In spite of widespread disappointment over military construction and housing, the base brought benefits to a few local interests. Contracts let by the U.S. military were, for the most part, small and temporary. A military spokeswoman in Comiso indicated that in their terminology the phrase, "the local community" could mean the province of Ragusa, the region of Sicily, or even all Italy. In 1983, for example, payments for temporary housing rentals for military personnel amounted to only $35,000. Similarly, in 1984 the base open bidding for contracts for office and storage space in town for

$150,000, but these contracts were to terminate by 1985 when the base facilities were near completion.[17]

According to military figures, the amount for "public contracts awarded within the region of influence" in 1984 was projected to be over $1 million, and in 1985, $2.9 million.[18] This is a relatively small amount, compared to a (1978) gross domestic product for the province of Ragusa of approximately $300 million, and $5 billion for Sicily as a whole.[19] Apart from few local politicians—for example, the head of the Christian Democratic Party who was awarded a cleaning contract—few townspeople were known to have received substantial contracts.

Comiso is the heart of the most productive agricultural area of Southern Italy, yet relatively little local produce was purchased for the base. Instead, enormous quantities of packaged and frozen foods were imported from the United States. The men at Comiso's wholesale market, which opens at 4:00 a.m., noted that the North Americans showed up at 10:00 a.m. only to complain that the remaining produce wasn't worth buying.

Merchants complained that the "soldiers" spent very little money. Some businesses refused to sell them large items such as cars and appliances because they did not pay the bills. A few bars and restaurants received some business from Americans. Servicemen bought gold jewelry in local stores, where it could be purchased for half the U.S. price. When asked to provide evidence of benefits to local businesses, however, a chagrined municipal employee once remarked, "There's nothing really. The presence of the North Americans just created an air of servility."

Mayor Catalano led townspeople to believe that the military base would benefit Comiso not just by spending and job creation, but by sharing its electric power and water supply, and by improving highways and railroad connections.[20] As of late 1985, this cooperation had not materialized. In fact, the town's infrastructure was severely taxed by the increased demand for water and use of local roads.

Comisani gradually discovered that their relationship to the base was not an equal one. The base became increasingly heedless of local concerns and garrison-like in mentality. Military representatives seldom saw any reason to consult with Comiso's municipal administration about the drastic changes the base brought to the town. Even a town council member who had strongly supported the base observed:

> There has been no relationship between the base and the municipal administration...Do you know not a single local official was invited to the inaugural ceremonies at the base? Comisani welcomed the Americans out of a customary sense of hospitality, but they have

behaved…badly. If Comisani had known they wouldn't find work
at the base, they would have all been protesting at its gates.

By 1990, the economic contribution of the base had dropped even
further, construction having been completed for some time. Only 240 Italian
citizens from across the province worked at the base, but they stood to lose
their jobs in 1991 with the removal of the cruise missiles. The base could not
guarantee even these few jobs. In the years of its operation, the base had
done nothing to reduce Comiso's official unemployment rate of 10 percent.

Worlds Apart: Social and Cultural Relations Between North Americans and Comisani

The U.S. military entered Comiso smoothly in 1982, but mutually
negative perceptions developed between the base and the town, leading to
an uneasy segregation. By 1985, approximately 1,800 U.S. servicemen were
on the base. The people of Comiso were never hostile to North Americans.
As one said, "We like them fine—those that don't come in uniform."

The U.S. presence in Comiso was most obvious in the beginning,
before on-base facilities were built. During 1983 and 1984, bewildered
off-duty servicemen could be seen wandering the quiet streets of the town.
Looking out of place, they would walk three or four abreast down the back
streets, startling the housewives. Elderly Comisani were reminded of the
German, then U.S., occupying troops during World War II, even though these
North American troops wore civilian clothes. A few servicemen visited the
local pizzerias and weekly open-air market, but this diminished by 1985.
Comisani surmised, "The Americans don't have to come into town now that
they have everything they need on the base." Social exchanges were
short-lived because of the language barrier. Few Comisani spoke English and
U.S. personnel rarely learned Italian because most were stationed at the base
for only one year.

Another social barrier involved relationships between U.S. military
personnel and local women. The servicemen complained that Comisani
women were not available for the casual relationships which North Americans are used to. Military officials paternalistically distributed a pamphlet of
guidelines for the proper behavior toward local people. It instructed the
servicemen not to encourage the local women, who were assumed to be in
search of North American husbands. A few marriages between U.S. soldiers
and local women did take place. In one case, the serviceman later left his
wife in Comiso, taking their child with him.

The initially open attitude of Comisani toward the North Americans
was not reciprocated by the military. Local people once rented a hall to invite

North Americans to a dance, but the enlisted men were told they would be court-martialled if they showed up! Intelligence officers attended to make certain that the servicemen stayed away. According to a U.S. civilian employee, the base commander "scared" the servicemen out of contact with Comisani whom he believed were "all out to get the Americans."

Organized events at which local and military people could mix often failed, but not for reasons of anti-Americanism. There were cultural clashes, to be sure, but local people were loathe to become involved in the conflict between base authorities and peace activists. For example, in August 1983 another provincial town hosted a basketball tournament to which a team from the base was invited. A few days before the scheduled game, police brutally attacked pacifists at the gates of the military base. In response, the young people who planned the tournament—with support from the town's mayor—decided to exclude the North Americans.

Several other incidents heightened mutual fears and prejudices. Two off-duty Italian soldiers target-shooting in the countryside accidentally shot a 63-year-old woman standing by the door of her house. She was paralyzed. The soldiers were immediately transferred from Comiso. The local paper reported that the soldiers were Italian, but many people believed they were really North American.

The military's attempt to take over local recreational areas also provoked conflict. Fence posts appeared suddenly in a national park at one of the province's most beautiful beaches in late 1984. A new sign declared the area to be military property. Rumors spread that the Italian authorities intended the public beach for the exclusive use of the military. Comisani leveled charges of apartheid at the U.S. servicemen who acted as if they were "too good to share the beaches." The fence posts were eventually torn down.

The base's public relations office lamely tried to manage holiday and sporting events to make a good impression on townspeople. News photos showed military officials giving Christmas gifts to local orphans, although Sicilians themselves do not customarily exchange gifts at Christmas. One young serviceman voluntarily joined a local bicycle race and was told by his supporters to keep up the good work, since he was "doing more good than the public relations office ever could."

But such efforts scarcely camouflaged the actual consequences of the military presence. In the end, local people saw through public relations devices to the real effects of the military presence, but there was little they could do—short of demonstrating hurt pride—to punish military transgressions. In retribution for the base's dumping large amounts of waste on town property without permission or compensation in 1986, the municipality refused permission to the NATO band to play in Comiso's main plaza.

The gap between Comisani and soldiers at the base remained wide. Even the Christian Democratic president of the provincial council, generally a supporter of the base, said in 1985 that the base left Comiso "dominated by a fatalistic logic of resignation" and subject to "a cultural graft that does violence to our traditions, our very conditions of life, while on the narrower economic plane producing dissolution and ruin." By 1990, political relations between the base and the town were nonexistent, except for overt politeness on the part of the authorities during ceremonial occasions. Social relations between Comisani and U.S. servicemen were increasingly rare, as military personnel were "ghettoized" by living exclusively on base. Apart from organized visits by groups of school children, the base remained an isolated entity.

Infiltration by the Mafia and the Increase in Crime

In Comiso, military and Mafia interests coexist in what people assume is a symbiotic relationship. The Mafia is not a phenomenon of the past. Today the Mafia is a widespread, sophisticated network of illegal and quasi-legal business and financial enterprises reaching the highest levels of the Italian government and using coercion in everyday operations. In an unprecedented wave of violence, the Mafia has openly murdered a dozen high-level, anti-Mafia officials and journalists since the late 1970s. In addition to La Torre in 1984, the Mafia also assassinated Giuseppe Fava, editor of *I Siciliani*, a progressive Catania-based magazine which supported the peace movement and documented Mafia involvement in Comiso.

The Mafia did not exist in the area surrounding Comiso before the early 1970s, although it is deeply rooted in much of the Sicilian political economy.[21] After the Allies drove Italian fascist troops out of Sicily in 1943, the U.S. military government restored Mafia leaders to prominent positions to aid the conquest of Sicily.[22] This legitimized the Mafia, whose code of honor demands silence before the law. The refusal to testify or to cooperate with the law makes accusations about Mafia activities difficult to prove. Nevertheless, Comisani and other Sicilians believe they know some things about Mafia activity in the area. In the 1970s and 1980s, social scientists and magistrates in Italy observed that the Mafia began moving into previously untouched geographic areas.[23] The Mafia began recruiting Christian Democratic and Socialist politicians and businessmen involved in real estate, construction, and contraband drugs and arms. Many observers believe that construction of the missile base provided major new opportunities for the Mafia in the Comiso region.[24] Flora Lewis of the *New York Times* wrote:

It has even been suggested that the decision to install nuclear cruise missiles at Comiso, was because the Mafia could be relied on to protect the site in return for the inevitable rake off it could exact on hundreds of millions of dollars in construction contracts for roads, housing and so on. Max Raab, the American Ambassador in 1983 when the site was being built, was said by aides to be philosophical about the situation, holding that the corruption was a problem for the Italian, not the U.S., government and that in any case the dollars would help stimulate the bedraggled Sicilian economy.[25]

Rather than stimulating the economy, the base was being used as a shelter for illegal activity. Given the scarcity of benefits for local people, most concluded that any profits from the military base have gone instead to outsiders such as the Mafia. The exploitative employment practices on the base seemed strikingly similar to those of the Mafia.

By the early 1980s, organized crime was prepared to capitalize on the missile base in Comiso. The "Mafia-style" methods observed among the firms constructing the base included forming sub-divisions to circumvent lawful hiring procedures, sub-contracting and retaining most of the profit, and taking kickbacks. These practices are typical of the Mafia-dominated western Sicilian construction industry, from which the great majority of the laborers at the base were drawn.

Identifying Mafia *cosche* (families) involved in the Comiso base is difficult, but members of the Gambino crime family were likely to have been involved. According to parliamentary investigations and court transcripts, the Gambino family is part of one of the largest Sicilian construction firms, which fronts for the largest heroin-trafficking crime group in Sicily. At a lower level of Mafia organization, one sub-contractor at the base was Biagio Cutrale, a feared boss of Vittoria whose "men of confidence" included prominent Christian Democrats of Comiso.

Mafia influence may well have extended beyond the building of the base. The Mafia entry to the territory surrounding Comiso was followed by a demonstrable increase in crime, although the Mafia presence may be only one cause among many for the increase. By 1983, criminal acts of intimidation such as the destruction of orchards, the killing of sheep, and knee-capping (shooting people in the knees to intimidate them) became common. More than 20 Comisani were condemned for extortion and low-level delinquency of the Mafia type in 1985. In the early years of the base's construction, anyone who frequented the main streets could observe the out-of-town prostitutes inside cars driven by pimps, but in this socially conservative town prostitution as a locally based business never caught on. But, in the 1980s, the number of addicts in Ragusa, Vittoria, and Comiso did increase by 10-fold.

In 1984, a local delegation comprised of the head of the merchants' association, the head of the civic association, and the owner of a large jewelry business visited the provincial police chief to demand more protection against the *cosche* behind the crimes. They told him, "You can't strip the town of police to guard the base where there are already enough military people. For what? To confront the pacifists?"[26] But Comisani spoke of the increase in crime with caution. The word "Mafia" raised eyebrows and shoulders, signalling a subject that could not be openly discussed. One local journalist in Comiso bluntly remarked, "People aren't talking. They're afraid of getting killed." This fear is new to Comiso. Because Comisani tend to repress awareness of the Mafia presence, the overt blame for Mafia practices falls on its apparent accessory, the U.S. military. U.S. officials in turn view the Mafia as "the Sicilians' problem" and insist they have no business interfering in such internal affairs.

Safe and Secure?

The military base brought Comiso political, economic, and social problems far outweighing any benefits to the community. It also made people feel less secure, an ironic result for an installation supposedly built for defense. Defense Minister Lagorio frequently assured Comisani that they were safe because the nuclear missiles would be dispersed across Sicily "like needles in a haystack" before launching. However, Comisani became truly frightened when the base was put on "red alert" after the U.S.-Libyan clash in the Gulf of Sidra in March 1986. Following this military engagement, the Libyan government secretly informed the Italian government that they considered Comiso an offensive target. Townspeople soon noticed armored cars circling the base, provincial hotels filling with U.S. advisors, and the postponement of the monthly missile deployment exercises in which the cruise missiles were moved on trucks in the surrounding countryside. Comisani heard rumors that radar coverage of all Sicily was put into effect. The mayor said he had "great concern for the danger which threatens the security of the civilian population." Within a week the danger seemed to have passed.

On the night of April 15, 1986, the United States bombed Tripoli, the Libyan capital. The island-wide radar watch was immediately made operational. At Sigonella on the east coast, and at the U.S.-Italian base near Trapani on the west coast, combat planes were reportedly prepared for take-off throughout the night. The entire southern coast of the island was surrounded by U.S. ships and planes of the 6th Fleet. Security was stepped up around the several military bases in Sicily, including Comiso.[27]

Comiso was not the target of retaliation selected by Libya. The next day a Libyan missile landed off the island of Lampedusa, the site of a U.S. communications facility 150 miles to the southwest of Comiso. According to a Sicilian newspaper, however, "The news of the attack on Lampedusa unleashed panic yesterday evening in Comiso. The gas stations were crowded with cars while rumors spread of entire families fleeing the city. For the first time since the missiles were installed, the sensation of real and imminent danger has emerged."[28]

From its inception the Comiso missile base created problems for people in the community, people who had nothing to say about the decision to build it nor recourse when it infringed on their rights and wishes. Politicians misled Comisani into thinking the military base would benefit them, as if it were a form of economic development rather than a self-contained nuclear weapons facility. The economic arguments for the base, although false, appear to have been the single greatest factor in quelling local opposition. Once construction of the base began, the gap between promises and reality became clear; the reality included municipal corruption, temporary and minimal employment, few contracts for services, negligible spending, housing shortages, social conflict, and crime. These are the conditions Comisani are learning to live with.

With the conclusion of the INF Treaty, the cruise missiles are being removed from the Comisani's backyards. Yet, in spite of this positive step, the U.S. base is an enduring example of how militarization can undermine not only a community's political and economic life, but also the democratic ideals it is supposedly intended to defend.

Notes

1. There were also strategic considerations behind the decision. NATO's "southern flank" was shifted to the Mediterranean in order to protect Western interests in Southwest Asia and to facilitate the operation of the U.S. Rapid Deployment Force (Hearings on H.R. 1816, Committee on Armed Services 1983), 331. The policy set priorities well beyond NATO's original mandate and geographic boundaries.

2. Gregory Treverton, "NATO Alliance Politics," in Richard K. Betts, ed., *Cruise Missiles: Technology, Strategy and Politics* (Washington, DC: The Brookings Institution.)

3. For reasons of morale the Air Force considers it more cost effective to maintain a family than a single person overseas. Its priority is a high "quality of life," particularly housing and amenities, for personnel. For 1984, the Air Force requested $26.9 million for construction, $3.4 million for leased family housing, and $12.9 million for schools at Comiso. For more detail see Hearings on H.R. 1816 (H.R. 2972) 1983 Military Installations and Facilities Subcommittee of the Committee on Armed Services, House of Representatives, 98th Congress.

4. Maria Guastella, "Come la pensano a Comiso," *Bozze '85*, 8:4, July/August, 89-123.

5. *La Sicilia*, 10 August 1981.

6. *Gazzetta del Sud*, 9 August 1981.

7. *Grionale di Sicilia*, 13 August 1981; *La Sicilia*, 22 August 1981; *L'Ora*, 29 August 1981.

8. *L'Ora,* 24 November 1984.

9. *La Sicilia,* 10 and 11 August 1981.

10. *L'Unita,* 11 October 1981.

11. *Il Giornale,* 6 May 1983.

12. *L'Espresso,* 20 June 1982.

13. *Giornale di Sicilia,* 26 March 1982.

14. *La Sicilia,* 17 October 1982; *L'Unita,* 13 November 1982; *Paese Sera,* 1 December 1982; *Il Manifesto,* 17 March 1983.

15. *L'Ora,* 6 May 1983; *La Sicilia,* 6 May 1983; *L'Unita,* 20 May 1983.

16. The military worried about housing with reason: hundreds of military families were reportedly on waiting lists or lodged in "unsuitable" private housing in 1982 at Sigonella Air-Naval Base, established 20 years before. But according to researchers of the Sicilian Committees for Peace, it is the nearby community, Motta S. Anastasia (population 6,500), which suffered most. Of 5,000 U.S. servicepeople stationed at Sigonella, 2,000 live in the town. Speculators initially benefitted from the militarization of the community, then the cost of living, drug-traffic, and Mafia-style tactics increased. The local trade union was repressed and a Christian Democratic-neofascist governing coalition was installed in the town.

17. *La Sicilia,* 5 September 1985.

18. Economic Resource Impact Statement, the Cost and Management Analysis Branch of the Comiso Air Station, Fiscal Year 1985.

19. Giorgia Chessari, *L'Altra Sicilia: L'Economia Della Provincia Di Ragusa Nel Contesto Regionale E Nazionale* (Ragusa: Centro Studi "Eliciano Rossitto," 1981).

20. *Il Giornale,* 6 May 1983.

21. Anton Blok, *The Mafia of a Sicilian Village, 1860-1960* (New York: Harper & Row, 1974); Judith Chubb, *Patronage, Power and Poverty in Southern Italy* (Cambridge: Cambridge University Press, 1982); Danilo Dolci, *Report from Palermo* (New York: The Orion Press, 1956); Filippo Sabetti, *Political Authority in a Sicilian Village* (Rutgers, NJ: Rutgers University Press, 1983); Jane and Peter Schneider, *Culture and Poltical Economy in Western Sicily* (New York: Academic Press, 1976).

22. See R. Faenza and M. Fini, *Gli Americani in Italia* (Milano: Feltrinelli, 1976); D. Mack Smith, *A History of Sicily* (London: Chatto and Windus, 1968), 526; M. Pantaleone, *Mafia e Politica, 1943-1962* (London: Chatto and Windus, 1962), 95.

23. Pino Arlacchi, *La Mafia Imprendatrice: l'etica mafiosa e lo spirito del capitalismo* (Bologna: il Mulino, 1983); Commissione antimafia, "Commissione parlementare d'inchiesta sul fenomeno della mafia in Sicilia," Vols. I, II, II, IV (Rome: Tipografia del Senato, 1976), document XXIII, V Legislatura.

24. P.A. Spampinato Gentiloni and A. Spataro, *Missili e Mafia: la Sicilia dopo Comiso* (Rome: Editori Riuniti, 1985).

25. Flora Lewis, *Europe: A Tapestry of Nations* (New York: Simon and Schuster, 1987), 153.

26. *Epoca,* 27 January 1984

27. Besides Comiso Air Base, there are three other important military bases in Sicily: Catania Navy Base and Sigonella Air-Naval Base, used by the U.S. 6th Fleet for communications and storage of nuclear weapons; and the Trapani-Birgi NATO base for AWACS. There are also several Italian military installations, firing ranges, and communication stations throughout the island.

28. *L'Ora,* 17 April 1986.

Chapter 5

A Feminist Perspective on Foreign Military Bases

Cynthia Enloe

Along with other concerns such as peace and sovereignty, the future and the dignity of thousands of women and children, as well as tribal groups, should be made an immediate and important reason for the dismantling or removal of the U.S. bases.

—*Nelia Sancho*
Manila, Philippines 1990[1]

A military base is more than a piece of land littered with barracks, rifle ranges, and runways, and it is much more than the concrete representation of a military doctrine. While it *is* both of these, a base is also a peculiar social creature, a web of human relationships—generally of *unequal* relationships between men and women of different races and classes. This pattern of relationships that constitutes a "base," furthermore, extends far beyond its physical parameters.

Military spokespersons for bases often ignore the impact of these dense social patterns on their personnel or on the communities that host the bases. Even progressive critics of the bases have preferred to discuss the feasibility of any base in the context of the end of the Cold War, "national security" threats, or the dangers of modern nuclear weaponry. All too frequently, both military policy makers and anti-bases activists have paid only superficial attention to the experiences of women who live and work on, or near, the base, women on whom the base relies for its very survival.

This political blindness is caused by portraying the military as a thoroughly masculine institution. Women are generally absent from battle paintings, historical studies about war, journalists' accounts of international alliances, and war comics and films—or they appear merely as minor characters, inserted to add intrigue and color. Women are not allowed to

95

drive the plot; in traditional media coverage of war, women's activities rarely are used to explain any nation's victory or defeat.

Swallowing this popular portrait, observers all too easily accept the official analysis of military operations. If women—lots of women—were featured on the canvas, a military might resemble a hospital or a school, both of which are dependent on the labor of women as nurses, teachers, administrators, secretaries, cleaners, and volunteers. That analogy is rarely drawn; for doing so might deprive the military of its special aura of masculinity and, with it, one of its chief political assets.

Yet the facts do not tell an exclusively male story. Long before the current spate of media features on women soldiers, military commanders were relying on women to do the physical, intellectual, and emotional work to support male soldiers. Yet women routinely have been treated by commanders with a shifting mix of condescension, irritation, even outright contempt. Women from impoverished classes or from "lower-status" racial and ethnic groups have been presumed to be mere "camp followers," single-mindedly pursuing soldiers for sex and rations, even while they were washing soldiers' clothes or tending to their psychological wounds. It is in this wider context of male military planners' ambivalent attitudes toward women—need plus contempt—that any military base must be understood.

Military Wives and Girlfriends

The U.S. military has depended on women married to soldiers to transform overseas bases into socially cohesive communities that are impervious to distracting external influences. The Defense Department expects these military wives to bolster their husbands' morale and to insure their readiness for combat. The *model military wife* will absorb her husband's devotion to his military mission into her marriage. She will remain faithful despite his long absences on military exercises. She will not complain about her loneliness or the extra work involved in acting as a single parent. Instead, she will devote herself to the wives' club and other base volunteer activities that help sustain the fiction of "the military family." After trying to be superwoman for months at a time, she will, however, gladly defer to her soldier husband as "head of the household" when he returns, being careful not to dampen his sense of masculine pride—a pride, military commanders believe, that enhances his soldiering.

The model military wife must also be willing to travel abroad when her husband is sent on longer tours, even if this means giving up her own career aspirations, losing close friends, learning a new language, and making a home out of borrowed quarters. Lonely in Germany, Korea, or Guam, she is expected to think of the military as her *family*. But that may not be enough to insure a stable home. Military social workers have reported that both wife and child abuse in U.S. military families occur at higher levels than in the civilian population.[2]

Given the hardships of being left behind in the U.S., it is not surprising that many women married to U.S. soldiers press to accompany their husbands on overseas assignments. In the 1990s, as the Defense Department is trying to make congressionally demanded budget cuts without sacrificing favorite weapons projects, more and more soldiers are being sent overseas without their civilian spouses. In this sense, the U.S. "Operation Desert Shield" in Saudi Arabia, deploying 400,000 military personnel without a single spouse, may be the forerunner of future bases-without-wives operations. Operation Desert Shield and its successors will only work for the U.S. military if the women married to deployed soldiers are willing and able to "do everything" without redefining the meaning of "wife."

Girlfriends of male soldiers likewise are expected to aid the military by maintaining their soldiers' morale and readiness. Left at home when their boyfriends are sent abroad, these women are expected to be loyal and eager to become military wives upon their soldiers' return. Better yet, they might rush into marriage just before their boyfriends are deployed. A *model girlfriend* should not be very demanding, lest she impose undue stress upon her soldier. His stamina instead needs to be reserved for such high-stress missions as flying jet fighters dangerously low over the sea, or repairing a computer-directed tank on a sand-blown desert. Men serving at an overseas U.S. base will be better able to concentrate on their officers' orders if they receive a steady stream of reassuring letters from their girlfriends back home, letters that do not dwell on the girlfriends' own doubts and worries.

Girlfriends are closer to overseas base life when they are women from the local host society. The Defense Department welcomes efforts by friendly governments to supply U.S. personnel with companionship. Australian women who have grown up in the port city of Perth recall being enlisted to join the "dial-a-sailor" program. Many Australian teenage girls say that they have enjoyed dating U.S. men and going to base dances, which often seem much more exciting than dates with local boys. With the outbreak of AIDS in the United States, however, teenage girls have begun to approach the dial-a-sailor program with greater circumspection. Feminists facilitating discussion groups with Perth's young women report that now girls who accept invitations to on-base dances are taking condoms with them.

All military marriages are stressful, but none more so than between U.S. soldiers and their girlfriends from Asian countries. Eighty percent of marriages between Korean women and U.S. servicemen end in divorce. The Reverend

Yu Bok Nim, a Korean Presbyterian minister, founded a counseling and
service center for local women who date U.S. servicemen in Korea. She has
watched many of these marriages come unravelled:

> When the U.S. soldiers were in Korea, their Korean wives helped
> them get by and have much healthier lives. Many of these men felt
> very lonely in a strange land and found these women, whom they
> came to love. So they got married. But once they return to the States
> the situation changes. Looking around them, they find that their
> wives are the only ones who have yellow faces which stick out like
> sore thumbs. These women…are also incapable of doing what is
> taken as basic—ordinary things like driving, shopping, and com-
> municating with others. So these men quickly change their minds
> and divorce their wives.[3]

Class and race distinctions inform all social relations between the U.S.
military and the host community. Thus the social construction of a U.S.
military base will not be identical in Germany, Italy, Puerto Rico, Hawaii, and
South Korea. If the U.S. soldiers are men—white, African-American, Latino,
Asian-American—who have grown up imagining that they are somehow
more modern or advanced than the local people, the relationships they enter
into with local women will be fraught from the start with paternalism and
perhaps later with tension and trauma. On the one hand, U.S. soldiers may
view these women as less sophisticated and therefore less demanding than
the "liberated" women they know back home. Still, their desire for a
submissive wife may clash with their need for a companion whom they see
as a peer. For her part, a young Asian woman may imagine a foreign soldier
to be more worldly than his local counterparts. If the young woman is from
a working-class or peasant family in a third world country, she may see in
her relationship with a U.S. soldier a route out of poverty and economic
insecurity. She may also be attracted to the relationship out of a sense of
daughterly duty. If she accepts a U.S. soldier's marriage offer, perhaps she
will be able to send money back to her parents from her new home in the
United States.

U.S. military chaplains and officers warn their men against marrying
foreign women, especially from the Third World, women they suspect of
dating soldiers out of a "crass" desire for upward mobility. These warnings
reveal a dilemma the U.S military has created for itself by its dependence on
overseas bases. Military officials imagine male soldiers as men whose morale
is sustained in part by social and sexual access to women wherever they are
stationed. This is not a universal assumption. It seems to stand in stark contrast
to Soviet military presumptions. Drawing on admittedly limited information,
it would appear that the Soviet policy has been to preserve "good relations"
with local governments (for example, in Poland and Afghanistan) by prohib-

iting Red Army men from dating local women or patronizing local brothels. The U.S. military has rejected this policy alternative, and thus has encouraged contacts between its soldiers and local women for the sake of "good morale."

On the other hand, U.S. military officials have demonstrated a fear and suspicion of those same local women: after all, such women might have their own motives and needs. Thus the chaplains' warnings and the bureaucratic obstacles are put in the way of soldiers marrying local women. In addition, some U.S. military advisors may also worry about the risks being taken by the local women who marry U.S. men, many of whom are motivated by myths of Asian feminine docility and U.S. feminine emancipation.

Outside the Fence

Of course, not all women who live in the towns surrounding U.S. bases see themselves as potential girlfriends or wives of military men. But this does not shield them from harassment by male soldiers. The legal protection for women who have been harassed by military personnel is typically flimsy. It depends on the fine print of each base-access agreement made between the United States and the host government.

Every U.S. base located in a foreign country is legally defined by a formal government-to-government agreement, including agreements on health provisions and police and judicial authority. It is here, in these technical agreements arrived at by usually all-male diplomatic bargaining, that local women's roles are presumed and rights are guaranteed—or bargained away. These agreements differ from country to country. Some host countries—for example, Germany, Italy, and Japan—may come to negotiations for basing agreements with impressive bargaining chips. Their diplomats *could* push for provisions assuring that local women were not subject to harassment by U.S. soldiers. But whether those local officials actually do take advantage of their position to write women's concerns into the bases agreement depends on whether there is a well-organized local women's movement making the bases agreement one of its own political priorities, and whether the government's bargainers are open to public pressure. Other governments, of course, come to the bases agreement bargaining sessions in a posture of relative, though never total, weakness, because their officials imagine that their country needs the U.S. base to bolster its economic or political security. In this situation—for example, in the Philippines, Diego Garcia, Honduras, or Kenya—even the activism of an alert women's movement might have a hard time affecting the health and policing provisions so that local women's well-being is not jeopardized by the opening of the U.S. bases.

In November 1990, President Bush and Singapore Prime Minister Lee Kuan Yew formally signed an access agreement which will allow an increase in U.S. training missions and visiting warships to Singapore. According to journalists' reports, the U.S. negotiators were concerned that Singapore's government's tough laws against drug possession would make U.S. soldiers vulnerable to arrests and long imprisonments. But in the end, the U.S. negotiators, badly in need of an alternative to their Philippines bases, gave in. They recognize in the final agreement " the sovereignty of Singaporean law" and will trust that a full briefing of U.S. soldiers and sailors will keep them out of the clutches of Singapore's no-nonsense police. But what the Singaporean government's stance on prostitution, on sexual assault, and on AIDS? Lee Kuan Yew himself has made determined efforts to control his female citizens' reproductive behavior, so it would be surprising if he and his appointed base agreement negotiator did not have firm ideas about sexual relations between U.S. soldiers and Singaporean women. Were these discussed? Were any local women's advocates asked to submit proposals? Newspaper accounts are silent. Perhaps Singaporean and Filipina feminists are sharing ideas about what lies in store for Singaporean women.

Each foreign community hosting a military base has its own peculiar police and prosecutorial relationship to the base. German women, for example, have discovered that a woman who wants to charge a member of the U.S. military with assault has only a very limited period of time in which she can carry those charges through a German judicial procedure. Thereafter, any charges fall under the authority of the U.S. military judicial system. Under that system, not surprisingly, a woman's claim is frequently treated with suspicion, sometimes even leading to investigations of her *own* sexual conduct.

Here in the United States, the political process of writing bases agreements proceeds with scarcely a ripple on the public's consciousness. Thus it is a rare occasion when U.S. women's groups join in an alliance with a Kenyan or Honduran or Italian or Japanese women's movement to coordinate lobbying efforts around a bases bargaining process. This is not simply a testimony of U.S. feminists' parochialness. It is a reflection of the way bases agreement diplomacy is pushed to the outer margins of the bureaucratic maze, where it is difficult for ordinary citizens to monitor, especially when the media decides such negotiations are not "newsworthy." It is also a reflection of the peace movement's often masculinized agenda: the experiences of local women living and working near U.S. military bases are rarely the subject of serious peace movement analysis and strategizing.

The exception may occur when bases become synonymous with prostitution, which in a country such as the Philippines has grown to such proportions due to the U.S. bases that U.S. male peace activists have had to take it into consideration. But frequently this consciousness takes the form merely of moral outrage. The women servicing U.S. male soldiers still are not listened to by peace activists as if they had light to shed on the *entire* political structure of U.S. bases at home and abroad.

The Base Sexualized

No assessment of any military base is complete unless it includes a serious investigation of the extent and character of military-generated prostitution. While military men relate to women in many ways that do not involve exchanging money for sex, prostitution merits discussion by base observers for three reasons: 1) it clearly reveals the race- and class-based inequalities between men and women that underlie military policy; 2) prostitution reveals the connections between *all* categories of women as they serve to maintain a military base; and 3) it reveals the deliberate choices that a governments' officials make about particular groups of women in their attempt to structure each base so that it serves foreign policy objectives.

When U.S. troops pulled out of South Vietnam in 1975, they left behind an estimated 500,000 Vietnamese working as prostitutes. Today in Olongapo City, in the Philippines, there are approximately 20,000 women and children working as prostitutes in an industry servicing the U.S. Subic Navy Base. The women who work in bars, brothels, and massage parlors around military bases are frequently non-white and non-European, unlike most of the male soldiers they are expected to attract. This situation reinforces the global dynamics of sexism and racism that have played an important historical role in colonialization and military expansion. In the microcosm of the base, soldier-clients learn to view their masculinity—and the prowess of the nation they represent—as dependent on their sexual domination of the women who live near the base.

Rather than address these deeper ramifications of prostitution, military officials often express only a more narrow concern about (male) soldiers' morale and readiness for combat. On one hand, military commanders presume that allowing men sexual access to local women is necessary to boost morale. On the other hand, soldiers must be protected from any health risks that endanger their readiness for war.

Local officials and business people, eager to lure or retain a base in their community, often adopt such a distorted view of life on the bases and the social policies that emanate from it. For example, the Philippine local health departments in the base towns accept U.S. funds on the condition that they help keep prostitutes "clean." In 1988, women working as prostitutes near Subic were required by local officials to be tested for VD and AIDS every two weeks.

For local nationalists, prostitution is striking evidence of their nation's compromised sovereignty. Yet women who work as "entertainers" around the U.S. bases rarely are asked to contribute to the broader political debate about the bases, even though they have their own understanding of what the bases mean to them, to their children, to their extended families. And, while local feminists have taken concrete steps to ensure that their analyses and future aspirations are included in the overall anti-bases agenda, so far these efforts have had only minimal impact on anti-militarist organizing. This seriously weakens these governments' capacity to plan for post-base development.

It would be a mistake to imagine that brothels are "natural," inevitable appendages of every military base in the world. They are not. Every military base—foreign or local, overseas or next door—has its own particular sexual politics. That politics is shaped by the local government's laws pertaining to prostitution; the local government's inclination toward enforcing or overlooking those laws; the level of impoverishment of the poorest women in the local society, and their economic alternatives to prostitution; the political influence of the men (and occasionally the women) who own the entertainment businesses near the base; the degree to which the central government of the country hosting the base is nervous about its political opposition using the "corruption of our women" as a launching pad for challenging the incumbent regime; the base commander's and his superiors' presumptions about what bolsters male soldiers' morale and their beliefs about the uncontrollability of men's "sexual drives"; the willingness—or unwillingness—of the military's political superiors (for example, the U.S. House of Representatives Armed Services Committee) to investigate and hold the military accountable for its implicit as well as explicit prostitution policies; the willingness of soldiers' wives and girlfriends to make common cause with local women working as prostitutes; the sexualized racial presumptions held by male soldiers and their officers—themselves usually of several races and ethnic groups—about the availability and erotic appeal of local women; the existence of a local women's movement able to develop an analysis of prostitution autonomous from, even if compatible with, the analysis of a mixed anti-bases nationalist movement; the local perception of the source of health (VD, AIDS) threats from sexually active male soldiers; the base commander's and his superiors' perceptions of the sources of AIDS and VD threats from local prostitutes.

This is a long list, and it could be longer. The point is not just to engage in social science "variable juggling." Rather it is to underscore the range of *politically constructed* variations in a military's sexual policy. If the policy toward military prostitution is just that—a policy—then it should be articulated as such; its makers should be held accountable by the sovereign people.

This has not happened in the United States. Instead, the prostitution business—with its exploitation of literally thousands of local women, especially in third world base communities—has been treated by U.S. citizens as though it were inevitable. While in recent years there has been increasing outrage over the proportions of military-based prostitution, there has been startling little political will to detail the precise *policy decisions* and *policy makers* which have created and supported this prostitution industry.

The 1990 U.S. basing strategy in Saudi Arabia places the political quality of military prostitution into sharp relief. By December 1990, over 300,000 U.S. military personnel were based in Saudi Arabia; 90 percent of those soldiers were men. There is no evidence to suggest that these U.S. male soldiers were chosen for Saudi deployment on the basis of their having distinctly different masculinized sexual attitudes or practices. Presumably these soldiers were interchangeable with—and some were the very same men as—male soldiers thought to have "naturally" needed access to local prostitutes when based in Germany, Honduras, South Korea, Puerto Rico, Guam, Kenya, or the Philippines. But "Operation Desert Shield" appears to have a very different sexual policy. The Saudi-U.S. government-to-government agreement carefully worked out to allow thousands of U.S. soldiers to be based in Saudi Arabia prohibits the establishment of brothels in Saudi Arabia starting in December 1990 (Filipinas have been brought to Bahrain to "serve" U.S. troops there), or the importation of poor women to sexually service U.S. male soldiers. If this policy has been possible in Saudi Arabia, why hasn't it been possible in the Philippines—or in Kenya or Puerto Rico?

Gaining Leverage, Redefining the Base

Against all odds, women seem to be gaining political leverage in military basing decisions. Groups of organized wives and of women soldiers are beginning to raise the kinds of issues that most military officials are ill-trained to address—sexuality, sexism, marital conflict, child care. This sort of organizing usually has been outside peace movements and usually gets little peace movement attention or support.

Some military wives in Canada and the United States, for instance, have insisted that child-care facilities on military bases be upgraded and expanded. Their demands have carried extra weight when they have persuaded their soldier-husbands to support them—going so far as to quit the service if their family needs were not met. In an era when militaries cannot financially afford to lose expensively trained soldiers, military wives' critical efforts to persuade their husbands have paralleled the evolution of child care into an issue of increasing importance in civilian society. More women, in and out of the military, have come to believe that their own and their children's long-range security depends on their having viable careers. To pursue jobs with more promise than working at a fast-food restaurant off base, military wives need not only base child-care facilities but also a radical change in base commanders' conception of "the military wife" and "the military family."

In the late 1980s, a group of U.S. military wives appeared before the House Armed Services Committee. They insisted that Congress instruct the Secretary of Defense to order all base commanders to stop withholding senior promotions from military men whose wives refused to put their own careers on the back-burner in order to perform unpaid volunteer labor on the base. The wives' representatives made their point. The Secretary of Defense instructed all base commanders to find some other way to socially glue "the military family" together. This change in policy may not be fully carried out in spirit—as some vocal wives are quick to note—but it has served to reconstruct the social meaning of a "military base."

One does not have to idealize the newly mobilized military wife in order to appreciate what her emerging feminist consciousness is doing to the Defense Department's use of bases as an instrument of foreign policy. First, most of the military wives who have become autonomously organized do so as women married to officers, often quite senior officers. Women married to non-commissioned officers and to rank-and-file soldiers have not been easily integrated into these fledgling organizations; thus *their* issues have not always had the political airing they deserve. Second, most of the military wives' advocates have been white women. Black, Hispanic, Asian, and Native American women married to U.S. soldiers are not the women publishing the newsletters, appearing before Congress, and developing political strategies. Third, Defense Department officials have not simply succumbed to the activist wives' demands. They have too much at stake—making military bases serve their military interests. Thus while the Defense Department speaks more these days of "wife abuse" and "child abuse" and "family services," each of these is vulnerable to militaristic interpretation.

In 1989, 60 Canadian native and white women met together to explore the effect on women of the proposed expansion of the NATO Air Force base in Goose Bay, Labrador. One morning they used a roll of masking tape to outline a map of Labrador on the floor of the community center. Then, one by one, the women stepped into the map and declared whom they represented. Some imagined themselves to be wives of local white businessmen; others became the native mothers of girls dating NATO pilots, men from

Germany, Holland, Britain, the U.S., and Canada; still others stepped onto the taped map to become local women desperately looking for paid work. Some women gathered there in the community center imagined themselves in the role of men whose sense of self derived partly from their relationships with local women, or the local base commander, who needed to keep up soldiers' morale. The role play was one of the many organizing activities white and native women undertook to resist the Canadian government's ultimately unsuccessful effort to expand the base in order to host NATO's low-level flight training.

Because of the women's imaginative resistance, Ottawa had to include a *gender* impact statement as part of its $4 million Environmental Impact Statement on the proposed NATO base. Never before had a government had to take so seriously the effects that a military base's operations have on women of different ages, social classes, and ethnic groups.

In fact, Ottawa's "EIS" included an assessment of the base's gender implications that was deemed superficial and inadequate by Labrador's native and white women anti-bases activists.[4] But the very mandate provided an unprecedented door through which feminists could gain an official hearing. Thus in 1990, they wrote a public critique of the proposed base that carried crucial legal weight. These documents—especially backed by native women's base sit-ins and nationwide speaking tours—are credited with persuading NATO to drop its plans to expand the Labrador base.

Conclusion

No such gendered impact statement requirement is imposed on the U.S. Defense Department. But the Labrador women's example is well worth American critics' attention. It has the great advantage of pushing women of different groups, on whom army bases depend, for the first time to see how they are linked together by the operations of that base.

There is another set of images that needs to be forged in the 1990s. Women share many common experiences involving the military, whether they live on or near Goose Bay Air Force base in Canada, Subic Naval base in the Philippines, or Elefis Army base in Greece. From Saudi Arabia to Ramstein, Germany and Palmerola, Honduras, from San Diego, California to Yokohama, Japan, women's knowledge and experience must be integrated into progressive critiques of militarization. If they are not, those critiques will be naive, and organizing flowing from them will be ineffectual.

In the eyes of military base negotiators, the world is a single market. If a base is forced to close in one place, it will have to relocate somewhere else. Consequently, women who live near bases now are connected to women who live in areas being considered for future bases. Unless women organize together and argue for a truly radical reassessment of global military strategy, dismantling a base in one country can represent a victory for peace in one country but increasing militarization in another, where women are perhaps less equipped to organize or resist.

Notes

1. Nelia Sancho is a prominent feminist and activist in the movement to remove the U.S. bases from the Philippines.

2. See Nancy Lee Hall, *True Story of a Drunken Mother* (Boston: South End Press, 1990), for a first-person testimony of a navy wife.

3. Yu Bok Nim, "Military Bases—In Whose Interest?" Conference on International Bases Transcripts, 7-8 April 1989, New York City.

4. See, for instance, Cynthia Enloe, "Technical Review of the Goose Bay EIS with Special Attention to the EIS's Consideration of Gender," in Peter Armitage, ed., *Compendium of Critiques of the Goose Bay Environmental Impact Statement* (Sheshatshit, Labrador, Nitassinan, Labrador: Naskapi Montagnais Innu Association, February 1990).

Chapter 6

Voices of Hope and Anger

Women Resisting Militarization

Aurora Camacho de Schmidt

I was born during World War II, in a peaceful and relatively small Mexico City. My country contributed a squadron in support of the Allies, and over the radio the President had told Mexicans that we were at war. But, to my young parents, the war was only visible in the scarcity of some products. My father, fearing food rationing, filled our garage with cartons of imported "Klim" powdered milk, which we hated and had to drink long after the war ended. From that awful powder my sisters and I acquired a precocious distaste for war.

Later, during the early 1950s, Hollywood brought a glamorous war to our imaginations. War movies were filled with noble images—tearful wives saying good-bye to young, heroic soldiers, and handsome pilots solemnly frowning under their helmets. If the Mexican Revolution was fought by peasant armies that raped, looted, and drew blood, this was a war of advanced technology conducted by kind people against the chaos of the world. Even in a foreign country, children were subject to the mythology that ennobled war. Perhaps reality would have been unthinkable. As World War II veteran Paul Fussell wrote, the horror of the war front is impossible to convey:

> The real war was tragic and ironic beyond the power of any literary or philosophical analysis to suggest, but in unbombed America especially, the meaning of the war seemed inaccessible. Thus, as experience, the suffering was wasted.[1]

In the last 45 years, the world has been inundated with images of the unmitigated horrors of warfare through the immediacy of electronic communications. The vivid images of human destruction in Vietnam, Northern

Ireland, Mozambique, the Middle East, Cambodia, El Salvador, and the Guatemalan highlands have also taken on a numbing power. Occasionally, personal testimonies and pictorial images break through our emotional defenses, and once more we are horrified and amazed. In those moments, sanitized words like "army," "military budget," "defense," and "missile" are revealed to mean dismembered bodies, rotting flesh, starving refugees, and burnt children. These are privileged moments when reality makes new demands of us.

In April 1989, I had the opportunity to think again about my reasons for rejecting war and militarism when I was invited to join "Voices of Hope and Anger," an international women's speaking tour about military bases which was organized by the American Friends Service Committee. I joined the tour as an interpreter for Martha Sandoval—our Honduran speaker— and as a chronicler. The tour was organized to raise the issues of foreign military bases within the U.S. peace movement and the wider U.S. public. The eight women worked with the media, spoke in churches, high schools, universities, and community centers and met with women's organizations, as well as with government officials. The tour focused on foreign military bases and consisted of women only, from Japan, South Korea, the Philippines, Puerto Rico, Honduras, West Germany, Poland, and the United States. They came to Philadelphia, meeting for the first time in a three-day orientation session during which they became their own most demanding audience. They next visited New York and Washington, before dividing into groups with separate itineraries and a final common destination on the West Coast. The women formed very strong bonds immediately, transcending differences in language, ethnicity, culture, age, and class.

Women and Anti-Militarism

All the women of "Voices of Hope and Anger" are involved in political action, but a feminist ideology was not their fundamental point of departure. If it is fair to say that they were feminists, each feminist position was cast in different terms. Their opposition to war was eminently practical, and in some cases it was a response to danger and threats to their survival and that of their families and communities. Each saw women's solidarity as an essential component of a global anti-militaristic movement. They saw prostitution as the effect of militarism and the devaluation of women. They all would have agreed with the conviction of Cynthia Enloe that

> as we have accumulated more and more evidence from more and
> more societies, we have become increasingly confident in our
> assertion that to omit gender from any explanation of how milita-
> rization occurs is not only to risk a flawed political analysis; it is to

risk, too, a perpetually unsuccessful campaign to roll back that militarization.[2]

When confronted with questions about feminist struggles in Honduras, Martha Sandoval gave complex answers. She explained that there is a widespread and strong popular mobilization in her country, in spite of shameless repression by the government. She said:

> Women are incorporated in this movement in two ways. First, the growing poverty brought about by the new level of militarization of the country has meant that men have agreed to let their wives and daughters enter the paid labor force. This has meant changes in the traditional family and a search for equality that is not easy and is not a given. Second, women have found opportunities for leadership as the whole population must respond to the assault by the government and the Honduran military aided by the United States. But Honduran women can't afford to split their struggles. The blows come to men and women alike.[3]

Popular struggles in the Third World typically synthesize several strands of opposition and resistance. They cannot be reduced to the familiar terms of the women's movement in the United States and Europe. [4]

Suzuyo Takazato, the speaker from Okinawa, was radicalized by her long experience working with prostitutes and ex-prostitutes who "served the sexual needs of Japanese and now American soldiers." The sorrow of these women, some of whom are now mental patients, convinced her that "military prostitution is the end of a chain of violence created by systems of control: the war system, the patriarchal system, the imperial system." She reminded listeners that mothers who are against war because wars kill their sons, "should also oppose wars because wars prostitute their daughters." For Suzuyo, Okinawa, which hosts an enormous concentration of U.S. military bases and installations, "is the prostituted daughter of Japan."

The understanding of the interlocking systems of power, through which militarism and sexism reinforce each other, gave "Voices of Hope and Anger" its collective identity. The first achievement of the tour was creating a space in which women could articulate convergent analyses about the effects of militarism on their countries as a whole, and on women in particular. In this regard Suzuyo Takazato provided a central insight early in the tour: the violation of a land and a people by an imperial military power is akin to the violation of a woman by a soldier.

Militarism, Gender, and Race

Prostitution has long been associated with the life of soldiers. But military prostitution in a subjugated country has other dimensions. Race is often a central, not accidental, element of militarized sexual exploitation. Consider Suzuyo Takazato's statement that "American men from the Kadena Air Base can be seen in town (Naha) wearing offensive T-shirts. They depict a woman with the letters LBSM. That means 'little brown sex machine.'"

Yu Bok Nim, our speaker from South Korea, also works with women in a center named "My Sisters' Place." Nim, soft-spoken and strong, explained that many prostitutes who work in Okinawa are from South Korea or the Philippines.[5] Given Japan's prosperity, Okinawan women have other work opportunities, but Nim also recounted how Korean women have been forced to serve the sexual needs of foreign armies in earlier times as well:

> [Fifty] years ago Korea was occupied by Japan. At that time 200,000 Korean women were forcibly drafted, kidnapped and deceived, and brought to China, the Philippines, Taiwan, some South Pacific Islands, and Malaysia to become prostitutes for Japanese troops.

Similarly, Lilo Klug, from Germany, reported that Asian women are brought to Europe to work as prostitutes serving NATO troops and other men, as relatively few European women need to play such a role.

Tour member Maria Socorro (Cookie) Diokno is a highly visible leader of the powerful Philippine anti-bases movement. She is not directly involved in assisting women who practice prostitution, but she knows the enormity of the problem around Subic Naval Base and Clark Air Base, where a combined sexual labor force of 23,000 registered prostitutes are at the service of U.S. military men. In the educational and political work of the Philippine anti-bases movement the situation of these women is a central concern. As Cookie explained, "They tell us that the bases bring jobs. Jobs that kill, like prostitution. Jobs that keep the worker forever poor and sick, like prostitution. We don't want those jobs!"

Yu Bok Nim is a skilled storyteller. In the course of the tour she described the lives of typical women who arrived at her center in search of help. The women are poor, and often have a history of early abuse. They have little formal education, but they can read and write, like most Koreans. The women arrive from their villages looking for work and wind up in the ring of bars that surround the military bases. Money is borrowed from the employer to set up her room: a bed, a tape recorder, a dresser. She is then ready to work in the club, dancing with customers, or more frequently, drinking with customers. She may be paid a commission for each drink. She may receive a percentage of the sexual service fee. She will never have enough to repay the initial loan. She must buy food and clothes, and often she sends money to her family—especially if she has children being raised by relatives. She will live like this until she is too sick to go on.

Poster calling for a march against U.S. Bases in the Philippines, produced by GABRIELA, a Philippine women's organization. The poster says, "Remove the Bases Now! Enough is Enough!"

Prostitution is not the only exploitative sexual interaction. Military men become involved with women in the community, and many of these relationships last several months, often with dreadful consequences for the women. "Every day one Amerasian 'souvenir' baby is born. Every day some of these babies are abandoned or sold," Cookie said, adding sobering facts about the prostitution of some of these children.

Martha Sandoval described poor Honduran women who are intent on getting pregnant by a U.S. soldier in the hope of becoming married and being taken to the United States. Nim too, has witnessed such hopes in the visitors who knock at her door at all hours of the day and night.

In Honduras, South Korea, the Philippines, and many other places, military prostitution is receiving a new level of attention because of the spread of AIDS. Overwhelming evidence indicates that the U.S. military has brought AIDS to the "host" countries, yet no branch of the Armed Forces has taken responsibility. Where the U.S. Navy inspects the health of prostitutes, it does so in order to protect the sailors as customers, but only in a haphazard way. In the Philippines the spread of AIDS around U.S. bases has fueled anti-U.S. sentiment. The military, however, remains aloof, and is apparently covering up the extent of the problem, both within its own ranks and with respect to the Philippine people. A recent article by Saundra Sturdevant describes this situation:

> At Subic Bay Naval Base, there is a display board that advertises local nightclubs with pictures of their female employees. When a woman tests positive for syphilis or gonorrhea, her photograph on the board is turned upside down. But no such attention is given to women who test positive for HIV, the AIDS virus. Their identity, as well as the extent to which AIDS has spread among the women who provide sexual labor for GI's, is one of the better-kept secrets in this part of the world.[6]

Thus, both the women and the young soldiers are victimized. Individuals who become ill are expendable, while the military institution remains intact. When prostitutes in Olongapo and Angeles, the Philippine cities that serve Subic and Clark bases, are found to have AIDS, they are simply sent away, and they are given no assistance by either the U.S. or Philippine governments.

According to Martha Sandoval, all of the identified cases of AIDS in Honduras can be traced to Palmerola, the largest U.S. military base in Honduras. A virulent form of venereal disease is known in her country as "la flor del Vietnam," another gift from U.S. personnel.

Racism contributes to the degradation of women as sexual objects for soldiers, but it operates in other military social transactions, both inside and outside the military. Fulani Sunni-Ali is an African American woman with a long history of political activism. Her participation in the speaking tour helped her foreign sisters to understand new connections between racism, poverty, and militarism in the United States. "I also come from a country occupied and impoverished by U.S. military bases: I come from the South of the United States," Fulani said.

Fulani spoke from long years of experience with African American men and women recruits and with communities suffering under the impact of military installations. She described the disillusionment of many young people in the military:

> The U.S. military will spend millions of dollars on recruits this year. It will promise job training, educational benefits, travel opportunities, improvement in the quality of life, and more. The ads will not tell women who are considering careers in the military that they can expect little respect from the male-dominated armed forces. They will not tell Black recruits that they will be victimized by racism.

Fulani equated the Southern states' economic dependency on military installations with the economic needs of military recruits of color. Neither has been fully free to choose, and society takes no responsibility for creating alternative sources of income for regions and alternative employment for individuals. This situation makes the military a self-perpetuating structure. The U.S. military is, in fact, a multi-layered structure with complex power relationships that replicate and magnify the problems of U.S. society at large.

Several of the foreign speakers had observed the unequal treatment of military personnel of color. In Korea for example, Nim noted that African American soldiers were often stationed in the most dangerous positions near the Demilitarized Zone (DMZ). Both Nim and Cookie reported that women who know they are carrying the child of a African American U.S. soldier are more likely to seek an abortion. In the Philippines, the child of an African American man brings less money if sold to illegal adoption rings. Many military prostitutes in South Korea and the Philippines believe that African American men and Latinos are undesirable customers. "Philippine 'bar girls'" Cookie said, "think of Black GI's as more violent. Clearly, we have internalized the racism of the U.S. military."

National Sovereignty and Human Rights

In a paper presented at the New York conference that launched the speaking tour, author Holly Sklar explained that, while the political debate in Washington centers on modes of intervention, the right of the United States to intervene—particularly in Latin America—is never questioned.

Martha Sandoval and Yu Bok Nim experience U.S. military bases in their countries as a form of intervention, all the more insidious because it is done under the pretext of defending their societies. The same has been true of Soviet foreign military bases. Elizbieta Piwowarska was the youngest participant in the tour, which she joined in much the same spirit as she had joined the dissident "Freedom and Peace" organization in Poland. She expressed her people's struggle for independence from the Soviet Union:

> Military dependence is only a small part of our general objection to the Soviet Union. There are approximately 40,000 Soviet troops in Poland and one anti-aircraft nuclear missile site. Even if the Soviet Union removed all of the Soviet Army from Poland, we wouldn't be freed from the domination. I want to emphasize Poland's lack of sovereignty and self-determination.

Particularly moving was Elizbieta's expression of pain at the Soviet officer's imposition of the Russian language on Poland. "We are an old, embattled nation. After a difficult history, we are still Poles. But Russian officers and their families expect to be served in the Russian language at restaurants and other public places."

Every speaker in the tour addressed the question of sovereignty. Even in West Germany, sovereignty was a serious issue. As Lilo Klug reported:

> West German sovereignty is limited by a series of conventions and treaties signed in 1952 and 1954. These treaties give the three victor powers, France, England, and the United States, the right to station military forces in West Germany as during the time of occupation.

In this period, before the Honneker government in East Germany was overthrown, Lilo advocated a peace treaty between the two German states and the victor powers as a means of recovering their sovereignty. Nim demanded "the right of North and South Koreans to make our own mistakes and defend ourselves." But nowhere was the question of sovereignty as pressing as in the case of Puerto Rico.

Maria Isabel Fidalgo is a staff researcher for the Caribbean Project for Justice and Peace. Based in Puerto Rico, the Project identifies itself as a regional institution, concerned with the militarization of the entire Caribbean and tensions in this "strategic" realm.

Maria Isabel described U.S. military installations in Puerto Rico as among the most formidable in the world, making the country a military target and impoverishing the nation. "Puerto Rico is in the grip of a colonial power," she explained. "We are a country under intervention: politically, culturally, ecologically, economically. The U.S. military presence in Puerto Rico is simply the culmination of a colonial relationship."

Maria Isabel's research has focused on the island of Vieques, where the U.S. Navy operates with little or no concern for its impact on the water, soil, health, and social structures essential to life on the island. Puerto Rican land has been used as a testing area for the deadly Agent Orange and other lethal chemicals. Maria Isabel put it succinctly for all the women on the tour: "Military installations mean ecological disasters." The loss of forests in Honduras to make way for maneuvers, the pollution of the Savannah River in Georgia near a military nuclear power plant, the devastation of farmland in West Germany, the destruction of fishing grounds in Vieques—all seriously damage the earth and endanger human life. To all this must be added the presence and dangers of nuclear weapons, often in defiance of a nation's constitution, and sometimes clandestinely stockpiled or transported through sovereign territories without the people's knowledge.

Militarization of these proportions takes a toll on community health, including mental health. While Martha Sandoval worried about the psychological effects of utterly unfamiliar foreign military equipment on the people of Honduras, Maria Isabel wondered about the effect of militarized life becoming *too familiar* for Puerto Rican children. "How do you explain to the children of Vieques," she asked, "that real life is not meant to be like this?"

The loss of farmland to military installations in Honduras is a central concern in the life of Martha Sandoval. Being a peasant, like the majority of Hondurans, she knows that U.S.-owned banana plantations have transformed farmers into serfs since the nineteenth century. Her work as an organizer is ultimately focused on the enactment of real agrarian reform, with the full participation of women as landowners. But the presence of U.S. bases makes that goal remote. As Cynthia Enloe has observed,

> Honduran feminists argue…that the entire militarization policy, of which the American bases are a central part, has served to deprive women of genuine security. Being deprived of farming land by an armed local elite and its soldiers and being infected with AIDS by an American soldier are part of a single militarizing process.[7]

A few times during the tour someone in the audience asked Martha why the Honduran government did not tell the U.S. military to leave. Beyond economic explanations, Martha spoke of the overt and subtle ways in which the Honduran government is complicit with the U.S. government.

How does the presence of a foreign military power increase the repressive power of a government that rules by force? In the Philippines, Honduras, and South Korea, the violation of human rights by national authorities escalates in direct ratio to the growth of popular resistance. Martha Sandoval moved many audiences with her stories about friends and colleagues, including her predecessor in the Women's Section of the Peasant Union:

> This woman is now an invalid. She disappeared for several days. When she came back to her town, she was unrecognizable. Her breasts—she was a nursing mother—had been beaten to a pulp; she had been gang-raped; her collar-bone was broken, and she had lost the capacity to move her legs. All this happened because she had attended an international conference on women and peace, denouncing the conditions in which we must live.

Cookie Diokno was clear on the same point:

> If you oppose the bases, if you work for human rights, if you are for land reform, you are considered a communist. The counterinsurgency program is not directed at people who bear arms: it is directed against people like us. Six of our human rights lawyers were killed in the past six months.

Cookie also spoke about the reality of torture which has continued into the Aquino era:

> There were two boys, a 19-year-old and a 21-year-old, who were putting up posters in Manila saying "Bases Out." They were arrested. They were kept inside the presidential palace for two days; they were slapped around and burned with cigarettes. The third night they were slashed across their necks with a shoemaker's knife. One died. The other is alive. I do not know how. He is walking, but he does not have any feeling on one side of his body.

The presence of military bases requires the acquiescence of the governments of "host" nations. In addition to the officially paid "lease fees," there is always unofficial money that makes a few key people too rich to want change. When popular organizations work to change social and economic structures from the grassroots, they become a "national security" problem in the eyes of their own government. The government and its military branch soon may be using training, equipment, and funds acquired from the United States to repress their own people. The bases can stay in Honduras, the Philippines, and South Korea only if the governments of these and other countries are effective in repressing opposition to the bases.

How is the repression targeted particularly against women? Martha Sandoval reported that in Honduras rape is one of many tools of repression. Looking at the situation in Latin America and the Philippines, Cynthia Enloe has taken the analysis one step further:

> [F]or the counterinsurgency strategist, it is the woman herself who has torn apart the social fabric when she has begun to stretch the confines of feminized domestic space to organize with other

women. Moreover, a woman who helps organize a day-care center, a soup kitchen, or a literacy class comes to be seen by military commanders and anti-communist vigilantes as doubly subversive...Rape has become integral to the implementation of low-intensity conflict doctrine insofar as it is meant to punish a woman for defying rules of respectability, a feminine respectability which serves to hold up the existing political order as well as the existing domestic order.[8]

A Demand for Solidarity

The women discussed many issues: the conversion of bases to economically productive uses; the reunification of Korea; the relationship between NATO and the Warsaw Pact, the future of a free Honduras and a free Puerto Rico, to name only a few. But the immediate, urgent agenda of the women can be stated simply: "Get the bases out!" The women of "Voices of Hope and Anger" agreed on the important role of the people of the United States in their struggles. Martha concluded many of her presentations by telling North Americans, "This is not a Honduran problem. This is your problem. Death is being dealt to the Honduran people, on *your* behalf, and *you* are paying for it."

The eight women came asking for solidarity. They asked people to take responsibility for being well informed. They asked that information be understood in a new critical framework, taking into account the experience of societies—and especially women within these societies—affected by foreign militarization. They asked for specific action: they demanded the dismantling of military bases. Often the women ended their presentations with the plea: "Bring your soldiers back. They are yours!" Suzuyo was eloquent on this issue:

> If men in the military rely on women prostitutes to alleviate their anger and frustration, it must be that being on a base on foreign soil is oppressive. A [male] soldier who has learned that women are disposable sexual objects eventually has to be reintegrated into [U.S.] society. What kind of relationships will he have with women? What kind of lover, husband, or father will he be? This is an issue for U.S. women to be concerned about.

At certain moments, audiences were asked to join fully in the struggle. This invitation meant more than most people expected it would. To a surprised group of college students, Martha said:

> You can write to your senators and representatives and you can join peace groups. But ultimately, nobody can help a social movement in another country until she has done something in her own. You have grave problems in your own society. Look at what

happens to poor people in your own town. Try to understand and take action! Then, maybe someday, I will come and offer you a bunch of Honduran solidarity.

The Women of 'Voices of Hope and Anger'

Maria Socorro Diokno (Cookie) is Secretary General of the Philippines Anti-Bases Coalition, Director of the Free Legal Assistance Group, Chair of the Asian Regional Council on Human Rights, and Secretary of the Philippine Health Professionals for Health and Human Rights.

Maria Isabel Fidalgo attended the University of Puerto Rico where she was active in the student pro-independence movement and in Catholic social action. She works for the Proyecto Caribeño de Justicia y Paz (Caribbean Project for Justice and Peace), focussing in particular on ecological issues and on the impact of the U.S. Navy on the Puerto Rican island of Vieques.

Lilo Klug is currently a member of the city council of Heilbronn, Germany, a town situated between a major U.S. military base and a Pershing II and ground-launched cruise missile site. She is the founder of the Union for International Exchange (a peace organization) and a writer.

Yu Bok Nim is the founder and resident director of My Sister's Place, a counseling, residential, and learning center for women who are involved with U.S. military men from the bases located near Uijongboo, South Korea. She attended Hankuk Theological Seminary in Seoul.

Elzbieta Piwowarska is a student at Jagiellonian University in Kracow, Poland. Elzbieta is a founding member of Freedom and Peace, an independent anti-military, pro-democracy organization.

Martha Sandoval was born in Santa Barbara, Honduras. She became a rural teacher, catechist, and organizer at the age of 14. She is the Secretary of the Women's Section of the National Federation of Honduran Peasants. Martha travels in the Honduran countryside organizing training groups for women and overseeing a network of peasant cooperatives.

Fulani Sunni-Ali is Director of AFSC's Disarmament Program in the Southeastern Region in Atlanta. Fulani has worked as a political organizer, teacher, and youth counselor. As a professional singer and dancer she performed with Miriam Makeba. In 1981, Fulani Sunni-Ali was imprisoned for nine months for refusing to cooperate with a federal investigation of Black political movements in the South.

Suzuyo Takazato is a social worker and currently serves on the City Council of Naha City, the capital of Okinawa. She works with prostitutes near Camp Butler Marine Corps. She is a leader in the Okinawa Christian Peace Center and the Asian Women's Association. She has written numerous papers for international peace gatherings and conferences on prostitution.

Notes

1. Paul Fussell, "The Real War, 1939-1945: An Experience in Horror and Madness," *The Atlantic*, August 1989.

2. Cynthia H. Enloe, "Beyond Rambo: Women and Varieties of Militarized Masculinity," unpublished paper, Conference on Women and Military Systems, Helsinki, January 1987.

3. Cynthia Enloe has written that machismo and U.S. militarization combine to produce the reality known as "Banana Republic": "The colonially seeded culture of machismo serves to legitimize local class and racial stratifications in ways that make the subjugation of all women perpetuate low wages and attenuate union organizing." See Enloe, "Bananas, Bases and Patriarchy," in Jean Bethke Elshtain and Sheila Tobias, eds., *Women, Militarism and War,* (Totowa, NJ: Rowman and Littlefield, 1989), 194.

4. University of Texas Professor Barbara Harlow writes about the ideological divergence of women in liberation movements in Asia, Africa, and Latin America from feminists in industrialized nations. She quotes Gayatri Chakravorty Spivak as deploring the "inbuilt colonialism of First World feminism toward the Third." See Harlow, *Resistance Literature* (New York: Methuen, 1987), 182-185.

5. "Currently there are between 80,000 and 100,000 Filipinas working in the entertainment-sex industry in mainland Japan. They work in cities and in the countryside. Their labor is primarily for Japanese males," Saundra Sturdevant, "Report on AFSC Conference on Women's Labor as Prostitutes Around U.S. Military Bases in the Southern Part of Korea, Japan, Okinawa, and the Philippines," unpublished AFSC report, Okinawa, 1988.

6. Saundra Sturdevant, "The Bar Girls of Subic Bay: The Military, Women, and AIDS," *The Nation,* 3 April 1989.

7. Cynthia Enloe, *Does Khaki Become You? The Militarization of Women's Lives* (Boston: South End Press, 1983), 35.

8. Ibid., 29.

Part II: The Pacific

Chapter 7

The United States in the Pacific

*Christine Wing**

On January 16, 1893, troops from the USS Boston landed in Hawaii. They did so at the request of U.S. Minister to Hawaii John Stevens, who asked them "to secure the safety of American life and property.[1]

But the streets were quiet and there were no signs of threat to U.S. life or property. The approximately 150 troops camped in the front of the Iolani Palace, home of Queen Liliuokalani. Two days earlier Liliuokalani had attempted to proclaim a new constitution for Hawaii. It would have invalidated the existing constitution that, when forced upon the previous king, had effectively disenfranchised Hawaiians while giving legislative control to the *haole* (Caucasian foreigner) minority. Liliuokalani was trying to reassert Hawaiian control over the sugar, professional, and merchant interests represented by the government.

Having engineered the Marines' arrival, a self-appointed "Committee of Public Safety" announced that the monarchy was dissolved, and proclaimed the creation of the Republic of Hawaii. They took over government buildings and set up a Provisional Government. Understanding the threat posed by the U.S. forces, the Queen surrendered her authority.

The Committee of Public Safety represented prominent *haoles* who wanted the United States to annex Hawaii. They hoped and expected that annexation would follow soon after they took power. In the short term they were disappointed. There was substantial anti-annexation sentiment in the United States, and eventually President Cleveland even called for Liliuokalani's restoration (a call which the new government in Hawaii

---

* The author wishes to thank Frank Brodhead and Nelson Foster for their comments and advice.

ignored). But within five years the annexationists got their wish. In the summer of 1898, in the wake of the Spanish-American war, the U.S. Congress passed a resolution annexing Hawaii. The Honolulu Advertiser exuberantly declared "Hawaii Becomes the First Outpost of a Greater America."[2]

These words were prophetic. Since annexation, Hawaii has become a crucial military center for the United States. Hawaii houses the headquarters of the entire Pacific Command, whose responsibility runs from the west coast of the continental United States to the east coast of Africa. Nearly 47,000 U.S. troops are regularly stationed in Hawaii.[3]

The military presence is not without controversy. Many native Hawaiians resent the loss of native lands to the military, and many Hawaiians do not relish the implications of storing over 300 nuclear warheads in Hawaiian territory.[4] Still, the military seems a firm part of the Hawaiian landscape, its presence shored up by the provision of many civilian jobs, and by arguments about Hawaii's contribution to national defense.[5] Thus Hawaii has truly become an "outpost" of the United States.

The United States and the Pacific

Queen Liliuokalani's overthrow was not the first time that representatives of the United States used military force to seize Pacific or Asian lands. Nor would it be the last such intervention. Although the Hawaiian situation was unusual in some ways,[6] these few days in 1893 foretold much about the later U.S. role in the Pacific: the importance of the economic and political interests of U.S.-based business, the availability of U.S. military force to pursue those interests, and the consequent assault on Asian and Pacific people's culture.

In addition to annexing Hawaii, the United States also acquired Guam and the Philippines following the Spanish-American War. These three territories became military (and to some extent commercial) way stations on the United States' path to becoming a Pacific power. U.S. interests in the Pacific grew steadily over the next 40 years, in search of the "China market," and other places to do business. Commercial conflict with the British and, especially, Japan eventually culminated in World War II—which in turn became the pivotal period for the U.S. role in the Pacific.

The United States emerged from World War II in a strong position, both economically and militarily. It also emerged from the war prepared to consolidate and build upon its relative power. In the Pacific, the United States' ability to do this was enhanced by the extensive territory acquired in the course of the war.

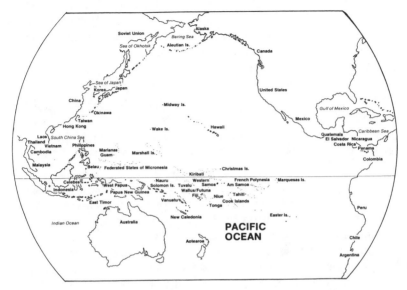

The Pacific. Courtesy of the Conference for a Nuclear Free and Independent Pacific.

In the immediate post-war period, the United States consolidated its control over bases or over areas where bases could be constructed—from Micronesia and Guam, to the Philippines, to Okinawa, and up to the Aleutian Islands. By the end of the Korean War, the military had added or expanded significant installations in South Korea and Japan, and had acquired base rights in Taiwan.[7] The basing structure which developed at the end of the war has remained largely unchanged since the early 1950s, with two exceptions: the addition of important communications, control, and intelligence facilities in Australia; and the downgrading of Taiwan as a military site.

All parts of the U.S. military have been represented in this basing network. But with an ocean twice the size of the Atlantic, and with no Army or Air Force presence on the North American continent itself, the Navy has long viewed the Pacific as its special province—and more than half of all naval operations take place in the Pacific. The military rationale for this network of U.S. bases has been:

- To project military power throughout the Pacific and into the Indian Ocean, allowing the United States to dispatch its military forces throughout the region.

- To encircle the U.S.S.R., denying the Soviet Union access to areas of military and/or economic interest to the United States; allowing the United States to fight a war close to the Soviet homeland, but far from U.S. shores; and creating the chance to "bottle up" the Soviet Pacific Fleet before it is able to "surge" into the open ocean.

- To protect ocean routes and "sea lines of communication" which are important to the United States and to U.S. allies. This includes the Malacca Straits which link the Pacific and Indian Ocean (and through which 90 percent of Japan's oil is transported.[8])

- To support the United States' ability to fight a global or regional nuclear war. The bases house troops, planes, ships, and missiles which would be used in fighting a nuclear war. They also include communication facilities which allow the military command to maintain contact with nuclear capable forces, and to target nuclear weapons against the U.S.S.R. Test sites in Micronesia have also played an important role in the development of nuclear weapons.

- To intervene immediately with massive fire power if South and North Korea were to go to war.

This military presence represents more than the *potential* for warfare. The basing network established in the years immediately following World War II provided the infrastructure for the Korean War, and the bases that were maintained and built after the Korean War supported the war in Indochina. The bases exist so that the United States can wage military aggression.

As we enter the 1990s, there is growing pressure for a new U.S. role in the Pacific. The pressure comes from popular movements and allied governments, from the erosion of the Cold War and changing Soviet policy, and from economic developments that challenge U.S. power and reshape relations among Pacific and Asian nations. Will the United States adjust? There is little evidence that it plans to do so voluntarily. Whether the United States can continue to avoid change is another question, to which we shall return at the end of this chapter.

The Evolution of the U.S. Basing Network

The network of U.S. bases in the Pacific[9] has been built on a foundation of widely varying bilateral relations. In the Philippines, Hawaii, and Guam, the relationship was initially colonial. The United States purchased Alaska. Japan was a World War II enemy and then subject to U.S. occupation. The United States occupied South Korea at the end of World War II, and within a few years was involved in a major war there. Many Pacific Islands came under U.S. influence through a political status newly created at the end of World War II, as "strategic trust territories."Australia, a member of the British Commonwealth, became a strategic center for U.S. forces during the war. It is illustrative of U.S. determination to control the Pacific—and of its post-war power to realize that determination—that these different relationships could be transformed into a reasonably integrated network of facilities devoted to projecting U.S. military power throughout the region.

While the growth of the U.S. basing network in the Pacific occurred mostly in the late 1940s and 1950s, some elements of this network were in place by the late nineteenth century, as the United States joined the race for colonial power. In the nineteenth century, merchants and missionaries from the United States were anxious not to be excluded from colonial opportunities, and, in addition to Hawaii, laid claim to Wake and Midway islands and American Samoa. As we have seen, the Spanish-American War brought Guam under U.S. domination, and hastened the ouster of Spanish colonialism from the Philippines. But it was the China market, in particular, that lured U.S. nationals across the Pacific. The growing U.S. role in the Pacific was justified in large measure as a step on the road to China, whose fabled markets were the goal of U.S. traders.

World War II was the pivotal point in the development of the U.S. bases network. The United States captured islands previously held by Japan, including many in Micronesia, and Okinawa, which military planners would come to see as essential to the U.S. "defense." The United States was the sole occupying force in Japan, and also received the Japanese surrender south of the 38th parallel in Korea. And the Philippines and Guam, lost to the Japanese during the war, also returned to U.S. control.

The United States emerged from the war determined to stake out a "Grand Area" open to U.S. trade and investment. There was widespread agreement among political and military leaders that the U.S. economy could only flourish in a healthy international economic environment, guided by principles of "free trade." Closed economic systems, such as the British sterling bloc of the pre-war period, could not be reestablished. Moreover, communism had to be "contained"; those areas of industrial and military power (real or potential) that were in the capitalist camp at the end of the war were to remain firmly capitalist in their economic organization.

What would this mean for U.S. policy? In one sense, U.S. interests in the Pacific did not change from the pre-war years. At their core, these interests continued to be the expansion and protection of capitalist business opportunities. But now the United States was taking responsibility for assuring that the context in which those interests were pursued was one of economic and political stability. World War II, and the changes which it brought, created new challenges to that stability and to the U.S. role. The Soviet Union came out of the war as a major military (if not economic) force. While the Soviet military could not directly threaten the U.S. homeland, U.S. leaders saw the Soviet Union as clearly hostile to U.S. interests. Many argued that the Soviets represented a real threat to U.S. allies. And the prospect of war with the Soviets was made more dangerous by the advent of atomic weapons, which U.S. leaders assumed would soon be developed by the Soviets. Finally, anti-colonial movements for national liberation gained momentum in the post-war period, and while the United States often favored the dissolution of the old European colonial relationships, these movements also represented a possible danger to U.S. economic prerogatives.

The military requirements posed by U.S. post-war interests were two-fold. The United States needed to be able to project power to areas of economic interest. This was a substantial share of the earth's surface, as the United States increasingly defined the economic well-being of its allies as a "U.S. interest." When the United States resolved that it wanted to revive the Japanese economy, for example, it became necessary to protect access to raw materials and markets in Southeast Asia—since the United States opposed the restoration of Japanese economic links to China, once China was "lost" to communism.

In addition, the United States needed to "contain" the Soviet Union. In the immediate post-war years there was still debate about the nature of the threat posed by the Soviet Union, and how the United States should address it: should the United States try to block Soviet and communist advances everywhere, or only in areas of "vital interest" to the United States? Regardless of how policy makers answered this question, there was consensus that the Soviet Union was fundamentally expansionist, and that U.S. interests—and those of its allies—must be protected from Soviet encroachment.

This was the context in which military and political leaders made decisions about the Pacific basing system. In 1943, even before the war was over, the Joint Chiefs of Staff and President Roosevelt had agreed on a global post-war base plan whose Pacific component assumed exclusive U.S. military rights to the Japanese mandated islands (including Okinawa), the Philippines, and the U.S. possessions in the Pacific.[10]

In the immediate post-war period, many military and civilian planners did not assume that U.S. interests required bases in the "home islands" of Japan,[11] nor did they consider Korea, or an ongoing U.S. presence there, to be critical. Rather, planners thought in terms of a "defensive perimeter," with advance bases in a line linking the Philippines, Guam, Micronesia, Okinawa, the Aleutians, and Alaska. (Hawaii would also continue to play a central role in the Pacific basing system, of course.) Such a basing pattern would guarantee naval and air access to Asia, the latter being especially important given the recent development of the atomic bomb. This strategy was also attractive to the budget-conscious Truman Administration because of its lower cost: the United States could protect its interests, and "contain" the Soviet Union, without incurring the expense of advance troops.

The United States moved quickly to put these Pacific bases in place at the end of the war, sometimes before the political status of the host lands was even determined:

- The Joint Chiefs-of-Staff argued strongly for annexation of the Japanese mandated islands of Micronesia. Instead of outright annexation, however, the Truman Administration opted in 1947 for a UN-sanctioned arrangement. The United Nations created a "Strategic Trust Territory" that gave the United States almost total control over the islands. This arrangement allowed the United States to use the islands for military purposes, in exchange for U.S. commitments to help "advance" the political and economic development of the islands. By August 1946, before the Trusteeship Agreement was established, the United States was conducting atomic bomb tests in Micronesia.

- In Okinawa, the United States proceeded to expand its bases well before the Okinawan political status was resolved.[12]

- When the Philippines gained formal independence in 1946, it was only on the condition that the U.S. bases could remain. In 1947, the United States and the Philippines signed a Military Bases Agreement which gave the United States full control over 23 bases and installations, rent free, for 99 years.

- Guam had been a territory of the United States since 1898, and after World War II, U.S. control of the island was firm. It quickly became a critical home to the Strategic Air Command's 8th Air Force.

The idea of a "limited" offshore defensive perimeter did not last. As the outcome of the Chinese civil war became apparent, and as anti-communism grew in both the domestic and international spheres, the political right in the United States was increasingly successful in calling for a larger military, which would be capable of fighting communism throughout the world. In 1949, the so-called "fall of China" became a major political issue with which conservative critics attacked the State Department's Asia policy. And also in 1949, the Soviet Union exploded its first atomic bomb. But the crystallizing event was the outbreak of the Korean War.

The Korean War and Its Aftermath

If World War II established the beginning of today's system of U.S. bases in the Pacific, the Korean War provided for that system's consolidation. It did this in several ways. The war resolved earlier debates about whether the United States should protect only "vital areas," or oppose communism on every front. By fueling fears about alleged Soviet and world communist expansionism, the war gave added weight to the latter position. The system of bases in the Pacific would expand. As U.S. troops returned to Korea in 1950, this country, once considered unnecessary as a military outpost for the United States, became an essential part of the U.S. "defense" system in Asia and the Pacific.

More broadly, the Korean War established that there could be conventional war in the atomic age—a relief to military services that were trying to define their mission in a world where atomic weapons seemed to have changed the course of warfare. At the same time, the tremendous cost of the Korean War—in both lives and dollars—made security planners reluctant to engage in another land war in Asia. This added significance to the U.S. nuclear arsenal, which was increasingly seen as a way of buying military might at a limited cost in dollars and U.S. lives.[13]

The Korean War confirmed Japan as the fulcrum of U.S. policy in the region. Even before the war began, U.S. policy makers had reached a consensus that U.S. economic and security interests required an economically strong Japan, not a totally subjugated society. The conduct of the Korean War itself helped Japan along that path, as Japanese industry supplied the U.S. war effort. Moreover, U.S. bases on the main islands of Japan played an active role in the war, and earlier thinking about withdrawing those bases was soon abandoned. During the war, the United States also extensively developed bases in Okinawa, taking over 40,000 acres of land, or 13 percent of total land area, for this purpose. [14]

When the Korean War began, the United States sent the 7th Fleet to the Taiwan Straits to prevent an attack by communist troops (and, according to some analysts, to assure that Nationalist Forces did not attempt an attack on the Chinese Mainland). The war thus resolved conflicts within the Truman Administration about defending Chiang Kai-Shek, and the United States proceeded to adopt defense commitments for Taiwan.

Finally, relatively early in the war, the United States secured mutual defense treaties with many countries in the region. These generally included provisions for U.S. base access. In 1951, the United States signed treaties with the Philippines, Japan, Australia, and New Zealand. These were followed by similar treaties with South Korea in 1953 and with Taiwan in 1954.

Between Korea and the Indochina War

For the remainder of the 1950s, the official objective of U.S. military policy in the Pacific was to prevent the growth of Soviet or communist influence. This propaganda line disguised the actual objective: to oppose the growth of any nationalist movements that would not cooperate with U.S. trade and foreign investment strategies. Maintaining and expanding Japan's access to markets and raw materials in Southeast Asia was particularly important, as the United States increasingly saw Japan's economic well-being as central to its own security. The commitment to keeping communism out of South Korea was also now firmly established. Earlier hopes about promoting a split within "international communism" by establishing friendly relations with China were abandoned in light of the Chinese role in the Korean War, and the apparent Sino-Soviet cooperation.

These commitments required a growing U.S. military presence in the region. Hundreds of U.S. bases and installations were constructed or expanded in this period. Robert Harkavy writes of this time:

> At its peak, the United States had some 3,800 military installations in Japan...of which over thirty were major facilities...Okinawa became, after 1945, virtually a vast U.S. island base, involving some 120 military facilities, including 19 major ones...
>
> While the United States had originally made scant use of the South Korean facilities before the 1950 invasion, the aftermath of the war saw significant forces left in place to deter another...From then until 1971, the United States deployed two army divisions in South Korea backed up by nuclear weapons...The U.S. Air Force, meanwhile, became entrenched at six major air bases in South Korea, which deployed some 100 combat aircraft...[15]

This was the period of extensive above-ground nuclear testing in the Marshall Islands as well. The United States exploded 66 atomic and hydrogen bombs in the Marshalls between 1946 and 1958. This included the 1954 "Bravo" test of a hydrogen bomb with 1,000 times the power of the Hiroshima bomb. It vaporized Bikini atoll, and dropped radioactive ash on 82 people living on nearby Rongelap atoll, as well as on 23 Japanese fishermen and 28 U.S. nationals at a weather station—and exposed many other Marshallese to lower levels of radiation. Miscarriages, birth defects, and other serious health problems—some fatal—were the result for many Marshallese.[16]

The War in Indochina

The theoretical focus in the 1950s may have been on "Massive Retaliation" and the development of the U.S. nuclear capacity, but a structure for intervention with conventional forces was also expanded in this period. The Kennedy Administration and its successors were willing to use this infrastructure for war in the Third World. In the 1960s, military strategy changed to highlight "flexible response": a readiness to respond at any time to any situation with whatever means were deemed necessary. And nuclear war planning began to emphasize the importance of being able to fight "limited" nuclear engagements. [17]

U.S. bases in the Pacific were integral to the Indochina War. Subic Bay Naval Base and Clark Air Field made the Philippines ideal as a major staging area and logistics hub for the war, with up to 50 transports daily flying out of Clark, and frequent ship visits to Subic (as many as 1,700 in 1968). [18] B-52's took off from Guam to bomb Vietnam and Cambodia. Yokosuka Naval Base in Japan was a rear base for four aircraft carriers of the 7th fleet; the Marine bases in Okinawa and Japan, and at Subic Bay, were rear areas for Marines fighting in Vietnam, as well as training areas. [19]

Bases in Southeast Asia also played an important role in the war. According to Harkavy, the military buildup in Southeast Asia began "around 1961-62, during the onset of the almost "secret" war in Laos, and several years before the serious beginnings of the U.S. involvement in the major conflict in South Vietnam." [20] Thailand became home to U.S. air bases, ground personnel, aircraft (including B-52's), and communications and intelligence facilities. Laos provided airstrips, and facilities to support CIA and Special Forces—all engaged in the Indochina War.[21] Within South Vietnam, the United States also built a massive military infrastructure. According to the authors of *American Lake*, "At the peak of the base construction in 1966, U.S. forces operated from 73 major air bases and airfields in South Vietnam, as well as four major and ten smaller military ports." [22]

With the loss of the war came the loss of many of these bases, including those in Thailand, where the United States was asked to withdraw. But the war also brought broader changes that affected U.S. bases and their prospects for remaining in the Pacific. The U.S. defeat and the domestic political upheaval during the course of the war provoked a crisis in U.S. foreign policy. Despite the application of massive amounts of military equipment, money, and hundreds of thousands of troops, including more than 50,000 U.S. lives, the United States found itself unable to enforce its will in this part of the globe.

The United States also faced growing economic challenges. Partly because of the demand created by the war effort, the economies of U.S. allies began to boom. At the same time, the U.S. economy experienced high inflation and slow economic growth engendered, in part, by the cost of the war. Moreover, third world countries began to organize for more control over critical natural resources, most notably oil, on which the U.S. economy depended.

Thus the United States found itself over-extended, without the political or economic capability to meet its commitments. President Nixon and Secretary of State Kissinger moved to adjust U.S. policy even before the end of the Indochina War. They sought "detente" with the Soviet Union, including negotiations on nuclear weapons. The Nixon Administration also initiated rapprochment with China. The Administration hoped to forge economic links with this large and populous country, and to further the Sino-Soviet split, which was manifest in the 1969 border war between China and the Soviet Union.

A second adjustment in U.S. policy was the "Nixon Doctrine," announced in Guam in 1969. President Nixon said that the United States would no longer provide the "manpower" for fighting wars when an ally was threatened by non-nuclear aggression. Allies (Korea, Japan, and Indochina, in the Asian/Pacific context) were expected to take up more of their own burden of defense.

These adjustments in U.S. policy were reflected in reduced force levels in the Pacific. With "Vietnamization," the number of U.S. troops in Indochina began to decline before the war was over. In 1968, there were 859,000 U.S. personnel in the Pacific (this includes personnel in South Korea, Japan and Okinawa, Thailand, South Vietnam, the "other Pacific" areas, and those afloat). By 1972, the number of forward forces in the Pacific had dropped to 275,000; by 1978, the figure was at 130,000.[23]

The war in Indochina also fostered greater local opposition to the U.S. presence in the region. Popular anti-war movements grew in Japan, Okinawa, the Philippines, Australia, and New Zealand. One consequence was the successful demand by anti-war forces for the reversion of Okinawa to Japan (although the bases remained). Anti-nuclear and pro-sovereignty sentiments also emerged and were strengthened at this time, fueled by a number of events: the decolonization of several South Pacific states, efforts to create a new political status for the Trust Territories of Micronesia, and continued nuclear testing, or plans for nuclear waste dumping, by big powers. Later in the decade, these would give rise to the Nuclear Free and Independent Pacific movement, which eventually connected with the emerging anti-nuclear and anti-bases forces in the "Rim" countries.

Into the 1980s

The retrenchment in U.S. forces in the Pacific was not to last. Between 1975 and the 1980 presidential election, right-wing discontent and power increased in the United States. Critics attacked both Kissinger and Carter for the "failed" policy of detente, arguing that this policy allowed the Soviets to gain nuclear superiority and pursue expansionist aims (as in the invasion of Afghanistan). The Carter Administration was also criticized for alleged weaknesses shown by the Iranian hostage problem and U.S. "losses" in Central America and Africa.

President Carter initiated a military buildup, which Ronald Reagan accelerated when he became President. The goals of this buildup appeared to be several: 1) to allow the United States to fight a global war, in more than one "theater"; 2) to acquire nuclear superiority over the Soviet Union; 3) to allow the United States to fight a "limited" nuclear war; and 4) to limit, if not reverse, the course of nationalist, socialist, or communist revolutions in the Third World.

The network of U.S. bases in the Pacific could readily support these directions in U.S. military policy. U.S. force levels increased again, and by 1988 they totalled 141,000 in the Pacific region.[24] A critical part of the military buildup was the newly articulated Maritime Strategy, which called for a substantial increase in Naval forces—the "600-ship Navy." The 600-ship Navy would have a new and expanded mission in times of war. It would attack Soviet submarines and ships in Soviet waters—including Soviet ballistic missile submarines. This larger Navy could engage Soviet forces around the globe (not only at the primary site of military conflict), thereby forcing the Soviets to pull resources from a main conflict. In recent years there have been some budget cuts in the Navy's plans for a 600-ship Navy, but the Maritime Strategy remains in place. In 1989, the Navy had 565 combat ships, compared to 480 in 1980.[25]

With the Navy's mission in the Pacific expanded, U.S. naval and air bases assumed increased importance in the region. The rapid escalation of the nuclear arms race also required expansion and modernization of U.S. facilities for command, control, communications, and intelligence (C3I). The 1980s thus brought continued further development of C3I facilities in the Pacific, continuing an expansion begun in the late 1960s. Finally, forward bases in Okinawa, Japan, and the Philippines played increasing roles in supporting U.S. military operations in the Persian Gulf and the Indian Ocean.

The Network of U.S. Bases Today

U.S. bases in the Pacific, from Hawaii to the Philippines, from the Aleutians to Australia, are linked through interdependent combat missions and strategic nuclear functions. Here is a brief overview of the most important bases:[26]

Hawaii

Hawaii is the headquarters of the Pacific Command. Located at Camp H.M. Smith at Oahu, the Pacific Command is headed by the Commander-in-Chief of the Pacific (CINCPAC), traditionally an admiral in the Navy. Pacific Command is responsible for planning and command of Navy, Army, Marine, and Air Force operations in an area which covers nearly half the globe's surface: from the west coast of North America to the east coasts of Asia and Africa.

There are more than 25 military facilities on the islands. The U.S. 3rd Fleet is based at Pearl Harbor. Pearl Harbor also serves as a rear base for the 7th Fleet, and as the headquarters of the Naval Forces of the Central Command (the Middle East and Southwest Asia). Hickam Air Force Base is headquarters to the Pacific Air Forces, as Fort Shafter is to the Army Western Command. A variety of C3I activities are also based in Hawaii.[27] In the mid-1980s there were 345 nuclear weapons stored at two sites in Hawaii, at Barbers Point Naval Air Station and West Loch, Pearl Harbor, both on Oahu.[28]

Guam

The next important way station for the Navy and Air Force is at Guam, about 4,300 miles west of Hawaii. A commonwealth of the United States, where the U.S. military controls 30 percent of the land,[29] Guam is pivotal to U.S. power projection in the Pacific. Facilities at Guam can support combat operations in Southeast and Northeast Asia and the Indian Ocean. They also play a role in preparation for strategic nuclear warfighting.

For many years the Strategic Air Command's B-52 bombers at Andersen Air Base carried nuclear bombs for use in possible strategic nuclear war with the Soviet Union. Recently the nuclear weapons have been removed. One squadron of B-52's remains, but it is armed with conventional bombs.[30]

Apra Harbor is a "vital transit point for the Pacific Fleet." [31] Formerly home base for the Polaris missile submarines (which have been phased out), Apra Harbor is now homeport to the Proteus, a submarine tender which services attack submarines in the Western Pacific. Apra also includes a ship repair facility for some parts of the 7th Fleet.[32]

Santa Rita has had the "main nuclear weapons storage site in the western Pacific." [33] In the early 1980s, over 200 nuclear weapons were stored here,[34] although the number may have decreased somewhat since then. Guam also houses various C3I facilities, including part of the Giant Talk-Scope Signal III system which is designed for communication with airborne B-52's.[35]

Philippines

The U.S. bases in the Philippines sit at the gateway between the Pacific Ocean on one side, and Southeast Asia and the Indian Ocean on the other. They link U.S. military forces in the two areas to support intervention and combat operations in Northeast and Southeast Asia, and in the Indian Ocean.

Subic Bay Naval Base, the largest U.S. overseas naval base, supports the U.S. 7th Fleet and "Task Force 77," a carrier task force which is assigned to the Indian Ocean. Subic Bay is also a major ship repair and storage facility. Clark Air Base is the second most important U.S. facility in the Philippines. It is a logistical and communications hub for the Air Forces's western Pacific operations.

Japan and Okinawa

Separated by narrow straits from the Soviet Union, China, and the tense Korean peninsula, Japan is close to countries which the United States has historically seen as military rivals. It hosts important bases for every branch of the U.S. military, including large deployments of troops and equipment ready for fighting in Northeast Asia, or southward.

In Japan, there are large U.S. naval complexes at Yokosuka (headquarters for the 7th Fleet), Yokohama, and Sasebo; an Army facility storing ammunition and equipment for Army headquarters in South Korea; and important C3I installations. Kadena Air Base in Okinawa "is one of the most important U.S. overseas bases, housing strategic tankers, reconnaissance aircraft and communications."[36] One Marine Corps Division is based in Okinawa, as well as pre-positioned equipment for fighting in Korea or the Middle East. There are also several large Signal Intelligence bases here.[37]

Korea

With the exception of Indochina, South Korea is the only place on the Asian mainland that the United States has deployed combat forces since World War II. It is also the only place in the region where U.S. forces are configured primarily to fight a war in the country where they are located.

Their main mission is to deter a war with North Korea or, depending on policy decisions, to fight and defeat North Korea.

Currently there are about 46,000 U.S. troops in Korea,[38] on about 40 bases and installations.[39] The great majority of these are Army forces. U.S. Forces-Korea has its headquarters at Yongsan in Seoul, and the Army's 2nd Infantry Division is based at Camp Casey, in Tongduchon. The Air Force holds important bases at Kunsan (8th Tactical Fighter Wing), Osan (314th Air Division), and Taegu (497th Tactical Fighter Squadron).[40]

In a situation unique in the U.S. basing and alliance system, a U.S. general commands South Korean troops in Korea. The Commander of United States Forces in Korea (an army general) also has under his jurisdiction the "Combined Forces Command," which includes all South Korean combat forces.

The United States stores about 150 nuclear weapons in Korea at Kunsan Air Base. At Kunsan, there are nuclear-capable F-16's, which would be capable of striking Soviet as well as North Korean territory.[41]

Alaska

Like Hawaii, Alaska is a U.S. state which nonetheless lies sufficiently "forward" (three miles from the U.S.S.R. at the nearest point!) that it would be the site of important operations in the event of war. Arkin and Fieldhouse list 42 facilities in Alaska that constitute part of the "nuclear infrastructure," and they report that its location makes Alaska a "significant strategic command and control headquarters."[42] They add:

> The main U.S. ASW [anti-submarine warfare] base is at Adak in the middle of the Aleutian Islands. In peace-time about sixty B-57 nuclear depth bombs are stored at Adak. P-3 maritime patrol aircraft fly regularly from the island; they collect information from the ocean surveillance network…and follow the movements of Soviet submarines and surface ships. In wartime the number of ASW aircraft based at Adak would increase.[43]

Micronesia

The most important military facility in Micronesia is the Kwajalein Missile Range. Since 1958 test missiles launched from Vandenburg Air Force Base and Point Magu Naval Station in California have landed in Kwajalein's lagoon. This tiny atoll in Micronesia has played a crucial role in the development of strategic nuclear weapons, including the MX missile. The Pentagon has used Kwajalein in tests of anti-ballistic missile defenses, and it plans to test parts of Star Wars there as well. The ALTAIR radar system tracks Soviet satellite launchings, providing targeting information for U.S. anti-satellite weapons.[44]

At Yap (in the Federated States of Micronesia), there is a component of the "Clarinet Pilgrim" shore-to-submarine communications system.[45] On other Micronesian islands, such as those in the nation of Palau, the United States seeks to retain military access, even if no major military installations are there at present. Micronesia would be of special interest to the United States if U.S. bases are forced out of the Philippines.

Australia

Australia offers several advantages as a site for C3I facilities.[46] It sits on the far side of the globe from the United States, offering coverage of areas not easily reached by other facilities, including parts of the Soviet Union, China, and Southeast Asia. Moreover, it is difficult for other nations to monitor secret transmissions from facilities in Australia's large, sparsely populated interior.

Three bases in Australia are considered especially important, and one—Nurrungar—is seen as essential to the U.S. nuclear war-making capability. Nurrungar is a ground station for the early warning satellites of the Defense Support Program (DSP), one of three such facilities in the world. Using infrared sensors, these satellites can detect launches of Soviet land-based missiles. DSP would provide early warning of a Soviet pre-emptive strike, or allow the United States to "reconstitute and retarget its forces in the tail end of a U.S. first strike."[47] The DSP can also collect information about atmospheric nuclear tests, and thus monitor compliance with the Comprehensive Test Ban.

At Pine Gap, the United States maintains an important ground station for a spy satellite which monitors the Soviet Union and China. At Northwest Cape, the United States communicates with Trident submarines that carry ballistic missiles. It is from here that targeting and firing orders would be sent to Trident submarines in the event of nuclear war.

Challenges to the Bases

The U.S. bases inevitably shape the political process in the countries where they are located. The United States grants friendly leaders economic and military aid (including assistance in putting down opposition movements) and, in some cases, political legitimacy. Through these mechanisms the United States helped to keep Ferdinand Marcos's dictatorship alive for many years, as well as a succession of repressive leaders in South Korea.

But this political influence can be a double-edged sword. In countries where the United States has supported dictatorships, the U.S. presence engenders resentment among those who do not benefit from the U.S. role. Even in countries where governments are more democratic, there is substantial opposition to the U.S. presence. This is due to the fundamental loss of sovereignty that accompanies the bases, the unwillingness of local populations to participate in the nuclearized superpower rivalry, and the social and environmental effects of the bases—particularly, their effects on women and children.

Opposition to the U.S. bases has grown in each of the countries discussed above. Moreover, there are growing *regional* networks of activists opposed to the U.S. presence. While some have a broader focus than only the U.S. bases, their work either explicitly or implicitly challenges the U.S. basing system itself. These include the movement for a Nuclear Free and Independent Pacific, the Pacific Campaign to Disarm the Seas, and networks of women opposed to military prostitution and the international trafficking in women.

The full range of anti-bases activity in the Pacific is too broad to cover here. The following three examples are chosen to illustrate the diversity of anti-bases work in the Pacific. The subsequent chapters on the Philippines and on Japan and Okinawa add to this picture.

The Question of Sovereignty in Korea

Pressure to remove United States bases from Korea has been growing rapidly within the past few years. Since World War II, the United States has played a determining role in the fate of people on the Korean peninsula. Following the division of Korea at the end of that war (a decision made by the United States and the Soviet Union), and the bloody and destructive Korean War, Korea became a major dividing line in the Cold War. The United States has the only foreign troops, and the only nuclear weapons, on the peninsula. Although Korean public opinion is divided, the U.S. military presence, and especially the nuclear weapons, are increasingly criticized.

The opposition to the U.S. presence is due in part to the U.S. role in creating and maintaining the repressive governments of the past 45 years. U.S. military, economic, and political support has shored up successive governments that have used brutal force to crush popular dissent. There has been no true political sovereignty in South Korea since the U.S. occupation. This is underscored today by the complex treaty structure which gives the U.S. Command authority over South Korean troops. In 1980, the U.S. Commander released some of these troops to participate in the repression of anti-martial law protests at Kwangju. Several hundred unarmed protesters were killed by South Korean military forces.[48] In South Korea, this incident is still much discussed, mourned, and cited as evidence of the true nature of the U.S. presence.

Many Koreans also object to the possibility that the United States would decide to use nuclear weapons in a war that would surely obliterate their land. And Koreans deal regularly with the range of other problems that typically accompany the U.S. military presence: the growth of prostitution and drug trafficking around bases, lack of jurisdiction over criminal activities of U.S. forces, and military exercises that disrupt daily life and agriculture. Because the U.S. presence is so dominant a factor in Korean life, there are other aggravations as well. For example, one television channel is reserved for U.S. armed forces viewing, and for years the Army has had a main base sitting on valuable property in the heart of Seoul (including a full 18-hole golf course!). But, reflecting growing sensitivity about the U.S. presence, there are plans now under way to remove this base from Seoul.

The issue of reunification is closely tied to the issue of the bases. Korea was divided against the wishes of its people, North and South. The desire for reunification is intense, even though the hostility between the two govern-ments has been great, and many people in the South are strongly anti-com-munist and distrustful of the North. (North Korean people may also have great fear and distrust of the South, but this is harder to know, given the secrecy of North Korean society.) Most people in one country have relatives in the other, often members of their immediate family. The pain of the division is still very real.

What's more, people in Korea believe that some kind of reunification of their country is possible, a faith encouraged by the fall of the Berlin Wall. But many within the opposition see the U.S. presence as an obstacle. Not only is the North unlikely to reunify with a United States-occupied country, but they believe it was the superpower presence—and the ongoing super-power rivalry—that created the problem. Finally, many believe that the United States itself favors the continued division of Korea: that a reunified Korea would upset the status quo in Northeast Asia, and that a unified Korea, functioning in markets of interest to the United States, but outside the political control of the United States, might eventually pose an economic threat.

Bases and the Sexual Exploitation of Women

The U.S. basing network relies on the sexual labor of Asian and Pacific women. Bases in the Philippines and Korea are surrounded by sex industries (as were bases in Okinawa until the reversion of Okinawa to Japan in 1972). The profits go primarily to bar owners and other proprietors in this industry. The women (and children) who are driven to work here out of economic desperation often find themselves locked into chattel-like working relationships, barely able to get out of debt to the bar owners, rarely able to escape.

Rather than being an uncontrollable side effect of the bases, this reliance on women's sexual labor is built into the military presence. Women "service" the U.S. sailor or soldier, and in the process create an economic base for the communities around U.S. facilities. This objectification rests on a fundamental racism and sexism that devalues the lives of Asian and Pacific women.

The systematic exploitation of Asian and Pacific women as part of the U.S. war-making effort can probably best be seen in the Indochina war, when both Okinawa and the Philippines offered "rest and recreation" to U.S. servicemen. Suzuyo Takazato, a political activist in Okinawa, analyzed the close relationship between the presence of the bases and the need for an economy based on prostitution:

> From a strictly economic point of view, this area [in Okinawa] certainly enjoyed a tremendous boom during the Vietnam War due to the existence of the base. In its heyday, there were more than 1,200 "approved" bars, night clubs and restaurants on Okinawa, and soldiers spent money freely. B-52 bombers were taking off from Kadena Base almost every day to bomb North Vietnam, while returning soldiers from Vietnam, with their chest pockets filled with dollar bills, sometimes spent all their money in one night. They felt anxious and frustrated not knowing how their lives would be the next day and hoped to receive temporary relief from the killings.

In relation to the political situation in Japan, the situation in Okinawa could be stated as follows:

> Japan used her daughter, Okinawa, as a breakwater to keep the battlefields from spreading over to the mainland until the end of [World War II, in which 150,000 Okinawans died]. After the war, she enjoyed economic prosperity by selling the daughter [to the United States]. In sold-out Okinawa, under the government of a different race, many families, in fact the whole island, managed to overcome the economic straits, directly or indirectly, by the earnings of prostitutes.[49]

Women throughout the Pacific are working to rid their countries of U.S. bases, organizing at every level, from community projects to national and regional efforts. Some of this work takes place in the context of a larger quest for national independence and economic self-sufficiency. In other cases, the organizing is built directly around prostitution and other sex-industry issues. An example is the work of the Philippine women's organization GABRIELA, which has made the situation of prostituted women around U.S. bases a major priority. GABRIELA runs a center for prostituted women in Olongapo (the city next to Subic Bay), campaigns for the removal of the U.S. bases, and collaborates with anti-bases and feminist struggles in other countries.

Self-determination, Nuclear Weapons, and Palau

The Republic of Palau ("Belau" is the spelling and pronunciation used by many people; the official spelling, however, is "Palau") contains numerous islands which stretch over a 300-mile area. Its population numbers about 15,000. Belau was part of the "Strategic Trust Territory" granted to the United States at the end of World War II. In taking over administration of the territories, the United States was given extensive military rights in Micronesia, in exchange for an obligation to promote economic and political development of the islands.

Unfortunately for Micronesia, the United States concentrated on its military opportunities rather than its economic responsibilities. As discussed earlier, in the Marshall Islands, atomic and hydrogen bomb tests vaporized atolls and radiated people, land, and water. To make way for the missile test range at Kwajalein, Marshallese were moved to the tiny atoll of Ebeye. Living conditions on Ebeye are very crowded and poor, public health problems abound, and Marshallese face profound discrimination in services, employment, and even travel rights.[50]

In the meantime, Micronesia's economies, once self-sufficient, have become increasingly reliant on the infusion of government funds from the United States. In 1987, for example, more than 50 percent of employed Palauans worked for the government, which received 90 percent of its budget as a direct subsidy from the United States. Throughout Micronesia, the production of basic commodities and foodstuffs has been undermined by imports from the United States and Japan, and more generally, by the selling of the "American way of life" which devalues the products of the local culture.[51]

Palauans adopted a new constitution in 1979 as part of the process of terminating the Trusteeship and creating a new political relationship with the United States. The Constitution prohibits nuclear weapons in Palauan territory, and forbids the use of eminent domain on behalf of a foreign entity. The Constitution also requires a 75 percent majority vote to overturn the non-nuclear provision.

The United States and Palau have been negotiating a "Compact of Free Association," which would define the new relationship between Palau and the United States. The Compact calls for unlimited military access and the right to transit nuclear weapons. The Compact would also provide about

$300 million to Palau over 15 years—a powerful incentive to this small debt-ridden island nation with relatively few economic alternatives.[52]

The Compact has not been approved in repeated voting, despite the economic incentives. Supporters of the Compact have been unable to muster a 75 percent majority, which is what the courts have said is required, since the acceptance of the Compact would implicitly overrule the non-nuclear provision of the Constitution.

There have been many votes on the Compact because both the United States and segments of the Palaun leadership have wanted the Compact approved. Palau is a traditionally peaceful culture which had previously made its decisions by cooperative consensus. But in the summer of 1987 the situation turned violent, with severe intimidation of those opposed to the Compact, and the murder of the father of a pro-Constitution activist. Since that time, the violence has calmed, but the political situation remains complex—and the Compact has yet to be approved.

What's Ahead for U.S. Bases in the Pacific?

The fate of U.S. bases in the Pacific will be determined by developments within the countries where they are located, by how the U.S. government perceives its interests and acts to protect them, and by whether the U.S. government has the ability to achieve its goals. Currently, pressure for change comes from three sources: the erosion of the Cold War, in addition to already changing Soviet policies in the Pacific; the growth of opposition to the bases, as discussed above; and economic challenges—constraints on the U.S. budget, combined with the broader and longer term problem posed by economic competition from Pacific Rim countries.

Created in the context of deepening East-West tensions, the network of U.S. bases in the Pacific might be expected to decline with the apparent demise of the Cold War. Indeed, the Bush Administration has demonstrated some interest in modest troop reductions in Korea and Japan, but the proposals are quite limited. For example, an April 1990 Department of Defense report on the future U.S. military posture in East Asia projected a force reduction of about 10 percent by the end of 1992. (Later reductions were anticipated, but not specified.) There does not appear to be any serious rethinking of the overall mission and responsibilities of U.S. forces in the Pacific.[53]

For several years, beginning before the dramatic changes in Europe, the Soviets have been indicating that they would like to see new U.S. and Soviet roles in the region. Eager to be a more active player in Pacific affairs (especially to participate in the booming economic activity of the region) and needing to reduce their military burden so as to attend to domestic economic needs, the Soviet Union has offered proposals to reduce military forces and to lessen the risk of war in the Pacific. In 1986, in Vladivostok, Gorbachev called for broad steps toward demilitarization and improved trade relations. The Soviets agreed to dismantle the intermediate range SS-20 missiles in the Soviet east (targeted on Asia) as part of the Intermediate Range Nuclear Forces (INF) agreement of 1987. Gorbachev has said the Soviet Union will also unilaterally withdraw 200,000 Far Eastern troops, cut back the Pacific fleet, and withdraw Asian-based forces that are not within Soviet borders—including those at Cam Ranh Bay.[54]

The United States has indicated relatively little interest in the Soviet proposals. However, U.S. allies in the Pacific and Asia have encouraged a more positive response from the United States. The apparent Soviet interest in a less militarized Pacific, as well as improved U.S.-Soviet relations, challenge the articulated rationale for much of the Pacific arms race of the last four decades, that is, the growing "Soviet threat."

Second, local and regional opposition to the bases is clearly of concern to the United States. For example, the U.S. military is exploring alternative sites for the functions now carried by Philippines bases. Even if the U.S. government is not forced to withdraw soon, apparently some in the United States military anticipate that the United States will be out of the Philippines within the next 25 years.

The *Discriminate Deterrence* report (discussed elsewhere in this book) also suggests that opposition to the bases may be shaping U.S. options. This report argues for less reliance on overseas bases to support U.S. pursuit of interests in the Third World. It calls for greater reliance on "low-cost satellites in space...[to] replace the communication and intelligence-gathering functions of overseas bases...[and] long endurance aircraft for surveillance...[and] naval options." The problem with overseas bases is that "We have found it increasingly difficult, and politically costly, to maintain bases [in the Third World.]"[55]

A third pressure on the United States is economic. In narrow terms, the pressure is that of the U.S. budget. There are two ways to think about reducing the military budget: cutting programs and "burdensharing." Modest program cuts may be made in the next few years, although no radical changes were presented in the budget proposals in the year that followed the collapse of the Soviet Union's Eastern European empire and the demise of the Cold War. Burdensharing is an active issue in discussions between the United States and Japan, and also with Korea. Both Japan and Korea are seen as economically strong, cutting into U.S. markets, and benefiting from trade surpluses with the United States. Their prosperity is taken as a further argument for encouraging them to assume greater responsibility for the U.S. military budget.

More broadly, the economic pressure on the United States derives from the changing place of the United States in the international economy, vis-á-vis Japan, Western Europe, and the Newly Industrialized Countries (NIC's) of Asia. The United States is no longer the unquestioned economic giant of the world capitalist system. "Free trade" worked well for the United States as long as the United States wielded disproportionate economic power; but that is no longer the case, and at least some sectors of the U.S. economy are suffering.

In the short term, this may actually increase Washington's motivation to hold on to bases in the countries with which it competes economically, particularly in Japan and Korea. Negotiations over the level of sharing "defense burden" for these countries gives the United States added leverage in negotiations over trade relations.

But in the longer term, this strategy is problematic. It is unlikely that the United States can afford its military commitments, nor that pressure on Japan and the NIC's will lead to long-term improvements in the U.S. economic position. Meanwhile, the United States faces the risk of forcing retaliatory moves in other countries if it presses its allies for special treatment. At some point, the United States will have to confront its changed economic circumstances in the Pacific and in the world, and try to structure a healthy U.S. economy in that context. Adjusting the U.S. military commitments will surely be a part of that process.

These three factors, taken together, suggest that the U.S. government needs to rethink U.S. interests in the Pacific—what they are today, and what they will be in the next century. But policy makers appear to be proceeding with the same view of U.S. interests that has guided U.S. policy for at least the last 45 years. In the short term, the United States still has options in regions where the U.S. presence is threatened. One option is to continue relying on governments which support the U.S. presence, even if this means continuing to accept the risks associated with backing a repressive leader. This may be the U.S. approach to Korea. Another option is to seek an accommodation that allows the United States to maintain its most important facilities in a country, while perhaps abandoning others (as Walden Bello discusses in his chapter about U.S. bases in the Philippines). Finally, the United States can seek other ways of projecting U.S. power, as suggested in the *Discriminate Deterrence* report. The recently strengthened Navy, with enhanced power in the Pacific, is a likely candidate for this task.

The many changes occurring in the Pacific, and the different pressures on the U.S. role, mean that progressive political activists face many opportunities. While individual anti-bases struggles may seem to face enormous odds, whether in Korea, Palau, Australia, or the Philippines, each is perhaps on the side of history. The cumulative effect of many such struggles will increasingly make the U.S. military feel unwelcome throughout the region. For those of us who live in the United States, our task seems clear, if not altogether easy: to support those individual anti-bases efforts while assuring that our support is region-wide, and that it argues for a regional U.S. withdrawal.

Notes

1. Quoted in Merze Tate, *The United States and the Hawaiian Kingdom: A Political History* (New Haven, CT: Yale University Press, 1965), 176. Tate gives the citation for this quote as a note from Minister Stevens to Captain Wiltsie (of the USS Boston), enclosed in "Stevens to Foster, Jan. 18, 1893, No. 79," in Papers Relating to the Foreign Relations of the United States, 1894, App. II, 208.

2. As quoted in Noel J. Kent, *Hawaii: Islands Under the Influence* (New York: Monthly Review Press, 1983), 56-68, from William Adam Russ, *The Hawaiian Republic, 1894-98* (Selingsgrove, PA: Susquehanna University Press, 1956), 367. The account of the coup in Hawaii is summarized from Roger Bell, *Last Among Equals: Hawaiian Statehood and American Politics* (Honolulu: University of Hawaii Press, 1984), 8-37; Kent, *Hawaii;* Lawrence H. Fuchs, *Hawaii Pono* (New York: Harcourt Brace Jovanovich, 1961, with new preface 1983), 21-39; and Tate, 155-193.

3. International Institute for Strategic Studies, *The Military Balance, 1989-1990* (London: International Institute for Strategic Studies, 1989), 26.

4. William M. Arkin and Richard W. Fieldhouse, *Nuclear Battlefields: Global Links in the Arms Race* (Cambridge: Ballinger, 1985), 186.

5. In 1980, one out of every seven people in Hawaii (all islands) either worked for the military or was a military dependent. Fuchs, x.

6. No blood was shed in this takeover, whereas in the Philippines, for example, hundreds of thousands of Filipinos were killed in the U.S. drive to claim the islands. Moreover, as noted earlier, there was widespread domestic opposition to the annexation of Hawaii. Nearly a half-century later, the United States would acquire islands in Micronesia with little public outcry (although U.S. allies objected vociferously).

7. Robert E. Harkavy, *Great Power Competition for Overseas Bases: The Geopolitics of Access Diplomacy* (New York: Pergamon Press, 1982), 130, 141-142.

8. The figure on Japanese oil flow is taken from Malcolm McIntosh, *Arms Across the Pacific: Security and Trade Issues Across the Pacific* (New York: St. Martin's Press, 1987), 44.

9. Much of the history and analysis in this section draws heavily on two works by Peter Hayes, Lyuba Zarsky, and Walden Bello, whose scholarship on these issues has greatly eased the task of others who want to understand the U.S. role in the Pacific. The first of these works is *American Lake: Nuclear Peril in the Pacific* (Ringwood, Victoria [Australia]: Penguin Books, 1986). The second is an unpublished manuscript, *Bases of Power,* also written in the mid-1980s, which the authors generously made available to me.

10. Elliot Vanveltner Converse, III, *United States Plans for a Postwar Overseas Military Bases System, 1942-1948* (Ph.D. Dissertation, Department of History, Princeton University, Princeton, NJ, June 1984), 48-49.

11. A 1947 base plan, approved by the Joint Chiefs of Staff and the State-War-Navy Coordinating Committee, put Japan in a third priority category of areas to be "kept under surveillance" as possible sites for a U.S. military presence. Japan was one of many such areas. This same plan identified nine primary base locations, and 15 subsidiary ones. See *Foreign Relations of the*

United States, 1947, Vol I. General: The United Nations (Washington, D.C.: U.S. Government Printing Office, 1973), 766-770.

12. In the immediate post-war period, Okinawa was under U.S. military administration. The United States retained administrative control following the signing of the Peace Treaty and Mutual Security Treaties between Japan and the United States in 1951.

13. Six months after the Armistice was signed in Korea, John Foster Dulles articulated what became known as the policy of "massive retaliation," arguing that the United States did not need to—and could not—be prepared to fight in every corner of the globe. Rather, "[t]he way to deter aggression is for the free community to be willing and able to respond vigorously at places and with means of its own choosing"—i.e. with nuclear weapons if necessary (quoted in John Lewis Gaddis, *Strategies of Containment* [New York: Oxford University Press, 1982], 147). Thus the United States accepted the necessity of being prepared to oppose communism at every point, but would do this at least partly through the use—or threatened use—of nuclear weapons.

14. Hayes, Zarsky, and Bello, *American Lake*, 45.

15. Harkavy, 130, 141.

16. The information on atomic tests is taken from Giff Johnson, *Collision Course at Kwajalein: Marshall Islanders in the Shadow of the Bomb* (Honolulu: Pacific Concerns Resource Center, 1984), 11-12.

17. Gaddis quotes Walt Rostow on these shifts as follows: "It should be noted that we have generally been at a disadvantage in crises, since the Communists command a more flexible set of tools for imposing strains on the Free World—and a greater freedom to use them—than we normally command. We are often caught in circumstances where our only available riposte is so disproportionate to the immediate provocation that its use risks unwanted escalation or serious political costs to the free community. This asymmetry makes it attractive for Communists to apply limited debilitating pressures upon us in situations where we find it difficult to impose on them an equivalent price for their intrusions. We must seek, therefore, to expand our arsenal of limited overt and covert countermeasures if we are in fact to make crisis-mongering, deeply built into communist ideology and working habits, an unprofitable occupation." Quoted in Gaddis, *Strategies,* 214. Gaddis cites a Rostow draft, "Basic National Security Policy," 26 March 1962, 173-174.

18. Roland Simbulan, *The Bases of Our Insecurity,* Second Edition (Quezon City [Philippines]: Balai Fellowship, 1985), 195-196.

19. Hayes, Zarsky, and Bello, *American Lake,* 103.

20. Harkavy, 144.

21. Ibid., 144-145.

22. Hayes, Zarsky, and Bello, *American Lake,* 103.

23. Caspar W. Weinberger, *Report of the Secretary of Defense* (Washington, D.C.: U.S. Government Printing Office, 8 February 1982), C- 5.

24. Frank C. Carlucci, *Annual Report to the President, Fiscal Year 1990* (Washington: U.S. Government Printing Office, 1990), 227.

25. William M. Arkin, "Troubled Waters, The Navy's Aggressive War Strategy," *Technology Review,* January 1989, 56.

26. In addition to the two works of Hayes, Zarsky and Bello, cited earlier, this section makes extensive use of Arkin and Fieldhouse, *Nuclear Battlefields.*

27. Hayes, Zarsky, and Bello, *Bases of Power,* 616-621. Arkin and Fieldhouse, 186-187.

28. Arkin and Fieldhouse, 186-188.

29. Ibid., 221.

30. Ibid., 221. Also "3 Nuclear Storage Depots to Close as B-52 Missions Change," *New York Times,* 16 May 1988, A18; and Major Rita F. Clark and CS Sgt. Herman F. Martin, *Strategic Air Command: Unit Mission and History Summaries* (Offutt Air Force Base, Nebraska, 1 July 1988), 11-12, 55-56.

31. Arkin and Fieldhouse, 221. Hayes, Zarsky, and Bello, *Bases of Power,* 731.

32. Arkin and Fieldhouse, 221.

33. Ibid.

34. Ibid.

35. Ibid., 80 and 221.

36. Ibid., 224.

37. Hayes, Zarksy, and Bello, *Bases of Power,* 707; Robert E. Harkavy, *Bases Abroad: The Global Foreign Military Presence* (New York: Oxford University Press, 1989), 181.

38. Carlucci, 227.

39. Hayes, Zarsky, and Bello, *Bases of Power,* 710.

40. Ibid., 710-712; Arkin and Fieldhouse, 231.

41. Arkin and Fieldhouse, 231.

42. Ibid., 172.

43. Ibid, 127.

44. Johnson, 45-46, 61.

45. Arkin and Fieldhouse, 245.

46. As discussed by Desmond Ball, *A Suitable Piece of Real Estate, American Installations in Australia* (Sydney: Hale and Iremonger, 1980), 15-16.

47. Hayes, Zarsky, and Bello, *Bases of Power,* 765.

48. Official accounts put the number killed at fewer than 200. Opposition forces claim that over 1,000 and perhaps 2,000 died. According to *Lost Victory,* a publication of the Christian Institute for the Study of Justice and Development, a Korean organization: "While the Chun regime claims that only 191 people, including 46 soldiers, died in the 'violent riot,' the Kwangju death statistics show over 2,600 people died that month, exceeding the monthly average by over 2,300." Christian Institute for the Study of Justice and Development, ed., *Lost Victory* (Seoul: Minjugsa/CISJD, 1988), 30.

49. Suzuyo Takazato, "Women on Base," *AMPO,* Vol. 14, 1982, 25.

50. Giff Johnson discusses the situation on Ebeye in detail, *Collision Course at Kwajalein: Marshall Islanders in the Shadow of the Bomb* (Honolulu: Pacific Concerns Resource Center, 1984), 19-25. A few examples of the living conditions of the Marshallese: "[T]here has never been a high school on the island, although at least 50% of the population is under 20 years of age. And the Kwajalein high school, just 3 miles away, is segregated for American children only," 22. Moreover, "To travel to Kwajalein which is their own island, the Marshallese must have passes, issued in limited numbers, for such purposes as banking or airline business... Furthermore, Marshallese must be off Kwajalein Island by nightfall or risk being arrested by security police," 23. Finally, "Miserable health and sanitation conditions on Ebeye have regularly brought on epidemics that are virtually impossible to control. In 1963, a severe polio epidemic swept Ebeye, spreading to other parts of the Marshalls. More than 190 people were left severely paralyzed at a time when polio vaccine had already been available to Americans for eight years...," 20.

51. American Friends Service Committee, "Self-Determination for Belau?" 13 May 1987.

52. Paulette Wittwer, "New Belau Vote: Same Old Problems," *Asian-Pacific Issues News,* January 1990 (published by American Friends Service Committee, Portland, OR), 2.

53. As reported in the *Far Eastern Economic Review,* 3 May 1990, 10.

54. "In Asia, His Cold War's Over," *New York Times,* 27 May 1990.

55. Commission on Integrated Long-Term Strategy, *Discriminate Deterrence* (Washington, D.C.: U.S. Government Printing Office, January 1988), 22.

Chapter 8

Moment of Decision

The Philippines, the Pacific, and the U.S. Bases

Walden Bello

As this is written, the clock is racing toward September 1991, when the current agreement on the U.S. bases in the Philippines expires. The future of these bases is the focus of an intense national debate in the Philippines. Clark Air Force Base and Subic Naval Base have so dominated U.S.-Philippine relations that Filipinos view Washington's every move through the prism of the bases issue. Thus, when U.S. F-4 Phantom aircraft flew "intimidation" missions against rebel forces during the unsuccessful coup attempt in December 1989, many Filipinos saw the gesture as an opportunistic attempt to convince them that the bases were necessary to "defend democracy."

At the heart of the bases debate is a struggle for Philippine sovereignty. In recent years the bases have become a focal issue for the whole Pacific region as well, having become the most important battleground in a struggle over two visions of the future of the Pacific.

The Philippine Bases and the 'Containment' Vision

One vision is the continuation of the 40-year-old reality of U.S. military supremacy in a broad arc from the North Pacific to the Indian Ocean. This massive military presence has been sanitized, in Orwellian fashion, as "forward defense," and packaged as "containment" for political consumption. Its imperial essence was described by Gen. Douglas MacArthur when he claimed that after World War II, "The strategic boundaries of the United States were no longer along the western shore of North and South America; they lay along the Eastern coast of the Asiatic continent." [1]

The Clark Air Base/Subic Naval Base complex was seen by many strategists as a major element, if not the centerpiece, of the U.S. posture in the Western Pacific. When Alvin Cottrell and Robert Hanks claimed in 1980 that Clark and Subic were "probably the most important basing complex in the world," [2] they were merely restating what earlier prophets of U.S. expansion in the Pacific had pointed out. Eighty years earlier another MacArthur—Arthur MacArthur, who led the military conquest of the is-lands—asserted that the Philippines constituted "the finest group of islands in the world. Its strategic location is unexcelled by that of any other position in the globe." [3]

The communist revolution in China, the Sino-Soviet alliance, and the rise of communist-led revolutionary movements in Indochina appeared to vindicate the dark vision of containment in the popular mind of North Americans in the 1950s. Better to engage the enemy across an ocean moat, 8,000 miles away, than to fight them in the streets of San Francisco! And from the Philippines to South Korea to Japan, local elites cooperated with U.S. authorities to create a McCarthyite atmosphere that would legitimize the U.S. military presence.

In the service of this vision, the Philippine bases were used as a key rear base during the Korean War from 1950 to 1953. They were used as springboards for intervention in the Taiwan straits and Indonesia in 1958, for intervention in Thailand in 1962, and as a main staging area for the war in Vietnam from 1964 to 1975.

In the 1970s and 1980s, the Sino-Soviet split, the Vietnam debacle, and the Sino-Vietnamese conflict undermined the viability of containment strat-egy in Asia and the Pacific, weakening the ideological rationale for the bases. Writing in 1977, George Kennan, the "father" of the containment strategy, called for the "immediate, complete, resolute, and wordless withdrawal of the facilities," on the ground that the "original justification for the maintenance of those bases has been extensively undermined." [4]

A New Lease on Life

In this same period, from the Pentagon's perspective, there were three developments that gave containment a new lease on life and reinforced the strategic potential of the Philippine bases. First, Great Britain, in line with its policy of withdrawing its military forces from "East of the Suez," withdrew its naval squadron from the Indian Ocean in the late 1960s. This created a "vacuum" that the U.S. Navy happily proceeded to fill in the early 1970s. Subic became the "principal logistics base" for the regular deployment of naval units in the Indian Ocean beginning in 1973.[5] Daily "Starlifter" flights origi-

Helicopter flying over Clark Air Force Base. Photo courtesy of NARMIC.

nating from Clark became the principal link with Diego Garcia, a strategically located island-base in the middle of the Indian Ocean.[6]

Securing the Persian Gulf and the Indian Ocean as far as the coast of East Africa became one of the two main pillars of U.S. policy in the Middle East. The other was the creation of regional gendarmes who could serve U.S. interests. When the overthrow of the Shah of Iran eliminated one of these gendarmes, out-of-area bases took on added importance as a means of projecting U.S. power into the Persian Gulf region. It was from Subic that the U.S. mounted the abortive mission to rescue the Embassy hostages from Teheran in 1980. Subic likewise served as the logistical hub for the U.S. naval intervention against Iran in the Persian Gulf at the height of the "Tanker War" in 1987-88.

Second, the expansion of the Soviet Pacific Fleet under Admiral Gorshkov was a lifesaver for disgruntled admirals who were staving off efforts by Henry Kissinger and Jimmy Carter to reduce U.S. Pacific forces in the aftermath of the Vietnam War. While some U.S. officials admitted that the Soviet base at Cam Ranh Bay was no more than a "minor repair facility"[7] which served Soviet ships and anti-submarine and intelligence aircraft, the Pentagon had a heyday depicting the base as the most formidable Soviet naval bastion outside Soviet home waters. According to the the standard line from the U.S. Pacific Command, Subic and Clark were well within the range of Soviet Badger bombers operating from Cam Ranh Bay.[8]

Thus, a new Southeast Asia mission for the Philippine bases was to counter the Soviet "buildup" at Cam Ranh Bay. A second mission served by these bases was to function as a transit point for military aid to Thailand to counter Vietnamese "expansionism" and to provide logistical assistance to the People's Republic of China in the event of war with the Soviet Union.

The third development was the formulation of the strategic doctrine of "maritime supremacy" within the Reagan Administration in the early 1980s. Forcefully espoused by Navy Secretary John Lehman, maritime supremacy was essentially the old forward-defense/containment doctrine, refurbished with a vengeance. It incorporated the Reagan Administration's commitment to "roll back" communism, and thus went beyond the classical containment doctrine.

This development represented a shift from the sea-lane defense doctrine of the Carter years toward an offensive that would "threaten the potential adversary in his most secure areas." [9] In the Pacific, this meant bottling up the Soviet Pacific fleet at its home base at Vladivostok.[10] In this context, Subic and Clark's traditional support role for U.S. forces in Northeast Asia acquired renewed importance, a point underlined by the participation of units from Clark and Subic in the massive annual "Team Spirit" exercises in Korea.

Thus, early in the "New Cold War" years of the Reagan era, the mission of the U.S. forces based in the Philippines was stretched to the full strategic potential as envisioned by Arthur MacArthur in the early 1900s, when he wrote that the Philippines:

> lies on the flank of what might be called a position of several thousand miles of coastline: it is in the center of that position. It is therefore relatively better placed than Japan, which is on a flank, and therefore remote from the other extremity; likewise India, on another flank. It affords a means of protecting American interests which with the very least output of physical power has the effect of a commanding position in itself to retard hostile action.[11]

The U.S. Base Complex Today: Some Considerations

By 1989 just under 15,000 U.S. forces were permanently stationed in the Philippines, with the number swelling to as many as 25,000 when aircraft carrier battle groups sailed into Subic Bay. The U.S. military complex in the Philippines consisted of two massive bases (Subic Naval Base and Clark Air Force Base); three support bases (San Miguel Communications Center, Wallace Air Station, and Camp John Hay); and 19 smaller communications and intelligence facilities.[12] Clark and Subic, two of the United States' largest overseas bases, covered approximately 25,000 acres, with the U.S. guaranteed access to another 152,500 acres that were returned to Philippine "jurisdiction" as part of the 1979 revision of the U.S.-Philippine Military Bases Agreement.

In addition to the roles played by Subic and Clark in "conventional" U.S. military interventions, U.S. bases in the Philippines play four other important roles:

- The bases are integrated into a U.S. strategy-of-power projection that uses both conventional and nuclear arms. Since Subic is the nuclear-armed 7th Fleet's "primary port, training area, and logistics support base," [13] it is safe to assume that nuclear arms regularly transit in and out of Philippine territory. Also, nuclear-armed hunter-killer submarines regularly visit the base, and nuclear-capable PC-3 Orion anti-submarine aircraft are based at Subic's Naval Air Station at Cubi Point.[14] While nuclear weapons do not seem to be stored routinely at the huge naval magazine, the military does have contingency plans to deploy nuclear depth charges and other naval nuclear weapons to the Philippines.[15]

- The bases have served not only to project U.S. nuclear threats from the North Pacific to East Africa; they have also contributed to U.S. capabilities to wage strategic nuclear war. To cite just a few examples: The PC-3 Orion squadron at Subic is designed to hunt and destroy Soviet ballistic missile submarines in the event of nuclear war. Clark Airfield is integrated into "Signal Scope," the global communications system of the Strategic Air Command. It has a receiver for intelligence data from the Pine Gap facility in Australia which controls the CIA's covert satellite surveillance of the Soviet nuclear defense system. The Navy's San Miguel communications station has had equipment used in tracking Soviet satellite launches and operates a low-frequency transmitter that provides "back-up" communications to U.S. nuclear missile submarines.[16]

- Subic and Clark have also functioned as bases for U.S. intervention in the internal affairs of the Philippines. Military aid to defeat the Huk insurgency in the 1950s was routed through Clark, which also served as a base for incendiary raids on Huk positions. During the Marcos dictatorship, the bases or base-connected military units occasionally assisted counterinsurgency efforts by providing the Armed Forces of the Philippines with

reconnaissance support to troops conducting anti-rebel
sweeps, assistance in "civic action" maneuvers, and training.[17]

- Finally, Subic and Clark have grown in importance as "rest-and-
recreation" centers for U.S. forces throughout the Pacific, as the
costs of "entertaining the troops" have risen in other areas. As
James Fallows noted, "In Japan, American servicemen are the
New Poor, and in Korea they're just more potential customers
for $8 direct-from-the-factory Reebok shoes. [But] in the Philip-
pines, they are princes." [18] More than 500 clubs, bars, sauna
baths, and other recreational facilities in Olongapo service
sailors from adjoining Subic, and another 450 in Angeles City do
the same for airmen from Clark. Wilkes and Leadbeater claim
that "Olongapo has what the U.S. military would regard as the
best bar and brothel facilities of any U.S. base in the world—and
keeping up force morale is not a trivial military objective." [19]

The Emergence of an Alternative Vision

The fulfillment of Clark's and Subic's "strategic potential" has come at
a high price: the erosion of the goodwill of the Filipino people. Through four
presidencies—Nixon, Ford, Carter, and Reagan—Washington supported the
dictatorship of Ferdinand Marcos because he guaranteed "unhampered use"
of the bases. By the end of the Marcos period, anger and resentment against
the United States was widespread among the middle class and politically
organized sections of the poor. The formation of the Anti-Bases Coalition
and the Coalition for a Nuclear-Free Philippines reflected this sentiment.
Traditional politicians, always sensitive to political winds, began to use
anti-bases rhetoric in public. Shortly before the fall of the dictatorship, key
political personalities, including soon-to-be Pesident Corazon Aquino,
signed a statement calling for the eventual withdrawal of the U.S. bases from
Philippine soil. Though the Reagan Administration managed to leap from
Marcos's sinking ship at the last minute, the severe damage to U.S.-Philippine
relations inflicted by 14 years of shameless *realpolitik* was not so easily
undone.

Fueled by resentment, a desire to regain sovereignty, and fear of the
country becoming a nuclear target, Filipino sentiment against the bases grew
against a supportive backdrop of escalating region-wide opposition to
nuclear weapons and superpower military presence. A vision of a new
Pacific that promised a future so different from the darkness of containment
was being forged in struggle throughout the region.

Anti-nuclear sentiment began in the early 1950s in the two nations victimized by nuclear explosions during war and atomic testing: Japan and the Marshall Islands in Micronesia. In 1979, in an effort to prevent a repetition of the Marshall Islands tragedy, the citizens of Belau, 600 miles east of the Philippines, approved the world's first nuclear-free constitution. Belau's example, plus the anger generated by French nuclear testing in Tahiti, contributed to New Zealand's banning visits by nuclear-armed and nuclear-powered warships in 1984. In 1985, 11 South Pacific island countries created the South Pacific Nuclear-Free Zone (SPNFZ), which, despite a number of loopholes, was an important symbolic advance. Today, anti-nuclear and anti-militarist movements are linked to movements for independence and indigenous people's rights in the vibrant Movement for a Nuclear-Free and Independent Pacific (NFIP).

It was against this regional backdrop that the Philippine Constitutional Commission adopted a provision making freedom from nuclear weapons a fundamental national policy in 1986: "The Philippines, consistent with its national interest, adopts and pursues a policy of freedom from nuclear weapons in its territory." The nuclear-free constitution was ratified in February 1987; in June 1988, the Philippine Senate, in an effort to strengthen the nuclear-free clause, approved a bill to ban the entry, transit, and storage of nuclear weapons. This was, of course, a thinly disguised vote against the presence of the bases.

The extent of U.S. political isolation was underlined in April 1988, at the beginning of the formal review of the bases agreement. After Ambassador Nicholas Platt opened the review by firing the usual salvo against "the Soviet buildup," Australian Foreign Minister Bill Hayden contradicted the U.S. position. He cited evidence gathered by Australian-U.S. intelligence sources of a 50 percent reduction in Soviet naval deployments.[20]

Like Australia, Indonesia and Malaysia were supposed to be strong U.S. allies. Yet at the December 1987 summit meeting of the Association of Southeast Asian Nations (ASEAN), the two countries sponsored a resolution creating a Southeast Asian Nuclear-Weapons Free Zone (SEANWFZ), which was adopted "in principle" as a goal for ASEAN over the objections of U.S. Secretary of State George Shultz.[21]

The increasingly independent policies of these two authoritarian U.S. allies cannot be divorced from the increasing popularity of anti-nuclear commitments in the region and the dramatic impact on the popular mind of Mikhail Gorbachev's and former Soviet Foreign Minister Eduard Shevardnadze's "Pacific peace offensive" in 1987 and 1988.

But the most serious blow against the containment rationale was delivered by Mikhail Gorbachev in September 1988, when he made explicit what he had hinted at two years earlier in his Vladivostok speech: The Soviet Union would withdraw from Cam Ranh Bay in exchange for U.S. withdrawal from Subic and Clark. Despite U.S. officials' attempt to dismiss the proposal as an opportunistic gambit designed to throw a monkey wrench into the ongoing review, Gorbachev's offer was widely seen in the context of broader Soviet policy decisions designed to reduce the Soviet Union's military commitments abroad in order to focus on *perestroika*.

From Containment to Dollar Diplomacy

As Gorbachev's peace initiatives eroded the credibility of the containment strategy that legitimized the bases' presence, U.S. apologists were driven to formulate alternative rationales. One influential defense analyst stated that it would be wise not to create a "power vacuum" in light of the "uncertainty of China's intentions in the 21st century—or even Indonesia's."[22] Others have dropped the pretense that the bases are good for anyone else except the United States, and have argued in strictly *realpolitik* terms. As Stephen Bosworth, former ambassador to Manila, put it recently:

> What we have to remember is that the bases were there even before the emergence of the Soviet problem. And if we want to continue doing what we have been doing to defend our interests in that part of the world, then we need the bases there.[23]

But imperial force without altruistic rationalization is repulsive. With the decline of the Soviet bogeyman, the U.S. resorted to dollar diplomacy to save its bases. The 1988 Shultz-Manglapus Agreement committed the White House to attempt to provide $431 million per year in compensation for the bases—up 140 percent from the $180 million a year provided between 1983 and 1989.

The U.S. has prepared propaganda on the "benefits" of the bases for distribution in the Philippines. The glossy pamphlet "Background on the Bases," emphasizes the ostensible impact of spending for the bases on the Philippine economy: $507 million in total spending, a $96 million payroll—the country's second largest after the government—for 68,500 workers, and for 2,000 local contractors.[24] The fact that much of the economic activity generated by the military dollar is underground in character, paying for prostitution, drugs, smuggling, and gunrunning, was conveniently ignored by U.S. officials who confidently claimed that there was "no credible plan to make the areas economically viable without a U.S. [military] presence." [25] In addition to producing propaganda, U.S. officials have apparently recently extended procurement of goods and services beyond the Olongapo, Angeles, and Metro-Manila areas to other parts of the country.[26] Construction of

Homeless Filipinos sleeping at the entrance of Clark Air Force Base. Photo by Joseph Gerson.

school buildings funded by the "Economic Support Fund" component of the bases compensation package was strategically located in almost all of the country's 73 provinces.[27] The political terrain was prepared for the possibility that the future of the bases might be decided by a national referendum, an eventuality provided for by the Constitution.

A more massive effort to influence Philippine public opinion is the U.S.-led effort to assemble a five-year, $10 billion "Multilateral Aid Initiative" (MAI, also known as the Philippines Aid Plan, or PAP) for the Aquino government, for which it has sought other donors including Japan, Germany, France, South Korea, Australia, and Taiwan. But prospective donors and many Filipinos have been suspicious that the initiative is linked to the retention of the bases. Indeed, critics of the so-called Mini-Marshall Plan have seen it as a ploy to utilize Japanese capital to achieve U.S. objectives. The hint of financial blackmail was not dispelled by Senate minority leader Robert Dole's frank assertion that there was, indeed, a link between the status of the bases and the MAI. "That is not a threat," he said. "It is a fact."[28]

In its game plan for retaining the bases, Washington has seen Section 25, Article 18 of the Philippine Constitution as its last line of defense. The article provides for a national referendum should the Philippine Congress decide to call one on the issue of the bases. As Stephen Bosworth put it, "If the Filipinos decide by a referendum, as provided for by their constitutional processes, that we should leave, then we will." [29] This strategy does not reflect respect for democracy. Instead it is a calculation of the strength of what Filipinos call the "colonial mentality." To a large degree, Washington appears to assume that the majority of Philippine voters would ratify their continued presence—an expectation based on polls that consistently show that a majority of Filipinos support the bases.

It is difficult to determine the reliability of political polls conducted in a country that has so recently emerged from an era of dictatorship. Under Marcos, keeping one's views to oneself was a widespread means of survival. In any event, according to an August 1988 survey conducted by the respected Ateneo de Manila University, 74 percent of those polled said they favored retaining the bases, 18 percent wanted them removed, and 6 percent were undecided. The figure favoring retention dropped to 57 percent if Washington would not increase financial compensation for the use of the bases beyond what the government was then receiving. [30]

How firm popular support for the bases is remains to be seen. A substantial portion of the population does not even know the bases exist, and an even larger section is not familiar with the issues raised by the presence of the bases. As the debate on the bases engulfs the country over the coming years, the opposition will reach out beyond the cities and beyond the middle class.

Washington worries about this opposition because, though still a minority, it is increasingly organized, and carries weight beyond its numbers. As one Filipino analyst put it:

> What was, however, indisputable is what the survey failed to reckon with: the widely acknowledged observation that among the politically keen and articulate Filipino middle class, intelligentsia, and organized militants the bases had to go. If not now then eventually. And if they are to be allowed to stay, then the country should be able to extract the maximum financial benefit from them. No longer are influential Filipinos convinced that the U.S. bases are in the Philippines... for the country's own security. [31]

In addition to the threat that the bases pose to Philippine national security and sovereignty, an increasingly persuasive argument used by the anti-bases forces is that the bases promote the systematic degradation of women and children through prostitution. Forty-five of the 76 identified AIDS carriers in the Philippines in late 1988 were women who worked in communities near the U.S. bases. As described in greater detail in Chapters 6 and 7, this has become another powerful reason for shutting the bases.

In contrast, the pro-bases position not only lacks a convincing ideological rationale; it also cannot rely on an organized base of supporters beyond the prostitutes, bar and brothel owners, and toughs that Olongapo's pro-bases Mayor Richard Gordon occasionally assembles for demonstrations.

The Elite and the Bases

The U.S. foothold on the bases is further undermined by the fact that as a result of pressure from the nationalist movement, the skeptical middle-class intelligentsia, and sectors of the lower class organized by the left, its traditional base of organized support—the Philippine elite—has fragmented. While the bases seem to meet with the approval of the majority of the population, as measured by current polls, many elite politicians understand that public opinion on the issue is volatile. They have become hesitant to take a pro-bases stance for which they could later be attacked.

This was brought home to Washington when the Philippine Senate voted to ban nuclear-armed and nuclear-powered warships from the country in June 1988. One U.S. analyst reported bleakly that "20 of the country's 24 senators have stated opposition to a granting of base rights after 1991." [32] If the opposition holds, ratification of a new treaty will be blocked. Thus U.S. officials hardly mention Senate ratification but instead constantly appeal for a popular referendum, which could supersede a Senate decision.

The Philippine elite's extreme reluctance to serve as pointman for Washington is evident not only in the Senate but also in the upper echelons of the Aquino Administration itself. Perhaps the individual most responsible for generating a controversy within the elite around the official 1988 bases review was the foreign minister, Raul Manglapus. Borrowing from Freudian imagery, he talked about the need to "slay the father"—meaning the United States. [33] Manglapus, in fact, practically disowned the agreement arrived at during the review, implying that the Philippines had been forced to accept a bad deal.

There are many political figures who appear to want the bases to remain; among them is Defense Secretary Fidel Ramos, who requested help from U.S. planes at Clark to bombard rebel positions during the December 1989 coup attempt. In September 1990, after the United States made the tactical maneuver of offering to "withdraw" from Subic Naval base over a 10-year period, President Aquino revised her public stance from keeping her "options open" to calling for the withdrawal of the U.S. bases, with the expectation that a "mutually acceptable and beneficial" arrangement could be negotiated. Given her great dependence on U.S. support, however, it is likely that the arrangement will allow the bases to remain in one form or another. This view is reinforced by the controversial opinion issued by Sedfrey Ordonez, the Secretary of Justice, who argued that President Aquino can legally sidestep the Constitution's anti-nuclear clause and conclude a new treaty that would allow the U.S. bases to stay beyond 1991 despite Senate opposition.[34] Unable to call openly for the extension of the bases treaty, pro-bases politicians now use calls for a referendum on the bases to cloak their real intent. Shortly before the visit of President Aquino to the United States in late 1989, the conservative-dominated House of Representatives passed a resolution calling for a national referendum. This was an effort to circumvent the anti-bases sentiment in the Senate, which alone has the power to ratify the treaty. President Aquino promptly endorsed the House action before meeting with President George Bush, sending Washington a strong positive signal. Neveretheless the fact that almost no Filipino politician wishes to openly call for extension of the treaty poses a serious dilemma for Washington. It means that U.S. officials must directly assume the burden of campaigning in any referendum on the bases—a role that would confirm charges of intervention in the Philippine political process.

Policy Contradictions and Bases Options

While maintaining Clark and Subic is a critical element of U.S. policy in the Philippines, it is not the be-all and end-all of this policy. U.S. interests go beyond the bases and include the more comprehensive objective of keeping the Philippines stable and within the U.S. sphere of influence. In the short and intermediate term, this means stabilizing President Aquino and marginalizing the nationalist left as a political force. Some U.S. officials believe that a hard-line approach on the maintenance of the bases could endanger long-term political stability by exacerbating nationalist fervor.

Fear of a sharpening contradiction among U.S. policy objectives was expressed by Fred Brown, an influential Republican analyst who served as a staff member of the Senate Foreign Relations Committee:

> Clark Air Base and Subic Naval Base are unique, undisputably the most valuable U.S. military facilities available to the United States west of Hawaii. Losing access to them would be inconvenient. But strategically what really counts is the relationship between the Filipino and American peoples. To have the Philippines pass under a resolutely hostile political system and to lose a Filipino people ultimately well disposed toward the United States would be catastrophic for the U.S. position in the Pacific and for the non-communist countries of Southeast Asia.
>
> The surest way to "lose" Clark and Subic is to tell Filipinos that the United States cares more about the military bases than the broader,

social aspects of the historical relationship, including the democratic spirit.[35]

Central to U.S. policy, Brown counseled, must be projecting Corazon Aquino as a nationalist, since "Nationalism has become an imperative of Philippine politics, and to survive Aquino must become her country's leading nationalist. She will no doubt twist Uncle Sam's tail in the process. She must also ride the tiger of nationalism without becoming its captive and without alienating international support."[36]

These implicit contradictions are likely to stoke heated debates within the U.S. national security bureaucracy, notably between the Navy and unreconstructed containment strategists on one side, and on the other side the national security "pragmatists," who are primarily ensconced in the State Department.

The military—and particularly the Navy—is likely to be the most powerful lobbyist for the status quo. This is hardly a surprise, because the Pacific has always been a Navy precinct. The Navy's attachment to Subic is deep, for it was Subic that provided the rationale for the expansion of the U.S. fleet into a two-ocean Navy in the early twentieth century. This powerful commitment to its Philippine bastion was perhaps best expressed by former Navy Secretary John Lehman, who told Congress in 1986: "We consider the Philippine bases critical to our strategy in the Pacific and Indian Ocean. We do not plan to leave." [37]

But over the last decade, a strong pragmatist bloc has emerged in the State Department. It was this group that eroded the link that the Pentagon and the White House had forged between the necessity of maintaining the bases and continued support for Ferdinand Marcos. Today, similar pragmatic solutions to the delicate relationship between the bases issue and political stabilization are being discussed.

Increasing domestic pressures to cut the defense budget—in light of the vanishing Soviet threat and U.S. economic needs—adds another factor to the debate. One recent high-level Pentagon study raised the possibility of shutting down both bases as part of a drastic global cutback of U.S. forces to meet budgetary constraints.[38]

Congressional Research Service Analyst Larry Niksch presented yet another option, one that has been given serious consideration in some circles: give up Clark but retain Subic. According to Niksch, who is associated with the State Department, Pentagon, and CIA, Subic is irreplaceable in terms of power projection, but Clark "could be replaced by other air bases in the region." Such a deal would be designed to "demonstrate a U.S. willingness to accomodate the more moderate elements of Filipino nationalism and, hopefully, isolate the extremists." [39] Support for the proposal has been expressed by Alvin Bernstein, chair of the Strategy Department of the U.S. Naval War College, who also believes that it "would enhance President Aquino's nationalist appeal, and so help to counter the communist insurgency in the Philippines." [40]

The Withdrawal Option: Costs and Benefits

What would happen if the Niksch option failed to defuse the nationalist movement and Filipino senators scuttled the ratification of a new treaty? Would the U.S. be willing to risk a bruising referendum to secure a "popular mandate" for the bases that could undercut President Aquino's legitimacy and harm U.S. relations with the Philippines over the long run? With the bitter reaction of many Filipinos to the use of U.S. warplanes to help save the Aquino government during the December 1989 coup attempt, Washington is wary of the referendum option.

The United States may well agree to a treaty providing for phased withdrawal if it becomes politically impossible to maintain Subic in the short run. This tactic might be viewed by U.S. officials as a way of buying time, hoping that within five or 10 years a more congenial atmosphere in the Philippines might permit another extension of the lease.

But should retention of Subic prove impossible in the intermediate term, the U.S. is studying a number of potential alternatives.[41] The consensus appears to be that the functions performed by Clark and Subic for projecting U.S. power could be performed from other sites, though less efficiently.[42] From the point of view of military planners, relocation would involve parcelling out the different functions now packaged together at Subic and Clark. The candidates for the dispersed forces and functions include Guam, Tinian, and Belau in Micronesia; Japan, Okinawa, and Korea in Northeast Asia; Singapore in Southeast Asia; and Brunei and Australia. In all these nations except Brunei, the United States already has military bases, facilities, or rights to build bases. Redeployment costs are estimated at $5-19 billion.[43]

Singapore is seen by many defense analysts as a possible substitute base for U.S. power projection to the Indian Ocean. Air Force "Starlifter" flights can begin in Guam, instead of Clark, refuel at Singapore and reach Diego Garcia, with full payloads. Navy anti-submarine aircraft currently operate out of airfields in Singapore, and U.S. ships visit Singapore's docks for repairs.[44]

The one resource that no alternative site can provide is the bargain-basement price paid for skilled Filipino labor. A Filipino base worker receives approximately one-eighth of the wage of that of a worker at a mainland U.S.

Navy yard; one-fourth of the wage of a Japanese base worker; and one-half of the wage of a Korean base worker.[45]

More important than the wage-cost differential is the quality of work. This is particularly true of workers at the Subic Base ship-repair facility. In the view of William Sullivan, former ambassador to the Philippines:

> Most of the workforce at Subic comes from families who have worked at least five generations at their trade, who served long apprenticeships learning the details of their work, and who can count on a career of at least 20 years in the employ of the U.S. Navy. I know of no more professional group anywhere in the world.[46]

For Sullivan, so central is the work-force issue that he believes the United States should plan how to relocate Subic's Filipino work force to Okinawa, Guam, or Darwin, Australia. In the view of the "pragmatists," two developments mitigate the potential loss of the Clark and Subic work force: the virtual annexation of Micronesia and technological advances in mobile basing. While the military places great value in redundancy, some in the national security establishment argue that withdrawal from the Philippines could be a case of "rational retrenchment."

Tinian and Belau, some 600 to 1,000 miles east of the Philippines, are likely to be the prime candidates for assuming the functions of Clark and Subic. Micronesia is a more politically secure area, compared to the Philippines. Indeed, over the last 15 years, the United States has been transforming Micronesia's status from that of a United Nations Trust Territory to a U.S. territory—that is, from de facto to formal control. This means, as analyst Alva Bowen approvingly notes, that "[a]ny political difficulty over the execution of this option in Micronesia would be settled as a domestic issue."[47]

The second offsetting consideration stems from developments in mobile basing. The pragmatists in the national security bureaucracy appear to take seriously the opinion of the Presidential Commission on Integrated Long-Term Strategy that foreign bases are in some cases more trouble than they are worth. The Commission suggested that advances in logistics technology make some third world bases less essential for the global reach of the U.S. military.[48]

Withdrawal and U.S. Post-Containment Strategy

The loss of the Philippine bases will not necessarily diminish U.S. capability to project power throughout the Western Pacific and the Indian Ocean. Without Subic and Clark, the United States will even retain the capability to intervene in the Philippines to keep a stable, pro-U.S. government in power in Manila.

The retention of substantial power-projection capability has become especially critical because U.S. intervention in the Pacific, Middle East, and other parts of the Third World is likely to increase rather than decrease in the post-containment era. As Admiral (Ret.) Stansfield Turner, Jimmy Carter's CIA chief, put it:

> Worldwide projection of power is the only mission that has involved our forces in combat in the past 44 years. There is little sign it will diminish in importance. There will be more Iran-Iraq wars, more instances of terrorism that call for rescue missions or bombing raids and more political instabilities in areas where we have a stake.[49]

Turner's viewpoint is shared by Henry Kissinger, Zbigniew Brzezinski, and the other authors of *Discriminate Deterrence*, whose argument for less reliance on fixed land bases is actually made in the broader context of reorienting U.S. defense strategy from its preoccupation with containing the Soviets to streamlining the military's capability for intervention in the Third World. All this underlines the fact that the withdrawal of U.S. bases from the Philippines cannot be a discrete objective for opponents of foreign military bases; it would be a severely limited achievement unless it is part of a pan-Pacific strategy aimed at dismantling the other keystones of the U.S. garrison state. This would involve not only withdrawing other forward bases in Diego Garcia, Korea, Okinawa, and Japan, but also struggling for the denuclearization and demilitarization of Micronesia.

The U.S. structure of power projection in the Pacific is more than the sum of its parts. A truly post-containment order in the Pacific, characterized by relations of equality and peace among nation-states, dynamic economic exchange, reliance on diplomatic solutions to conflict, and the absence of superpower competition, can only be secure if it is built on the dismantling of the entire U.S. transnational garrison state from Diego Garcia to Micronesia.

Notes

1. "Conversation between Gen. of the Army MacArthur and Mr. George Kennan, 5 March 1948—Top Secret," in Thomas Etzold and John Lewis Gaddis, eds., *Containment: Documents on American Policy and Strategy, 1945-50* (New York: Columbia University Press, 1978), 229.

2. Alvin Cottrell and Robert Hanks, *The Military Utility of the U.S. Bases in the Philippines* (Washington, D.C.: Center for Strategic and International Studies, 1980), 34.

3. Quoted in William Manchester, *American Caesar: Douglas MacArthur* (New York: Dell, 1978), 48-49.

4. George Kennan, *Cloud of Danger* (Boston: Little Brown, 1977), 97-98.

5. Larry Niksch, "Philippine Bases: How Important to U.S. Interests in Asia?" Issue Brief of the Congressional Research Service, 1 August 1980, 7.

6. Owen Wilkes and Marie Leadbeater, "The Asia-Pacific Situation," paper presented at Asia-Pacific People's Conference on Peace and Development, January 1989, 6.

7. Rear Adm. John L. Butts, "Testimony," in U.S. Senate Committee on Armed Services, *Department of Defense Authorization for Appropriations for Fiscal 1984, Part 6: Sea Power and Force Projection, Hearings* (Washington, D.C.: U.S. Government Printing Office, 1983), 2975.

8. United States Information Service, *Background to Bases: American Military Facilities in the Philippines,* Second Edition (Manila: United States Information Service, 1988), 11.

9. Quoted in Chalmers Hood, "The Face That Launched 600 Ships," *Defense and Foreign Affairs,* December 1983, 11.

10. Cited in "Soviets Buttress Naval, Ground Forces in the Pacific," *Defense Week,* 14 February 1984, 16.

11. Manchester, 48-49.

12. See "Book Reportedly Identifies 25 U.S. Facilities," *Foreign Broadcast Information Service: East Asia,* 10 April 1989, 59-60.

13. United States Information Service, 10.

14. For more information, see Walden Bello, "Springboards for Intervention, Instruments for Nuclear War," *Southeast Asia Chronicle,* No. 89, April 1983, 10.

15. William Arkin, "Contingency Overseas Deployment of Nuclear Weapons: A Report," Washington, D.C., Institute for Policy Studies, February 1984, 4.

16. For further details, see Bello, 10-12.

17. For further details, see Walden Bello and Severina Rivera, eds., *The Logistics of Repression* (Washington, D.C.: Friends of the Filipino People, 1977), 23-28, 138-140.

18. James Fallows, "The Bases Dilemma," *The Atlantic,* February 1988, 21.

19. Wilkes and Leadbeater, 10.

20. "Soviet Activity in Asia-Pacific Declining, Says Hayden," *Singapore Straits Times,* 13 April 1988.

21. Fred Greene, ed., *The Philippine Bases: Negotiating for the Future; American and Philippine Perspectives* (New York: Council on Foreign Relations, 1988), 61.

22. Fred Z. Brown, "Letter to the Editor," *Pilipinas: A Journal of Philippine Studies,* No. 11, Fall 1988, 105.

23. *Kwitny Report,* Public Broadcasting System, New York, 8 March 1989.

24. United States Information Service, 16, 19.

25. David Lambertson, Deputy Assistant Secretary for East Asian and Pacific Affairs, State Department, Testimony before U.S. House of Representatives Foreign Affairs Committee, Subcommittee on Asia and the Pacific, Washington, D.C., 7 March 1989, 15.

26. Personal communication from Stephen Rosskamm Shalom, 7 March 1989.

27. United States Information Service, 48-68.

28. Quoted in Alyson Pytte, "Proposed 'Mini Marshall Plan' Encounters Budget Strains," *Congressional Quarterly,* 18 March 1989, 602.

29. *Kwitny Report.*

30. "Survey Says Majority Favor Aquino, U.S. Bases," *Foreign Broadcast Information Service: East Asia,* 10 November 1988, 43-44.

31. Danilo-Luis Mariano, "Basis for Dissatisfaction," *Philippines Free Press,* 29 October 1988, 7.

32. Larry Niksch, "Salving Bitter Memories," *Far Eastern Economic Review,* 16 February 1989, 26.

33. "Talks on Bases Spur Defiance Toward U.S.," *New York Times,* 25 June 1988.

34. "Aquino Can Let Bases Stay," *Sing Tao International,* 21 July 1988.

35. Fred Brown, "Side with Masses in Manila," *San Jose Mercury News,* 22 February 1988.

36. Ibid.

37. John Lehman, Secretary of the Navy, "National Security Interests in the Philippines," testimony presented at hearing of U.S. Senate Committee on Armed Services, Subcommittee on Military Construction, 10 April 1986, 4.

38. Patrick Tyler, "Cheney, Powell Are Told U.S. Can Cut Korea Forces, Give Up Philippine Bases," *Washington Post,* 20 December 1989, A7.

39. Niksch, 27.

40. Kim Gordon-Bates and Mathews George, "Joint Manoeuvres in Uncle Sam's Wake," *South,* March 1989, 33.

41. Lambertson, 17.

42. Capt. (Ret., USN) Alva M. Bowen, Jr., "U.S. Facilities in the Philippines," in Greene, 112.

43. Alva M. Bowen, Jr., "Letter to the Editor," *Pilipinas,* No. 11, Fall 1988, 110.

44. Fallows, 27-28.

45. "Special Report: U.S. Bases in the Philippines," *Philippine Agenda,* May 1988, 7; William Sullivan, "Relocating Bases in the Philippines," Washington Quarterly, Spring 1984, 117. The differential between Philippine and Japanese labor has increased beyond this figure due to the vastly increased value of the yen.

46. Sullivan, 117.

47. Bowen, in Greene, 117.

48. Presidential Commission on Integrated Long-Term Strategy, "Discriminate Deterrence," (Washington, D.C.: Presidential Commission, 11 January 1988), 11.

49. Stansfield Turner, "Arm for the Real Threat," *New York Times,* 10 April 1989.

Chapter 9

Japan

Keystone of the Pacific

Joseph Gerson

> If containing Soviet expansion was all we cared about, we might be tempted to withdraw. But that is not what we intend to do...it should be clear that the United States could not ever think of a withdrawal from Asia.
>
> —*Secretary of Defense Richard Cheney*
> New York Times
> *February 25, 1990*

During the more than 200 years, between 1640 and 1854, that Japan closed itself to foreign influence, it permitted Holland to maintain a fortress on an island in Nagasaki harbor. That fortress provided a base for Dutch traders and diplomats, giving them an exclusive Western influence in Japan while providing Japan the narrowest of windows to the technology and thought of the West.

For many Japanese, the presence of the Dutch fortress was a national humiliation. Japanese soil was being occupied by foreigners. Yet very few people in Holland knew of the existence of the distant fortress. So, in 1861, when Japan sent its first diplomatic mission to Europe, the following exchange took place in Amsterdam between Japanese diplomats and their Dutch hosts:

"Is the sale and purchase of land in Amsterdam freely permitted?"
"Certainly it is free."
"Do you sell land to foreigners also?"
"Yes, as long as a foreigner is willing to pay for the land, we would sell any amount of it to any person."

"Then, suppose a foreigner were to put down a large sum of money
to purchase a great tract of land in order to build a fortress, would you
allow that too?"

"We never had occasion to think of such a case...we do not believe
any merchant would spend money on such a venture."[1]

More than a century later the situation has changed less than one would
expect. U.S. Secretary of State James Baker called the U.S. alliance with Japan
the most important Pacific partnership for the United States and the world,
and former Ambassador Mike Mansfield has frequently described it as "the
most important bilateral relationship in the world, bar none." Yet, even as
Japan reemerges as a world power, the United States maintains more than
100 military bases and installations, with 48,000 troops, on the main islands
of Japan and on Okinawa. Even as people in the United States complain
about the invasion of Japanese goods and capital undermining U.S. security,
few have any inkling of the continuing U.S. military occupation of Japan—or
its meaning for the Japanese people.

Before World War II ended, national security planners in Washington
saw Japan as more than a defeated enemy. Japan could, they believed, serve
as the "keystone" of U.S. power in Asia and the Pacific. General MacArthur
described the new order in unmistakable terms: "Now the Pacific has become
an Anglo-Saxon lake and our line of defense runs through the chain of islands
fringing the coast of Asia. It starts from the Philippines and continues through
the Ryukyu archipelago, which includes its broad main bastion, Okinawa.
Then it bends back through Japan and the Aleutian Island Chain to Alaska."[2]

Since the end of World War II, the United States has maintained an
enormous military presence in Japan. These "forward deployed" U.S. forces
have served five primary functions: 1) encirclement of the Soviet Union; 2)
a jumping off point for U.S. military intervention in Asia, the Pacific, and more
recently the Indian Ocean and Persian Gulf; 3) a command, control, communications, and intelligence center—also known as C3I; 4) as tripwires
against an invented or perceived Soviet threat; and 5) as a lever for U.S.
influence and power within Japan.

The powerful U.S. military presence in Japan was conceived by U.S.
policy makers as a military necessity and as an appropriate consequence of
World War II. From the popular U.S. perspective, it was the U.S. prerogative
and responsibility to ensure that Japan would never again threaten the United
States or Japan's Asian and Pacific neighbors. This post-war relationship and
the U.S. bases were legitimized by the Treaty of Mutual Security and Cooperation, negotiated—or more properly, imposed—in 1951 at the end of the
official U.S. occupation of Japan. The treaty has since been at the core of

Japanese debates over war and peace, Japanese-U.S. relations, and the limitations of Japanese sovereignty.

Relations between Japan and the United States have since undergone enormous changes. The conqueror and occupier became the senior partner, and over time, the debtor. The evolving relationship has been legitimized at critical moments through surrender documents, a U.S.-imposed constitution, and the Mutual Security Treaty. It has been modified in recent years by the communiques of presidents and prime ministers. Through all these changes, one thing has been relatively constant—the enormous U.S. military presence throughout Japan. However, unlike the early period of occupation, or the 1960 *ampo* revolt of Japanese against the renewal of the Mutual Security Treaty and the bases, the U.S. military presence in Japan has become invisible to most people in the United States.

Forty-five years after the end of World War II, U.S. perceptions of Japan are confused, uncertain, and changing. The emerging world order is, itself, still being defined. As the initial response to Iraq's invasion of Kuwait indicated, it may be marked by cooperation among the dominant powers of the coming era—the United States, Japan, and a united Europe—at the expense of the Third World. It may be dominated by conflict between dollar, yen, and ecu (Euro Currency Unit) trading zones, not entirely unlike the period that preceded World War II, with the Third World being squeezed to serve the needs of the northern-dominated trade zones. Or, we may see a reversion to old-fashioned balance-of-power politics and conflict.

During this period of declining U.S. power and growing uncertainty about the future, the range of the policy debate in the United States has been enormous, exacerbating the anxieties of the Japanese people and government. Some in Congress have called for severe trade sanctions against Japan, while a "revisionist" school of journalists and scholars has called for controlled trade and continued political pressure on Japan. At the other end of the spectrum, successive presidents and national security planners have called for increased U.S.-Japanese partnership. Zbigniew Brzezinski has gone so far as to call for cutting a new global deal, the creation of "Amerippon"—integrating the elites of the United States and Japan.

Though economics plays a critical role in Japanese life, the military dimensions of U.S.-Japanese relations are of equal and possibly greater importance to many Japanese. Former Japanese Prime Minister Nakasone put it simply. In 1983, he horrified many Japanese by bragging that Japan "is a floating aircraft carrier" for the United States. When he retired in 1988, he warned his country that "security relations" between the two countries are at least as important to Japan as economic relations. More recently the Kaifu government swallowed its considerable pride, making major trade concessions to the Bush Administration in order to stabilize the partnership.[3]

If there are tensions in the United States over trade with, and dependency on, Japan, the same can be said of Japanese attitudes toward the continued presence of U.S. bases and troops in their country. The Mutual Security Treaty and the U.S. bases have often led the United States to place its strategic interests above those of the Japanese people. For many Japanese, U.S. bases mean the presence of nuclear weapons, despite the fact that they are outlawed by Japan's post-war pacifist constitution. Despite *glasnost* and *perestroika,* the Cold War tensions and structures of power linger in the North Pacific. Being an "aircraft carrier" for the United States means continued tension with the Soviet Union.

The U.S. military presence is not, however, without its Japanese supporters. Until recently it has guaranteed a secure environment for the ruling political establishment installed by the United States during the early post-war years. It has also allowed this establishment to concentrate on economic reconstruction and profit for its corporate allies. Japan's role as the primary staging ground for the United States' wars in Korea and Indochina also provided an enormous boost for the retooling of Japan's industrial sector and released a massive flow of dollars into the Japanese economy for resources and services needed for the wars.

U.S. bases have done more than undermine the constitutional basis of Japanese government and stimulate the Japanese economy, however. In Okinawa, where U.S. bases occupy 20 percent of the land, they have meant the seizure of farmers' land, decades of prostitution, and little room for the growth of Naha, the island's major city. The U.S. military inflicts the crushing noise of low-level flight exercises on countless Japanese communities; military accidents take a toll in Japanese lives and security, and environmentally important natural resources are regularly destroyed by the U.S. military presence. For many Japanese, the U.S. military presence means, at the deepest level, the continued military occupation of Japan 45 years after the atomic bombing of Hiroshima and Nagasaki, an occupation supported and partially financed by the Japanese government itself.

Japan's Strategic Role in U.S. Power Projection

The authors of *American Lake* have described Japan as "America's single most important ally in [the] Pacific Command," more important than any other U.S. bases in the Pacific or Europe. U.S. base sites in Japan, Okinawa, and South Korea form an "iron triangle," concentrating air and ground power on the Soviet Far East and reinforcing intervention to the south and west.⁴ U.S. bases in Japan are not only a remnant of the Cold War, but they are well placed for post-Cold War U.S. power projection.

Japan's strategic importance, and many of Japan's own strategic concerns, are functions of its geography. Japan consists of four main islands, and many smaller ones, that lie parallel to the Asian coast. Okinawa is little more than 300 miles east of the central Chinese mainland, and it is closer to Taiwan than it is to Tokyo. Three of the four main islands of Japan—Kyushu, Shikoku, and Honshu—stretch around and past Korea and Chinese Manchuria to a point just 250 miles east of the Soviet Union's major Pacific port, Vladivostok. Hokkaido Island and the Kurile Islands (the latter seized by the Soviet Union following World War II) rise to the Soviet Union's strategically vital Kamchatka Peninsula, closing the Sea of Okotsk. Since the arrival of Admiral Perry's "Black Ships" in 1853-54, Japan's geographic location and economic power have made it a focus of U.S. strategic planning.

There has been continuity in the U.S. approach to Asia and the Pacific since that time. In the 1890s, President McKinley was clear that "[w]e want our own markets for our manufactures and agricultural products; we want a foreign market for our surplus products." In 1935, during the Great Depression and the increasing tension with Japan that would lead to war, President Roosevelt remarked: "Foreign markets must be regained if America's producers are to rebuild a full and enduring domestic prosperity for our people. There is no other way if we would avoid painful economic dislocations, and unemployment."⁵ Contrary to public assertions by the Truman Administration and popular understanding, it was Japan's strategic importance to the U.S. in the anticipated Cold War that was the primary motivation for the atomic bombings of Hiroshima and Nagasaki. Truman sought to end the war with Japan before the Soviet Union could enter it, thus ensuring that Washington would not have to share its influence in Japan with Moscow.⁶ And today the United States and Japan remain major competitors for economic influence in China—a potential market of one billion people. This continuity informed Ronald Reagan's Secretary of the Navy, John Lehman, when he wrote:

> Today, the United States has an Asian orientation at least equal to its historic engagement in Europe...in 1980 the value of U.S. trade with the Pacific rim nations was roughly equal to trade with the country's Atlantic partners. Four years later, Pacific trade exceeded that with Western Europe by $26 billion.

Lehman noted that U.S. naval forces and strategy were being restructured accordingly.⁷ Since then the United States' trans-Pacific trade has grown to $271 billion per year, and exceeds its trans-Atlantic trade by almost $100 billion a year, leading Secretary of State Baker to call for "a deepening military and economic partnership." [8]

In reviewing recent history it is also worth noting that although Cold War fears in the United States focused primarily on the possibility of war in Europe, it was during the Chinese Civil War, the Korean War, and the U.S. war in Indochina that the fiercest East-West conflicts and nuclear threats occurred. It was Asia, not Europe, that witnessed the most intense military confrontations between Western capitalism, led by the United States, and communism, led by the Soviet Union and China.[9]

Since its defeat in 1945, Japan has served the United States as a base for controlling Soviet and Chinese ports and as a jumping off point for intervention to the south and west (Taiwan, Indochina, the Philippines, and the Middle East). It has served as an economic and technological resource for U.S. power. Japan also has become an important military ally whose protection of the Home Islands and the vital straits around Japan has freed U.S. forces for more distant missions.

U.S. military planners have traditionally seen "Japan's main utility as a physical barrier blocking Soviet naval egress from the Sea of Okhotsk and the Sea of Japan where the...Soviet Pacific Fleet has its main base at Vladivostok."[10] U.S. naval forces, and increasingly the Japanese "Self Defense" Navy, use bases in Japan to control the strategically important Sova, Tsugaru, and Tsuchimi straits around Japan and thus contain the Soviet Fleet in its Vladivostok harbor. More than naval bases are involved. Airfields across Japan serve as bases for PC3 Orion anti-submarine planes designed to carry nuclear depth charges. These aircraft are part of an integrated anti-submarine warfare system that includes sound surveillance microphones seeded on the ocean floor and intelligence facilities in Japan that collect and interpret the data.

Though U.S. forces based in Japan have repeatedly been used for intervention in Asia and the Pacific throughout the Cold War, the Soviet "threat" served to rationalize the U.S. military presence in Japan. While there have been fears of a Soviet threat to Japan, they have had little basis in reality. According to the U.S. Pacific Command, "China is the primary Asian concern of Soviet military planners...90 percent of Soviet ground forces in the Far East are directed against China and are preoccupied with the 'growing Chinese nuclear capability.'"[11] Though the Soviet Pacific fleet did expand during the early and mid-1980s, it was primarily in response to tension with the Chinese, the Reagan Administration's maritime strategy, and Japanese remilitarization. As William Arkin and Richard Fieldhouse have written, the Soviet Pacific Fleet remains primarily defensive. It is structured "to protect the Pacific flank of the Soviet Union," to protect Soviet ballistic submarines, and to "provide limited

U.S.S. Midway at Yokuska Navy Base. Photo courtesy of Gensuikyo.

interdiction."[12] The same cannot be said of U.S. forces in Japan. Again quoting Arkin and Fieldhouse, U.S. forces "have an offensive structure to counter deployable Soviet forces and to 'project' U.S. power ashore, primarily to attack Soviet bases, troop concentrations, and nuclear weapons facilities on the Soviet homeland."[13] When the Soviets look east, they still see U.S. nuclear weapons in the seas around Japan.

The strategic relationship of the Korean Peninsula to Japan, and thus to the United States, is frequently overlooked. More than 100,000 U.S. soldiers and two million Koreans were killed and wounded during the Korean War. Twice during the war, the U.S. threatened to use nuclear weapons to ensure that the war ended on terms acceptable to Washington. To this day, the U.S. maintains 44,000 troops in 21 bases and installations in South Korea, and they are armed with more than 150 nuclear weapons.

For U.S. military planners, Korea's strategic importance lies in its proximity to Japan and, thus, in its potential strategic threat to the Japanese economy. Since the turn of the century, when Russian and Japanese ambitions clashed in Manchuria and the Korean peninsula, Korea has been seen as a "sword pointing at the heart of central Japan."[14] This is a "sword" that they believe must, under no circumstances, come under Soviet domination. In the early days of the Cold War, U.S. military strategists resolved to use "any means necessary" to prevent Japan from falling into the Soviet orbit, lest it tilt the balance of power in Asia and possibly the world. In large measure it was to protect this strategically important economic resource that the United States went to war in Korea in 1950.[15]

Japan has also served the United States as an offensive platform for intervention throughout the Pacific, Southeast Asia, and the Middle East. In 1950, the U.S. used Sasebo as its base of operations while the 7th Fleet occupied the Straits of Taiwan, "effectively preventing a communist invasion of Taiwan." In the words of one Japanese observer, this made Japan "a forward military base for intervention in the Chinese communist revolution," ruling out any possibility of friendly Japanese-Chinese relations for many years to come.[16]

With the escalation of the war in Indochina in the 1960s, the United States again used Japan as a base of operations and as its primary overseas source of arms. Bases in Okinawa were used to train troops, as the launching point for bombers, and for R&R ("rest and recreation").

More recently, U.S. forces based in Japan were used to reinforce U.S. influence in the Philippines during the 1986 uprising that toppled Ferdinand Marcos. The aircraft carrier Midway and amphibious assault ships loaded with Marines were dispatched from Okinawa to the Philippines. Special forces were sent from Okinawa to the Philippines for "military exercises," and F-4 Phantom jets were moved from Kadena Air Force Base in Okinawa to Clark Field in the Philippines "for runway construction."[17]

From Defeat to Alliance

Japan was a devastated nation when U.S. occupation forces landed there in late August 1945. Atomic bombs had left the people and cities of Hiroshima and Nagasaki in cinders, with survivors envying the dead. Much of Tokyo had been reduced to ashes by prolonged and deadly fire bombings. Japan, which had brutally conquered and occupied Southeast Asia, Korea, and much of China and the Pacific, was now an occupied nation which had suffered eight million casualties. The Japanese people were stunned and ready to welcome an end to their agonies. Popular resentment, to the extent that it existed and could be expressed, was directed primarily against the generals and admirals who had led Japan into and through the war.[18] Never before had Japan been militarily defeated or occupied.

The road from occupation to alliance passed through at least four stages: 1) the end of the occupation and the signing of the U.S.-Japan Mutual Security Treaty in 1951; 2) the traumatic 1960 treaty revision; 3) the 1969 Nixon-Sato communique which provided for the reversion of Okinawa to

Japan and a growing role for the emerging Japanese military under the Nixon Doctrine; 4) and, finally, the Reagan-Suzuki and Reagan-Nakasone communiques, which restructured the alliance to reflect Japan's enormous economic and technological power. Though the missions of U.S. bases in Japan have been adjusted to respond to changing U.S. priorities, the number and importance of U.S. forces in Japan have remained nearly constant.

The U.S. occupation of Japan was marked by the competing visions and interests of policy makers, as two contending approaches vied to shape U.S. policy toward post-war Japan. The "China hands," primarily Foreign Service officers who had served in China, viewed Japan through the lenses of suffering caused by the Japanese conquest and occupation of much of China. They sought to demolish the structures of Japanese military power and to impose major democratic reforms on Japanese culture and politics. The "Japan crowd" sought to make Japan the "keystone" of U.S. interests in Asia. To this end they attempted to maintain much of Japan's pre-war economic structure and to reduce, but not eliminate, Japanese military power. MacArthur, who had suffered military defeats at the hands of Japan's old order, was initially unsympathetic to the advice of the "Japan crowd," but in time he was rehabilitating war criminals and reconstructing the Japanese military. As the "loss of China" approached, and the Cold War with the Soviet Union intensified, the "China hands" lost influence to the "Japan crowd" and their allies. U.S. industrialists, who saw more profit in controlling the *Zaibatsu* (the great industrial combines that served Japan's war economy) than in destroying them and who feared the emerging power of Japanese labor unions, made common cause with ideological militarists in Washington, who wanted to use every possible resource to fight communism.

With a clear message coming from the Truman Administration, MacArthur's staff reversed direction. Major General Charles Willoughby, MacArthur's "lovable Fascist," recruited former right-wing leaders of the Imperial Army and Navy and the *Yakuza* (organized crime) to identify, attack, and purge "communists" and many labor organizers. Communists, however, were not the only victims of the purge, which included the dismissal of 20,000 civil servants and teachers, police raids against newspapers and radio stations, and the ouster of leftist professors from the universities. Previously ousted war criminals were rehabilitated. Those who had served as the foot soldiers of the democratic reforms were disowned.

The United States was preparing to use Japan as the springboard for future operations. In August 1946, the *Baltimore Sun* ran the headline, "U.S. Army Foreseen Staying on Indefinitely in Japan." It reported that, "[a]lthough the military phase of the occupation is nearly completed, American forces may remain indefinitely in Japan to hold what is regarded here as the eastern anchor of a worldwide American line against the Soviet Union and communism."[19]

The post-war democratic state that the Occupation forces constructed to replace the occupation was not based on any single legitimizing principle. It ambiguously incorporated three mutually exclusive principles: 1) the pacifist Constitution...2) the military alliance with the United States... through which Japanese military and...diplomatic functions were largely relegated to the United States, and 3) the somewhat surreptitiously but stubbornly preserved continuity from the prewar imperial state" in the form of Emperor Hirohito remaining on the throne.[20] Though the final peace treaty was not signed until 1951, preparations for formal transition of power began early in the occupation. Three major agreements had to be negotiated: a constitution for an independent Japan, a peace treaty ending the war and the occupation, and a "security" agreement which would legitimize the continued U.S. military presence in Japan.

In February 1946, when General MacArthur directed the government section of SCAP to begin drafting a constitution for Japan, he underlined three elements that he expected to be included. The Emperor was to remain head of state but be responsible to the people. All the vestiges of the feudal system were to be abolished. So was Japan's ability to wage war. MacArthur was not disappointed on any of these points. Article 9 of the U.S.-imposed constitution read:

> Aspiring sincerely to an international peace based on justice and order, the Japanese people forever renounce war as a sovereign right of the nation and the threat or use of force as a means of settling international disputes.

> In order to accomplish the aim of the preceding paragraph, land, sea, and air forces, as well as other war potential, will never be maintained. The right of belligerency of the state will not be recognized.

The peace treaty was complemented by the U.S.-Japan Mutual Security Treaty. In exchange for U.S.-sponsored reconstruction of Japan and the rehabilitation of much of the old order (limited by a decidedly more democratic constitution),

> the United States asked only for the right to utilize bases in Japan as part of a global strategic network. As a minor corollary to this approach, the United States also gradually pressured Japan from the beginning to help out where it could by bolstering its nascent armed forces. [21]

In April 1951, the Mutual Security Treaty was signed within hours of the official ceremony at which 49 nations—excluding the Soviet Union and China—signed the peace treaty formally ending the war with Japan. The

Security Treaty was later described by Secretary of State Christian Herter to be "pretty extreme from the point of view of an agreement between two sovereign nations."

The United States was granted the right to use bases in Japan without consulting the Japanese government about operations that affected Japanese interests in Asia. The United States had the freedom to bring whatever weapons it chose into Japan. Japanese police forces created by MacArthur to compensate for the dispatch of U.S. troops to Korea were legitimized and transformed into "Self Defense Forces" through provisions that mandated the initial rebuilding of the Japanese military to "increasingly assume responsibility" for the defense of Japan. The United States, however, was not required to defend Japan.

In a provision that seriously subverted Japan's sovereignty, the United States was permitted to deploy forces to combat internal disturbances in Japan. The United States also retained the extraordinary power to veto any arrangements the Japanese government might make with other countries to bring military forces into Japan. And the treaty contained no provisions for termination except by mutual consent. The few restrictions on U.S. power in Japan did not apply to the concentration of U.S. forces in Okinawa, a province which continued under formal U.S. occupation. As Assistant Secretary of State Graham Parsons testified in 1960: "This first treaty of 1951 was not one which was entered into by Japan voluntarily." [22]

The 1960 treaty revision resulted from questions raised before the initial treaty was signed. Even the Japanese elite debated whose interests were served by the treaty, and until 1960 the focus of friction in U.S.-Japanese relations was the Mutual Security Treaty. Many Japanese were frightened by the presence of U.S. nuclear weapons, and they were affronted by their deployment in Japan. Others were resentful of the many privileges still afforded to U.S. military forces in Japan. The continued U.S. occupation of Okinawa offended Japanese nationalist sensibilities, and powerful figures in Japan were deeply concerned that the 1951 agreement made no provisions for the United States to defend Japan in time of war. The Eisenhower Administration was not averse to renegotiating the treaty and removing some of its extremes.

Ignoring most popular concerns about the treaty's provisions, U.S. and Japanese negotiators focused on the defense of Japan and the presence of nuclear weapons. When the minimal modifications had been negotiated, Prime Minister Kishi forced his cabinet to approve the revised treaty which relegitimized U.S. bases in Japan. Though the new treaty provided for a slight reduction in the number of bases, this was of dubious value because the bases and installations were consolidated, and the number of U.S. forces in

Japan remained essentially unchanged. The United States committed itself to the defense of Japan, and in turn the Japanese government committed itself to continue rebuilding its military to defend the home islands. The United States also agreed to prior consultation with the Japanese government before major deployments of U.S. forces to Japan or major changes in U.S. equipment (including nuclear weapons).

The United States was not willing, however, to consult *formally* with Japan about the presence of U.S. nuclear weapons in Japan, nor was it willing to end the occupation of Okinawa, where the greatest number of bases were located. In essence, the United States agreed to withdraw the nuclear weapons it had secretly stored in Japan in exchange for their continued presence in Okinawa and for transit rights. The agreement also provided for the use of U.S. forces should they be requested by the Japanese government to put down internal disturbances.

The lack of fundamental change in the revised treaty, and its continued assault on Japanese sovereignty, incensed vast numbers of Japanese and led to "internal disturbances." In the words of one diplomatic observer, the protest that followed was "a watershed in post-war Japanese history. Socialists, Communists, labor unions, leftist intellectuals, and radical student groups combined to rampage through Tokyo and other major cities demanding the resignation of Prime Minister Kishi, the scrapping of the Mutual Security Treaty, and the withdrawal of the invitation to President Eisenhower to visit Japan."[23]

Within days of the ratification of the renegotiated treaty, Kishi was forced to resign. President Eisenhower, with considerable loss of face, was forced to cancel a scheduled good-will visit to Japan. But by steering public attention toward economic development, Kishi's successor, Ikeda Hayato, quelled the crisis, leaving the revised treaty and U.S. bases intact.

The third stage in the evolution of the U.S.-Japan alliance came in 1969 at the Nixon-Sato summit. Twenty-five years had passed since the end of World War II, and the Japanese economy was largely rebuilt. Japan was becoming a "superstate." Tied down in Vietnam and facing a tide of popular opposition to the war, President Nixon had developed a doctrine to compensate for the relative decline in U.S. power. The doctrine was designed to create a structure of sub-imperial powers, from Iran to Indonesia and Argentina to Israel. These countries were to fight to maintain the United States' global empire while pursuing their own foreign policy interests. The leaders of Vietnam called this "changing the color of the corpses," and Japan had a crucial role to play in the new doctrine.

The communique issued after the Nixon-Sato meeting reaffirmed the Mutual Security Treaty and the continued presence of U.S. bases in Japan. It thus confirmed the United States' strategic position and power in the region. Changes in the strategic relationship were reflected in Sato's proclamation of "the beginning of a 'new order' in the Pacific based on the American-Japanese alliance."[24] As part of this new order Sato pledged that the Japanese "Self-Defense Forces" would play a larger regional role. Under pressure from popular opposition against the use of U.S. bases for the war in Indochina, which was heightened by the crash of a B-52 bomber in a densely populated district, President Nixon returned nominal sovereignty of Okinawa to Japan and allowed the naval base at Yokosuka to formally revert to Japanese control.

Sato projected himself as a nationalist who had ended the last vestiges of the U.S. occupation. He appeared an equal in an alliance with the United States, even as he presided over the deepening integration of Japan into the U.S. military infrastructure.

The alliance matured and became more deeply institutionalized in the last years of the Carter Administration and throughout the Reagan years. In 1978, the two allies agreed to guidelines for joint military operations. Following the 1979 overthrow of the Shah in Iran and the Soviet invasion of Afghanistan, the division of labor established in the U.S.-Japanese alliance became more critical to Pentagon planners. Japan began planning how to respond to crises in South Korea and preparing to blockade the straits between the Soviet Union and the Pacific. In times of crisis, the U.S. 7th Fleet could now more easily be committed to the Rapid Deployment Force (which became the Central Command) for operations in the Indian Ocean, the Arabian Sea, and the Persian Gulf.

Though U.S.-Japanese relations in the 1980s were marked by economic friction, the Reagan Administration used those pressures to demand, and receive, greater "burdensharing." During the Reagan-Nakasone relationship, the Japanese government assumed greater financial responsibility for the costs of the United States bases in Japan. Through agreements to assist in Star Wars research and the co-production of weapons like the FSX fighter, the United States struggled to reverse the direction of technology transfer and to deepen the integration of Japan's scientific establishment into the U.S. Military Industrial Complex.

In recent years the majority of U.S. strategic analysts have taken the U.S. military infrastructure in Japan for granted. They have concentrated their energies on "burdensharing," and have pressed Japan to augment its own military power to complement the structure of U.S. military forces—for example, during the U.S. intervention in the Iraq-Iran war and again following the Iraqi invasion of Kuwait. Economic limitations on future U.S. military spending are reinforcing this trend. This was most recently seen in the Japanese debate over how to respond to U.S. demands for help in paying for its 1990 Persian Gulf intervention and for the deployment of Japanese military forces to the Gulf. As evidenced by huge mass demonstrations in Japan against the proposed deployment of Japanese troops to the Middle East in December 1990, deep and popular Japanese resistance to increases in Japan's military spending and to Japanese militarism will continue. In the future this resistance is likely to be aimed at both the role of Japan's own military as well as at the United States' military presence in Japan.

The U.S.-Japanese alliance, like all other military alliances, is based on the cooperation and strategic integration of military forces. Though Article 9 of the Japanese Constitution prohibits the maintenance of "land, sea and air forces, as well as other war potential," under constant U.S. diplomatic and economic pressure, by 1990 Japan's Self-Defense Forces were financed by the world's third largest military budget.

Former U.S. diplomats have described how bewildered most Japanese were when Vice President Nixon visited Japan in 1953 and urged the Japanese to rearm.[25] Hadn't the United States imposed a pacifist constitution and destroyed the last vestiges of Japanese militarism? Nixon's proposal, however, was not a new initiative. The Korean War accelerated U.S. efforts to rebuild Japanese military forces, which had begun in 1948. The first divisions sent to Korea were drawn from U.S. occupation forces in Japan, and by September 1950 it was clear to military planners that the United States could not leave its bases in Japan unprotected. Thus, the decision was taken to transform the existing Japanese police force into a 75,000-man National Police Reserve. "It was made clear that the NPR was to be the nucleus of the future Japanese army."[26] Many of its officers were drawn from the ranks of the purged Imperial Army. In a pattern that became familiar over the next four decades, President Truman pressed Prime Minister Yoshida to build an enormous force of 350,000. Yoshida and many Japanese feared this would lead to their direct military involvement in Korea, which was—and remains—unthinkable following the devastating consequences of World War II.

Compared to U.S., Soviet, and Chinese military forces, those of Japan remain relatively small. However, in the words of one military observer:

> [D]espite the ridicule to which they sometimes are subjected, the Self-Defense Forces are reasonably formidable armed forces. In size (180,000) they rank eighth in the world; in terms of capability, their anti-submarine forces are among the world's best...their firepower surpasses that of their imperial predecessors...[27]

As an island nation whose strategic power, and role in the U.S. global system, depends on control of the seas, the Japanese Navy receives the largest portion of the Japanese military budget. By the end of 1990, Japan is scheduled to have 60 destroyers, twice the number of the 7th Fleet. It will also have 100 PC3 Orion anti-submarine aircraft and 260 F-4 and F-15 jet fighters—not an insignificant military force, by any means.

Structure of U.S. Bases in Japan

The presence of so many U.S. military bases in Japan reflects the depth of Japanese integration into the United States' global military infrastructure. One hundred and five U.S. installations, including at least 20 major bases, stretch from Okinawa to Hokaido.[28] The bases are concentrated in Okinawa and the Tokyo area, where the commanders of the U.S. 7th Fleet and the 5th Air Force have their homeports and headquarters. Twenty miles from Tokyo, at Yokosuka Naval Base, the nuclear armed U.S. aircraft carrier Midway and its fleet of supporting ships—some equipped with nuclear-armed Tomahawk cruise missiles—have their homeport. This vast military presence ensures that U.S. Army, Navy, Air Force, and Marine commanders and staffs have daily contacts with their Japanese counterparts, reinforcing the ties of the Japanese military to the U.S. system.

The bases serve a variety of military functions. Though the Air Force, Navy, and Marines have the highest visibility in Japan, Japan serves as a warehouse for U.S. Army forces in Korea. Three Army storage sites in Hiroshima prefecture (Akizuki, Hiro, and Happonmatsu) "store enough ammunition for 5 divisions...to use in 12 days at the rate of 10,000 tons a day."[29] Training for counter-insurgency warfare has been a staple of the U.S. presence in Japan, particularly in Okinawa, since the 1950s. It was in Okinawa that many soldiers bound for Vietnam received training in jungle warfare, and in the early 1960s officers based in Okinawa were dispatched to observe and advise the first U.S. forces sent to fight in Southeast Asia.

Two other military functions have made Japan the "keystone" of the Pacific: C3I and intervention. The proximity of U.S. bases in Japan to the Soviet Union made the island nation an important base for Cold War encirclement of the Soviet Union. U.S. forces in Japan have closely observed Soviet military activity and even in the post-Cold War order remain prepared to support U.S. nuclear attacks on Soviet military installations and cities. C3I operations have included processing data collected from daily P3C Orion flights monitoring Soviet submarine activity in the seas and ocean surrounding Japan; linking communication between the Japanese, Korean, and U.S. militaries; and, potentially, issuing fire orders for nuclear-armed Strategic Air Command bombers. The Air Force Base at Misawa, in Hokaido, is less than 400 miles from Soviet shores. Nuclear capable F-16's based there can reach the vital port and naval base of Vladivostok and return without refueling. They can also wreak havoc on Soviet shipping in the Sea of Japan.

Major U.S. Bases on the Home Islands

Atsugi	Commander Fleet Air, Western Pacific Naval Air Facility
Iwakuni	Marine Corps Air Station
Kamiseya	Command Patrol & Reconnaissance Force of 7th Fleet Headquarters Patrol Wing I (Navy)
Misawa	Japan Air Patrol Group 432nd Air Base Wing Naval Air Facility
Sasebo	Fleet Activities
Yokohama	Military Sealift Command, Far East
Yokota	Headquarters of US Forces in Japan (under Pacific Command Headquarters, 5th Air Force 475th Air Base Wing 316th Tactical Airlift Group
Yokosuka	Command of US Naval Forces in Japan (under Pacific Fleet) Command of 7th Submarine Group (under Pacific Fleet)
Zama	Headquarters, US Army Japan IX Corps US Army Garrison, Japan

---

The bases have also served as a jumping off point for U.S. military intervention in Asia, the Pacific, and the Persian Gulf in much the same manner as they did during the U.S. wars in Indochina and Korea. The Army's Mobile Command Center at Camp Zama is designed to be rapidly relocated for operations anywhere in Asia. Sasebo Navy Base, on the Sea of Japan, serves as a fuel and munitions storage center. Both Sasebo and Yokosuka are integrated with the Marine Air Station at Iwakuni, where Marine fighters and helicopters are based for intervention in Korea and the Soviet Union. Recent operations have included the dispatch of warships, F-15 fighters, and Marines to the Philippines during the turmoil that led to the ouster of Ferdinand Marcos. President Reagan's military interventions in Lebanon and the Persian Gulf were supported by Naval and Marine units based in Japan, and Marines were sent back to the Gulf from bases in Japan in 1990.

Japan has been "burdensharing" from the beginning. Since the conclusion of the Mutual Security Treaty, the U.S. has had rent-free access to its bases in Japan. The Status of Forces Agreement provided that Japan would pay for all costs of Japanese labor related to the bases, exclusive of wages. This includes the costs of housing, transportation, and retirement for 21,000 Japanese and Okinawan base workers. In one form or another the Japanese government paid about 54 percent of the $6.2 billion costs of the U.S. bases in Japan in 1988, a greater percentage than any other host government.[30]

Major U.S. Bases in Okinawa

Camp Courtney	3rd Marine Amphibious Forces (7th Fleet)
Camp Hansen	9th Marine Regiment
Camp Schwab	4th Marine Regiment
	3rdy Marine Reconnaissance Battalion
	1st. Tracked Vehicle Batallion
Futenma	36th Marine Air Group
Kadena	Okinawa Fleet (under command of 7th Fleet)
	313 Air Division under the 5th Air Force
	18th Tactical Fighter Wing
	376th Strategic Wing (Strategic Air Command)
	Naval Air Facilities
Makiminato	Army Troops
Tory	Army Troops
Zukeran	12th Marine Regiment
	Headquarters 1st Marine Air Wing
	Camp Smedley D. Butler

Under pressure from the U.S. Congress in the first months of the 1990 U.S.-Iraq confrontation, the Japanese Government indicated it might augment its subsidies for U.S. bases by as much as $3 billion a year.

U.S. Bases in Okinawa

The greatest concentration of U.S. troops and bases in Japan is located in Okinawa, where they occupy 20 percent of the land. These bases limit the growth of cities and towns, occupy rich farmland, and dominate the economic, social, and cultural life of the island. Though it is formally part of Japan, Okinawa has suffered from centuries of Japanese imperialism as well as decades of U.S. militarism. It remains a military colony of the United States.

Okinawa is the largest island of the 400-mile-long Ryukyu island chain which stretches parallel to the eastern coast of China. It is 860 miles southwest of Tokyo and nearly the same distance from Manila and Hong Kong. It was long an independent kingdom influenced by both China and Japan, and it served as a buffer through which Japan could conduct trade during Japan's two centuries of self-enforced isolation from the world. In 1872, after the forced opening of Japan obviated this role for Okinawa, it was conquered and formally annexed by Japanese imperial forces, and the Japanese language was imposed over distinct native dialects.

Okinawa's distance from the main islands of Japan and the collapse of its former economic role led Okinawa to become the poorest prefecture of

Japan. Today Okinawans are second-class Japanese citizens, suffering racial discrimination at the hands of many Japanese. From the Okinawan perspective, the concentration of U.S. bases in their communities and on their farms is deeply resented and represents the continuation of Japanese willingness to sacrifice Okinawan security, culture, quality of life, and values for the sake of Japan. World War II almost by-passed Okinawa.

Until the summer of 1944 there were virtually no military forces on the island. Then, as U.S. forces moved toward the Japanese mainland, taking one Pacific island after another, a Japanese army was organized and deployed to hold Okinawa for as long as possible. Japanese military leaders saw the battle as a means to buy time for the imperial mainland and to experiment in planning for the defense of the home islands. The battle was to be fought to the last person, and it nearly was. In Okinawa today, people's memories remain scarred by images of life in caves, flame throwers, suffocation, and maggots eating the dead and wounded. There are bitter memories of the Emperor system sacrificing more than 200,000 lives to buy time and a better deal in the months before the atomic bombings of Hiroshima and Nagasaki.

The U.S. Army concentrated massive military power on Okinawa to win a front-line base of operations against Japan. The "Typhoon of Steel," the intense shelling of the island, was preceded by the massing of 1,500 warships and more than half a million personnel. When the fighting was over, 95,000 Japanese soldiers and conscripts had died, as had 12,500 North Americans. An estimated 150,000 noncombatant Okinawan civilians were killed in the battle or in the early days of the occupation—one-quarter of the Okinawan population. Okinawans died in the cross fire. They were killed by Japanese soldiers afraid of spies. They were pressed to commit suicide rather than suffer the "humiliation" of surviving the defeat. And they died of hunger and disease when they were confined to concentration camps following the U.S. victory.[31]

When Okinawans were released from internment camps, many found U.S. forces occupying their property. To secure its control over Okinawa and its newly won bases, the United States suppressed the political rights of the islanders.[32] With few economic options available to them, widows and their daughters served the occupiers as prostitutes. In 1949, Congress responded to the establishment of the People's Republic of China with an allocation of $58 million for "improving" its Okinawan bases. The signing of the Peace Treaty and the Mutual Security Treaty in 1951 legitimized the U.S. military colonization of Okinawa and the other Ryuku islands.

Though legal Japanese sovereignty over Okinawa has been restored, U.S. domination of the island cannot be ignored. In the words of one observer:

In Okinawa one is constantly reminded of the U.S. presence. Apartments housing U.S. personnel with huge U.S. flags painted across their tops, statues of Uncle Sam and the Statue of Liberty, advertisements for American Bakery; discos, stores selling surplus military equipment or merchandise made to look like surplus are but a few visual examples. On the highways and central streets there is the regular movement of U.S. military personnel in combat fatigues from one camp to another or to maneuvers some place in the islands. And the sound of aircraft is constant. Military exercises, training and performances ensure that the intrusion on Okinawan life is constant.[33]

Naha, the capital city, and other towns are surrounded by the bases and have little room to grow. Fertile farmland is paved over with runways and military highways and is used for training exercises, including the use of live ammunition which cannot always be contained within the bases.

The missions of U.S. bases in Okinawa parallel those on the main islands, but the Okinawan bases play a greater role in third world intervention. During the Korean War, Okinawa was transformed into a staging ground, especially for B-29 bombers. After the war, it served as a base for missiles and aircraft aimed at China. During the Indochina War, Okinawa was a logistical center. Okinawa also served as a training ground and rear area for U.S. Marines deployed in Vietnam. Tankers based at Kadena Air Force Base met B-52 bombers from Guam on their way to Vietnam. Okinawa also had the largest medical depot in the world, dressing GI war wounds from Vietnam.[34]

Today one-quarter of the U.S. Air Force's planes in the Pacific fly from Okinawa. These include short-range bombers, nuclear bombers, fighters, transport and refueling aircraft, spy planes, and PC3 Orions. The Marine complex includes troops and equipment for rapid deployment throughout the region and to the Middle East. Their equipment includes artillery capable of launching nuclear, chemical, and biological weapons.[35] Intelligence facilities collect electronic information from China and Korea, and the "Giant Talk" facilities at Kadena Base are designed to send orders to B-52 bombers during nuclear war.

Women have paid a disproportionately heavy price for the U.S. military presence in Japan. This is especially true in Okinawa. Few GIs bring their U.S. wives to Okinawa. Eating places, pool halls, souvenir shops, and clubs surround the bases. In many cases, these services are owned or controlled by the *Yakuza,* Japan's organized crime. It is to the clubs of these areas that GIs go to find relief and escape.

During the formal occupation, most women who worked as prostitutes were the widows and daughters of men killed during the war. During the

Korean and Vietnam wars more than one in 30 Okinawan women worked as prostitutes. Some served more than 20 men a night. Their sexual labor was an important, but degrading, source of the money that rebuilt the Okinawan economy.

Today, few Okinawan women work as prostitutes. Instead, 4,000 poor Filipina women have been imported to serve the GIs. When they are not working, many are confined to rooms that they share with other women. Drugs and alcohol often serve as their only form of escape. Some have died when fires swept through their locked quarters.

Many Okinawans oppose the U.S. occupation of Okinawa—60 percent according to a recent poll.[36] Popular protest began when farmers struggled for the return of their land in the early 1950s. In 1969, a bomb-laden B-52 crashed at Kadena, nearly hitting a densely populated housing district and a munitions dump believed to contain nuclear weapons. This ignited massive demonstrations. The 1969 Nixon-Sato communique, providing for the reversion of Okinawa to Japan in 1972, was designed to quell these protests and others which had been mounted in opposition to the use of the bases against Vietnam. Okinawans were disappointed when the final agreement reaffirmed continued U.S. access to the bases. Despite popular Japanese expectations that Japanese sovereignty would mean the end of U.S. nuclear weapons in Okinawa, this was not to be the case.

Nuclear Weapons in Japan

Japan is the only nation ever to suffer attack by nuclear weapons. The *Hibakusha* (surviving victims who witnessed the atomic bombings of Hiroshima and Nagasaki) and their children have impressed the meaning of nuclear weapons and nuclear holocaust deep into Japanese consciousness, and this has led to meaningful limits on U.S. and JSDF (Japan Self Defense Forces) militarism in Japan. The presence of nuclear weapons on U.S. bases and in Japanese ports has thus been a painful affront to the Japanese people as well as a violation of their Constitution.

The U.S. policy of neither confirming nor denying the presence of nuclear weapons on bases, naval vessels, aircraft, or other weapons systems has not been sufficient to hide the presence of the U.S. nuclear arsenal in Japan. Former Army intelligence officer William Arkin named 29 U.S. facilities in Japan that serve U.S. preparations for nuclear war. Japan, he wrote, is "the most extensive forward nuclear infrastructure in the Pacific region." In addition to the nuclear weapons regularly brought into Japan aboard U.S. warships, they are regularly based in Yokosuka aboard the aircraft carrier Midway and its support fleet. Air Force documents indicate nuclear weapons have been stored at Kadena Air Force Base in Okinawa,[37] and Lance missiles have been displayed at Yokota base during military exercises, as have nuclear capable anti-submarine missiles. Air Force training documents describe frequent training to cope with nuclear weapons accidents and the fact that such accidents have happened. A slideshow designed for safety education for the 313th Air Division indicated U.S. forces in Japan have suffered five "bent spears" (nuclear incidents) and 65 "dull swords" (incidents of safety deficiency involving nuclear weapons).[38]

In addition to the nuclear weapons based or present in Japan, C3I installations in Japan play important roles in preparations for nuclear war. Communications facilities are concentrated at Kadena. Bases at Owada, Tokorozawa, Yosami, and Misawa also support training for nuclear warfighting and are designed to receive nuclear weapons in wartime.

Despite Japanese fears and opposition to nuclear weapons, the Peace Constitution, and the "Three Non-Nuclear Principles" (that Japan would not possess, manufacture, or introduce nuclear weapons into Japanese territory), successive Japanese governments have conspired with the United States to allow the introduction of nuclear weapons into Japan. The 1951 Mutual Security Treaty gave the United States the freedom to base any weapons it desired in Japan, and the United States had few limitations on its actions in Okinawa until it reverted to Japanese control in 1972. Opposition to the suspected presence of U.S. nuclear weapons in Japan helped fuel opposition to the bases through the 1950s and played a role in forcing the 1960 renegotiation of the Mutual Security Treaty. The refusal of the two governments to directly address these concerns sparked the 1960 *ampo* rebellion which toppled the Kishi government. At the time it was not known that an agreement providing for the transit of nuclear weapons through Japan "was appended as a top-secret document to the 1960 United States-Japan mutual security treaty."[39]

Though the Japanese government continues to deny the presence of U.S. nuclear weapons in Japan, the charade was revealed in 1981 in an interview with former Ambassador Edwin Reischauer. "Right from the start," Reischauer said, "I had been informed that the meaning of 'introduction' meant putting nuclear weapons ashore or storing them. It had always been our understanding that this didn't prevent us from moving weapons through Japan.[40] The uproar that followed the Reischauer interview was reinforced by another interview given by retired Navy Admiral Gene La Rocque. He reiterated that U.S. ships did not and could not off-load nuclear weapons before entering Japanese waters. La Rocque said "the only people in the world who don't know [that U.S. ships carry nuclear weapons] are the Japanese."[41]

Prime Minister Suzuki attempted to dampen the controversy in 1981 by maintaining that "Japan has always trusted that the United States has faithfully lived up to agreements in connection with the U.S.-Japan Security Treaty and will continue to trust U.S. fidelity."[42] The revelation, six years later, of the 1960 top-secret amendment to the security treaty confirmed the accuracy of Reischauer's and La Rocque's statements and revealed the complicity of the Japanese government in introducing nuclear weapons into Japan.

Opposition to U.S. Bases

Though some conservative voices of dissent are beginning to be heard, U.S. bases in Japan have received consistent support from the Liberal Democratic Party (LDP), which has controlled the Japanese government for the last 40 years, and from several opposition parties in the Diet (the Japanese parliament). Opposition to the bases, however, has been an important thread in Japanese politics, running through the entire post-war era. It even has been enough to topple governments, as Prime Minister Kishi discovered in 1960.

The LDP has used the bases as a means of ensuring Japanese security throughout the Cold War, allowing the government to concentrate on economic growth instead of military spending. Fundamental questions have been ignored by the LDP: questions of Japan's role in war and peace, the presence of and the threat posed by nuclear weapons, the sovereignty of Japan, and the immediate impact of the bases on the lives of the Japanese people. These unresolved questions have made the massive U.S. military presence a running sore in Japanese politics and in U.S.-Japanese relations.

A study prepared for the Brookings Institution by Fred Greene summarized the broad opposition to the bases and concern about their impact. The Mutual Security Treaty, it began, has never been accepted by the Japanese public. It is "regarded at best as a necessary evil...Antagonism to the U.S. force and base presence has grown, especially as Japan has recovered its economic strength."[43] The need to defend Japan against a possible Soviet attack has never been taken seriously by the Japanese, and there is a widespread view "that the U.S. military installations served American rather than Japanese interests."[44]

The most vocal opposition to the bases comes from the Japanese left which is structured more along party lines than the U.S. left. The annual October 21st "National United Action" against the Mutual Security Treaty, with rallies and demonstrations, is held in every prefecture each year. These and other anti-bases protests are initiated mainly by the Communist and

A protest assembly against U.S. military live ammunition firing exercises in Kim Town, Okinawa. Photo courtesy of Kazuo Kuniyoshi.

Socialist parties and by the peace movements and labor unions which are related to them.

The protests of the left cover a broad range of activities and constituencies. Community organizing and work within party structures reinforces the deep Japanese antipathy to militarism and has resulted in hundreds of town and city councils, academic research centers, and ports declaring themselves nuclear-free zones. The widely respected declaration of Kobe City requires all ships entering the port to make a positive declaration that they are nuclear free. As a result there have been no port calls by U.S. ships to Kobe for more than a decade. Demonstrations are frequently held outside U.S. bases, and the number of demonstrators is occasionally large enough to encircle a base.

While many people in Japan are highly politicized, it is the day-to-day impact of the U.S. bases and U.S. troops that angers people the most and fuels opposition to the bases. As one journalist observed, "In a country as small as Japan, sensitivity to safety is a necessity."[45] The noise and sonic booms of military aircraft doing low-level exercises over towns and cities would traumatize anyone, but they are even worse assaults in a culture which places high value on peace and tranquility.

People have been killed and houses destroyed when U.S. military aircraft have crashed. Homes have been sprayed with bullets from U.S. firing ranges. Japanese Coast Guard ships, well outside designated zones for military training, have been fired on by guided-missile destroyers. Tens of thousands of traffic accidents involving U.S. military personnel have occurred. Even in universities the U.S. military presence is felt. The integration of Japanese scientific research into the Reagan-Bush plans for "Star Wars" has contributed to the passage of a new State Secret's Law, limiting the freedom of many Japanese scientists.

Opposition to the bases is by no means limited to the organized left. In recent years, the left has frequently supported initiatives of people whose ties to the land and cultural values led them to launch community-based campaigns against the bases. For years, farmers in Okinawa refused to sign lease agreements to legitimize the seizure of their land for the bases, and their resistance remains strong. More recently, residents of the Tokyo suburb of Zushi and the more isolated Miyakejima Island have been opposing the expansion of U.S. bases.

Ikego Forest in Zushi has become "one of the most hotly contested pieces of real estate in Japan."[46] In the search for more housing for Navy personnel stationed in Yokohama, the U.S. and Japanese governments struck upon the wooded hills of the 800-acre Ikego Forest. With little apparent forethought, the central government began the process of seizing the forest from the city. People in Zushi and neighboring communities responded quickly and forcefully, circulating petitions and voting to ensure that their mayor and city council would resist the seizure and destruction of the forest. They even sent delegations to the United States to lobby in Congress, to demonstrate in front of the White House, and to build political support for their resistance.

The urbanization of Japan has created a metropolitan corridor between Yokohama and Tokyo which is far more densely populated than the Washington-Boston urban corridor on the East Coast of the United States. Under the assault of this urbanization, the most fundamental values and self-interest of the Japanese people—preservation of nature and the quality of life—are threatened. Mayor Tomino of Zushi has described the fight against the base expansion and destruction of Ikego Forest as a fight against the "slow death of environmental and social destruction."[47]

Miyakejima Island, also known as "Bird Island" because it has attracted bird watchers from around Japan and the world for decades, became the center of national and international controversy in 1983. The U.S. Navy was seeking an alternate base where fighter pilots could practice night landings when the aircraft carrier Midway was at its homeport in Yokosuka. Without practice, the Navy said, its pilots risked losing the skills required to land on a ship pitching wildly at sea. To keep the landing skills of F-4, A-6, and E-2 pilots sharp, the U.S. and the LDP government proposed building a mile-long runway and airport over much of the island's forest and farmland.

The Navy had formerly used Misawa and Iwakuni air bases, far from Yokosuka. Training was moved to Atsugi Base in the Tokyo suburbs, but local residents protested the constant and disturbing noise. They even filed a lawsuit to stop the landing practices at night. The more isolated and politically conservative Miyakejima Island, 110 miles south of Tokyo, which has long been under the protective status of the Japanese Environmental Agency because of its ecological importance, was selected as the new site for night landing exercises. In December 1983, the village council voted in favor of construction of the base.

As in Zushi, the response was swift. Protests to the council and petitions followed immediately, and the next year a strong opponent to the proposed base was elected mayor. In subsequent years base opponents elected a majority to the city council, held many demonstrations, and built support for their anti-base commitment across the country. Like the residents of Zushi, the fishermen, farmers, and other residents of Miyakejima are fighting to preserve an environment and a way of life that is deeply integrated into their personal identity and their vision of the future of Japan.

While larger U.S. bases in Okinawa and across Japan have been the focal point of opposition and protest, they have not sparked the broad-based national concern and opposition that the proposed facilities at Zushi and Miyakejima have engendered. There are several reasons. Bases at Zushi and Miyakejima threaten commonly held and fundamental Japanese values. The opposition to the bases transcends traditional political concerns and debates over sovereignty. It rests on the defense of Japan's existence and identity. The proposed bases in Zushi and Miyakejima, unlike those in Okinawa, are to be built in or near the communication and cultural center of the Tokyo-Yokohama corridor. While many Japanese are willing to let Okinawa be a "prostituted daughter," they resist the prostitution of what they see as the heart of the nation.

For the Future

The U.S.-Japanese relationship has become a profound alliance of economic and technological superpowers, with the United States stressing the military elements of the partnership. Though much attention and concern were focused on Euromissiles and the arms race in Europe during the Reagan years, the North Pacific was the focal point of the U.S. escalation of the arms race. In the same period Japan assumed increasing responsibilities in the U.S.-Japanese alliance. Not surprisingly, Prime Minister Takeshita was the first foreign head of state Bush welcomed to Washington; Japan was the first overseas nation that President Bush visited after his inauguration; and Prime Minister Kaifu hurried to Washington to affirm his commitment to the Mutual Security Treaty within weeks of becoming the Japanese leader in August 1989.

The United States remains deeply committed to "forward deployment" and to its bases and installations in Japan. In 1992, agreements that provide the U.S. access to land for some of its bases are scheduled to expire. This may provide the context for some minor cutbacks, over and above the 10 percent reduction announced by Secretary of Defense Cheney in 1990, but the Pentagon has been clear about its future plans: "In Japan, beyond some personnel reductions, we envision little change in current deployment patterns."[48]

Destabilizing and humiliating forces eat at the core of the relationship, however. U.S.-Japanese interdependence is threatened by the two countries' economic rivalry, and Japan remains a junior partner in the military alliance. The military dimension of U.S.-Japanese relations has remained essentially unchanged since the signing of the Mutual Security Treaty. The United States uses Japan as a base for forward deployment and intervention. In exchange for providing Japan's "security," the United States continues to control many aspects of Japan's foreign policies, including the flow of vital economic resources.

In recent years, the terms of this relationship have again been clearly revealed in the demands of the Bush Administration and the U.S. Congress for Japan to help finance the U.S.-led interventions in the Middle East.

To offset the costs of U.S. intervention to guarantee U.S. control of the flow of oil, Japan has increased its flow of Overseas Development Aid and other financial assistance to strategically important U.S. allies, including Turkey, Egypt, Pakistan, Jordan, the Philippines, and Panama. While financially powerful, Japan's ambitions are limited by its lack of energy and food resources, its history, and continued U.S. military domination.[49]

Japan has choices. Most disturbing to those with memories of World War II is the possibility that Japan will ride its dependence on the United States through the next decade, using the time to transform itself into a military—even nuclear—superpower, freeing itself of U.S. bases and rivaling the power of the United States and a unified Europe. It is in this context that calls from the U.S. Congress and from within the leadership of the Japanese LDP to dispatch elements of the Japanese "Self Defense Forces" in support of U.S. military operations in the Middle East, and to revise or reinterpret Japan's peace constitution, should be read.

There are, however, strong forces within Japan pressing it to concentrate on economic development and financial power while accepting U.S. military leadership. Political and economic forces unleashed by the end of the Cold War, the relative decline of U.S. and Soviet power, and the Japanese desire for peace and sovereignty could also presage a neutral Japan in a truly pacific ocean.

Though the military core of the U.S.-Japanese relationship remains unchanged, Japan's arrival as an economic superpower and the relative economic decline of the United States are placing strains on the old order. Increasingly, the Japanese government is demanding power sharing rather than burdensharing. Tokyo "is willing to shoulder more of the cost of U.S. international commitments, so long as it receives more decision making power in return."[50] The hope in many of Tokyo's elite circles is that a version of Zbigniew Brzezinski's "Amerippon" will prevail. "Amerippon," as described by Brzezinski, is increasing economic competition *and* interdependence between interlocking Japanese and U.S. elites—with Japan playing a greater role in financing U.S. military power. Japan is, however, demanding a price for its subsidies. For example, during the Structural Impediments negotiations, Japan placed explicit demands on the Bush Administration to put the U.S. financial house in order. Closer to home, Japan has won increased freedom of action in its relations with China as it competes there with the United States for economic and political influence.

However, international forces that reinforce the "Mutual Security" order are powerful. Japanese conservatives see the U.S. presence as a cheap price to pay for protection against an unlikely threat to Japanese "security." Though it formerly railed against the U.S. military presence in Japan, the People's Republic of China now supports the Mutual Security Treaty as a means of balancing Soviet power and containing the forces of Japanese militarism. Unlike Europe at the end of the Cold War, there were no diplomatic structures in place for regional arms-control negotiations.

While they are unlikely to prevail in the short term, there are strong forces militating against the continued presence of U.S. bases in Japan. The collapse of the Cold War order removes the rationale of the Soviet threat that long legitimized the bases in the minds of the U.S. and Japanese electorates. In the future, tensions in the Asia/Pacific region may be dominated by traditional balance-of-power contests. Moscow wants Japanese technology and investments in its Far Eastern regions, and it is offering peace proposals to sweeten the diplomatic environment. If the Japanese government considers the Soviet Union's proposals seriously, perhaps in exchange for reversion of the Kurile Islands to Japanese sovereignty, the rationale for maintaining U.S. bases in Japan would be severely undermined. Ecological and traditional Japanese values, as manifested in the protests against base expansions in Zushi and Miyakejima, could add force to the demands of Japanese leftists, pacifists, and concerns from within the Japanese establishment, for true independence, sovereignty, and peace. If it becomes increasingly clear to people in the United States that their youth are serving as mercenaries for "Amerippon," there may be increasing demands for change.

Should the balance of political forces and human imagination change, the withdrawal of U.S. bases from Japan need not create a vacuum to be filled by Japanese militarism. There are serious political visions of a "Pacific Economic Community" including all the Pacific Rim nations, with the Pacific Ocean becoming a sea of peace, freedom, and mutual benefits. Concrete proposals, which need to be further developed through negotiations, have been advocated by Gorbachev and others. They call for the reduction of nuclear and conventional arms in the Pacific, the creation of a nuclear-free zone, and Soviet withdrawal from its base in Cam Ranh Bay in Vietnam in exchange for a U.S. withdrawal from Subic Bay in the Philippines. At least four models for different economic alliances and unions are under study in Tokyo, Washington, and other Pacific Rim capitals. Such proposals, which would deepen the economic integration of the region, can serve as the basis for debate and negotiations for the creation of a nuclear-free, independent, and economically secure Pacific Basin, which includes the United States.

Notes

1. Yukichi Fukuzawa, *The Autobiography of Yukichi Fukuzawa* (New York: Columbia University Press, 1960), 130.

2. John Dower, "The Eye of the Beholder," *Bulletin of Concerned Asian Scholars II*, October 1969, reprinted in Jon Livingston, Joe Moore, and Felicia Oldfather, eds., *Post War Japan: 1945 to the Present* (New York: Pantheon Books, 1973), 236.

3. "Kaifu Uses Trade Reform in Power Bid," *Japan Times*, Weekly International Edition, 19-25 March 1990.

4. Bello, et al., *Bases of Power*, unpublished manuscript, 669.

5. William Appleman Williams, *The Tragedy of American Diplomacy* (New York: Delta, 1959), 16, 161.

6. Gar Alperovitz, *Atomic Diplomacy: Hiroshima and Potsdam: The Use of the Atomic Bomb and the American Confrontation with Soviet Power* (New York: Vintage Books, 1965).

7. John Lehman, "The 600-Ship Navy," *Proceedings*, January 1986.

8. James Baker, 26 June 1989 speech provided by State Department.

9. Joseph Gerson, ed., *The Deadly Connection: Nuclear War and U.S. Intervention* (Philadelphia: New Society Publishers, 1986), 36-60.

10. Edward A. Olsen, *U.S.-Japan Strategic Reciprocity* (Stanford, CA: Hoover Press, 1985), 43.

11. William M. Arkin and Richard W. Fieldhouse, *Nuclear Battlefields: Global Links in the Arms Race* (Cambridge, MA: Ballinger Publishing Co.: 1985), 117.

12. Ibid., 123.

13. Ibid., 124.

14. Bello, et al., 668.

15. See Olsen, 4-6 and 55-58. See also Ian Nish, *The Origins of the Russo-Japanese War* (New York: Longman, 1985), which provides historic perspective on Korea's geo-strategic relationship to Japan and what has become of the Soviet Union.

16. Council Against Atomic and Hydrogen Bombs, Proceedings of 1986 Okinawa International Conference for Prevention of Nuclear War, Elimination of Nuclear Weapons, and a Nuclear Free Pacific, 86.

17. Ibid.

18. John K. Emerson and Harrison M. Holland, *The Eagle and the Rising Sun: America and Japan in the Twentieth Century* (Reading, MA: Addison Wesley, 1988), 57-58.

19. Dower, 234.

20. Livingston, Moore, and Oldfather, 69.

21. Olsen, 7.

22. Fred Greene, *Stresses in U.S.-Japanese Security Relations* (Washington, D.C.: The Brookings Institution, 1975), 25-26.

23. Emerson and Holland, 7-8.

24. Saundra Sturdevant, unpublished study on the impact of U.S. military bases in Korea, Japan, and the Philippines (Hong Kong, July 1988).

25. Emerson and Holland, 8.

26. Livingston, Moore, and Oldfather, 239.

27. *Christian Science Monitor,* 28 February 1989.

28. Council Against Atomic and Hydrogen Bombs, 78.

29. Council Against Atomic and Hydrogen Bombs.

30. Sturdevant. See also "Japan agrees to pay more for U.S. Bases, *Boston Globe,* 3 March 1988, 3.

31. *An Oral History of the Battle of Okinawa, Guide to the Okinawa Prefectural Peace Memorial Museum,* Welfare Department, Okinawa Prefecture, 1985. Material in this section is also drawn from personal interviews in April 1986 by the author with survivors of the invasion of Okinawa and of the "relocation" camps.

32. Ibid., 701.

33. Sturdevant, 10.

34. *Okinawa Information Guide and Business Directory 1967-68* (Naha, Okinawa: International Inspection Co., 1967), 50-51.

35. Arkin and Fieldhouse, 224-226.

36. "Okinawans reject bases," *Philippine Daily Inquirer,* 17 May 1990.

37. Council Against Atomic and Hydrogen Bombs.

38. Evaluation Team Report, 30 September 1977, and photograph from 313th slideshow provided to the author.

39. *New York Times,* 7 April 1987.

40. *Mainichi Shimbun,* 18 May 1981, 1-2, as quoted in Olsen.

41. Olsen, 25.

42. Ibid.

43. Greene, 1.

44. Ibid., 2.

45. *Christian Science Monitor,* 28 September 1988.

46. From a video program shown by a delegation headed by Mayor Tomino of Zushi in Cambridge, MA, 19 February 1988.

47. Statement by Mayor Tomino during visit in Cambridge, MA, 19 February 1988.

48. "Pentagon sees 'little change' in Japan troop deployment," *The Japan Times,* Weekly International Edition, 30 April-6 May 1990. The 3 May 1990 *Far Eastern Economic Review* listed Kadena as one of 34 facilities it is considering closing.

49. Tetsuya Kataoka and Ramon H. Myers, *Defending an Economic Superpower: Reassessing the U.S.-Japan Security Alliance* (Westview Press: Boulder, 1989), 103; Bruce Cummings, "Power and Plenty in Northeast Asia: The Evolution of U.S. Policy," *World Policy Journal,* Winter 1987-88, 79, 82.

50. *New York Times,* 7 March 1989.

Part III: Europe

Chapter 10

The Burdens and the Glory

U.S. Bases in Europe

Diana Johnstone and Ben Cramer

Europe is the center of the United States' overseas basing network. The United States maintains bases and military facilities in nine European NATO countries: Britain, Germany, Italy, Turkey, Greece, Spain, the Netherlands, Belgium, and Iceland. It has bases in the offshore territories of two other countries: Greenland (Denmark) and the Azores (Portugal). Officially, there are no U.S. bases in Norway or Luxemburg, both NATO members, or in France, which left the NATO integrated military command in 1966 while remaining a member of the Atlantic alliance. However, it is impossible to be sure of the precise numbers and locations of all U.S. bases in Europe. Their establishment is usually decided by bilateral executive agreement without consulting the parliaments of the countries concerned. U.S. facilities remain shrouded in a secrecy even more dense for citizens of host countries than for U.S. Congressional researchers.

Of a total of more than 1,600 U.S. military installations, bases, and facilities located overseas, more than 1,200 are in Europe, and at least 892 in the Federal Republic of Germany (FRG). In this densely populated, highly industrialized country, which before the reunification with East Germany had 62 million inhabitants in an area the size of the state of Oregon, the United States has maintained approximately 250,000 military personnel equipped with the most advanced conventional and nuclear weapons. These personnel have regularly used the entire country, including its highways, farmlands, and airspace, as their military exercise terrain.

The officially stated military mission of this imposing array of armed forces has been to prevent a Soviet invasion of Western Europe. Such an invasion was always a most unlikely hypothesis. In practice, the huge military presence has lent concrete reality to the idea of the war that never happens. The fact that no war has ever happened could be interpreted to mean that the danger was exaggerated, or perhaps never existed. On the contrary, the official interpretation is that the vast military deployment was necessary to ward off the Soviet threat and succeeded in keeping the peace.

If the danger never really existed, then it can be argued that a primary mission of U.S. forces in Europe in reality has been to *maintain* the Soviet threat. So long as vast U.S. forces were arrayed in Western Europe in a position to attack (or counterattack) the Soviet Union, the Soviet Union would itself remain in a position to attack (or counterattack) the U.S. forces in Europe. The Soviet and U.S. "threats" maintained each other, and thus their double military hegemony over the European continent.

The mutual-threat system collapsed at the end of the 1980s. Many factors contributed to this collapse. In political terms, the most significant factor was the rise of the peace movements in NATO countries, especially in West Germany, expressing the growing opposition of West European populations to the nuclear arms race. This in turn encouraged Mikhail Gorbachev to take a bold, constructive way out of the crippling arms race by calling for an end to the Cold War.

The rapid changes in Eastern Europe must raise questions about U.S. bases in Western Europe. Except in Germany, the country on the front line of the Cold War battlefield, U.S. bases in Europe were not designed for the defense of the countries where they were located. Rather, from the time NATO was established, they have been part of the vast global military deployment surrounding the Soviet Union. This deployment has ranged from nuclear submarines to vast amounts of electronic and other forms of surveillance and intelligence gathering technologies, with immediate political as well as eventual military uses.

In addition to its theoretical military function of deterring a supposedly global Soviet threat, the U.S. base structure in Europe has exercised the political function of keeping the European NATO allies in a subordinate role within the U.S. sphere of influence. Not only allied military structures, but also their intelligence agencies have been under U.S. control, often with covert effects on European political life. The structure has also maintained Europe as a primary market for the U.S. arms industry. The costs to the European host countries, especially those where U.S. facilities are most extensive—Germany, Britain, and Italy—are impossible to calculate with precision.

How They Got There

.U.S. bases in Europe have a double historical origin: World War II against Germany, which brought them there, and the Cold War against the Soviet Union, which kept them there. The changing perceptions and purposes of U.S. bases in Europe can be summarized in five phases.

Phase 1: Liberation and Conquest

World War II gave the United States access to whatever facilities it wanted in liberated Europe and in conquered Germany itself. The United States also used bases in Britain and in various outposts of the British Empire around the world. After the war, U.S. forces in Europe were rapidly demobilized, dropping from 69 divisions in 1945 to only one in 1950. Before Cold War lines hardened, European allies hastened to recover facilities from the United States. The Azores base was returned to Portugal, Iceland asked U.S. military personnel to leave, and Denmark was attempting to dislodge the U.S. from Greenland.[1] Occupied Germany had nothing to say in the matter.

It was, primarily, the Red Army that defeated the German Wehrmacht. While the United States became the supreme power in the Pacific by defeating Japan, in Europe the Red Army was the strongest force on land. In his *Memoirs*, George Kennan compared the United States in Europe to

> a man who has let himself into a walled garden and finds himself alone there with a dog with very big teeth. The dog, for the moment, shows no signs of aggressiveness. The best thing for us to do is surely to try to establish, as between the two of us, the assumption that the teeth have nothing whatsoever to do with our mutual relationship...[2]

Although the Red Army never showed any sign of crossing the line agreed to at Yalta, U.S. leaders worried about those "teeth." The victorious new president, Harry Truman, had teeth of his own to show: the atomic bomb. This threat continued despite mass demobilization. A month after the first bombs were dropped on Hiroshima and Nagasaki in August 1945, the Joint Chiefs of Staff began secretly planning to seize airfields in Britain and the Far East for an atomic "first blow" against the Soviet Union.

Harry Truman had publicly reacted to the Nazi invasion of the Soviet Union by declaring: "If we see that Germany is winning the war we ought to help Russia, and if Russia is winning we ought to help Germany and in that way let them kill as many as possible." The later U.S. disinclination to make diplomatic compromises was greatly strengthened by its sole possession of the atomic bomb. Disagreements were turned into "threats," and shows of military strength were the U.S. response.

US and Soviet Military Forces in Europe

Iceland

Norway

Sweden

Finland

USSR

Denmark

Ireland

United Kingdom

Netherlands

Belgium

Luxembourg

East Germany

West Germany

Poland

Czechoslovakia

France

Switzerland

Austria

Hungary

Rumania

Portugal

Spain

Italy

Yugoslavia

Albania

Greece

Bulgaria

Turkey

AFRICA

Countries in which more than 1,000 U. S. troops were deployed in 1989.

Countries in which more than 1,000 Soviet troops were deployed in 1989. (All Soviet troops are supposed to be removed from Czechoslovakia and Hungary by mid-1991, and from Germany by 1995 at the latest.

The more noble version of U.S. post-war policy toward the Soviet Union was developed by diplomat George F. Kennan, whose February 1946 "long telegram" from Moscow to the State Department stressed the specifically internal Russian sources of Soviet conduct ignored by U.S. policy makers in Washington. In May 1947, Kennan was placed in charge of foreign policy planning by Secretary of State George C. Marshall. His July 1947 article in *Foreign Affairs* on "The Sources of Soviet Conduct" introduced the concept of "containment" that ostensibly governed U.S. policy toward the Soviet Union from then on.[3]

The Soviet Union and the United States emerged from the war in opposite conditions with correspondingly opposing interests. Soviet leaders had one overriding economic interest: reparations, in order to rebuild their own devastated country. They had an even more imperative security interest: to prevent another invasion from the West such as they had just suffered. United States policy makers had good reasons for opposing German reparations. Heavy reparations payments had undermined German democracy after World War I. Moreover, U.S. economic planners soon realized that they needed German economic recovery in order to give U.S. production a European market to replace the war market that had brought the United States out of the Depression.

Such differences could conceivably have been resolved by diplomacy, but social revolution in Russia had broken the elite network which traditionally makes diplomacy function between Western states. Kennan's argument that the Russians had their own impervious way of thinking led the United States to proceed and to present the Kremlin with accomplished facts. In 1946, the U.S. occupation authorities suspended reparations deliveries from the U.S. zone of occupied Germany to the USSR. This policy incited the Russians to intensify exploitation of territories they occupied.

The British and the United States took the first step toward division of Germany by merging the administration of their occupied zones—amounting to most of the territory of the future Federal Republic—as the Bizone in January 1947. In the anti-communist ideological mindset, Soviet reparation demands came to be interpreted as a deliberate effort to impoverish the West and thus to promote communism.

In June 1947, Secretary of State George Marshall made his famous speech launching the "Marshall Plan." In April 1948 Congress passed the Foreign Assistance Act, preparing the ground for the Marshall Plan, which in four years distributed just under $13 billion through the Economic Cooperation Administration. Meanwhile, in July 1947, to preserve the economic independence of the Soviet Union, Stalin refused to participate in the Marshall Plan.

The final break between East and West came with the surprise Anglo-American reform of the West German currency in June 1948. All old Reichs-marks became worthless and had to be exchanged for the new Deutschmark. When the Western occupation powers extended the reform to Berlin, the Russians panicked and, on June 24, shut the land routes to the city. This was Moscow's rude way of demanding negotiations on the future of the whole of Germany. Instead, the United States took it as a challenge to the "Free World," and responded with the 11-month Berlin Air Lift. This provided the founding saga that justified the historic switch of alliances bringing West Germany into the anti-Soviet Western alliance.

Moscow and Washington interpreted each other's moves with suspicion. Both were reductionist and pessimistic. Washington interpreted Moscow's policies and actions as a purposeful drive toward expansion of political power. Soviet analysts correctly forecast a worldwide expansion of U.S. capitalism, especially into war-wrecked Europe, and feared that such expansion would restore the pre-war "cordon sanitaire" of hostile neighbors along the Soviet Union's western border.

Cold War ideology rested on the identification made by each World War II victor, the United States and the Soviet Union, of the other with Nazi Germany. For the United States, the Soviet Union, like Nazi Germany, was "totalitarian." For the Russians, the United States, like Nazi Germany, was "imperialist." Both these labels fell short of the full truth. Both fostered enemy stereotypes and the vision of the other as a threat comparable to Hitler.

"American decision-makers misinterpreted the Soviet Union's security policy as proof of unlimited Soviet expansionism, and reacted by refusing further cooperation," concludes West German historian Wilfried Loth. "The Soviet leadership misinterpreted this refusal to cooperate as proof of the necessarily aggressive character of expanding U.S. capitalism and reacted by further hardening its security policy. In the years after 1945, this vicious circle was never broken; and so the building of blocs became more and more definitive."[4]

Phase 2: The Atlantic Alliance

By obliging the Eastern European countries to join the Soviet Union in rejecting the Marshall Plan, Stalin took the decisive step toward suppressing the fragile democracy of the "people's democracies." To defend this unpopular course, the Soviet leadership revived the international communist movement that had been dissolved with the Comintern as a sacrifice to the war-time alliance with the West. In September 1947, when the "Cominform" was created at a meeting of Communist Parties in Poland, Andrei Zhdanov laid down the "two-camps" line, dramatically describing the Marshall Plan as a "plan for enslaving Europe." Communist Parties were called upon to lead the resistance of the "anti-imperialist democratic camp."

The massive strikes that shook France and Italy in the following months, fanned by their Communist Parties, brought the Cold War into European domestic politics. The result was certainly counter-productive from the Soviet viewpoint. The Communist Parties were expelled from coalition governments in both France and Italy. Socialist Interior Minister Jules Moch sent nearly 40,000 troops to put down strikes in northern France, and the CIA helped anti-communist unionists split the French labor movement.

It was French leaders who pressed the United States to form a military alliance against the communist threat. Washington knew at the time that there was no threat of Soviet invasion. But France's political class was weak and nervous. Few had forgotten France's ignominious collapse in 1940. The glorification of the Resistance had primarily benefited the French Communist Party, which received more than a quarter of the vote in post-war elections and which had, by far, the largest membership of any party in France. De Gaulle had retired to wait for his ungrateful nation to need him. The politicians in Paris sought U.S. protection against their own communists.

The late 1940s were years of bloc building marked by the creation of the Atlantic Alliance and by the division of Germany. There is a French myth of a Soviet-American deal to partition Germany. Evidence indicates otherwise. In the first months of the occupation, when Germany was run by four occupation powers—the Soviet Union, the United States, Britain, and France—it was France that systematically obstructed efforts to build a unified German administration. The Soviet Union, on the contrary, wanted to keep Germany as a single unit in order to demand reparations from the whole country. Official Soviet policy was to blame fascism, rather than the German people, for the crimes of Hitler's era, and to favor a single, neutral German state.

The division of Germany was the result of the incorporation of West Germany into the Western economic, monetary, and—finally—military systems. Each step of the way—the creation of a German state and the establishment of a military alliance—it was the United States which moved first and the Russians who followed. Throughout this phase, Soviet diplomacy was characterized by a certain brutal pessimism. In contrast, the United States innovated boldly and successfully. Washington had the advantageous role. Europeans naturally preferred being occupied by a rich power that was handing things out rather than by a poor power that was carting things away.

Ironically, the Berlin blockade accelerated the two developments it was intended to stop: the North Atlantic Treaty was signed in April 1949, and the Federal Republic of Germany was proclaimed a month later.

Phase 3: NATO Militarizes the Cold War

The year 1950 was a watershed year. The Atlantic Alliance was transformed into a permanent U.S. military occupation of Western Europe. "Containment," initially a rich (and thus necessarily misunderstood) political concept, was reduced to a military doctrine.

The new policy was spelled out in April 1950 by Paul Nitze, who succeeded George Kennan as head of the State Department's planning staff, in the famous National Security Memorandum NSC-68.[5] In cahoots with Dean Acheson, Nitze set out to frighten the Truman Administration and Congress into a major increase in military spending. NSC-68 laid the doctrinal foundations of the military Keynesianism which has dominated U.S. policy ever since.

According to NSC-68:

> One of the most significant lessons of our World War II experience was that the American economy, when it operates at a level approaching full efficiency, can provide enormous resources for purposes other than civilian consumption while simultaneously providing a higher standard of living.

World War II taught that the cure to the Depression was both guns and butter. The "purposes other than civilian consumption" were the redevelopment of military power. NSC-68 warned that "more positive government programs" were necessary to avoid "a decline in economic activity of serious proportions." The programs were military buildups, and the pretext was the "Soviet threat." NSC-68 declared that "a substantial and rapid building up of strength in the free world is necessary to support a firm policy intended to check and rollback the Kremlin's drive for world domination."

NSC-68 portrayed the diabolical threat justifying these expenditures in melodramatic tones. The United States was threatened by a Soviet Union "animated by a new fanatic faith, antithetical to our own" which "seeks to impose its absolute authority over the rest of the world." The proof of this mortal danger lay not in any visible threats but in the very nature of the Soviet Union, "inescapably militant because it possesses and is possessed by a worldwide revolutionary movement, because it is the inheritor of Russian imperialism and because it is a totalitarian dictatorship." The proof of Soviet expansionism was not in anything it did, but in what it was—an ideological allegation impossible to prove or disprove.

The Korean War began two months later—just in time to support this vision. Truman's recent promise to cut defense spending was forgotten. Military appropriations for fiscal 1951 were hastily increased from $13.5 billion to $48.2 billion. Thanks to the ideological concept of a monolithic "communist threat"—quite contrary to Kennan's initial pluralistic analysis[6]— the Korean War, even though it was in Asia, served as the pretext to build up U.S. forces in Europe. In September 1950, the decision was taken to send four divisions back to Europe to build a NATO force under the command of General Dwight D. Eisenhower. Acheson called this "a complete revolution in American foreign policy." It transformed the Atlantic alliance into something entirely new: a military organization bringing the European allies largely under U.S. command.

In 1951, Iceland, which has no armed forces, turned over responsibility for its defense to the United States on behalf of NATO. The United States was granted use of a tactical air-defense radar site at Hofn and the base at Keflavik near Reykjavik, the capital. In the same year Denmark granted the United States basing rights in Greenland. Port facilities were obtained in Bordeaux (France), Livorno and Naples (Italy). In 1953, basing agreements were signed with Greece, which belonged to NATO, and Spain, which did not.

Considering the hostility that prevailed between the Soviet Union and the United States, each identifying the other with Nazi Germany, war might indeed have broken out. But what would it have been about? What exactly was the "threat" each posed to the other?

The Soviet Union never showed the slightest inclination to overstep the Elbe boundary agreed to at Yalta. Soviet forces withdrew from Finland and Austria. In short, there was never the slightest evidence of Soviet military expansionism. The "threat" of the Communist Parties in Italy and France was also grossly exaggerated. In fact, neither had a revolutionary agenda.

The Western threat to the Soviet bloc was more plausible. The West contested the legitimacy of the Eastern bloc regimes, and West Germany had territorial claims in Poland and the western Soviet Union. The "rollback" policy was supported in the United States by Eastern European exiles, many of whom had worked with the Nazis in World War II.

There was never any Soviet challenge to Western legitimacy. The only conceivable Soviet military threat was to the Western sectors of Berlin. But Soviet offers to negotiate a permanent settlement of the German problem, including Berlin (made first by Stalin and later by Khrushchev), were rejected in favor of NATO and the status quo. The linkage of the "Soviet threat" to internal "communist subversion" was a pretext for U.S. interference in Europe's domestic political affairs, facilitated by subordination of allied intelligence agencies to the CIA. The "common enemy" was invoked to promote the Western European economic integration sought by the United States in the framework of Atlantic unity.

Phase 4: Flexible Response, or 'Anything Goes'

By 1960, the original doctrine of "massive retaliation" was collapsing as the Soviet Union also accumulated sufficient forces to retaliate massively itself. U.S. strategists then developed the doctrine of "flexible response." The change, pursued while Robert McNamara was Defense Secretary, was motivated by the more than justified horror at the apocalyptic prospects of "massive retaliation."

With "Mutual Assured Destruction" (MAD), the two superpower arsenals deterred each other from the Apocalypse. But did they deter anything else? "Flexible response" was an attempt to maintain the global order through nuclear deterrence, including lesser threats to the prevailing order, such as minor border violations, for which blowing up the world was hardly a credible response. In practice, the new doctrine led to the proliferation of nuclear weapons of various types and ranges, accompanied by ever more abstruse theories about their use.

Flexible response brought contradictory results: a huge military buildup in West Germany, in order to be able to respond flexibly; and the onset of growing European doubts about nuclear deterrence. Flexible response meant that U.S. nuclear weapons could no longer be counted on to deter the Russians or to strike them all dead in a pre-emptive attack; instead these weapons might destroy the Europe they were deployed to defend. To prepare for this possibility, the number of nuclear weapons grew and the presence of military forces became more intrusive. The climax came in 1979 with the decision to deploy U.S. cruise and Pershing II nuclear missiles in five European NATO countries. This set off the Euromissiles controversy of the 1980s.[7]

Moreover, just as Europe was becoming more prosperous and self-confident, U.S. policy makers reasserted U.S. leadership. "Logically, flexible response reinforced the need to centralize control of all NATO forces under an American Supreme Allied Commander," noted David Calleo.[8]

The 1960s saw the first stirrings of independent policy-making in Western Europe. In 1966, de Gaulle withdrew from the joint military command of NATO and expelled U.S. military bases from France. The French stressed the distinction between the Atlantic Alliance with the United States, whose value they did not question, and the integrated military organization of NATO under U.S. command from which they withdrew. De Gaulle's France rejected Flexible Response and committed France to a miniature version of Massive Retaliation. The shift in German attitudes was more gradual, but in the long run more decisive. Through the 1960s, the "rollback" policy of Adenauer was gradually abandoned in favor of a new approach toward Eastern Europe, the Ostpolitik championed initially by the Social Democratic Party (SPD) before being eventually accepted by the German political establishment as a whole.

Phase 5: Redistribution of Empire

"Flexible response" was by no means limited to Europe. It involved responding to "challenges" around the world and included waging anti-insurgency war in Indochina. The war in Vietnam aroused European awareness that NATO was part of a global military machine engaged in conflicts contrary to European judgment or interests.

After Vietnam, the Pentagon turned to surrogates in the Third World and sought to devolve some of its global policing to its European NATO allies. In the 1980s this change of policy was reflected in U.S. demands for greater "burdensharing" by the European allies and for "out-of-area" (outside the NATO treaty area) operations. European forces would either assume responsibilities for these operations, or they would replace U.S. forces in Europe—freeing them for other theaters such as the Persian Gulf. This phase is marked by the shift of the perceived "threat" from the communist East to the third world South, a shift that began before Gorbachev. It is also marked by a shift from heavy to lighter military forces, from ground forces to highly mobile aeronaval forces that can be moved rapidly to trouble spots anywhere in the world. To accomplish this shift, U.S. military planners have been more willing to reduce force levels rather than to dismantle bases which can continue to be used in the Pentagon's policing of the global system. The future of U.S. bases in Europe may depend largely on how European policy toward the third world South develops in the 1990s.

Changing Missions in Northern and Southern Europe

The role of U.S. bases in Europe has differed from time to time and from country to country. From the beginning, a geographical hierarchy has distinguished the nations of Northern Europe, taken by the United States as serious partners, and the more subordinate allies of Southern Europe. The most "serious" partners were Britain, the United States' principal ally in World War II and the imperial power whose global role the United States inherited; and West Germany, the major continental power whose industrial and military capacity the United States chose to revive under its own hegemony.

Britain

The United States and Britain emerged from World War II with close ties but very unequal power. Britain was exhausted and the United States was at the pinnacle of world economic and military power. The U.S. establishment set about replacing *Pax Britannica* with a *Pax Americana* more firmly based in a world system that was no longer fragmented between rival European empires. Obliged to surrender its empire, the British establishment clung to the "special relationship" that made it the United States' most privileged partner in *Pax Americana*. To a considerable extent, declining Britain acted as tutor in global hegemony for the United States. Britain provided the fundamental model for exercising global hegemony by means of power projection through a network of far-flung military bases.

The takeover began early in World War II, when the United States obtained bases in the British West Indies in exchange for lend-lease economic aid to the British war effort. In 1941, the United States was granted bases in Jamaica and Bermuda. In 1947, a secret agreement called UKUSA provided for a global system of electronic spying called "signals intelligence" (Sigint), using the far-flung facilities of the British Commonwealth and involving the whole English-speaking world in surveillance of the rest of the planet.[9] Britain was the center of these activities, which fell increasingly under U.S. control.

Concern with retaining the "special relationship" made British governments uniquely indulgent when it came to U.S. demands for basing rights, as Duncan Campbell documented in his book, *The Unsinkable Aircraft Carrier*. The United States withdrew from most of its United Kingdom bases within a few months of the May 1945 victory over Germany, but as early as mid-1946 the U.S. Air Force obtained permission to use British bases for atomic bomb missions in an emergency, and construction began to equip five Royal Air Force (RAF) bases with atomic bomb loading pits. At the start of the Berlin blockade in June 1948, the British government secretly agreed to let U.S. bombers use British bases, and nominally RAF bases began being placed under U.S. control. "Since the U.S. Air Force returned in 1948," writes Duncan Campbell, "there has been a *de facto* policy of 'open house.'"

In the early 1950s, the U.S. Strategic Air Command settled into Britain, using it as the primary forward base for "Massive Retaliation" against the Soviet Union. The basing rights were never defined in any treaty or executive agreement, much less submitted to Parliament for approval.

The only public document on use of bases in an emergency was a January 1952 communique by President Harry Truman and Prime Minister Winston Churchill issued from the presidential yacht Williamsburg declaring that: "Under arrangements made for the common defense, the United States has the use of certain bases in the United Kingdom. We reaffirm the understanding that the use of these bases in an emergency would be a matter for joint decision by Her Majesty's government and the United States government in the light of the circumstances prevailing at the time."

The "understanding" was, in fact, an institutionalized misunderstanding. Under questioning from members of Parliament, British government leaders maintain from time to time that the "understanding" gives Britain a right to veto U.S. nuclear attacks launched from British soil. However, U.S. officials have repeatedly denied the existence of such a veto. Because they are the ones who control the bombs, it is the U.S. understanding that is operational.

U.S. nuclear weapons in Britain are an incalculable hazard to the population and the environment. In July 1956, a serious accident involving a nuclear weapon at the Lakenheath air base sent U.S. forces stampeding away in panic. No warning was given to the local population, and the incident was kept secret until 1979. At least 20 nuclear accidents occurred between 1947 and 1964.

The British government provides the United States with rent-free land for its bases, and buys more land when the United States decides to expand. Such purchases cost Britain $70 million between 1973 and 1982. In addition, Britain has paid well over a billion dollars per decade into the NATO infrastructure funds that pay for base facilities in Europe used by the United States.

So uncontrolled was U.S. base expansion in Britain that when, in the 1980s, curiosity was whetted by the cruise missile controversy, nobody could say for sure how many bases and smaller facilities the United States was actually using in Britain. In the last few years, investigators have set the figure as high as 135.

This carte blanche is all the more remarkable in that the U.S. bases are all in service of the United States' global strategy; none of them have to defend the British Isles as such. On the contrary, British forces are supposed to defend the U.S. bases. The British anti-nuclear movement has pointed out that the presence of these U.S. bases decreases British security by making Britain a prime target for Soviet nuclear attack in case of conflict.

Less conspicuous than the Air Force bases are the intelligence facilities of all kinds located in the British isles: everything from electronic ears that bug private telephone conversations in Western as well as Eastern Europe, to a CIA arsenal set up during the Cold War to arm guerrillas for the "liberation" of Eastern European countries. One example is the medieval Chicksands Priory near Bedford, used by the RAF since 1941 for electronic spying on northern Germany and Poland. It was taken over by the U.S. Air

Force in 1950, and the United States has been there ever since. From Chicksands Priory, the United States not only spies on the Russians but it monitors its *allies'* diplomatic communications. This "NATO" facility serves only the United States, which does not allow NATO allies access to information gathered at Chicksands.[10] Another example is the National Security Agency station at Menwith Hill near Harrogate. Since 1966 it has fed private international telecommunications messages of citizens, businesses, and friendly governments into its computers.[11]

There is an an immeasurable political dimension to U.S.-British cooperation: espionage. "In the secret world, the Anglo-Saxon intelligence axis has been durable and powerful," writes Duncan Campbell. "No feature of the special relationship, other than the trade in nuclear weapons know-how, has been of comparable importance in binding together the British and American political and military establishments."

The special relationship that began in July 1948 with a 30-day "temporary" visit by several B-29 squadrons has transformed Britain into the overseas base for one-fifth of all U.S. Air Force strength abroad. The huge Lakenheath base in Suffolk, as well as 10 other air bases, a naval base, communications and intelligence centers, and nuclear weapons storage bunkers are facilities that the Pentagon has all to itself. It uses them for its own purposes, as the April 1986 bombing raid on Libya from bases in Britain clearly illustrated. Indeed, the use of bombers based in Britain was widely seen as dictated by political rather than military considerations: it was a way of implicating NATO allies in a unilateral "out-of-area" mission massively disapproved by public opinion in all NATO countries, including Britain.

Germany

While the Cold War expansion of U.S. bases transformed Britain from an ally into an occupied country, the same process transformed West Germany from an occupied country into an ally. This was the process deliberately and shrewdly promoted by the first West German Chancellor, Konrad Adenauer, recommended by a group of former Wehrmacht officers who managed, with astonishing speed, to make themselves indispensable military advisers to the U.S. occupation forces by turning their attention to the unfinished conquest of the East. These were officers who blamed Hitler for plunging Germany into a two-front war. They argued that Germany should have made peace and even alliances with the Western allies, the better to pursue the crusade against Bolshevism in the East. After the war, such German officers found friendly ears in the U.S. officer corps for their accumulated expertise in making war against the Soviet Union. Thus General Franz Halder, the former German Army chief of staff, was absorbed into the

U.S. Army's Operational Historical German Section and was awarded for his "lasting contribution to the tactical and strategic thinking of the U.S. Armed Forces."[12]

In the last year of the war, Wehrmacht General Hans Speidel proposed the so-called West Solution involving a cease-fire with the Allied Expeditionary Forces which would have allowed them to occupy Berlin and most of Germany before the Soviets. It also would have freed the Wehrmacht to concentrate on halting the Red Army. Hitler rejected the proposal, and Speidel was mildly disgraced—good for his rapid post-war rehabilitation. By 1946, Speidel was a member of Prince Max Eugen von Furstenberg's select circle which planned future German policy with prominent political leaders, notably Adenauer. These consultations were discreet, since both the Allied High Commission and the German people were opposed to any revival of German militarism.

At an October 1950 meeting in the Himmerod cloister in the Eifel Mountains, Speidel and 14 other senior Wehrmacht officers drafted what was later called the Magna Carta of German Rearmament. They understood that to revive the German Army, it had to be conceived as a contribution to a Western army. They thus sought to have the Western Allies shift the western defense line from the Rhine to the eastern boundary of Germany, and to include West Germany in the Western security system. The Himmerod gathering concluded that: "The restitution of the stolen Eastern territories is an unalterable necessity for the existence of the German people." The continuity between the thinking of Third Reich officers who wanted to ally with the West against the Soviet Union and the formation of a Western alliance including Germany, on the advice of some of those same officers, was strikingly clear to Soviet leaders. Seen from Moscow, this Western-plus-German alliance appeared to be aimed at the "rollback" called for by right-wing politicians, with the objective of regaining German territories lost to Poland and the Soviet Union.

It was the outbreak of the Korean War that permitted the clandestine post-war German general staff to succeed. Adenauer saw and seized the opportunity to recover German sovereignty, which he identified with the possession of armed forces, by dramatizing the similarities between the situation in Germany and the causes of the war in Korea. The two situations were totally different, not least because Secretary of State Dean Acheson had officially excluded South Korea from the U.S. global defense perimeter, whereas the Berlin Airlift had already illustrated U.S. determination to hold every bit of German territory occupied by the Western Allies.

Although West Germany did not actually join NATO until May 1955, due largely to French stalling tactics, the alliance between U.S. and German remilitarization was founded in 1950 on the basis of Nitze's NSC-68 doctrine. The alliance rested on a coincidence of interest between German partisans of rearmament and sovereignty, and U.S. advocates of military Keynesianism—the use of military spending to avoid recession and unemployment. (Ironically, this economic use of military spending was initiated by Hitler's National Socialist Workers Party to pull Germany out of the 1930s Depression.)

In 1950, U.S. bases in West Germany were a mark of recovered German sovereignty. Adenauer managed to persuade the U.S. to hasten the change in the function of its forces from "occupation" to "protection." Moreover, the better to justify the creation of a German army, the Germans demanded a Western buildup of forces in West Germany, including more U.S. forces, to which the Germans would then also contribute. In 1950, the United States had 145,000 troops in Europe. By 1955, the level had risen to 405,000. The U.S. buildup confirmed the notion that there was a mortal threat from the East, and thereby justified German rearmament.

In November 1951 talks in Bonn and Paris between Acheson, Anthony Eden, Maurice Schumann, and Adenauer resulted in a treaty lifting the occupation status. Article 7.3, known as the "binding clause," specified that "a reunited Germany will be bound to" the Federal Republic's treaty engagements. This made it impossible for Bonn to accept Stalin's March 10, 1952 note proposing the reunification of an armed but nonaligned Germany.

The paradox was that, inasmuch as rollback was a slogan and not a real option, the price for the type of sovereignty sought by Adenauer was the division of Germany—and a military occupation under the guise of "defense." With jets screeching overhead, tanks rumbling through villages and maneuvering armies trampling across their fields, many Germans, particularly in the 1980s, heard and saw more clearly the limits to the sovereignty achieved by Adenauer and his military advisers.

Southern Europe

The United States historically has sought to use Southern European bases without granting the host countries even a pretense of shared regional leadership. U.S. policy makers originally intended the North Atlantic Alliance to be just that. Italy was included only because France insisted on balancing Norway with a Latin country.

A 1979 report to Congress observed,

> Since World War II, Southern European countries have been governed by a combination of unstable democracies and "stable" but undemocratic regimes. For a number of years, U.S. policy generally accepted the stability of authoritarian right-wing regimes in some

Southern European countries as preferable to the possibility of political chaos.

The North-South hierarchy was not solely a matter of political stability. Economic clout was also a factor. "The Southern European countries do not in general have a decisive input with respect to the management of the international trading system," the report noted.[13]

From the official U.S. vantage point, its bases in Southern Europe were not so much an extension of the peer partnership with the British and the Germans as they were a transition toward the global power projection of bases in the Third World. They marked the United States' succession to Britain as world hegemonic power.

The turning point came on February 21, 1947, when the British Foreign Office officially informed the State Department that Britain could no longer maintain its forces in Greece, which were then fighting the communist-led war-time resistance forces on behalf of the local Anglophile oligarchy. Post-war Britain was too poor to continue policing the Eastern Mediterranean, even if Stalin had long since written Greece off as belonging to the Anglo-American sphere of influence. State Department planners were thrilled. One diplomat exulted, "Great Britain had within the hour handed the job of world leadership, with all its burdens and all its glory, to the United States."[14]

Conservative Republican congressional leaders were skeptical. To convince them to finance the burdens and the glory, Under Secretary of State Dean Acheson "pulled out all the stops" in a flight of fantasy whose traces endure to this day. Soviet pressure had reached the point at which

> highly possible Soviet breakthrough might open three continents to Soviet penetration…The corruption of Greece would infect Iran and all the East. It would also carry infection to Africa through Asia Minor and Egypt, and to Europe through Italy and France, already threatened by the strongest domestic Communist Parties in Western Europe. The Soviet Union was playing one of the greatest gambles in history at minimal cost.

Whereas Stalin had written Greece off as part of the Western sphere, refused to aid the communist partisans there, and was hardly about to "gamble" on three other continents, the United States habitually has had an eye on more distant horizons, especially where there is oil. The United States took over from Britain, turning the Mediterranean into an "American Lake," with bases and alliances controlling the straits at Bosphorus and Gibraltar.

U.S. bases in Italy have been outposts of interference in Italian democracy, considered unsafe because of the large Communist Party. When U.S. forces landed in Sicily in 1943, the first thing the OSS (Office of Secret Services, predecessor to the CIA) did was to rush to free the Mafia bosses jailed by the Fascist regime.[15] To combat the "Communist threat," the United States put the Mafia back on its feet in Sicily—perhaps the most lasting accomplishment of *Pax Americana.*

Even George Kennan, the most enlightened of senior U.S. policy makers of the period, recommended in March 1948 that the United States should provoke "civil war" in Italy rather than let the Communists win a "bloodless electoral victory." Sicilian separatists with Mafia connections were also encouraged, for possible use in the future against an Italian government that moved too far left for U.S. taste.

U.S. bases in Italy thus became part of the militarization of domestic Italian politics. Communist labor organizers were eliminated from Fiat factories "for security reasons," ostensibly because of military contracts, to the delight of management. Italian and U.S. intelligence agencies cooperated against the enemy from within. Whether or not the United States would have intervened militarily from its Italian bases to overthrow an elected left-wing government remains a matter of speculation. The widespread Italian belief that it would do so cannot be contested, and this belief has been a significant factor in Italian politics. Politicians, from the Christian Democrats to the neo-fascists, soon learned how to manipulate Washington's neurotic fear of communism to win favors.

In Southern Europe, U.S. bases were clearly a sign of the limitation of sovereignty—a limitation sought and fostered by local ruling parties in order to exclude the left opposition, particularly Communist Parties.

France

In U.S.-occupied post-war Europe, France's strategic position was between North and South. Formally, France was one of the victorious allies, a permanent member of the United Nations Security Council, and one of the four occupation powers in defeated Germany. France still had a colonial empire, the second in size after Britain's. France was thus one of the Atlantic nations (with the Netherlands, Belgium, and Portugal) that had shared in the West's global hegemony under *Pax Britannica.*

But the military collapse of 1940 demoralized France's ruling elite, and only the eccentric General Charles de Gaulle had managed to create the illusion that they were on the winning side. Like Italy, France had a large Communist Party and seemed, politically, even more unstable and unreliable.

The often schizophrenic nature of French foreign policy stems from the impossible contradictions it faced. Enfeebled France needed the Atlantic Alliance with the United States to pursue its traditional goals: holding German power in check in Europe, and preserving its colonies abroad. However, the United States favored independence for colonies and a privileged alliance with Germany.

The United States favored independence for colonies because it was assuming the "burdens and the glory" of *Pax Britannica*. Former French foreign minister Christian Pineau recalled that Eisenhower's Secretary of State, John Foster Dulles, "was convinced that in case of war, neither France nor Great Britain were militarily or psychologically capable of assuring the protection of the territories whose defense was entrusted to them." Pineau explained that "United States policy...consist[ed] in eliminating the French and British from the strategic points held by them in the world in order to replace them with American forces."[16]

The dramatic upshot of this certainty that the United States could succeed where France had failed was that the United States took over the French war in Vietnam, rather than allowing it to be resolved at the peace table.

The rapprochement between U.S. policy makers and German advocates of rearmament caused dismay in Paris. In late 1950, French statesmen led by Jean Monnet contrived a plan (named for the prime minister of the moment, René Pleven) for a European Defense Community (EDC) that would keep Germany's revived military forces out of German control. After being amended to increase German autonomy, the EDC was rejected by the French parliament in August 1954. This was a Pyrrhic victory of Gaullists, communists, and other guardians of French independence. Prime Minister Pierre Mendes-France allowed the EDC to be defeated, the better to ram through West German membership in NATO.

The Federal Republic of Germany was brought into NATO by way of the Western European Union (WEU), a 1948 mutual defense treaty signed by Britain, France, and the Benelux states directed against Germany. The WEU's history is a history of paradoxes. Originally sold to Western public opinion as a sign of the "Third Force," a European independent initiative, it was stimulated from behind the scenes by the United States, which demanded steps toward European unification in return for a protective alliance. In October 1954, the WEU treaty was revised to include West Germany.

In April 1949, France had signed a North Atlantic Treaty that seemed to formalize and perpetuate the victorious alliances of the two world wars. The Alliance was to be directed by a standing military committee of the Big Three: Britain, France, and the United States.[17] Five years later, France was bullied into admitting West Germany into an Alliance that had changed from a classical alliance to a military organization: the North Atlantic Treaty Organization, with a U.S. supreme commander who made decisions without consulting the French—or anybody else. France had always wanted the Alliance. In de Gaulle's view, on the other hand, the Organization was "the price France had to pay for the Marshall Plan."

Meanwhile, the United States had secured its bases in France through a series of secret accords: a major air base at Chateauroux in central France in 1951, four other Air Force bases accommodating 62,000 U.S. military personnel in 1952, an Army base at Saint-Germain-en-Laye near Paris in 1953, as well as communications and transport facilities.

When General de Gaulle returned to power in 1958, he asked the U.S. NATO commander, General Lauris Norstad, to tell him how many U.S. nuclear warheads were based on French soil, and where. General Norstad replied that he could not reveal this vital information to the French chief of state. De Gaulle also asked Eisenhower and Macmillan to restore the original three-power consultations on Alliance policy. When they refused, the French leader decided to steer France on its own course, both inside and outside of the NATO area.

In 1959, de Gaulle ordered the United States to remove its nuclear weapons, wherever they might be, from French soil. The Eisenhower Administration transferred U.S. nuclear weapons and nuclear-capable bombers to bases in Britain and West Germany.

By 1966, the international context had changed considerably. De Gaulle had ceded independence to Algeria, and France was free of its debilitating colonial wars. The United States, rejecting the Indochina settlement negotiated after France's 1954 defeat at Dien Bien Phu, had taken up where France left off, confident that it could do better.

Unable to convince the Anglo-Americans to coordinate "out-of-area" policy with France, de Gaulle took advantage of France's new freedom from colonial war entanglements to pursue a "third worldist" foreign policy. This new course was jeopardized by French membership in a military organization headed by the superpower intent on pursuing a lost war in Southeast Asia.

In March 1966, France withdrew its forces stationed in Germany from the NATO command and invited the United States to withdraw all its NATO bases from France. That August, as guest of Prince Norodom Sihanouk in Phnom Penh, de Gaulle called for neutrality of the Indochinese peoples and warned that pursuit of the U.S. war in Vietnam could lead to the worst misfortunes. One month later, NATO headquarters were transferred from Paris to Brussels.

The French case is exceptional: France is the only European ally that expelled all U.S. bases. The policy was popular at the time—polls showed a majority of French people favored both continued membership in the

Atlantic Alliance and withdrawal from NATO—and created the basis of a lasting consensus in French defense policy. In France, the removal of U.S. bases pulled the rug out from under the Communist Party's "Yankee go home" campaign, and even secured a certain unavowed support from communist leaders. Abroad, limited rhetorical anti-Americanism was helpful in maintaining the largest remaining neo-colonial sphere of influence in Africa, as well as territories in the Western Hemisphere and the Pacific.

In or Out of Area?

U.S. bases in Europe have served one constant purpose: they have been the actual and symbolic core of a worldwide system of U.S. military power. The establishment of NATO placed the U.S.-Soviet ideological confrontation at the center of U.S. global deployments. The standoff in Central Europe provided a definition of purpose for U.S. forces everywhere; all were engaged in "containing Soviet expansionism." This global ideological mission obscured the historical continuity with the imperialist power projection of U.S. bases in third world countries like the Philippines during the nineteenth century.

Theoretically, all other conflicts were extensions of the European confrontation between the Soviet communist bloc and the "free world." This interpretation was never accepted in Europe as it was in the United States. In the 1990s, with the collapse of the Soviet bloc in Eastern Europe, it has lost all credibility. New rationales will be required to maintain Europe as a base for U.S. "out-of-area" interventions.

U.S.-European cooperation in relation to the Third World has been marked by three periods. In the first phase the United States was supremely self-confident after having emerged from World War II victorious, rich, and in sole possession of the atomic bomb. The United States supported independence for the third world colonies of Britain, France, the Netherlands, and Belgium, in the expectation that it could do a better job in keeping those nations inside the "free world"—i.e., the capitalist free-trade area. The emblematic event of this phase was United States' disavowal of the joint 1956 Franco-British-Israeli invasion of Egypt to recover the Suez Canal.

The second phase followed when U.S.-supported decolonization failed to function smoothly. The United States put its earlier beliefs to the test by intervening militarily to set things straight: in the Belgian Congo, Lebanon, and Laos. The high, or low, point of this phase was the Vietnam war.

The third phase opened when the United States realized it could not manage the world as easily as the wise men of Washington had anticipated. The United States then began turning to the former colonial powers for help.

The 1980s were thus marked by U.S. exhortations to its allies to share the burdens in the Persian Gulf, Africa, and elsewhere.

It was the second phase, and notably the U.S. war in Vietnam, that finally aroused broad European opposition to the U.S. global posture, including the U.S. presence in Europe. The Vietnam War demonstrated a lack of U.S. wisdom about the world that alienated European (and world) opinion across the political spectrum, from the extreme of Gaullist "national interest" to the radical German left. Among Allied governments, however, only the French expressed open misgivings, bringing Franco-American relations to their nadir before de Gaulle was retired in 1969.

In April 1966, de Gaulle's Foreign Minister, Maurice Couve de Murville, justified French withdrawal from NATO's military structure, and the consequent expulsion of U.S. NATO bases from France, by pointing to the danger of being dragged into U.S. wars outside the NATO area. The integration of command structures under the leadership of an "infinitely more powerful partner" may influence a government "to orient its policy in a direction quite different from the one it would have spontaneously chosen," Couve observed. "Who doesn't see the hazards of such a system for France's security in case of a major conflict in which America would be involved without France being involved itself?" Couve suggested that French public opinion was aware of such a danger since the development of crises "not in our regions but on the distant confines of the Asian continent."

In Germany, left-wing opposition to the war in Vietnam centered on the moral imperative of refusing involvement in—yet again —a "genocidal" war. The emphasis of the German movement was on German complicity resulting from membership in NATO and the presence, on German soil, of essential elements of the military machine that was waging war against the Vietnamese people.[18]

As the United States has used its bases in Europe to support interventions in the Middle East and North Africa, European doubts and opposition have grown. During the 1967 Arab-Israeli war, personnel from the USAF's 66th Tactical Reconnaissance Wing based at Upper Heyford in Britain were secretly flown to Israel to take part in Israeli Air Force operations against Egypt.[19] Six years later, in the 1973 October War, the United States was denied use of all European bases for resupplying Israel. The sole exception was the mid-Atlantic Lajes air base in the Portuguese Azores islands. Portugal, which at that time was still under fascist dictatorship, was too weak politically to refuse U.S. requests.

In the early 1980s, when the Pentagon was obsessed by fears of a Soviet thrust toward the warm waters of the Persian Gulf, Defense Secretary Caspar Weinberger brought forward the concept of "horizontal escalation."[20] If the

United States were at a disadvantage against the Soviet Union in one region of the world, it could open a second front in a more favorable theater. For example, if the United States found itself at a disadvantage in the Gulf, it could threaten to invade Cuba or exploit anti-Soviet movements in Poland. Thus it came to be understood, particularly in the German peace movement, that U.S. bases in Western Europe could be used to create crises in Eastern Europe as a means of defending U.S. interests in another part of the world.

In the absence of any remotely credible danger of a Soviet invasion, U.S. NATO bases in Europe are more clearly seen as staging areas for "out-of-area" operations. The "threat" has been moving steadily "out-of-area." But what is that threat? Neither the Reagan nor the Bush Administration has solved the problem of defining the ostensible source of danger to the satisfaction of the European Allies of the United States.

The Reagan Administration favored "terrorism" as the ideological substitute for a fading communist threat. But the terrorist threat is geographically too far from the United States to remain credible. In Europe, terrorism is seen as a dubious ideological by-product of the most obscure episodes of the Israeli-Arab conflict.

The differences between U.S. and European perceptions of the "terrorist" threat were clearly revealed in October 1985, when U.S. Delta Force commandos and Italian *carabinieri* nearly came to blows at the Sigonella NATO air base in Sicily. The Delta Force commandos had been dispatched to arrest four Palestinians aboard a Boeing 737 that had been intercepted by U.S. warplanes and forced to land at Sigonella. While U.S. public opinion was apparently willing to approve of whatever methods might be used to arrest the Palestinians alleged to have planned the hijacking of the "Achille Lauro" cruise ship, Italian opinion strongly supported Prime Minister Bettino Craxi's refusal to turn the Palestinians over to the United States. In that event, the political costs of battling Italian allies were too high, and the Palestinians were released to the custody of the carabinieri.

Britain allows the United States a much freer hand than other Allies, as the bombing raid against Libya in April 1986 demonstrated. The raid was officially justified by allegations that Libya had organized the bombing of a West Berlin discoteque in which a U.S. soldier was killed, but no definitive proof was ever presented. Despite support from the Thatcher government, which approved the use of bases in Britain for the attack on Libya, it was opposed by the majority of the British population. There were also protests in Germany over the involvement of U.S. NATO installations in Germany in planning the raid. As is often the case, U.S. media singled out France for criticism after the French government reportedly refused to allow the U.S.

warplanes to fly over French territory. Spain took the same position, and refused to let the United States use its Spanish bases to launch the attack.

In the early 1990s, before Iraq's invasion of Kuwait, the Bush Administration shifted emphasis from the War Against Terrorism to the War Against Drugs. But this was primarily a Western hemisphere affair and did not justify U.S. bases in Europe. If U.S. bases are to remain in Europe as part of a global deployment, a more convincing rationale, acceptable to Europeans, will need to be found—a formidable task.

The collapse of the Warsaw Pact makes large-scale withdrawal of U.S. forces virtually inevitable. But the removal of forces is one thing, and the removal of the bases is another. As it withdraws cruise missiles from Europe, the Pentagon is seeking funds to build new facilities at Greenham Common, as well as other bases in Britain. The prospect of a powerful unified Germany has revived speculation that the French might welcome U.S. bases that it will be obliged to withdraw from Germany. Whether this happens will depend on the extent to which France remains bound to traditional balance-of-power thinking and fears of German preponderance.

After the collapse of the Warsaw Pact, the only major remaining argument in favor of the U.S. bases in Europe is that they are there. They are maintained in Europe by powerful vested interests and institutional inertia, while their champions devise new rationales in the face of growing critical scrutiny and opposition from the people of the host nations.

Notes

1. Robert E. Harkavy, *Great Power Competition for Overseas Bases: The Geopolitics of Access Diplomacy* (New York: Pergamon Press, 1982).

2. George Kennan, *Memoirs: 1925-1950* (New York: Pantheon, 1967), 407.

3. John Lewis Gaddis, *Strategies of Containment* (London: Oxford University Press, 1982), 26-53.

4. Wilfried Loth, *Die Teilung der Welt 1941-1945* (Munchen: Deutscher Taschenbuch Verlag, 1980).

5. Widely echoed at the time, but published only 25 years later in the *Naval War College Review*, May-June 1975, XXVII, 51-108.

6. Gaddis, 28-53.

7. Diana Johnstone, *The Politics of Euromissiles: Europe's Role in America's World* (New York: Schocken, 1984).

8. David Calleo, *Beyond American Hegemony* (New York: Basic Books, 1987), 45.

9. Duncan Campbell, *The Unsinkable Aircraft Carrier* (London: Paladin, 1986), 20.

10. Ibid., 153-159.

11. Ibid., 161-168.

12. Hans-Peter Hubert, "Der Weg der BRD in die NATO," *Die BRD in der NATO, Kumentationsstelle Friedens-und Sicherheitspolitik* (Munster, 1985).

13. April 1979 Report to Senate Foreign Relations Committee on "United States Foreign Policy Objectives and Overseas Military Installations."

14. Richard Barnet, *The Alliance* (New York: Simon & Schuster, 1983), 111.

15. Roberto Faenza and Marco Fini, *Gli Americani in Italia* (Milano: Feltrinelli, 1976), 13.

16. Christian Pineau, *1956 Suez* (Paris: Robert Laffont, 1976), 93.

17. See David P. Calleo, *Beyond American Hegemony, A Twentieth Century Fund Book* (New York: Basic Books, 1987), 32.

18. In May 1973, Andreas Baader's Red Army Faction (RAF) attacked a computer center at the U.S. Air Force headquarters in Heidelberg. For their trial, defense lawyer Otto Schily (who went on to become a leading Green member of the Bundestag) sought unsuccessfully to call U.S. military witnesses to support RAF contentions that the Heidelberg computer was used to program air raids in Indochina. A deposition by former National Security Agency analyst and *Counterspy* founder Winslow Peck testified that U.S. military operations in Indochina had been partly worked out in NSA offices in the old I.G. Farben Chemical firm in Frankfurt, which the United States had selected during the war as its future headquarters and had carefully spared in wartime bombing raids.

19. E. P. Thompson, *Mad Dogs* (London: Pluto Press, 1986), 28.

20. Secretary of Defense Caspar Weinberger's Annual Report to Congress for Fiscal Year 1983.

Chapter 11

U.S. Military Presence in Germany
Yarrow Cleaves

When the planes come the baby starts screaming with fear. She clings to my legs. I can't calm her. Her whole body trembles. When she started walking, she would run in panic every time, not seeing where she was going. Several times she fell and hurt herself badly. When I'm not there, she throws herself on the ground with her hands over her ears and won't stop screaming.[1]

This child, living in a military low-level flight training zone during what was called peacetime, was born in the Federal Republic of Germany. Her country, which is often compared with the state of Oregon for size, was occupied by a standing army of 495,000 and by another 399,000 foreign military forces under NATO.[2] For more than 40 years its eastern border marked the line between East and West in the political order that took shape after World War II. NATO called it the Central Front, and all its war games began with, or in anticipation of, the crossing of that line. Weapons and strategies changed through the decades, but throughout the Cold War the heart of the battlefield in Europe remained fixed in Germany.

That battlefield, superimposed on daily life in the Federal Republic of Germany (FRG)—and complemented, in the German Democratic Republic (GDR), by a Soviet occupation force of about 375,000—was an enormous burden. NATO strategists, taking the battleground for granted, ignored the burden on the populace and their many protests in favor of the interests of Alliance members. The single most influential of these, certainly the dominant power throughout the Alliance's 40-year history, has been the United States. To remain a "European power" since the end of World War II, Washington required access to and control over military bases and forces. Its allies have provided this, the FRG above all.

The bloc confrontation, which had served as the rationale for standing armies in Central Europe, collapsed at the end of 1989. Indeed, Gorbachev's initiatives to re-orient Soviet military strategy along defensive lines and his

225

willingness to agree to highly asymmetrical arms reductions had already undermined the assumptions governing NATO policy. When the governments of Hungary and then Czechoslovakia allowed East German emigrés to cross frontiers that had long been sealed, when the government of the GDR in desperation opened the Berlin Wall, and when the ruling orders in one nation after another fell beneath the demands of people in the street, a new European order was born with a Soviet commitment to non-intervention.

While the new governments of Warsaw Treaty Organization members were successfully demanding the withdrawal of Soviet forces from their territories, the governments of NATO allies were facing strong popular pressures to cut military budgets and to withdraw troops from the FRG. However, events in Germany offered a new—or at least a transitional—justification for maintaining the status quo in Western Europe.

As soon as the border between the two German states lost its significance as the Central Front, the possibility of German reunificaton, pressed by West German Chancellor Helmut Kohl, could not be avoided. In fact, the constitution of the Federal Republic had long ago framed the probable dynamics of reunification by extending full and automatic citizenship to any German from the GDR who could arrive to claim it. When it became possible for large numbers of people from the GDR to do so, the exodus created crises in both German states. Images of reunification, defined and funded by West German political parties for their East German counterparts, dominated the GDR's campaign for the March 1990 election. Euphoria and anxiety in the mainstream political imagination was manipulated in such a way that speed seemed the only way to bridge the gap.

In its early phases, this orchestrated stampede toward unity, with the anticipated power of a unified German state—so powerful economically, so strategically placed, and so startlingly imminent—raised fears internationally. The new governments of Eastern Europe agreed with those of the NATO Alliance that a united Germany should belong to NATO, and only NATO, and that U.S. and other NATO forces should remain in Germany to restrain potential nationalistic ambitions. Once President Gorbachev and Chancellor Kohl reached an accord on this issue in mid-July 1990, the way to German unification was clear. The new European order would present no *immediate* fundamental challenges to existing power structures in the West.

On September 12, 1990, the foreign ministers of the two German states and the four allied powers of World War II signed the Treaty on the Final Settlement with Respect to Germany, possible at last only because the Cold War had ended. The two German states, on behalf of the unified state that would exist weeks later, provided security guarantees, and Britain, France, the Soviet Union, and the United States agreed to relinquish the last of the occupation rights they had established 45 years earlier.

The United States emerged from Europe's year of great change with its power to deploy forces in Europe intact. The NATO summit declaration of July 6, 1990, which proposed to members of the Warsaw Treaty Organization that "we are no longer adversaries," explicitly confirmed the place of the U.S. military in Europe, stating: "The significant presence of North American conventional and U.S. nuclear forces in Europe demonstrates the underlying political compact that binds North America's fate to Europe's democracies."[3] It could hardly be stated more precisely. These political bonds have been demonstrated in the form of military force.

In 1990, the "significant presence" of U.S. forces in the Federal Republic of Germany stood much as as they had through the 1980s. There were hundreds of U.S. military installations in the FRG—depending on how they were counted. A 1986 atlas published by the Green Party, enumerating every single military facility in the FRG and the GDR, listed 902 for the United States.[4] A 1989 study by the Stockholm International Peace Research Institute, which combined closely associated facilities, yielded a total of 625.[5] At that time the U.S. Department of Defense said that 224—nearly two-thirds—of its 374 main operating bases abroad were in the FRG.[6]

These installations included storage depots for conventional, chemical, and nuclear weapons; artillery ranges; radio terminals; tank training areas; satellite relay stations; border observation points; fuel depots; missile sites— some on perpetual combat alert status; a huge cargo terminal; various command headquarters; and bases for the U.S. 17th Air Force and the two corps of the U.S. 7th Army.[7]

In 1989 the U.S. military had 249,411 military personnel—about three-fourths of its European-based forces—stationed in the FRG.[8] In addition, it employed 31,474 U.S. and 55,838 German civilians.[9] U.S. troops and civilians were accompanied by 214,373 dependents.[10]

Prevailing terms of diplomatic negotiations and budget setting have reduced the issue of the U.S. military presence in Germany to power games and numbers—questions of troops, tanks, nuclear warheads, missiles, air-planes, and dollars. However, the U.S. military occupation of Western Germany has a history which has impacted the life of the FRG's people for many years.

This chapter describes that history and impact. It outlines the origins and design of the military relationship of the United States to the Federal Republic of Germany, framed since the mid-1950s by NATO, and summa-rizes the succession of doctrines concerning the "European theater." It describes the main features of the U.S. military deployment as the 1990s began, and the effects of that presence on the people and environment of the FRG. After discussing the issue of sovereignty in relation to U.S. military operations beyond German borders, it summarizes prospects for future deployment. A sketch of the opposition concludes with a discussion of the possibilities for building a new European order based on peace.

An Ambiguous Sovereignty

U.S. military presence in Germany was established when the United States, with its Soviet, British, and French allies, defeated the Third Reich and occupied defeated Germany. After two world wars, the four occupying powers sought to limit and control German power. The Soviet Union, unlike its wartime allies, also sought reparations and extracted what it could from its zone of occupation in the East. The administration of the British, French, and U.S. zones, by contrast, focussed on German economic recovery and its integration into the U.S.-dominated economy of the post-war West. As the guiding ideology in the Western occupation zones shifted from "denazification" to anti-communism, the mission of U.S. troops shifted from containing Germany through occupation to containing the Soviet Union through combat readiness.[11] The North Atlantic Treaty Organization (NATO), for which the United States negotiated with great determination, soon came to serve the function of containing German power and integrating it into the security structures of the West. Thus, political interests and tensions became—or remained—enshrined in the structures and dynamics of military deployments and strategies.

The Federal Republic of Germany was created in September 1949. Britain, France, and the United States ended their formal military rule in 1951, but the occupation regime remained in effect until May 1955, and the agreements that ended the occupation maintained the authority of U.S. (and other) military forces within the FRG's borders. The amended Convention on Relations Between the Three Powers and the Federal Republic of Germany, signed in Paris on October 23, 1954, gave the FRG "the full authority of a sovereign state over its external affairs," yet stipulated that the United States, Britain, and France retained certain rights "relating to Berlin and to Germany as a whole, including the reunification of Germany and a peace settlement," and "to the stationing of armed forces in the Federal Republic [for]...the defense of the Free World, of which Berlin and the Federal Republic form part."[12]

Through the diplomatic agreements which ensured the continued basing of foreign troops on its territory and limited its fundamental rights and powers of self-determination, the Federal Republic of Germany remained in many ways an occupied country. Officials finessed the subject when they could not avoid it. At the December 4, 1989 NATO summit, when George Bush said that there must be "due regard for the legal role and responsibilities of the Allied Powers" in relation to the issue of German reunification,[13] he was reiterating the hard fact of U.S. power in German affairs.

On May 5, 1955, the day after the Conventions and Protocol came into effect and the occupation regime ended, the FRG joined NATO on the condition that its new military forces would be under U.S. command in NATO and that its reconstructed arms industry would be monitored by the Western European Union. The forces of NATO were thus augmented by German power, while that power was bound under the control of the United States and Western European nations.[14]

NATO, which was established on the basis of an agreement between states that an attack upon one would be considered an attack upon all, soon came to function primarily as a permanently mobilized military organization. As Dan Smith and Richard Barnet have described in detail, the United States has essentially dictated NATO's policies through a combination of pressure and bureaucratic finesse.[15] For example, the High Level Group, established in 1977 to plan and advise on the modernization of nuclear forces in Europe, is chaired by a Pentagon official, and the Pentagon provides all its staff work.[16]

NATO's integrated military command hierarchy is headed by the Supreme Allied Commander Europe, a position which not accidentally has always been filled by a U.S. general. This general is also U.S. Commander-in-Chief Europe, with authority over a command area encompassing Europe and all the countries around the Mediterranean, including Libya, Syria, and Israel. This general heads several other U.S. commands as well, one of which extends as far east as Pakistan, and as far south as Kenya. U.S. military personnel head five additional principal NATO commands.[17] In these ways, U.S. power in NATO has avoided subordination to any other authority.

NATO Strategy and the Nuclear Dimension

NATO's first Supreme Allied Commander, Dwight Eisenhower, regarded nuclear weapons as a less costly and more fearsome deterrent than huge troop deployments, and in 1952 U.S. military planners decided to store nuclear weapons in Europe.[18] In 1954 NATO began basing its war plans on their use.

U.S. nuclear missiles were first deployed in the FRG in 1955, and the first NATO exercise premised on the use of nuclear weapons—called "Carte Blanche"—was held there that June. Post-exercise calculations showed that West German casualties in the first two days would have been one-and-a-half million dead and three-and-a-half million wounded.[19] That shocked European governments and the German public, which protested having its country turned into a nuclear battlefield. In a public opinion poll three years later, only 13 percent of the population wanted nuclear missiles in the FRG.[20]

Under the Eisenhower Administration's "New Look" strategy, the United States attempted to minimize its deployment of conventional ground forces in Europe by threatening the Soviet Union with massive nuclear retaliation in the event of a Soviet attack on Western Europe. This nuclear threat was also supposed to ensure that Moscow did not attempt to counter U.S. intervention in the Third World. When Kennedy Administration strategists arrived in Washington, they were alarmed to find that the top-secret Single Integrated Operating Plan for war called for the simultaneous firing of every nuclear weapon in the U.S. arsenal. They soon developed the concept of "flexible response."[21]

NATO adopted this strategy with reluctance. Governments that had felt protected from Soviet military adventures by the U.S. threat of massive retaliation believed that flexible response now made war more likely. Whether the United States used nuclear weapons only when NATO's (mostly European) conventional forces were in danger of defeat, or only if the Soviet Union used its nuclear weapons first, Europe—and the FRG especially—would still be devastated.[22]

Nuclear weaponry proliferated under the doctrine of flexible response. Between 1960 and 1979, the United States deployed approximately 7,000 tactical nuclear warheads in Europe, with 10,000 more stored in the United States for immediate transfer. Their yields ranged from 1 to 1,000 kilotons, and they could be fired from artillery, airplanes, and short-range missiles.[23] For a time, the arsenal even included nuclear land mines, some small enough to fit in a soldier's backpack, for use along the inter-German border. The collective overkill of this nuclear arsenal was claimed to be a deterrent that justified its existence. Most of the warheads in Europe were, and remain, in Germany.

Awareness of the scope and nature of the European deployment of nuclear weapons increased dramatically in 1977, when NATO clashed with European public opinion over the "enhanced radiation weapon," or neutron bomb, which *minimizes* blast damage to factories and other structures and *maximizes* radioactive emissions that kill. President Carter said he would deploy the weapon in Europe only if Alliance members—the FRG in particular—requested it publicly. Chancellor Helmut Schmidt, caught between army officers who wanted the weapon and an angry public that did not, chose to support the military and made the request. Five months later, Carter reversed his decision, suspended the project, and left Schmidt angry and politically vulnerable at home.[24]

Pershing II Depot in Mutlangen, March 1984. Photo courtesy of Erika Sulzer-Kleinmeier.

Meanwhile, the newly established High Level Group began meeting in October 1977 with the mandate of redesigning Europe's nuclear strategy, and NATO began planning a major new deployment. It took great care this time to present a united front. After internal objections were raised that the new weapons could sabotage arms control negotiations, NATO set up a special group to develop an arms-control approach which could be tied to the new weapon. On December 12, 1979, in a scrupulously prepared "dual-track" decision, NATO committed itself to basing 572 intermediate-range U.S. cruise and Pershing II nuclear missiles in five European countries.[25] All the Pershing II's and 96 cruise missiles were slated for deployment at bases in Germany.

In the years between the Euromissile decision and the first deployments late in 1983, the U.S. Army adopted a significant new military doctrine. AirLand Battle—a doctrine which involves co-ordinated ground and air systems attacking deep into enemy territory with nuclear, conventional, and chemical weapons in an electronically controlled battlefield—first appeared in the 1981 edition of the Army Field Manual. The next year, the U.S. Army Chief of Staff and the Army Inspector of the FRG signed a document stating that the two armies agreed in principle on applying the doctrine.

AirLand Battle raised a storm when it came to public attention in the FRG the next year. First, NATO's *public* doctrine had traditionally been defensive, countering the offensive Soviet posture in Eastern Europe.[26] Second, under the new doctrine the FRG could serve as a staging area for AirLand Battle strikes *outside* Europe altogether, while the Pershing II and cruise missiles targeted on Soviet command and control centers held the Soviet Union at bay. These fears were confirmed during the 1986 U.S. attack on Libya and subsequent crises in the Gulf of Sidra, as people monitoring Pershing II and cruise bases watched missile convoys speed to dispersal sites in the countryside on full alert status.[27]

NATO incorporated the AirLand Battle doctrine into its official strategy of Follow-On Forces Attack (FOFA), which featured military strikes far behind the Central Front in Czechoslovakia and the GDR to destroy Warsaw Pact reinforcements and the roads, railroads, and bridges that would carry them to the battle front. A 1988 congressional study estimated the costs of developing and deploying FOFA systems through the year 2008 at approximately $50 billion.[28] By the end of 1989, the political order on which this strategy was predicated had crumbled.

U.S. Deployments in the FRG

NATO based its war plans on the concept of forward defense. Because the FRG is densely populated, heavily industrialized, and geographically relatively narrow, the only defense acceptable to West German governments was one that would minimize German casualties by concentrating forces on its eastern border. This required a large armed force, and the expense of maintaining it was a source of chronic tension between the United States and other members of NATO, especially the FRG.

To demonstrate its military commitment to Europe within the constraints of a congressionally set ceiling of 326,000 U.S. troops, the United States developed a rapid-reinforcement plan for transporting another six divisions, a Marine amphibious brigade, and about 60 squadrons of tactical fighters to Europe within 10 days of a decision to mobilize. One crucial element of this plan was a program of pre-positioned stocks of vehicles, munitions, and supplies stored and organized so that about half the reinforcement units could go directly to the depots and leave fully equipped for battle. Even more essential to the plan was logistical support provided by NATO allies, with which the United States has Wartime Host Nation Support treaties. The WHNS treaty with the FRG, signed in 1982 after secret negotiations, committed the FRG to providing U.S. forces with extensive logistics support, including 93,000 trained and equipped reservists.[29]

U.S. military facilities are concentrated in southern Germany, formerly the U.S. occupation zone. There are also U.S. installations in Berlin, which remained under the military authority of the Four Powers, and at the port of Bremerhaven in the north. Forty of the bases or constellations of closely associated facilities employ more than 2,500 people; of these, 11 employ more than 10,000.[30]

Department of Defense statistics for fiscal year 1988 put the number of Army personnel stationed in the FRG at 249,411 (70 percent of its troops in Europe and about one-fourth of its entire active force). The U.S. Air Force had 40,272 personnel (about half its European deployment) in the FRG,[31] with 371 of its 800 European-based combat and attack aircraft.[32]

While they may not appear as important as nuclear missile sites or bases for thousands of soldiers, the microwave radio links, satellite communication terminals, and transmitters for military communication and guidance systems are essential elements of a functioning nuclear command. Furthermore, they fill crucial roles in the global reconnaissance, surveillance, and intelligence-gathering networks of the United States. In 1986 the United States had 133 communication and 45 intelligence-related installations in the FRG.[33] It will not casually relinquish this strategic infrastructure.

U.S. nuclear deployments in the FRG are in a state of flux. Ground-launched cruise and Pershing II missiles eliminated under the INF treaty are still being withdrawn. A year after the May 1989 NATO summit at which the FRG made it clear it would never host a successor to the short-range, ground-launched, nuclear-armed Lance missile, President Bush announced cancellation of plans for a replacement. Most of the nuclear arsenal in the FRG has consisted of artillery—about 4,000 nuclear-capable guns with a range of 18 kilometers (11 miles), which can fire warheads with yields of one-half to 10 kilotons.[34] (The bomb dropped on Hiroshima was about 13 kilotons.) These weapons have lost their European mission, and the emerging NATO consensus is that they will be withdrawn.

With ground-launched nuclear weapons passing from the European scene, U.S. and NATO modernization is concentrating on air- and sea-launched nuclear systems. One is a new short-range Tactical Air-To-Surface missile (TASM, or SRAM-T for its more vivid designation, Short-Range Attack Missile—Tactical). It will fit many types of aircraft and it eludes all existing arms limitation categories.[35] NATO strategists want to deploy it in 1995 and hope that TASM's will face less opposition in Germany than Lance missiles did because other NATO countries would also receive them, and because their targets would not be Germany's immediate neighbors. According to a senior British official, "TASMs are absolutely the key, the key to all of it."[36]

Living with the Threat of War

The U.S. Army put one of its Pershing II missile bases inside the city limits at Heilbronn, half a mile from the nearest house in what was once a nature reserve where people loved to walk on Sunday afternoons.[37] Noticing construction there in 1975, the people of Heilbronn were first told that it was for a baseball field and later that it was for a U.S. Army training area. By the time NATO made its dual-track decision, fortifications were in place and storage bunkers were ready.

The missiles were kept on Quick Reaction Alert, meaning that a certain number were always armed and ready to launch. In 1985 an accident on the base left three soldiers dead, 16 severely injured, and a missile burning. The Pershing Unit had neither an ambulance nor fire-fighting equipment. The city sent its own, not knowing what had happened, whether a warhead was involved, or what it should do to protect the community.

In this way, the people of Heilbronn learned that there was no evacuation plan for them. Despite its having deployed the densest concentration of nuclear weapons in the world in the FRG, the United States acknowledged the possibility of accident only insofar as it developed evacuation plans for U.S. personnel and their households—but not for notifying or evacuating neighboring communities. Road blocks would be set up to keep local residents from getting in the way.

Local people resisted the deployment from the first. They climbed trees and took photographs of missiles inside the base when its use as a Pershing II site was still a rumor. Like grassroots activists at other cruise and Pershing bases, they tracked convoys to their "secret" launching practice sites and mapped the locations. They watched as convoys sped to launch sites on combat alert during the U.S. attack on Libya and the crisis in the Gulf of Sidra. They organized demonstrations, blockades, concerts, religious services, conferences, and peacewalks, and they began addressing the global policy that put the missiles in their backyards. In 1990, persuaded by a campaign of letter writing and 23 demonstrations in Heilbronn's central plaza, the Pentagon decided to turn the base over to the German Ministry of Defense. Local people want to convert it into a cultural center.

West of the Rhine is Hunsrück, a region of forests, fields, meadows, and lovely valleys. It is sparsely populated; only 90,000 people live in its 133 villages and five small towns, but one cannot walk more than three miles in any direction in Hunsrück without encountering a fenced-in military installation—an air base, munitions dump, or communications station. Unemployment is high, and almost half of Hunsrück's workers depend for employment on either the German military or the U.S. air base at Hahn, where 72

Hawk missiles during a maneuver in a German village. Photo courtesy of Wolfgang Bartels.

nuclear-certified F-16's are kept and exercised. Six hundred people who lived near the base consented to relocation because the noise of jet landings and takeoffs was unbearable.

Five facilities are known to house nuclear weapons. One, Hasselbach, served as a base for 96 cruise missiles. Once the missiles arrived in November 1983, the base also became the site of prayer services held every Sunday afternoon by local people, and in 1986, 180,000 gathered there in West Germany's last massive demonstration against the Euromissiles.

The Daily Presence of U.S. Forces

Most U.S. troops do not come prepared to engage with German people or to understand the effects of their presence. Few learn the language, and most tend to keep to themselves. In an area like Hunsrück, where more than 10,000 U.S. soldiers are stationed—one for every nine local inhabitants—the pressure on local communities can be overwhelming. The farming village of Lautzenhausen, which has virtually disappeared beneath the casinos, nightclubs, fast-food joints, and video stores of what they call "Little America," is Hunsrück's nightmare.

Because of the FRG's general prosperity and its social welfare system, the bases have generated relatively little prostitution, and it is not regarded as a significant problem. However, the macho culture that emanates from military bases is oppressive to women, who complain of distorted social relationships and a sense of physical insecurity. GI's accused of rape are tried in U.S. military—not local—courts, so that a woman who brings charges has none of the rights that are hers under the German Constitution, not even the right of appeal.

Women's lives and local economies both reflect the costs of suppporting children fathered by U.S. servicemen, whether the women are single, married to GI's whose income cannot support a family, or divorced and returning home with their children. According to a study by the Institute for German Economy, the annual cost to city budgets for this purpose is $60 million.[38]

U.S. military forces have inflicted heavy damage on the natural environment. Exempt from German anti-pollution laws, the U.S. military has polluted the soil, the water, and the air. Leaking fuel pipelines and storage tanks, and toxic wastes from the military dumps—to which civilian authorities have no access—are poisoning the ground water. Routine operations of U.S. forces consume enormous amounts of power; fumes from the sulfurous coal that fires the heating plants and vehicle exhausts poison the air, but local conservation and anti-pollution measures do not apply to U.S. military operations. The Army has estimated that air pollution reduction measures would cost $150 million, and that dealing with the water would take another $450 million.[39] Airplanes have accidentally dumped fuel, ammunition, and missiles. Because there are no wide-open spaces; most have fallen in fields and villages. Germany's growing population has forced cities to grow up around firing ranges that were once in the countryside, while nature reserves taken over for military training exercises look like ripped-up construction sites. As the U.S. reduces its presence in Germany, will it leave anything to rectify the damage it has done to the environment, or will the U.S. simply dismiss the damage as one of the costs of freedom that Germans must bear?

The answer may lie in the Status of Forces agreement, which defines the legal status of U.S. forces and their dependents in NATO countries. This agreement protects U.S. military personnel from prosecution by the host country for any harm done in the course of official duties. An on-duty soldier who causes a fatal traffic accident or endangers roadside protesters or terrorizes school children during field maneuvers cannot be held accountable under the law of that country. The agreement stipulates that when damage to property results from the performance of official duties, the United States reimburses the host nation for 75 percent of the settled amount,[40] yet the U.S. reimburses the German Defense Office for no more than half the cost.[41]

War Games Take a Toll

Through the end of the 1980s, about 5,000 military exercises, each involving up to 2,000 troops, took place on public and private land every year. Another 85 exercises a year were larger. The largest, the annual Reforger (REturn of FORces to GERmany) exercise, designed to demonstrate, practice, and develop the U.S. rapid-reinforcement plan, airlifted thousands of U.S. troops to their prepositioned equipment and designated support personnel to join other units already in the field for combat maneuvers.

The September 1988 Reforger used 125,000 ground troops, 103,000 of whom were U.S. soldiers, and 30,000 vehicles, 7,000 of which were "tracked vehicles" (tanks, heavy artillery, and missile launchers),[42] for maneuvers across 16,000 acres of central and southern Germany. The most destructive exercise ever conducted, Reforger 1988 killed seven people, five of them German civilians. In one village, soldiers fought mock combat from house to house, aimed their weapons at high school students in the schoolyard and then, without warning, began driving tanks into the yard until the principal blocked the way with his car. Near another village, tank crews broke into barns and dragged out farm machinery so they could hide their tanks inside, throwing smoke bombs at the farmers who protested. Elsewhere, four tanks rampaging through fields destroyed half the corn crop. One tank ruined the festival grounds and several streets of a village. In North Hessen alone 1,500 damage claims were registered. Damage claims, not counting lost crops, were 3 million marks in Bavaria and Baden-Württemberg, where troops caused 506 accidents, 106 injuries, and the seven deaths.[43]

The 1982 annual report of the U.S. Secretary of Defense noted that "our allies make their contribution to the potential war effort in the form of the totality of their civilian infrastructure."[44] NATO strategy has tested this infrastructure through WINTEX-CIMEX (Winter Exercise/Civilian-Military Exercise), staged every two years in various NATO countries. National, regional, and local officials are called upon to manage the civilian population so that roads, railways, airports, hospitals, and supply and communication systems function according to military needs. Engaging in two- to three-week pre-war crisis scenarios, they attempt to address problems of draft resistance, desertions, anti-war protest, refugees, public hysteria, sabotage, and runs on banks and grocery stores. They prepare for the detention of politically troublesome people and for commandeering civilian labor, vehicles, homes, radio stations and hospitals for military use. Above all, they practice their own subordination to military authority.[45]

The mayor of Würzburg refused to participate in the February 1989 WINTEX. After informing the district administrator that there would be no war in his city that year, he went public. "Twenty-five nuclear bombs are supposed to be dropped on our heads," he said, "and being the mayor of this town, it would be my duty to take care that nobody can leave the city. I suppose they expect me to shoot at our own citizens. The plans NATO generals developed for the people of this country are the craziest thing I have ever come across in my political career." After the mayor received a warning from the Bavarian Minister of Internal Affairs that there would be legal consequences, a citizen of Würzburg filed suit against him, charging violation of secrecy, the penalty for which is up to five years in prison.[46]

Efforts to resist this perpetual brink-of-war condition grew from below for years, but the full weight of NATO and U.S. policy pressed from above, and the national government provided more mollification than leadership. Low-level training flights, however, have imposed so much suffering on so many people for so long that by the late 1980s, the political mainstream had become the vehicle for public outrage.

Low-Level Flights

Allied aircraft have been flying about 580,000 sorties annually over the FRG, and about one-fifth of these are low-level flights (under 1,500 feet).[47] Two-thirds of the country is designated as a low-level flight zone;[48] only cities with populations over 100,000[49] and a margin along the eastern border are exempt. Within this zone, seven areas are designated for flight altitudes as low as 250 feet—treetop level.

Children who live in low-level flight areas in any country suffer hearing damage, headaches, sleeplessness, hypersensitivity, and fear. They have trouble concentrating and learning. The birth weights of newborns are lower than average, and physicians have observed that rates of miscarriage and premature birth are higher.[50] Stomach and heart problems occur with greater-than-average frequency among adults. So alarming were the results of a 1985 study of low-level flight effects on animals and human beings that the German Ministry of Defense reportedly suppressed the results.[51]

The public faces other dangers beyond health damage from "noise terror" (which NATO calls "the sound of freedom"). More than 375 military aircraft have crashed in the FRG since 1973. In 1988 alone, 40 USAF planes crashed, half of them F-16 fighters;[52] three F-16's crashed in a single day.[53] The danger is immeasurably compounded by the number of nuclear reactors and nuclear (and chemical and conventional) munitions depots on the ground. In June 1987, a U.S. F-16 crashed a few flight seconds from a nuclear reactor.[54] In March 1988, three NATO aircraft crashed within three days. The first, an F-16, plowed into a row of houses in Forst, nine miles from a nuclear reactor;

the next, a French Mirage, crashed six flight seconds from another nuclear reactor; and the third, another F-16, crashed 650 feet from a munitions depot.[55]

Two crashes late in 1988, neither connected to low-level flight training, heightened organized public opposition. At the annual Ramstein air show in August, three Italian stunt planes collided, and one fell flaming into the crowd, killing 70 people and injuring 400. Then, in December, a U.S. A-10 Thunderbolt hit the top floor of an apartment building in the city of Remscheid. A-10's are attack aircraft armed with 30-mm shells that have a special ingredient, depleted uranium, that makes them particularly effective against tanks. Only the next day did a U.S. military spokesman state that the ammunition that had detonated in the flaming ruins was only practice ammunition.[56] Nevertheless, the pilot and five Germans died, 50 people were injured (many seriously), and 50 more lost their homes.

Organized resistance to low-level flight training over the FRG began growing in the early 1980s and now has a very strong provincial and civic base with roots in the work of local peace and ecology groups. There are towns now that fly huge helium balloons, some painted with friendly faces, 330 feet in the air at the end of steel cables bolted down at street corners. After the Remscheid crash, 25,000 people signed a statement against low-level flights and, hoping to bring the issue before the civil courts, many citizens pledged to file a complaint with local police against the Ministry of Defense each day that low-level flights passed over their homes.[57]

This placed the government of the FRG in an awkward position. After the Ramstein crash, Defense Minister Rupert Scholz announced a permanent ban on military air shows, but it was pointed out that under the Status of Forces Agreement he lacked authority to do so. A week after the Remscheid crash the governors of the 10 states and the mayor of West Berlin agreed unanimously to seek substantial reductions in low-level flights. But a poll that same month showed that only 28 percent of West Germans favored reducing the number of the flights; 71 percent wanted them banned altogether. With NATO military leaders insisting that they were absolutely necessary, the most that Chancellor Kohl would press for in 1989 was the maximum feasible reduction.[58] The next year, though people might have anticipated relief with the end of the Cold War, the U.S. Air Force announced plans to begin nighttime low-level training flights.

The U.S. military buildup in the Persian Gulf that began in August 1990 demonstrated the role of the bases in Germany in the post-Cold War world. During the first phase, more than 100 transport planes were landing every night at the Ramstein and Rhein-Main bases to refuel. The first fatal accident of the deployment took place when a cargo plane headed for Rhein-Main crashed on take off from Ramstein in the middle of the night. Troops and battle helicopters were transferred from Germany to Saudi Arabia, and local activists think it is likely that stocks from rapid-reinforcement depots allocated for NATO operations may also have been flown out.

Sovereignty and Out-of-Area Operations

The issue of national sovereignty applies beyond maneuvers on German territory and has been raised a number of times with respect to U.S. and NATO military operations against targets outside Germany. The restoration of full sovereignty following the terms of the treaty signed on September 12, 1990 does not lay the issue to rest. In November and December 1990, more than 100,000 U.S. troops and their heavy battle tanks were airlifted to Saudi Arabia.

NATO guidelines allow ground, air, or naval forces to use German territory for military actions outside the country *if* those actions are carried out within the area and framework of the treaty. Article 53 of the NATO troop statute also allows the United States to do what it deems necessary to be combat ready or to fulfill its national defense priorities, although it cannot legally take measures that conflict with Federal Republic or international law.[59]

NATO and U.S. interests may often coincide, but they are not identical. To integrate the command areas of NATO's Supreme Allied Commander (SACEUR) and the U.S. Commander-in-Chief Europe (CINCEUR) under the authority of the same general reflects and simultaneously denies the possibility of conflict, for surely the CINCEUR might sometimes find the NATO framework restrictive.

While the primary mission of the U.S. European Command (USEUCOM) is to support NATO, the U.S. attack on Libya in 1986 illustrated that this is not its only mission. USEUCOM headquarters in Stuttgart coordinated the operation, which used U.S. aircraft based in Britain, but CINCEUR Bernard Rogers arranged to be absent from USEUCOM headquarters at the time. He was in Belgium at his office in NATO's Supreme Headquarters Allied Powers in Europe—on the hotline to his USEUCOM headquarters.[60] He avoided compromising the SACEUR, because the SACEUR was not on the scene and as CINCEUR, he avoided compromising the secrecy of the attack because, to inform NATO's high command as he was bound to do, he had only to tell himself.

In 1987, the UN General Assembly included in its definition of aggression "the action of a State in allowing its territory, which it has placed at the disposal of another State, to be used by that other State, for perpetrating an act of aggression against a Third State."[61] The attack on Libya involved Germany, without its knowledge or consent, in violating the closest thing we have to international law. Later the same year, the United States secretly shipped 500 missiles to Iran from its base at Ramstein as part of the weapons-for-hostages deal. In this, too, Germany was an unknowing participant in a charged international situation.

Out-of-area operations will remain controversial as long as the United States maintains a military presence in Europe. In 1981 at the 18th annual Wehrkunde Conference in Munich, deputy Secretary of Defense Frank Carlucci outlined the Reagan Administration's thoughts on meeting military threats in and beyond Europe. The United States would, he said, take most responsibility for dealing with contingencies outside Europe. While some allies would probably send token forces to the area, their more important military contribution would be to take the place—in Europe—of U.S. forces diverted to action outside Europe.[62] This was classically illustrated when U.S. naval forces intervening in the Persian Gulf during the Iraq-Iran war were joined by ships from France, Britain, Belgium, the Netherlands, and Italy,[63] while FRG ships, for the first time in the history of NATO, moved from their assigned areas in the North and Baltic Seas into the Mediterranean to replace allied vessels deployed to the Gulf.[64]

Direct military contributions from NATO allies followed a similar pattern when the Bush Administration sent troops to the Persian Gulf. However, the discrepancy between the massive U.S. deployment—150,000 troops within one month—and the limited participation of allies, especially Germany, angered U.S. supporters of the mobilization. One member of the Senate Armed Services Committee said, "I feel we are under no obligation to maintain our present military commitments to Germany unless Germany provides greater support to our efforts in the Gulf. Sending a few vehicles and dispatching a few ships to the Mediterranean is not the response of a great state or a true ally."[65]

This statement illustrates two crucial prevailing assumptions: first, that U.S. forces are in Europe to protect Europe, and second, that the use of a foreign territory—Germany, in this case—to serve a military campaign enforcing U.S. political and economic aims (even in another region of the world) is taken so for granted that it counts for nothing. The impact of U.S. displeasure moved Chancellor Kohl to announce that he would seek a constitutional amendment to allow the foreign deployment of German forces—forbidden since the defeat of the Third Reich.

The Prospects for Future U.S. Deployment

Europe has not been the focus of a potential military crisis involving the United States since the Berlin Wall was built in 1961. U.S. presidents and their Pentagon advisors favor other arenas for their military engagements.

U.S. Chief of Naval Operations Admiral C.A.H. Trost, advocating the continued global deployment of a nuclear Navy, put it succinctly: "Since 1980 alone, the President has employed naval forces in crises and contingency operations almost 50 times. Virtually none of these had anything to do with East-West confrontation."[66] With the collapse of the Cold War at the end of 1989, U.S. national security leaders felt free to admit that they saw little need to remain committed to bloc confrontation, and U.S. Army Chief-of-Staff General Carl Vuono pressed for the Army to function as a fast-reaction force able to strike anywhere in the world with airborne, air assault, and light infantry divisions.[67] The U.S. invasion of Panama provided a timely demonstration of this concept.

Current Pentagon plans call for reorganizing the U.S. military into a structure conspicuously designed to project power at will. It consists of a Pacific Force to deal with Asia, an Atlantic Force to deal with Europe and the Persian Gulf, a Contingency Force to make fast strikes and spearhead larger invasions, and a Strategic Force of long-range nuclear weapons. The Atlantic Force would base two of its five active Army divisions and three to four of its five or six tactical fighter wings in Europe.[68] Under this design Army deployment in Europe would be reduced by about two-thirds, the Air Force by about half.

In 1989 the numbers of domestic and foreign military personnel on active duty in the two German states totalled a staggering 1,439,000. The July 1990 accord between Chancellor Kohl and President Gorbachev provided for the total withdrawal of Soviet forces from eastern Germany by 1994. The treaty of September 12, 1990 included a provision limiting the armed forces of a unified German state to 370,000 by 1995, and Pentagon cutbacks are likely to halve the 1989 U.S. deployment level. In sum, the number of troops stationed in Germany may be slashed by nearly one million within five years of the opening of the Berlin Wall.

Germans will experience significant relief from the pressures of occupation by large standing armies poised for battle, but though the rights of occupation have passed from the Four Powers, and Germany is regarded as a full sovereign state, there are no commitments to change the relations between German society and U.S. military forces under the aegis of NATO.

The future U.S. presence in Germany is likely to resemble that in Britain, which has always been a distant second to Germany in terms of the number of U.S. troops it "hosts." It is the site of many strategic U.S. facilities for surveillance and reconnaissance, communication and control systems, command centers, and more. Nuclear-armed U.S. aircraft are based on its soil, and U.S. nuclear submarines controlling the North Atlantic are based in its harbors. Low-level flights scream through the mountain valleys of Scotland and Wales. Its own military forces and civilian police are charged with guarding U.S. facilities; its courts prosecute those who engage in nonviolent direct action to protest the U.S. presence. Its Host Nation Support Treaty with the United States grants the U.S. commander sweeping powers over civilian life in times of crisis, including the power to declare and enforce martial law. No U.S. troop and weapon deployments have ever been subjected to democratic process; indeed, cruise missiles were imposed over enormous protest. Thus, while the U.S. military presence in Britain may be less overwhelming physically than it has been in the FRG, it is dangerous and politically insidious nonetheless. Peace activists there experience it as an occupation.

U.S. airbases and facilities for communications and surveillance will only increase in strategic importance as elements of the AirLand Battle strategy. Germany will continue to provide storage sites for U.S. reserves and for operations in the Middle East. As long as Germany accepts U.S. bases, it will continue to be one of the foundation stones supporting the empire of the United States.

The Active Opposition

After World War II many Germans felt deep revulsion toward war. The rearmament Konrad Adenauer negotiated with the United States in the early 1950s encountered strong protest, but once remilitarization was under way, opposition retreated largely into the private realm. West German activism re-emerged in the late 1960s in the political and cultural ferment among students, and another wave gathered at the end of the 1970s, beginning with opposition to the neutron bomb and Euromissiles.

Pershing II and ground-launched cruise missiles were two more weapons in an already genocidal and suicidal arsenal, their European deployment one more symbol of "NATO unity" and of U.S. military power not only in—but over—Europe. When mass protests did not prevent this deployment, grassroots activists in Europe confronted the war machine itself. They blockaded bases and convoys and tracked down the secret woodland launch sites. But in West Germany, with brutal arrogance, the United States erected its missile launchers not only in secret but in the open as well, in town squares and school playgrounds, and on the highways Hitler originally built to speed his armies on their way.

Grassroots opposition demonstrated that these weapons could not function among people with a democratic spirit, at least not with the efficiency required of high-technology warfare. The enforcement measures and court prosecutions required to counter active resistance were too awkward to be carried on indefinitely in a European setting. So now the attack missiles built for the electronic battlefields of NATO and the United States are to be launched from the air and the sea, out of sight and out of reach of most popular direct opposition.

West German activists have been working for years to analyze the links between the militarization of "Western" society (their own in particular), the economic exploitation and political manipulation of third world peoples, and the destruction of the planet's life-system. Concentrated at the community level, their work created the conditions for effective mainstream protest. A 1983 U.S. Army publication noted that every U.S. military development had now become a political issue, that military operations were taking longer to carry out than they used to and were sometimes no longer possible to do, and that complaints and lawsuits against the Army were on the rise.[69]

Opposition to U.S. military deployments has been carried on in many ways and by many kinds of organizations—church groups, professional associations, community networks, study groups, research institutes that monitor Congressional hearings to give the public information that the German government tries to conceal from them, city officials like the mayor of Würzburg, and parliamentarians who publicize the plans and operations of the U.S. military and work for democratic process. In the summer of 1990, claiming a share of responsibility for a threat to other countries going forth from Germany, activists began preparing for the nonviolent disarming of U.S. European Command headquarters in Stuttgart.

Looking to the Future

George Kennan, who framed the U.S. policy of Soviet containment after World War II, commented in November 1989 that the alliances of the Cold War were obsolescent and needed to give way to a new framework of European security in a world in which the great enemy is not the Soviet Union but the catastrophic deterioration of the planet,[70] but the United States has only NATO on which to base its European presence. Its military power, particularly its nuclear force, provides the United States a lease on life as a European power. Within NATO, the stated U.S. public mission is now three-fold: still deterring and, if need be, defending against any imaginable Soviet aggression; once again containing German power; and, as President Bush described it, countering Europe's new enemies, "instability and unpredictability."[71] Europe's function as a forward base for "out-of-area" interventions in the Middle East and North Africa, the fourth and most substantial mission of U.S. forces deployed in Europe, has not been a subject for public discussion among NATO and U.S. strategists, but it is no secret in Germany.

For the time being, the U.S. military presence in Germany remains firmly institutionalized, but now that it is no longer framed by the East-West bloc confrontation, its role in projecting coercive power beyond Europe to enforce U.S. "interests" is more easily seen. As Europeans, feeling a new sense of community, explore possibilities for European security based on trust and co-operation, they will repeatedly confront the influence and obstacles of U.S. political and military pressures on their governments. The people of Germany in particular will be called by their own consciences to confront the continuing U.S. military presence with the promise, contained in the September 12, 1990 Treaty on the Final Settlement with Respect to Germany, that in the future "only peace will emanate from German soil." The people of the United States owe them full solidarity in fulfilling this promise.

Notes

1. *Overseas* (Heilbronn, Fall 1989), 24.
2. Simon Duke, *United States Military Forces and Installations in Europe* (London: Oxford University Press, 1989), 56.
3. "Text of the Declaration After the NATO Talks," *New York Times,* 7 July 1990.
4. Burkhard Luber, *Militäratlas von Flensburg bis Dresden* (Bonn: die Grünen, 1986).
5. Duke, 94-168.
6. Ibid., 56.
7. Ibid, 96-148; Luber.
8. U.S. Department of Defense, *Selected Manpower Statistics, Fiscal Year 1988* (Washington: U.S. Government Printing Office), 45.
9. Ibid., 130, 135, 138, 141.
10. Ibid., 165.
11. Duke, 59.
12. Ibid., 72.
13. Alan Riding *New York Times,* 5 December 1989.
14. Diana Johnstone *The Politics of Euromissiles* (London: Verso, 1984), 36-37.
15. Richard J. Barnet, *The Alliance* (New York: Simon and Schuster, 1983), 127.
16. Dan Smith, *Pressure: How America Runs NATO* (London: Bloomsbury Publishing Ltd., 1989), 8-16.
17. Duke, 324-325.
18. Barnet, 177.
19. Ibid., 176.
20. Ibid., 221.
21. Ibid., 195.
22. Ibid., 318-319.
23. Ibid., 370.
24. Ibid., 376.
25. Ibid., 377.
26. Johnstone, 198.
27. "For an End to Bloc Confrontation in Europe," *VIA Newsletter,* No. 2 (Spring 1986), 19.
28. Congressional Budget Office, *U.S. Ground Forces and the Conventional Balance in Europe* (Washington, DC: U.S. Government Printing Office, 1988).
29. Duke, 351-352.
30. Ibid., 388.
31. U.S. Department of Defense, 45.

32. Institute for Defense and Disarmament Studies, *Cutting Conventional Forces* (Brookline, MA, 1989), appendix 7b-2. This figure excludes combat-capable training aircraft and 530 held in storage; it includes naval land-based aircraft.

33. Luber.

34. Duke, 87-88.

35. Oxford Research Group, "The Missiles NATO Isn't Talking About," *Media Bulletin*, No. 1 (November 1989), 1-3.

36. R.W. Apple, Jr., *New York Times*, 29 April 1990.

37. Narrative materials on which descriptions of Heilbronn and Hunsrück are based were provided by Lilo Klug, chairperson of the Association for International Exchange, Heilbronn.

38. Janice Hill, "Women and the Military," *Field Notes* (Stuttgart, Germany, Spring 1990).

39. *Construction Hearings, FY 1989*, Part I, 427.

40. Duke, 407-411.

41. Ibid., 74-75.

42. Timothy Aeppel, *Wall Street Journal*, 6 November 1989.

43. Bob Aldridge, "U.S. Military Exercises in West Germany," *The Monthly Planet* (Santa Cruz, CA), Vol. 5, No. 2, March 1989.

44. Amerika Dienst (America Service), ed., "Europe Chapter of the Annual Defense Report," (Bonn), 17 February 1982, 10.

45. From "WINTEX-CIMEX, Die Geheimen Kriegspiele der NATO," *Kontaktstelle für Gewaltfrei Aktion und Föderation Gewaltfreier Aktionsgruppen*, October 1986, in *VIA Newsletter*, No. 6 (Winter 1987), 16.

46. From "Tageszeitung," 25 August 1989, in *Overseas*, Fall 1989, 14.

47. Duke, 378.

48. Informationsbüro für Friedenspolitik, *FriedensBrief*, Starnburg, No. 1/2 (January-February 1989), 1.

49. Thomas Kleine-Brokhoff and Joachim Riedlt "Die Zeit," April 1988 in *VIA Newsletter*, No. 8 (Summer 1988), 5.

50. Dr. Hahn, Medical Director, St. Vinzenz Hospital, Coesfield, and Dr. Karl Heinz Daumer, Monchsroth, cited in a January 1989 bulletin from Lilo Klug, Heilbronn.

51. "Deutsche Volkzeitung," in *Overseas*, Fall 1989, 24.

52. Aldridge, 16.

53. James M. Markham, *New York Times*, 10 August 1988.

54. Werner May, *MoP Newsletter*, August 1988, in *VIA Newsletter*, No. 8 (Summer 1988), 4.

55. Kleine-Brokhoff and Riedlt.

56. Informationsbüro für Friedenspolitik, 1.

57. Ibid., 2.

58. Robert J. McCartney, *Manchester Guardian Weekly*, 8 January 1989.

59. Duke, 75-77.

60. Duke, 324-325.

61. Duke, 77.

62. William Mako, *U.S. Ground Forces and the Defense of Central Europe* (Washington, D.C.: The Brookings Institution, 1983), 98-99.

63. Smith, 111-112.

64. "How Far Away Is War in the Persian Gulf?" *VIA Newsletter*, No. 7, (Winter/Spring 1988), 10.

65. Michael R. Gordon, *New York Times*, 2 August 1990.

66. C.A.H. Trost, *New York Times*, 1 January 1990.

67. Michael Gordon and Bernard E. Trainor, *New York Times*, 12 December 1989.

68. Gordon.

69. U.S. Army Europe and 7th Army, eds., "The German Context Within Which USAREUR Must Live and Operate," Heidelberg, 1983.

70. George Kennan, *Manchester Guardian Weekly*, 19 November 1989.

71. H.D.S Greenway, *Boston Globe*, 28 April 1990.

Chapter 12

NATO's Southern Flank and U.S. Bases

Low-Intensity Conflicts and Out-of-Area Operations

Mariano Aguirre

When the U.S. Government launched its massive deployment of forces to the Persian Gulf in August 1990, following Iraq's invasion of Kuwait, the activity on most U.S. bases in the Mediterranean region was frenetic. In a matter of weeks tens of thousands of soldiers and enormous amounts of war materiel were moved across the Atlantic Ocean and European skies. "I couldn't sleep on many nights" said a neighbor of Torrejon de Ardoz, a U.S.-Spanish base near Madrid.[1]

The cause of his sleepless nights was the U.S. Galaxy transport planes that used the base as a steppingstone to the Persian Gulf, and the F-16 bombers that were redeployed from Spain (and Italy and Turkey) to Saudi Arabia. The prediction of peace researchers and activists, who argued that the Spanish integration into NATO and the Western European Union (WEU), and the negotiation of the most recent U.S.-Spanish Military Agreement would make Spain a platform for U.S. intervention in the Third World, was sadly fulfilled.

Not only was Spain used as a platform for intervention, but three Spanish Navy ships—one corvette and two frigates—with young soldiers doing their compulsory military service, were dispatched to the Middle East from Cartagena and Rota in the name of "international solidarity." Similar deployments to fill the gaps in the U.S. 6th Fleet were made by the French, Italians, Dutch, Belgians, and Germans.

On December 1, 1988, Spain signed an agreement renewing the defense treaty in which Spain ceded bases and military installations to the United States. Despite the fact that the socialist government of Felipe Gonzalez had promised a "progressive reduction" in the North American military presence in Spain, the new text guaranteed the passage of nuclear arms through a country that has declared itself de-nuclearized. Moreover, the agreement stipulates that authorization for using the bases for NATO out-of-area actions, as well as for the installation of nuclear weapons in the country, must be sought, not from the Spanish Parliament, but from the government of the day. Possible disputes arising from the U.S. military presence shall be settled, not according to Spanish law, but under U.S. jurisdiction.

In January 1989, one month before he was rejected by Congress as U.S. Secretary of Defense, John G. Tower called upon the NATO allies to provide more support for security outside the defense area established in the North Atlantic Treaty, arguing that this was necessary in order to confront challenges emanating from the Third World. This topic, along with the modernization of short-range nuclear missiles, was one of the central themes of Tower's first meetings with the European allies, indicating the importance that Washington attaches to the international coordination of military actions in the Third World.

These two events—the renewal of the defense treaty between Spain and the United States and Tower's call for greater European support of intervention in the Third World—are each important in themselves. They are also interrelated. The United States saw renewal of the Spanish-U.S. treaty as essential to maintaining credibility as a world power. From the military viewpoint, Spain is an excellent platform from which to launch troops, in particular from the air and naval base at Rota, situated in the southwest of Spain on the Atlantic coast. As early as the 1950s, Western strategists were claiming that Rota was essential to the safeguarding of Western security.

The base at Rota is crucial for the passage of U.S. troops toward the Middle East or North Africa, as envisaged in the Maritime Strategy. The principal objectives of this strategy are to control commercial and military shipping routes in time of peace; to intervene in the Third World in times of crisis; and to engage in conventional or nuclear conflict against the Soviet Union in case of war.[2] Rota is an important support base for the U.S. Sixth Fleet, which has been patrolling the waters of the Mediterranean uninterruptedly since 1946. Despite Spain's supposedly nuclear-free status, the nuclear weapons carried by this fleet entered Spanish ports on more than 300 occasions in 1988.[3]

The pressure exerted by the United States on its allies to participate in NATO out-of-area activities, and the principle—tacitly agreed upon by

Madrid and Washington in the 1986 negotiations on the renewal of the defense treaty—that Rota was non-negotiable and would remain under U.S. control are both related to the recent re-evaluation of NATO's Southern Flank. Equally significant is the fact that Spain has signed an annex to the agreement of 1988 guaranteeing that it will not solicit information from the United States about the type of weaponry carried by U.S. ships (and, by implication, planes) in Spanish waters (and airspace).

This chapter describes the dual role of the U.S. bases in the Mediterranean area—to assist in nuclear deterrence of the Soviet Union and to support the United States in a wide range of conflicts in the Third World. It also sketches the political situation in Western Europe at the end of the 1980s and the beginning of the 1990s, and the prospect that a new "international division of labor" will develop with respect to military tasks, with the possible creation of a "European pillar" of NATO. This chapter raises questions about the role of the U.S. bases in Spain in the redefinition of the strategic role of the Southern Flank—in particular with respect to out-of-area operations. To address these questions, it is necessary to describe the general situation in the Mediterranean.

There are a number of reasons to pay special attention to the Spanish case. First, these bases play highly significant roles with respect to nuclear conflict and to intervention in the Third World. Second, the last defense agreement between Spain and the United States may well serve as a blueprint in negotiations with other countries. Third, the military relations Spain has maintained with the United States since 1953, although of a bilateral nature, drew Spain into practically all the structures of what is referred to as "Western defense." The Spanish case also merits particular attention because, despite strong popular opposition to membership in the Atlantic Alliance, Spain is now at the forefront of efforts to construct a European pillar of NATO.

The Rediscovery of the Southern Flank

At this writing, the East-West conflict, which provided the justification for the post-war growth of international militarism, is in a process of fundamental transformation which is likely to lead to a greater equilibrium between East and West in terms both of conventional and nuclear arms. Although this equilibrium would not signify disarmament, it would create a firmer climate of political confidence between East and West.

In the Third World, political, economic, and social questions are complex and explosive. Structural problems of underdevelopment produce: the drug economy with its Mafia leadership and peasant base that depends on the narcotics trade for its survival (as in Bolivia, Colombia, Afghanistan, and Pakistan); the massive exodus from countries in which the conditions of life are miserable to others that are equally poor and plagued by starvation or war (sub-Saharan Africa); popular uprisings provoked by material need (Venezuela, Morocco); massive anti-racist protest (South Africa); the protests of young people who find themselves without social or economic prospects (Algeria); and the steady pressure of immigration from the South to the North (for example, from Central America to the United States and from North Africa to Western Europe). The crises, and the established system's lack of adequate answers to any of these pressing problems, favor the rise of simplistic—and for that very reason highly effective—forms of religious fundamentalism, which reach far beyond the borders of any individual country and are in themselves an additional destabilizing factor.[4]

At any moment a combination of these factors could provoke radical change in countries or regions of the Third World, threatening what the Western world (that is, the United States, Western Europe, and Japan) views as its interests. The Gulf War (1979-1987), for instance, in which so many nations profitably participated as merchants of arms, came to be seen as a threat to oil supplies when the warring parties began shifting their attention to shipping in the Persian Gulf and attacking the adversary's oil refineries. Both the United States and some European nations intervened with warships to protect the transport of crude oil through the Gulf.

Faced with an increasingly complex and multi-faceted world, the United States and some other members of NATO are altering their military organization, as well as the theoretical assumptions on which military doctrines are based. The problems with which these nations see themselves confronted are no longer merely those that relate to movements of national liberation or revolutionary governments; rather, a whole gamut of situations in the Third World present potential threats to the established interests of the West. In the United States, the 1980s has seen the development of a strategy for "low-intensity warfare" precisely in order to confront these "changing threats" in "a security landscape dominated by shades of gray rather than blacks and whites."[5]

Low-intensity conflicts (LIC) are not necessarily less severe than mid- or high-intensity warfare. They are conflicts involving counter-insurgency, pro-insurgency (that is, the destabilization of governments "hostile" to the West), and "preventive" anti-terrorism. Like other levels of warfare, LIC seeks to defend U.S. access to or domination of natural resources, to aid friendly governments, and to achieve U.S. geostrategic goals. In recent years, the U.S. attack on Libya, actions against Nicaragua and Angola, economic and military aid to the government of El Salvador, arms transfers, the presence of military advisors in Morocco and Chad, and the training of ultra-right-wing para-military groups in the Philippines have provided examples of "low-intensity" actions subsumed under the heading of counter-insurgency, pro-insurgency, or rapid actions in "times of peace."[6] One of the regions which has experienced a number of such low-intensity conflicts is the Mediterranean. A conservative French weekly has described the area as "the typical model for the type of areas with 'low-intensity' conflicts where peace never reigns but a full-blown conflagration is improbable."[7]

A Region Potentially at War

At the end of the 1940s the Mediterranean Sea was viewed by Western military planners as a highway for the transit of supplies and reinforcements in a war against the Soviet Union. The Mediterranean was of secondary importance in the conflict with the Soviet Union; NATO was constructed on the assumption of a conventional attack launched against Central Europe by the Soviet Union and its allies.

The priorities in the so-called Southern Flank were of a political nature: to control the Communist Parties which had been strengthened in the resistance to Italian Fascism and German Nazism in Italy, France, and Greece. As in the rest of Western Europe, the aim was to reconstruct moderate governments that accepted the free-market economic system, parliamentary democracy, and the nuclear hegemony of the United States. In a few cases this option was not available because the choice was between anti-communist, anti-democratic governments or popular opposition forces of doubtful reliability. In such cases support was given to dictatorships, including Franco in Spain, Salazar in Portugal, and military dictatorships in Greece (1967) and Turkey (1980).

In the Middle East and the Eastern Mediterranean, the United States took the place of Great Britain and France, the two former colonial powers. In 1946, as the strategy of containment was being developed, the United States sent the first units of the Sixth Fleet to the Mediterranean. Forty years later, they are still there. A specialist at the Rand Corporation has described the military role of the United States in the Mediterranean:

> The United States, as the major Western military power in the region and the most influential politically, remains…the most capable Western power with the potential for integrating the defense area, and for arbitrating regional conflict political disputes…The global definition of U.S. interests combines with American membership in NATO and the nature of its role in the Gulf to make the United States the paramount link between European security and the Western defense of the Gulf.[8]

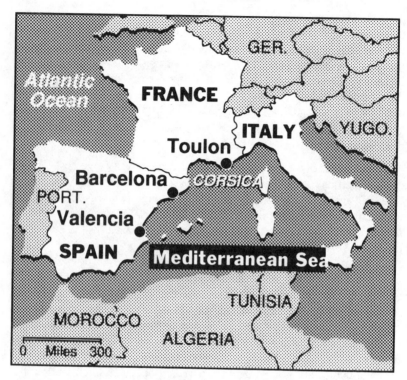

In reality the United States, far from being a stabilizing force, has provoked grave crises or aggravated existing conflicts, as in its military interventions in Libya and Lebanon.

Over the past 15 years, the Southern Flank has received increased attention. Various factors have influenced the enhanced assessment of its strategic significance. The first of these factors was the greater presence of the Soviet Navy. In 1968 the Soviet Union declared that, being a Black Sea naval power, it had the right to be present in the Mediterranean. The decision to use the Soviet Navy in forward defense was taken in response to the aggressive deployment of U.S. systems of sea-based nuclear weapons. The Soviet Union, however, has no permanent bases in the Mediterranean, although it uses maintenance facilities in Syria, Yugoslavia, Algeria, and Libya. In any event, its position in the Mediterranean is far from firm. In times of conflict the straits of the Bosphorus and the Dardanelles, which are controlled by Turkey, could be closed, thus denying the Soviet Union direct access to Mediterranean waters. But this East-West warfare scenario is outdated. With *perestroika* and *new thinking* in Soviet foreign policy, Moscow has made a number of proposals for the demilitarization of the Mediterranean in recent years. These proposals can be summarized as calling for a freeze on U.S. and Soviet naval forces, followed by negotiations for their withdrawal from the region, and the implementation of confidence-building measures. All signs indicate that the Soviet Union wants to withdraw its naval force from the Mediterranean in the broader context of the current negotiations on nuclear and conventional forces.

A second factor in the reassessment of the Southern Flank was the greater degree of commitment shown by the Soviet Union to the Palestinian cause and the Soviet friendship treaties with Egypt (repudiated by Egypt in 1975) and with Syria and Libya. The oil crisis of the 1970s and the possibility that the oil-producing nations might use oil as a weapon with which to blackmail the West have also focussed attention on the region's strategic significance. In Washington the Soviet Union is no longer seen as a competitor in the Middle East, allowing regional conflicts to be separated from the dynamics of East-West conflict. While this was an important development, the Iraqi invasion of Kuwait confirmed the political power of the Western fear of "enemies" controlling the region's oil reserves.

Today the Mediterranean Sea lies between the detente in the North and actual or potentially explosive situations in the South. In 1988, in his last lecture as Director of the International Institute of Strategic Studies, Robert O'Neill stated: "Virtually every type of security problem, subnational or international, from terrorism to the superpower nuclear relationship, exists in the Mediterranean region."[9] East-West relations are becoming more relaxed and, consequently, the traditional functions the Southern Flank was supposed to fulfill, both in peace and war, are losing their validity. As Diana Johnstone has written of the Italian armed forces, they grew tired of waiting for an attack from the East for 40 years and decided to direct their attention once more to the problems in the South.[10]

The southern border of the Mediterranean and the Eastern Mediterranean contain the roots of future conflicts. Economic, social, and religious conflicts predominate, and there are legacies of colonialism and of the region's older culture and history. The process of conventional rearmament and, in some cases, chemical and even nuclear armament, is influenced by local conflicts and follows its own course, apparently uninfluenced by the progress in Central Europe.

Military intervention in the region has taken the form of "surgical" strikes made in the name of "anti-terrorism": "surgical" Israeli attacks against Palestinian positions in the Middle East and North Africa; the dispatch of U.S.

Marines to Lebanon and the Israeli invasion of the same country in 1982; the U.S. attack on Libya in April of 1986; the constant show of U.S. naval force in the region, and the massive 1990 U.S. military buildup in the Persian Gulf.

There is an increasing tendency to view the Mediterranean area as part of a larger geopolitical structure, including North Africa, the Arab Peninsula, and the eastern part of the Atlantic Ocean. Within NATO, the Mediterranean is seen as a bridge uniting different areas. "The key word in Mediterranean strategic planning is 'join,'" according to U.S. Admiral Harry Train. "Rather than representing a barrier, the Mediterranean 'joins.' It joins Middle East oil with Western Europe. It joins Indian Ocean shipping with the Atlantic Ocean. It joins Soviet ice-free Black Sea ports with the Atlantic and Indian Ocean trade routes. It joins together the southern NATO partners. And it joins some of the West's most important industrial nations with their markets and resources."[11]

Nuclear Arms in the Mediterranean

Over the past four decades, the United States has established a powerful presence in the Mediterranean area; today, the United States has roughly 200 naval and air installations in countries as distant as Portugal and Egypt. The presence of U.S. troops in the area is considerable: some 8,600 in Spain, 16,100 in Italy, 3,300 in Greece, and 4,800 in Turkey. In addition, approximately 1,200 U.S. troops are based in Egypt and an unspecified number are in Morocco, where they have advised the army of the dictator Hassan II in his struggle against the Polisario Front. Israel is a privileged ally of Washington in the Eastern Mediterranean and in the Middle East. In Israel the United States has access to three air bases and two naval bases, and the country is frequently viewed as an extension of NATO in the Middle East. Egypt is another important ally, sharing with Israel a significant part of the U.S. military aid allotted to the area ($2.12 billion and $3 billion respectively in Fiscal Year 1988), and the United States has the use of eight airports, a naval base, and two other naval facilities in Egypt.

Washington has bilateral agreements with almost all the countries on the northern shore of the Mediterranean—Greece, Turkey, Italy, Spain, and Portugal. The only exceptions are Albania and Yugoslavia, neither of which belongs to any military alliance, and France, which demanded the withdrawal of U.S. troops and bases from its territory in 1966. However, military coordination between the French and U.S. navies has been considerably strengthened in recent years.

France possesses its own nuclear force. U.S. nuclear weapons are deployed in Greece, Italy, and Turkey. Portugal, Spain, Italy, Greece, and

Turkey all host elements of the military infrastructure required by the United States for the use of its land, sea, and air-based nuclear weapons. Military bases, control and communications centers, and radar networks comprise this infrastructure.

Spain hosted nuclear weapons on its territory and nuclear submarines based at Rota until 1979. The Portugese Constitution is ambiguous on the issue of nuclear weapons. It has been alleged that the Portugese island of Lajes and mainland ports are used for the transit of nuclear weapons.

During the course of the Reagan Administration, the headquarters of the Commander-in-Chief of U.S. Naval Forces in Europe was transferred from London to Naples. The Commander-in-Chief of Allied Forces in Southern Europe and of all NATO naval forces in Europe is a U.S. admiral, also with headquarters in Naples. William Arkin of the Institute for Policy Studies says:

> Consolidating U.S. and NATO commanders in the Mediterranean and stressing the improved "command relationship" of a U.S. Admiral command on all naval forces in the southern region and Europe is indicative of growing NATO interest in regions outside of its traditional focus.[12]

Great Britain maintains a base on Gibraltar, a point of strategic significance for NATO, plus two bases and an important communications center on Cyprus. The communications center is also used by the United States. None of these installations is controlled by the Republic of Cyprus.

France has a considerable military, economic, and diplomatic presence in the area. Paris attempts to maintain its influence in Arab countries and to operate at times as a partner and at times as a rival to the United States. French leaders are negotiating agreements on naval and airforce cooperation as well as cooperation agreements in intelligence for air-detection and early-warning systems with Italy and Spain.

The most powerful instrument of control that the United States possesses in the area is the 6th Fleet. According to the official version, the fleet has the task of protecting commercial maritime traffic, deterring the Soviet Union and supporting the United States' allies in the area, in particular Israel. However, Esther Barbe, a researcher at the University of Barcelona, maintains that the 6th Fleet operates at two levels: "as a guardian of European interests, basically expressed in terms of economic security, and as a direct defender of U.S. interests, adopting a position of controlling regional events."[13]

The 6th Fleet has been involved, directly or indirectly, in Mediterranean conflicts throughout the past 40 years: the Suez crisis (1956), Lebanon (1958, 1982-83, 1987), wars in the Middle East (1967, 1973, and 1977), Cyprus (1974), and Libya (1986). It carries some 300 nuclear weapons which can be used in land attacks or in anti-aircraft and anti-submarine warfare. It includes one, and on occasion two naval combat groups, each including more than 90 airplanes, six submarines, an amphibious group, and forces for anti-submarine warfare. Strategic submarines equipped with Poseidon nuclear weapons patrol the Mediterranean under NATO command.[14]

In the course of 40 years, the superimposing of military interests among the European NATO allies and the United States has led to confusion about these interests. Thus U.S. Secretary of Defense Caspar Weinberger was able to state—erroneously—in December 1986 that the U.S. forces in Spain on the basis of a bilateral treaty between Madrid and Washington were "NATO forces."[15]

Rapid Deployment and Naval Forces

Forty years after the arrival of the 6th Fleet in the Mediterranean, containment has acquired a different objective in accordance with Washington's new priorities. The founding of the U.S. Central Command (CENTCOM) in January 1983, which incorporates the Rapid Deployment Force (RDF) and whose action radius comprises an extensive area ranging from Egypt to Pakistan, the Persian Gulf, and Northeast Africa, coincided with a revival of the debate within NATO on the possible use of Alliance forces outside the geographical limits established in the Treaty of Washington. Retired Italian admiral Falco Accame commented: "For the Reagan government the Mediterranean has become a route from the Azores to the base of Diego Garcia in the Indian Ocean."[16]

To guarantee support for the RDF, Washington initiated an active campaign to extend the network of bases and supporting installations in the Mediterranean and the Indian Ocean, and between these two regions and the Persian Gulf. Thus, the U.S. bases in the Philippines are essential for the transit of the RDF, as are also those in the Azores and Diego Garcia. Equally important are authorizations for the use of airports and military bases that have been granted by allied Arab countries, from the Saudi monarchy to the Moroccan dictatorship. The projection of forces and naval strategy require that the infrastructure of bases, ports, installations, and electronic control centers be extended. It has also been necessary to increase the number of aircraft carriers—naval fortresses that reduce U.S. dependence on foreign bases—combat groups, logistical support, and rapid intervention forces.

The Mediterranean is experiencing an accelerated process of militarization and strategic reorientation. The modernization of Spain's aeronaval forces since the country's entry into NATO, and a similar modernization of Italian forces, coincides with a growth in French naval power. The construction of a "European defense" or a "European pillar" within NATO rests on two basic axes: first, the Paris-Bonn axis, and, second, the Paris-Madrid-Rome axis. The increased importance attached to naval forces is in accordance with the policy begun during the Reagan Administration—development of a maritime strategy to reinforce the aggressive projection of forces in the pursuit of U.S. global interests. This strategy seeks to fulfull three functions: to maintain a U.S. presence in times of peace, to intervene in crises in the Third World, and to deter or combat the Soviet Union in the case of nuclear or conventional war.[17]

Bases and Containment

In the years following World War II, the United States signed agreements with many Mediterranean countries, permitting it to establish military bases throughout the area. In many cases, reference was made to Article III of the North Atlantic Treaty, which provides: "In order more effectively to achieve the objectives of this Treaty, the parties, separately and jointly, by means of continuous and effective self-help and mutual aid, will maintain and develop their individual and collective capacity to resist armed attack." Reference to this clause gave rise to an ambiguous situation in which it was not absolutely clear whether NATO or U.S. bases were being established.[18] These defense agreements enabled the United States to strengthen the chain of bases intended to contain the Soviet Union. But in many cases they were also crucially important in facilitating U.S. control over the domestic politics of the countries in question; the counter-insurgency tactics that have become a central element in low-intensity conflict were first developed and put into practice in the Mediterranean in the immediate post-war years.

In 1951, the United States signed an agreement with France to establish five military bases in Morocco, then a French colony. That same year, the Portugese dictatorship, in an executive agreement with Washington, permitted the U.S. military use of the strategically placed Azores Islands "within the framework of the North Atlantic Treaty." Beginning in 1947, Greece received special assistance from the United States. In 1952, it became a member of NATO, and the following year, a bilateral treaty was signed between Washington and Athens, much of which remains secret to this day. In 1969, a Defense Cooperation Agreement was signed between Greece and the United States; the agreement was classified secret and, as in the case of the 1953 treaty, the full text has never been made public.

In 1947, an important program of military aid was also put into effect in Turkey which, in 1952, became a member of NATO. In the two years following Turkey's entry into the Alliance, a number of agreements relating to defense and mutual security, both public and secret, were signed between

Washington and Ankara. Washington's aim was to create a ring of bases in Iran, Turkey, and Greece, as part of the strategy to contain the Soviet Union. The United States also gained access to the air base at Wheelus in Libya, although this had to be abandoned in 1970 following Muammar Qadhafi's accession to power.

Italy: Stopping the Spread of Communism

U.S. bases were initially installed in Italy as a consequence of the U.S. military presence there at the end of the war and later by virtue of the Agreement on NATO forces. Rome and Washington exchanged notes in 1952 and signed an agreement in 1954; since then, a number of bilateral agreements between the two countries have been signed, none of which have required parliamentary ratification and all of which remain secret.

Italy offers a particularly striking example of the connection between the installation of military bases and the maintenance or construction of a political and economic system congenial to U.S. interests. Establishing a U.S. military presence in Italy, bringing that country into NATO, and marginalizing Italian communism were separate, but related, aspects of the U.S. strategy of stabilization in post-war Europe.

The U.S. military presence was used by the Truman Administration as an element of political pressure. The Administration openly supported the Italian Christian Democratic Party in the general elections of 1948, fearing that the Communist Party would nevertheless be victorious. A document of the National Security Council (NSC) dating from that year states:

> The United States should make full use of its political, economic, and, if necessary, military power in such manner as might be found most effective to assist in preventing Italy from falling under domination of the U.S.S.R. either through armed attack or through Soviet dominated communist movements within Italy.[19]

The NSC also suggested that one way of helping the Christian Democratic Party would be to encourage Italy's participation in NATO, which was established the following year. A series of official U.S. documents dating from this period indicate that, had the Italian Communist Party (PCI) won any elections, the United States would have expected Italy to request assistance from other members of NATO. This would have been a case of "confronting the communist threat," the precise purpose for which NATO had been formed.[20]

Greece and Turkey: The Truman Doctrine and Dependence

In the case of Greece, the installation of U.S. bases and the relationship of complete military, political, and economic dependency were preceded by the United States' first major post-war counter-insurgency operation. Greece was virtually destroyed during World War II, having been subjected first to Nazi occupation and then to a British invasion in 1944 which was intended to prevent the People's Liberation Army (ELAS), a broad-based popular front formed in 1941 as a resistance movement against the Nazis, from taking power. London imposed a government that was conservative, monarchical, and authoritarian, provoking the outbreak of civil war in 1944. The following year an armistice was reached, due in part to the fact that Stalin provided no assistance to ELAS since he regarded Greece as being within the British sphere of influence. But in 1946, the war erupted with renewed force. Britain, unable to continue carrying the economic and military cost of intervention in Greek affairs, appealed to the United States to assume this role. For three years, the U.S. Military Mission in Greece was responsible for planning the conduct of the war against ELAS and providing the right-wing forces with arms, equipment, and financial assistance. The Greek army was reorganized to equip it to carry out anti-guerrilla operations until ELAS was finally defeated in 1949. From then on, political parties that were permitted to operate had to accept the premise that Greece depended on both NATO and on a close relationship with the United States—the new dominant power in the Mediterranean.[21]

In a study of the Greek civil war, sociologist Todd Gitlin has written: "British and American policy were, under the surface, as crude as the strategy that governed them: not to contain foreign aggression but domestic revolution; not to bring democracy but to maintain its absence; not to avoid violence but to thwart radical change by violence if necessary; not to bring freedom, but bases."[22] Similarly, Lawrence Wittner's study of the same period concludes that U.S. policy "contributed to Greece's desperate political, social, [and] economic problems [and] encouraged the establishment and maintenance of a right-wing dictatorship as the only way to keep Greece in line with their [i.e., Washington's] aims."[23]

Greek dependence on the United States was revealed most dramatically in the assistance given by Washington to the Greek military dictatorship that ruled between 1967 and 1974. The leader of the coup d'etat that established the dictatorship, Colonel George Papadopoulos, had worked previously in liaison between the CIA and the Greek intelligence services. The United States feared an election victory for Dimetrios Papandreou of the

Panhellenic Socialist Movement (PASOK), in the elections due to be held in July 1967. A report drawn up by the CIA in Athens stated that if Papandreou triumphed, this "would seriously damage vital U.S. interests in the eastern Mediterranean area, weaken the Southern Flank of NATO and seriously destabilize...delicate Greek-Turkish relations."[24]

Economic and military relations between Greece and the United States since the 1950s have left Greece in the role of a client. Greece has paid high interest rates for U.S. loans and has received minimal decision-making powers in the unequal relationship. In exchange, the United States has the use of several bases (Souda Bay, Khania, and Iraklion on Crete; Nea Makri and, until recently, Hellenikon in mainland Greece), a series of communications facilities, and five NATO early-warning communications posts in mainland Greece and Crete. These installations provide information to the 6th Fleet, carry out intelligence, reconnaisance, and monitoring of naval traffic in the Mediterranean, link the Eastern Mediterranean militarily and electronically with North Africa, the Middle East, Spain, and Italy, as well as control the Balkan area.[25]

Looking back on his country's experience, the retired Greek general G. Koumanakos declared in 1987:

> When a military base gets installed in a country, a whole network—under the label of security—covers progressively and with the utmost secrecy the entire public and a large part of the private life of the host country... It is rather difficult, if not impossible to have real peace under foreign military presence. This presence is constituted by the foreign fleets, foreign bases and foreign military bases. The bases are not positive or useful installations for any host country. The country and its citizens become nuclear targets and national sovereignty and independence are violated.[26]

Following the military coup in Turkey in 1980, the United States repeated the Greek model of supporting a military dictatorship to guarantee stability and access to strategic bases there. In 1987, while the United States and NATO claimed Turkey's "transition to democracy" was in full swing, Amnesty International listed 15,000 political prisoners and condemned the frequent practice of torture. Only a handful of security forces were brought to trial for human rights violations. At the same time, the Turkish government was practicing religious and ethnic persecution, especially against the Kurds, and carrying out forced relocations of the population in the southeast of the country; trade unions and peace groups were prohibited; 300,000 Turks were denied passports; and over 13,000 exiles were stripped of their citizenship.[27] Washington's claim that Turkey was making progress toward democracy stemmed from Turkey's increased strategic significance to the United States after the fall of the Shah of Iran in 1979. During the 1990 Gulf crisis, Turkey played an important role in alliance with Washington and London. One of its open intentions was to gain membership in the European Economic Community.

Spain and the Southern Flank

The United States signed a treaty with Spain in 1953 through which it gained access to military bases. From then until the death of dictator Francisco Franco in 1975, Spain was integrated into the Atlantic defense system "via the back door." [28] In 1982, Spain formally became a member of NATO and, since then, has become progressively more integrated into the so-called Western defense system. Yet the country formerly had a tradition of neutrality, and a majority of its citizens opposed Spain's participation in military blocs. Nevertheless, Spain's military integration has proceeded at such a spectacular pace that the country is now at the forefront of plans for West European defense. It also "hosts" U.S. bases that serve important functions in the North-South and East-West conflicts.

In the immediate post-war period, Spain was in a unique position among West European countries. Though it had not participated directly in the war, it had been ideologically close to the Axis powers, whose assistance contributed to Franco's victory in the Spanish Civil War. Later, the Spanish dictatorship contributed forces to the German invasion of the Soviet Union in 1941.

As a result, Spain was excluded from the United Nations when it was formed in 1945, and it received no assistance under the Marshall Plan. Within the context of U.S. foreign policy, the brutal nature of the Franco dictatorship was less significant than its decidedly anti-communist character. Madrid signed commercial agreements with France and Great Britain in 1948, and from 1949 onwards, Spain also received U.S. economic aid, albeit indirectly, via private bank loans. Thanks to Washington's good offices, Spain was able to enter the United Nations in 1955.

As early as 1950, the U.S. Joint Chiefs-of-Staff had decided that, in one form or another, Spain must be incorporated into NATO. In a scenario which assumed that Central Europe would be the battlefield, Spain was seen to be important precisely because of its distance from the East-West demarcation in Central Europe, as well as for the role it could play by allowing the United States to project forces via the Mediterranean into North Africa and the Middle East.

Spain's Mediterranean Functions

The functions assigned to Spain in the 1980s differed little from those it was given in the 1950s. These were defined by the strategist Hanson Baldwin in 1953 in terms which have lost none of their relevance:

> Spain's bases help to seal the Western gateway to the Mediterranean; her Atlantic islands aid in controlling and protecting trans-Atlantic shipping lanes, and the Iberian Peninsula provides additional dispersed sites for light, medium and heavy bomber strips. And Spain, behind the ramparts of the Pyrenees, provides a last line of defense if the rest of Western Europe should fall, and offers a springboard for offensive land, sea and air operations. Her bases are particularly important as an alternative to the great bomber strips in Morocco, surrounded by political and social unrest...[29]

On September 26, 1953, the Eisenhower Administration and the Spanish dictatorship signed the Madrid Treaty, which granted the United States the use of air and naval bases, anchorage rights, underground storage installations, and oil pipelines, as well as the right to use all these facilities in the case of nuclear war, a right not subject to permission being granted by the Spanish government.[30] Spain began receiving U.S. military aid and training, economic aid, and other forms of military assistance. In 1970, 70 percent of Spain's military materiel was of U.S. origin, a degree of dependency that persists to this day. The Madrid Treaty was of enormous importance to Franco, allowing his regime to emerge from the international isolation to which it had been subjected. The *generalísimo* presented the treaty as clear proof of Spain's alignment with the West.

The Madrid Treaty provided for joint Spanish-U.S. use of airbases at Torrejón de Ardoz, Zaragoza, and Morón, and the aeronaval base at Rota. From the 1960s onward, Rota facilitated communication, the ships of the 6th Fleet. At the end of the 1960s, a U.S. naval squadron with nine nuclear-powered missile submarines, each armed with 160 nuclear weapons, was based at Rota. Other U.S. nuclear weapons were moved about Spain on U.S. B-52 bombers. These bombers, like those then deployed in Libya and the fighter planes of the 6th Fleet, were intended to carry out nuclear strikes against Eastern Europe and the Soviet Union. With the development of submarine-based, long-range nuclear missiles, the strategic role of NATO's Southern Flank in the East-West conflict declined.

When Spain entered NATO in 1982, several studies on its role in Western defense were published. These identified a number of roles for Spain:

- infrastructure (such as ports, roads, electronic communications and control centers, and pipelines);
- transit for the arrival or evacuaton of U.S. or Canadian troops in the event of conflict in Central Europe;
- a communications center between Western Europe and the United States;
- practice grounds for NATO troops;
- strategic "depth";
- storage of arms and munitions;
- contribution of forces to the mobile forces of the Allied Command in Europe (ACE) to strengthen the Southern Flank;
- a transit platform for out-of-area operations or activities on the Southern Flank;
- control of the Mediterranean Sea, the Straits of Gibraltar, and the Eastern Atlantic (Canary Islands); and,
- part of the United States' nuclear infrastructure through provision of key bases and facilities for command, control, communications, and intelligence (C3I).[31]

Maximum Coordination

In the course of the 1980s, the Spanish armed forces were restructured: the Navy and Air Force were strengthened, while the Army's relative importance diminished. This was a response to Spain's military requirements, given the country's potential conflict with Morocco over Spain's colonies, Ceuta and Melilla, on the North African coast. The reform of the Spanish armed forces also coincided with NATO's strengthening of the Southern Flank. If the 6th Fleet was to be transferred to the Persian Gulf, Washington would require the European allies to fill the vaccuum thus created. In May 1987, Spain confirmed that it would be prepared to assume this function.[32] Furthermore, Spain's entry into the Western European Union (WEU) enabled Spain to participate in WEU-coordinated out-of-area operations, as it did in August 1990,[33] following the lead taken by France and Italy, Spain created a rapid action force in 1988.

The functions assigned to Spain within NATO thus reflect Washington's interest in establishing an international division of military labor; they also relate to the creation of a "European pillar" of NATO.

Spain plays a very active role in the effort to construct a European defense; it accepts the view advanced by Francois Mitterrand that European political unity will depend on first establishing military unity.[34] A text published in the Spanish Defense Ministry's official journal states: "The Spanish government considers...that the authentic construction of Europe will remain incomplete if there does not exist a pillar of defense and security."[35]

While the government of Felipe Gonzalez, supported by all of Spain's right-wing political parties, has involved the country in as many Atlantic military activities as possible, Spain nevertheless has not freed itself from its dependency on the United States. On December 1, 1988, a new Spanish-U.S. agreement was signed. While the Spanish government did achieve a measure of success with the agreement to withdraw 72 U.S. F-16 jets from Torrejón over a three-year period, the Italian government has agreed to their redeployment at Crotone (Sicily), despite the protests of the local population. However, the United States maintains control over the bases at Zaragoza, Morón, and Rota. Moreover, in spite of the March 1986 referendum that committed the Spanish government to a nuclear-free Spain, the government has given the United States assurances that it will not request any information as to whether U.S. ships or planes entering Spanish territory are in fact nuclear armed.

Like previous agreements, the renewed treaty grants criminal jurisdiction in cases involving U.S. military personnel to the United States. Similarly, Spanish workers contracted by the Spanish Ministry of Defense to work on these bases do not enjoy the protection of Spanish labor law. Although the agreement states that the bases are Spanish, it provides for U.S. command over them. Furthermore, in contrast to previous agreements which were renewable every five years, this treaty remains in force for eight years.[36]

Maintaining Forward Deployment

Given pressures in the United States to reduce its foreign military expenditures, some U.S. troops will be withdrawn from Europe and some U.S. military bases and installations in Europe will be abandoned. U.S. strategy, however, remains dependent on the cooperation of Washington's European allies in guaranteeing its global interests. Each of the allies will be expected to take care of its own sphere of influence and to coordinate its policy with that of other members of NATO—for example, France, Italy, and Spain will be required to cooperate in the Mediterranean and the Persian Gulf. The United States will continue to maintain a strategic presence, but it will be more limited. U.S. troops withdrawn from Western Europe may then be assigned to NATO out-of-area operations.[37] The British journal *Jane's Weekly* stated as early as December 1988 that the United States was beginning to reduce its military presence in Europe, starting with the Southern Flank.[38] The present situation in the Mediterranean, whereby the United States, through its allies (Turkey, Egypt, Spain, Morocco, and Italy), controls all routes of access to this sea, represents the model Washington will adopt to maintain its influence.[39]

The U.S. Congressional Panel on Burdensharing in NATO, presided over by Representative Patricia Schroeder (D-CO), affirmed in 1988 that the annual permit costs for U.S. bases overseas have risen since the mid-1970s— from $1 billion in 1974 to $4.6 billion in 1986, even though the number of U.S. bases fell during the same period. The Panel concluded "that forward deployment of U.S. troops should remain the cornerstone of U.S. military strategy in the near-term but not necessarily at the levels the United States currently maintains in all areas of the world."[40]

The Panel argued that if there are reasonable possibilities of asymmetrical reductions in conventional arms between NATO and the Warsaw Pact, the United States should perhaps withdraw U.S. troops stationed in certain regions. At the same time, it maintained that the allies should be capable of defending themselves with less direct military assistance from the United States.[41] In the same vein, following a seminar organized by the International Institute of Strategic Studies in the Mediterranean, Robert O'Neill concluded that "the growing view that Mediterranean security can be handled by the littoral states with little or no assistance from the United States will be a powerful incentive for those seeking to cut defense budgets or deployment levels, particularly in Washington."[42] These recommendations have been integrated into the the Bush Administration's approach to prevailing in the post-Cold War order. In the first month of the 1990 Gulf crisis, President Bush turned to U.S. allies (including Germany, Japan, Britain, the official government of Kuwait, Saudi Arabia, the United Arab Emirates, and South Korea) to share the cost of the military deployments to the Gulf. Meanwhile, his most loyal ally, Margaret Thatcher, called on NATO to change its formal rules to provide for military actions outside the area defined by the NATO treaty.

Seen in this context, the recent Spanish experience is particularly noteworthy, as it may serve as the prototype for future agreements between the United States and its allies. The U.S.-Spanish agreement has resulted in a reduction in the number of U.S. troops stationed in Spain; withdrawal of the Tactical Wing 401 from Spain and its redeployment in Italy, the costs of which will be borne by all NATO allies; U.S. control of the base at Rota so that U.S. ships may continue to patrol the Mediterranean and protect forces deployed in out-of-area operations in the Middle East or North Africa; and the cancellation of direct military aid, it henceforth being the function of private banks to provide the credits that will enable Spain to buy U.S. weaponry. Furthermore, Spain is now responsible for the maintenance costs of the base at Torrejón de Ardoz, even though NATO is permitted to deploy squadrons there in times of crisis.[43]

As far as out-of-area operations are concerned, Spain imposes limits on the use of U.S. bases for such activities. Permission for such use is granted or withheld on a case-by-case basis. Nevertheless, it is disturbing that the new agreement between Spain and the United States leaves these decisions in the hands of the Spanish government of the day. In August 1990, Madrid authorized the use of the U.S. bases for intervention in the Gulf without any parliamentary debate. Given that MP Miguel Herrero de Minon, one of the leaders of the Partido Popular, the main opposition party, is one of the principal European advocates of out-of-area operations in cooperation with the United States, the terms of the agreement arouse concern.[44] As far as the nuclear question is concerned, the agreement with Spain is significant in establishing the precedent that a nation that has declared itself non-nuclear reaffirms its limited sovereignty by guaranteeing Washington (and Paris and London) that their nuclear weapons are more important than the popular will of its citizens. A similar agreement was reached with the newly installed conservative Greek Government in July 1990. The bases at Hellenikon and Makri "are too close to Athens and hence too much a symbol of the American presence in Greece to be ignored."[45] They are slated to be closed. In exchange for 342 million dollars in military credits, the remainder of the U.S. bases will remain for the eight-year duration of the treaty. "The new agreement," *The Independent* of London explained, "ensures the continued operation, with some functions transferred from Helenikon and Nea Makri, of the Souda Bay air and naval complex near Chania and an electronics surveillance station at Gournes."[46] From Greece, the United States can control naval activity in the Eastern Mediterranean, North Africa, and much of the Middle East.

A New International Military Division of Labor

Within the context of efforts to rationalize its defense spending, political and military circles in the United States have responded with increasing favor to efforts to construct a "European pillar of NATO"—as long as such endeavors do not marginalize the United States. The Congressional Panel on Burden sharing "applauds recent efforts through the Western European Union and other avenues (for example, the agreement between France and Germany to create a Franco-German brigade) to strengthen the so-called European pillar of the alliance."[47] Similarly, the Supreme Allied Commander in Europe, General John Galvin, declared in 1988: "If we were to see some kind of European military unity that did not include the other side of the Atlantic, that might be damaging to NATO." Galvin saw no such danger, noting: "...I don't see French-German military cooperation leading in that direction; the French very much want the United States in the Alliance."[48]

Two weighty opinions in favor of increased West European defense collaboration are those of Henry Kissinger, who has stated that the United States should abandon "its historic reserve and welcome a European identity in defense,"[49] and of Ronald Reagan who, in the course of a radio program broadcast in Europe in November 1987, declared that the United States applauded "what we see as a new willingness, even eagerness, on the part of some of our allies to increase the level of cooperation and coordination among themselves in European defense."[50]

Before the collapse of the Cold War, Professor David Garnham foresaw that, sooner or later, the United States would materially reduce its commitment to the defense of Western Europe; Europeans would then have to organize a defense union that had as its core France and the Federal Republic of Germany, possibly within the framework of the WEU, as well as Portugal, Spain, and some Scandinavian countries.[51] Such a process would lead to a general reformulation of relations between the allies. The future of U.S. bases in such a scenario would be among the most important questions to be settled.

In this respect, certain proposals have already been advanced in the United States. The Congressional Burdensharing Panel has suggested that those allies that wish to retain U.S. bases on their territory as vital to their defense "should be prepared to defray more of the added costs the United States incurs as a result of its large deployments overseas."

This new approach to U.S. bases is finding support in Europe. A report of the North Atlantic Assembly, drawn up by the French parliamentarian Loic Bouvard, affirmed that:

> negotiations will not evolve as in the past...The issues of foreign aid and base rights are distinct. Within an Alliance of democratic nations committed to collective security, it is not natural that the status of U.S. bases should be made contingent upon foreign aid and periodic review.[52]

In this respect, too, the recent agreement between Spain and the United States, which does not make reference to any type of economic compensation to be paid by the United States in return for maintaining bases in Spain, may serve as a model for future agreements.

Searching for Alternatives

Although the United States is prepared to abandon some bases in Europe (and has a direct economic interest in doing so), U.S. policy makers remain concerned that these bases should still be available in times of crisis. Such an agreement has been reached concerning the Spanish base at Torrejón de Ardoz, which the U.S. Air Force will be permitted to use in case of war. Despite such caveats built into U.S. withdrawals from former bases, the United States has no intention of renouncing all its bases in foreign countries, least of all its aeronaval bases. There is a direct relationship between the development of NATO naval forces and the need to be able to rely on such bases.

Washington will try to retain control of those bases it regards as important for naval deployment in the Mediterranean and for the protection of forces directed against the Third World. In this context, the Spanish base at Rota, the Portugese base at Azores, the Greek naval base at Souda Bay, and certain Turkish, Italian, and Moroccan bases are crucial to U.S. strategy. Nevertheless, Washington is confronted by the political problem that almost all the countries of the Southern Flank are reticent about permitting these bases to be used without restriction by the United States for out-of- area operations.[53] Similarly, Great Britain would confront political problems with Cyprus if it were to permit the United States to use its base at Akrotiri for military intervention in the Persian Gulf. And though Egypt may permit the United States the use of its base in Ras Banas, it does not wish to see a strong and permanent U.S. military presence installed there.

The Turkish government has also been hesitant to let the bases at Erzurum, Mus, and Batman be used for operations in the Persian Gulf. Turkey's Islamic population might mount a powerful reaction if Turkey were implicated in any operation which could be interpreted as being directed against the Arab world. Nevertheless, various U.S. studies insist that this country "is ideally located to support American power projection to the Persian Gulf."[52]

Confronted with the reticence of the European allies, Washington sees two partial solutions. First, the allies should assume responsibility for the strategic needs of the United States; second, the United States should seek other alternatives. Major General David E. Wates, Director of Logistics of the U.S. Central Command, suggested in 1988 that Morocco might be an alternative to the U.S. base in the Portugese Azores and stated that the U.S. airforce had been improving Morocco's air bases so that these might be of use to the United States.[55]

Given that the debate on out-of-area operations continues, believing that military cooperation to meet unconventional threats will be intensified, and assuming that members of NATO accept the postulated "danger from the South," situations may well arise in which the strategic interests of Western Europe do coincide with those of the United States. A good example of such cooperation was the joint U.S.-French naval exercises carried out in February 1989, in the course of which the participants also practiced the rescue of 600 U.S. and French citizens from an unnamed country "due to serious domestic disturbances." These exercises were particularly significant because U.S. forces operated for the first time under the command of a French admiral.[56]

Many of the U.S. bases in the Mediterranean have become anachronisms; worse, they are also militarily destabilizing forces. With the advent of a new phase of detente, the bases are not necessary to maintain the policy of containment elaborated at the end of the 1940s and in the 1950s. In addition, Western Europe has embarked on the road toward greater autonomy in its own defense, whether constructing a bloc around French and British nuclear arms or searching for a shared security in a denuclearized Europe. In either of these two options, the U.S. bases appear as elements belonging to the past, although many of them will remain during a long transitional period.

However, the anachronism becomes a danger to the extent that the United States and its NATO allies accept the idea that future wars will take place in the Third World. The U.S. bases in the Mediterranean area will then play an important role in interventionist actions, as the 1990-91 Persian Gulf crisis showed.

For the countries of the Third World, the bases represent a source of instability. In June 1987, the foreign ministers of the Mediterranean members of the non-aligned movement (Algeria, Cyprus, Egypt, Lebanon, Libya, Malta, Morocco, the PLO, Syria, Tunisia, and Yugoslavia) declared:

> [T]he constant growth of the military arsenals and the fleets of the great powers, of their nuclear potential, their bases and support points, as well as the repeated recourse to force and demonstrations and threats of the means of force, directly or indirectly, represent one of the principal causes of instability in the Mediterranean.[57]

With the Cold War ending and East-West relations evidently relaxed and stable, there is a serious risk that the "European pillar"—favored by politicians ranging from the right-wing to French and Spanish socialists—will not only see danger emanating from the Third World, but will also develop its own interventionist military forces, particularly for "resource wars" to protect what are seen as European interests. A clear example of such thinking is the view held in Paris that French military intervention would be necessary to guarantee stability in Tunisia in the case of a popular uprising against the present regime.[58] In this context, the creation of rapid action forces in France, Italy, and more recently Spain, is a disturbing sign. Mauricio Cremazco, an expert at Italy's Instituto Affari Internazionali (IAI), believes that "in the long term, the European rapid deployment forces could constitute the hard core of a truly 'European' military intervention capacity in out-of-area contingencies involving vital European interests."[59]

Western Europe should be searching for non-military alternatives in order to promote security in the Third World; specific peace initiatives in the Middle East; cooperation agreements that must include a joint North-South effort to conserve natural resources; development aid conducive to greater economic diversification and self-reliance in the developing countries; studies of alternative energy supplies; the reduction, if not complete elimination, of the official arms trade; a serious effort to halt the illegal traffic in arms; campaigns in favor of new models of consumption; the development of joint employment programs involving North and South; and support for the United Nations and its multilateral mechanisms of conflict resolution which should obviate the recourse to the unilateral use of force. Such initiatives should be taken in an effort to prevent further military intervention, whether on the part of the "European pillar" or by the United States.

Notes

1. The author wants to thank those who facilitated either resources or advice for this essay: Nicolau Barcelo (Greenpeace, Spain), Fabrizio Battistelli (Archivio Disaro, Rome), Bruce Birchard and Joseph Gerson (AFSC), Laura Guazzone (IRDISP, Rome), Priscilla Hayner (ACCESS, Washington, D.C.), Victor Millan (FLACSO, Santiago de Chile, SIPRI, Stockholm), Malcom Spaven (Armaments and Disarmament Information Unit, Sussex), Gini Sherry (Lawyers Committee for Human Rights, New York), Robert Matthews (New York University), Carlos Taibo (CIP, Madrid), and The Center for Defense Information (Washington, D.C.).

2. See William M. Arkin, "The Nuclear Arms Race at Sea," *Neptune Papers* No. 1 (Washington D.C.: Institute for Policy Studies/Greenpeace, October 1987).

3. Nicolau Barcelo and Joan Buades, "La Presencia de Armas Nucleares en los Puertos Españoles," in Mariano Aguirre and Carlos Taibo, eds., *Anuario del CIP 1988-89* (Madrid: IEPALA/CIP, 1989), 189.

4. About the international political use of fundamentalism see Samir Amin, *La Desconexión, Chapter 7* (Madrid: IEPALA, 1988); see also Sara Diamond, *Spiritual Warfare* (Boston: South End Press, 1989).

5. Frank A. Carlucci, "A Policy Warning: the 'New Era' Isn't All That New," *International Herald Tribune,* 28-29 January 1989.

6. About the theory of low-intensity conflict and its implementation in El Salvador, Nicaragua, the Philippines, and Afghanistan see Michael T. Klare and Peter Kornbluh, eds., *Low-Intensity Warfare* (New York: Pantheon, 1988).

7. *L'Express,* Paris, 24 July 1987.

8. Ciro Elliot Zoppo, "American Foreign Policy, NATO in the Mediterranean, and the Defence of the Gulf," in Giacomo Luciani, ed., *The Mediterranean Region* (London: Croom Helm, 1985), 294-295.

9. Robert O'Neill, "Conclusion," in *Prospects for Security in the Mediterranean,* Adelphi Papers No. 231, London, Spring 1988, 61.

10. Diana Johnstone, "Italy to the Gulf—and Back," *MERIP Report,* March-April 1988, 32.

11. Admiral Harry Train, "Maritime Strategy in the Mediterranean," in *Prospects for Security in the Mediterranean,* Adelphi Papers No. 229, London, Spring 1988, 32.

12. William M. Arkin, "Evolving Military and Political Role of U.S. Military Forces and Nuclear Weapons in Italy," paper presented at the International Conference on Nuclear Weapons and Arms Control in Europe, Castiglioncello (Livorno), Italy, 21-25 October 1985.

13. Esther Barbe, "La Región Mediterránea y el Flanco Sur," *Afers Internacionale,* Nos. 3, 4, and 5, CIDOB, Barcelona, 1984; see also Vicens Fisas Armengol, *Paz en el Mediterráneo* (Lerna/Barcelona: Greenpeace, 1987).

14. William Arkin and Richard Fieldhouse, *Nuclear Battlefields: Global Links in the Arms Race* (Cambridge: Ballinger, 1985), 113.

15. *El País,* Madrid, 6 December 1986.

16. Falco Accame, "Sigonella: La OTAN al Desnudo," *Mientras Tanto* No. 25, Barcelona, February 1986.

17. See Karsten Voigt, "General Report on Alliance Security: Towards Conventional Stability in Europe and The U.S. Maritime Strategy and Crisis Stability at Sea," North Atlantic Assembly, Brussels, November 1986, Ref.: AF 216 MC(88), 6, 35.

18. This ambiguity has, on occasions, led to acrimonious disputes between the United States and the European NATO allies. The Achille Lauro incident, for instance, led to open confrontation between the United States and Italy, with Italian Prime Minister Bettino Craxi publicly stating that "NATO bases in Italy can only be used for specific NATO ends in conformity with existing accords." The U.S. raid on Libya in April 1986 also created tension between Rome and Washington. See Mario Tedeschini Lalli, "Il Difficile Status Delle Basi Italiane, NATO o Statunitensi" ("The Difficult Status of the Italian Bases: NATO or U.S.A.?"), *Il Messaggero,* April 1986.

19. National Security Council Papers 1/2, 10 February 1948, U.S. Department of State, Papers Relating to the Foreign Relations of the United States (FRU.S.), 1948 (Washington D.C.: U.S. Government Printing Office, 1968), quoted in E. Timothy Smith, "U.S. Security and Italy: The Extension of NATO to the Mediterranean, 1945-49," in Lawrence S. Kaplan, Robert W. Clawson and Raimondi Luraghi, eds., *NATO and the Mediterranean* (Wilmington, DE: Scholarly Resources, 1985), 138.

20. National Security Council Papers 1/3, 8 March 1948, FRU.S., quoted in Smith, 141.

21. See a very good analysis of the Greek-American relationship in Chapter X of Theodore A. Couloumbis, John A. Petropulos, and Harry J. Psomiades, *Foreign Interference in Greek Politics* (New York: Pella, 1976); and Theodore A. Couloumbis and John O. Latrides, *Greek American Relations* (New York: Pella, 1980).

22. Todd Gitlin, "Counter-Insurgency: Myth and Reality in Greece," in David Horowitz, ed., *Containment and Revolution* (Boston: Beacon Press, 1987), 180.

23. Lawrence S. Wittner, *American Intervention in Greece, 1943-1949* (New York: Columbia University Press, 1982), 312.

24. Quoted in Richard Barnet, *The Alliance* (New York: Simon and Schuster, 1983), 347.

25. Richard F. Grimmett, *United Military Installations in Greece,* Library of Congress, Congressional Research Service, Report No. 84-24 F., 16 February 1984.

26. Presentation at Conference, "Peace in the Mediterranean," Madrid, May 1987.

27. See Human Rights Watch/Lawyers Committee for Human Rights, "Critique, Review of the Department of State's Country Reports on Human Rights Practices for 1987," New York, 1988, 154-158.

28. Center for Defense Information, "The Spanish Connection: A Wider U.S. Commitment in the Making," *The Defense Monitor,* Vol. V, No. 2, February 1976.

29. *New York Times,* 29 September 1953, quoted in Arthur Whitaker, *Spain and Defense of the West* (New York: Harper & Brothers, 1961), 48.

30. See Angel Vinas, *Los Acuerdos Secretos de Franco* (Madrid: Grijalbo, 1981).

31. Examples of these studies are William Heiberg, *The Sixteenth Nation, Spain's Role in NATO* (Washington: National Defense University Press, 1983); Max G. Manwaring and Alan N. Sabrosky, "Iberia's Role in NATO's Future: Strategic Reserve, Reinforcement and Redoubt," *Parameters,* Vol. XVI, No. 1, January-March 1986.

32. *El País,* 30 June 1987.

33. Mariano Aguirre, "Ingresar en la UEO Puede Implicar a España en Acciónes Fuera de Area de la OTAN," *El Independiente,* 4 November 1988.

34. See the essay by an important advisor of President François Mitterrand: Jacques Huntzinger, "L'Avenir de la Defense de l'Europe Occidentale: Une Alliance a Deus Piliers," *Politique Etrangère,* Paris, April 1985.

35. *Revista Española de Defensa,* No. 3, May 1988, 34-36.

36. See Mariano Aguirre, "El Nuevo Acuerdo Hispano-Norteamericano," *Papeles para la Paz,* No. 33, (Madrid: CIP, 1988).

37. Christopher Layne, "Atlanticism Without NATO," *Foreign Policy,* No. 57, Spring 1987, 45.

38. *El País,* 20 December, 1988.

39. Herve Coutau-Begarie, "Mare Nostrum: Esquisse de une Geostrategie de la Mediterranee," *Herodote,* Paris, *La Decouverte,* April-June 1987, 31-60.

40. Report of the Defense Burdensharing Panel of the Committee on Armed Services, House of Representatives (Washington, D.C.: U.S. Government Printing Office, August 1988), 52-53.

41. Ibid., 56.

42. O'Neill, 231.

43. *El País,* 26 May 1988.

44. See Miguel Herrero Rodríguez de Miñon, "Final Report of the Subcommittee on Out-of-Area Security Challenges to the Alliance" (Brussels: North Atlantic Assembly, May 1986), Ref: AD 81 PC/OA [86], 1.

45. Bruce R. Kuniholm, "Rhetoric and Reality in the Aegean: U.S. Policy Options Towards Greece and Turkey," *SAIS Review,* Vol. 6, No. 1, Winter-Spring 1986, 151.

46. *The Independent,* 23 July 1990.

47. "Report of the Defense Burdensharing," 57.

48. *Time,* 14 March 1988.

49. Henry A. Kissinger, "A New Era for NATO," *Newsweek,* 12 October 1987.

50. Ronald Reagan, "Remarks by the President to Worldnet" (Washington, D.C.: Office of the White House Press Secretary, 3 November 1987).

51. David Garnham, *The Politics of European Defense Cooperation: Germany, France, Britain, and America* (Cambridge: Ballinger Publishing Co., 1988), 184. Paul Kennedy, in his *The Rise and Fall of the Great Powers* (London: Unwin Hyman, 1988) also predicted the end of the bipolar world and the development of a German-French (with Italy and Britain) power; see 538.

52. Loic Bouvard, "General Report on the Alliance Political Developments in 1987-1988: Arms Control, Bases, the Gulf," (Brussels: North Atlantic Assembly, November 1988) Ref.: AF 225 PC [88] 5.

53. See the conclusions for every country from Portugal to Turkey in Congressional Research Service, Library of Congress, U.S. Military Installations in NATO's Southern Region, "Report for the Committee on Foreign Affairs, U.S. House of Representatives" (Washington, D.C.: U.S. Government Printing Office, 7 October 1986).

54. Jed C. Snyder, "Strategic Bias and Southern Flank Security," *The Washington Quarterly,* Vol. 8, No. 3, Summer 1985, 34.

55. Quoted in John Ausland, "Mediterranean Bases: Thinking of Oil Might Help," *International Herald Tribune,* 5 May 1988.

56. *International Herald Tribune,* 11 February 1989.

57. Final Statement of the Meeting of the Non-Aligned Countries of the Mediterranean, quoted in "Mediterranee: Politique et Strategie," *Problemes Politiques et Sociaux,* No. 582, La Documentation Francaise, Paris, 15 April 1988.

58. O'Neill, 72.

59. Mauricio Cremazco, "Do It Yourself: The National Approach to the Out-of-Area Question," *The International Spectator,* Vol. XXII, No. 3, Rome, July-August 1987, 150.

Part IV: The Middle East

Chapter 13

Middle East Bases

Model for the Future

Denis F. Doyon

Many people in the United States were taken by surprise when large numbers of U.S. troops were sent to Saudi Arabia in August 1990. Within weeks of the Iraqi invasion of Kuwait, more than 150,000 troops were rushed to the Middle East: some 70,000 soldiers to military bases and advance posts in the Saudi desert and another 45,000 Marines and 40,000 Navy personnel on ships offshore. The size and speed of the initial U.S. intervention put the world on notice that U.S. military power was still a force to be reckoned with in the post-Cold War world.

Ten years earlier, the United States had been unable to launch a major military response to the Iranian revolution and the Soviet invasion of Afghanistan. The United States had no permanent ground troops in the region, and it had no way to move them there quickly from other parts of the world. Requests to base U.S. troops in friendly Arab countries were rebuffed. The ill-fated hostage rescue mission in Iran only served to underscore the image of U.S. impotence in the region.

These two events frame a period of tremendous change in U.S. military and strategic planning. From the end of the post-Vietnam era to the beginning of the post-Cold War era, the United States developed a new doctrine of low-intensity conflict, a new strategy of rapid deployment, and a new capability of using its overwhelming military power to meet threats to U.S. interests anywhere in the world.

Nowhere are these changes more evident than in the Middle East. When Iraq invaded Kuwait on August 2, 1990, the United States had no facilities in the Gulf comparable to the sprawling military bases so common in Western Europe, East Asia, and the Pacific. Relatively small numbers of

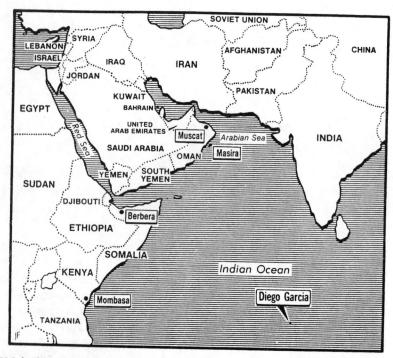

U.S. builds shield for southwest Asia's oil, by Joan Forbes. Reprinted by permission from the *Christian Science Monitor* © The Christian Science Publishing Society. All rights reserved.

U.S. military personnel were stationed in the region, serving in peacekeeping units in the Sinai Peninsula or performing support functions for U.S. planes and ships. The only permanent U.S. naval base to be found in the entire region was on the island of Diego Garcia, 1,900 miles south of the Strait of Hormuz, in the middle of the Indian Ocean. To the casual observer, little had changed since 1980, when critics bemoaned the inability of the United States to project military force to the Middle East. Over the past decade, however, the United States has directed a $1 billion military construction program to develop access to a wide array of modern military facilities in a dozen nations across North Africa, the Middle East, and Southwest Asia.[1] These facilities, and other projects under construction, give the United States access to seven airfields and three ports in the immediate Persian Gulf area, and provide a capability for air and sea support from Diego Garcia, Morocco, and Portugal.[2] By 1986, six years after the United States started building its basing network in the region, its program was virtually completed.[3]

This network of bases has been erected without significant public debate or wide public knowledge, in part because the Pentagon's program does not rely on the construction of massive U.S. military bases, as in East Asia or Western Europe. Nearly all of the bases included in Pentagon planning for the region, though built and paid for by the United States, are formally controlled by the host nations, which in return grant access rights to U.S. forces for specific contingencies. This arrangement diverted public scrutiny from U.S. military objectives and capabilities in the Middle East.

Since the late 1970s, the United States has been preparing for an increased military role in the Middle East. It has developed a strategy for meeting a wide variety of threats in the region and has established the military forces and acquired the weapons and equipment needed to carry out this strategy. When Iraq invaded Kuwait and (by some accounts) threatened Saudi Arabia, the United States was ready for the rapid mobilization of U.S. forces. Their quick deployment to the Gulf testified to an impressive logistical capability and years of planning and training. Within 60 days, the United States was prepared for a major war half way around the world.

Following the collapse of the Cold War in Europe, and with plans for a light and mobile U.S. Army, the infrastructure for intervention built in the Middle East and North Africa may suggest how the United States will respond to developments in Latin America and Africa, where it does not have large military bases but faces threats to its "interests." Because the recently built U.S. basing network in the Middle East may more accurately represent U.S. strategic thinking for the future than the basing posture inherited from Cold War-era commitments in Europe and Asia, it suggests what future basing patterns will be in regions where the United States may be forced to relinquish control of major overseas military bases.

U.S. Bases and U.S. Intervention in the Middle East Before 1979

The United States came late to intervention in the Middle East, as compared to its history in Latin America and East Asia. With a few exceptions, such as the naval attacks on the North African "Barbary Coast" in the early nineteenth century, for most of its history the United States had neither the interest nor the capability for intervention in the region. It was only during World War II that the United States became deeply involved in the Middle East and Southwest Asia.

The Allied invasion of North Africa in 1942 left in its wake a string of Army and Navy bases in Morocco, Algeria, and Tunisia. The most important U.S. installations were the naval bases at Casablanca in Morocco, Oran in

Algeria, and the naval air station at Port Lyautey, Morocco.[4] Since these bases were constructed to support combat operations, most were dismantled or turned over to host governments soon after the end of the war.[5]

With the creation of the Persian Gulf Command in August 1942, the United States deployed forces to the Gulf region to assist the Allied transport of supplies to the Soviet Union. U.S. forces controlled an airfield at Abadan in Iran and used British airfields in Iraq, Bahrain, Sharjah, and Aden. In addition, the ruler of Muscat allowed the United States to use facilities and erect buildings at Salala, Masirah, and Ras al-Hadd in Oman, and to station aircraft there. Approximately one-quarter of all war-time aid shipped from the Western Hemisphere to the Soviet Union passed through the Gulf region.[6]

At the close of World War II, U.S. objectives in the Middle East revolved around oil. Inexpensive oil from the Gulf had been an important strategic resource during the war, and it was now needed to fuel the reconstruction of Europe and Japan. U.S. strategy in the region was thus designed to control the flow of oil and to keep prices low.[7] In order to achieve both of these objectives, U.S. planners tried to establish close relationships with regimes throughout the Middle East. In most of the region, however, Britain lingered as the preponderant political, economic, and military power. At the close of the war, British military bases stretched from Morocco, through Egypt and Palestine to Iran, Pakistan, and India. British officers trained and sometimes commanded local armies. British advisers counseled traditional monarchs, and British corporations dominated regional commerce.

Though its influence began to decline soon after the war, Britain remained the most important military power in much of the region for several years, and in the Gulf itself until the early 1970s. Although the United States and Great Britain were close allies, they were often at odds in the Middle East, where U.S. political and military initiatives challenged British hegemony.

Like other areas of the Third World following World War II, the Middle East and North Africa witnessed numerous armed conflicts in the 1940s, 1950s and 1960s. Colonial wars were fought in Palestine, Kenya, Algeria, and the Spanish Sahara. Border clashes between Somalia and Ethiopia were frequent after 1963. A series of wars were waged between Israel and Arab states. Civil wars erupted in Sudan, Lebanon, Iraq, Ethiopia, North Yemen, South Yemen, Oman, and Chad.[8]

In contrast to conflicts in other areas of the Third World, however, these clashes only rarely prompted direct intervention by U.S. troops. The dispatch of Marines to Lebanon in 1958 was the exception, not the rule. The United States often provided advisers and trainers to allies and clients in the region, and many of the wars were fought with U.S.-supplied weapons. The United

States carried out intelligence and covert operations in the region, and used shows of force and nuclear threats to intimidate adversaries. Yet the level of direct U.S. military intervention in the Middle East was far lower than in East Asia or Latin America.

One reason was that the Pentagon was committed elsewhere: to the Cold War in Europe and to massive interventions in Korea and Vietnam. Perhaps more important, the British military presence in the Middle East offered an alternative to U.S. planners. British troops fought colonial wars in Palestine and Kenya, invaded Nasser's Egypt in 1956, and provided extensive support for pro-Western rulers in Aden and Oman in suppressing internal rebellions. To a great extent, Britain, not the United States, took on primary responsibility for maintaining "stability" and protecting Western interests against indigenous threats in the Middle East. This served British interests because it allowed Britain to maintain its political and economic influence in the region; despite occasional tensions with Britain, it also served U.S. interests because it advanced shared Western objectives at little cost.

British power, however, was not sufficient to meet the perceived Soviet threat to the Middle East. The region had become a theater of the Cold War, a "third front" between Europe and East Asia for the containment of the Soviet Union. The vast oil reserves of the Gulf were seen as a likely target in a general war with the Soviet Union, and as a Western resource that needed protection. For this task, the military might of the United States was necessary.

The United States relied on a structure of military bases to project its military power. The first line of defense was NATO's southern flank: U.S. bases in Greece and Turkey. British military bases in countries of the Baghdad Pact—Iran, Iraq, Pakistan, and Turkey—buttressed this line. Other U.S. bases established during World War II, including air and naval bases in Morocco and the sprawling Wheelus Air Force Base in Libya, were stitched together into a regional network.

In the Gulf itself, Saudi Arabia played a central role in U.S. strategy. Ever since oil had been discovered in commercial quantities near Dhahran in 1938, the Saudi royal family had had close relations with the United States. A U.S. military mission had been established in Riyadh during World War II. In February 1943, reportedly under pressure from U.S. oil companies developing Saudi oilfields, President Roosevelt declared that the defense of Saudi Arabia was vital to the defense of the United States, opening the door to U.S. military aid.[9] During this period, a large U.S. Army/Air Force base was built at Dhahran in the oil-producing eastern province of Saudi Arabia, as an air link between Cairo and Karachi.[10] Throughout the 1950s, Strategic Air Command bombers flew from Dhahran to the Southern borders of the Soviet Union.

The U.S. military presence at the Dhahran air base became an important issue for opposition groups in Saudi Arabia inspired by the Arab nationalist ideology of Nasserism. Opposition to the base, as well as other expressions of dissatisfaction with the regime, was stamped out ruthlessly, even within the ruling family. In 1961, Prince Talal ibn Abdel Aziz was dropped from his post as Finance Minister when he called for abrogating the security treaty with the United States and closing the Dhahran base. In August 1962, after more public statements against the base and calls for a constitution for the country, his ties to the regime were cut, his passport was withdrawn, his property was confiscated, and some of his supporters in the country were arrested. He then moved to Egypt, where with his brothers and a cousin he formed the "Free Princes" and broadcast denunciations of the royal family.[11]

By the 1960s, developments in the arms race had altered the regional calculus. Intercontinental ballistic missiles replaced heavy bombers as the most potent strategic weapon in the U.S. arsenal. In order to deploy newly developed Polaris nuclear submarines to the northern Indian Ocean, where their missiles would be within range of the southern Soviet Union, the Navy needed a new communications base in the region. Existing communications facilites in Asmara, Ethiopia and Cockburn Sound, Australia could not cover the vast expanse of the Indian Ocean.[12]

These new strategic considerations revived the U.S. Navy's plans for a base in the Indian Ocean, which dated from the early post-war period. In the early 1960s, the Pentagon set its sights on the small, isolated island of Diego Garcia. The site had three advantages: First, it was strategically located near the center of the Indian Ocean; as one naval officer remarked, "as Malta is to the Mediterranean, Diego Garcia is to the Indian Ocean."[13] Second, the atoll surrounded a six-square-mile lagoon which could accommodate submarines as well as an entire carrier battle group.[14] Finally, Great Britain was the sovereign power; in negotiating a basing agreement, the U.S. would be dealing with a trusted ally, not a suspicious third world regime.

Diego Garcia, 11 square miles of low-lying sand and coral 400 miles south of the equator, is the largest island in the Chagos Archipelago, which has been under British control since it was taken from France in the Napoleonic Wars. Prior to 1965, it was attached administratively to Mauritius, a British colony scheduled to become independent in 1968. Negotiations between the United States and Britain led to the detachment of the Chagos Archipelago from Mauritius in 1965, when it was declared to be "British Indian Ocean Territory."[15] This paved the way for a 1966 executive agreement between the United States and the United Kingdom making the islands available to both countries for military purposes for 50 years.[16] Britain agreed to eliminate local opposition to the deal by expelling the entire population

of Diego Garcia—1,200 copra plantation contract workers and their families—to Mauritius and Seychelles.[17]

In the Fiscal Year 1970 budget, Congress appropriated $5.4 million to
build the Navy's long-sought communications facility and lengthen the
island's airstrip to accomodate C-130 Hercules cargo aircraft. Between 1971
and 1974, an additional $48 million was spent on dredging the lagoon,
enlarging the airfield, and building shops, quarters, and warehouses. By late
1973, the Navy had a modern communications base, anchorage for its largest
ships, and fuel, provisions, and repair facilities.[18]

This period witnessed a striking decline in British military power in the
region, which had begun with the demobilization following World War II
and the withdrawal from India. At the close of World War II, British bases
were scattered throughout northern and eastern Africa, the Middle East, and
India. By the late 1970s, Britain had turned over the last of its military bases
in the region (except Cyprus) to the host countries.[19] This posed an immense
problem for the United States. Britain's withdrawal ended its usefulness as a
regional police officer, even as civil wars continued in Chad, Ethiopia, Iraq,
Oman, and Sudan. The outbreak of fighting between Palestinian forces and
the Jordanian Army in 1970, which threatened to escalate into a major
regional confrontation involving Syria and Israel, highlighted the continuing
instability in the Middle East and the consequent threat to U.S. influence in
the region. The United States could not replace the departing British forces,
largely because of its commitments in Southeast Asia. This combination of
factors contributed to the articulation of the Nixon Doctrine, whereby
regional allies would protect U.S. interests with weapons, training, and advice
from the United States. In the Middle East, the "twin pillars" of Israel and Iran
were to keep the forces of Arab radicalism in check.

An important aspect of the Nixon Doctrine was that it did not require
the overseas deployment of U.S. troops, nor the establishment of U.S. military
bases in areas of third world instability. During the period when the Nixon
Doctrine shaped policy, Diego Garcia was the only formal military base the
United States maintained in the Middle East/Indian Ocean region, and this
was probably because the primary function of the base (at least until 1979)
was to support U.S. strategic capabilities against the Soviet Union.

During the 1970s, the Soviet Union developed or acquired fleet facilities at Aden and Socotra in South Yemen, Hodeida in North Yemen, and
Berbera in Somalia.[20] Since U.S. client regimes could not counter this Soviet
naval buildup, the United States rushed to enhance its own naval capabilities
in the Indian Ocean.

In 1976, the United States and Great Britain signed an agreement to
further expand the anchorage, airfield, and base facilities at Diego Garcia.

The base's stated mission was revised to provide air terminal operations, search and rescue, aerology services, aviation shops, and fuel and supply support for planes and ships in the Indian Ocean.[21] By April 1977, Diego Garcia included an 8,000-foot runway, fuel storage tanks, and satellite and radio communications systems. Its deep-water anchorage was able to handle aircraft carriers. But more was being done; earthmoving equipment operated 24 hours a day, filling swamps and clearing coral for another 4,000-foot extension of the runway and expanding the parking area for military jets. Five miles away, foundations were laid for a huge oil tank farm to hold 640,000 barrels of jet fuel.[22]

The construction of the U.S. base at Diego Garcia was not carried out without opposition, even though all the inhabitants of the atoll had been deported. Several nations in the region, led by India, sought to limit the U.S. and Soviet military buildup. International opposition found an outlet in the United Nations General Assembly, which on December 16, 1971 voted to adopt a "Declaration of the Indian Ocean as a Zone of Peace," calling on the major powers to refrain from building military bases in the region.[23] For years, Indian Ocean countries repeatedly reaffirmed their support for the declaration.[24]

A New Need For Bases

By the end of the 1970s, the Middle East had become extremely important to U.S. global interests. The dramatic rise in oil prices had focused attention on the importance of the Gulf's oil resources—60 percent of the world's proven oil reserves—to Western economies. Many strategic analysts began to assert that U.S. interests in Southwest Asia had assumed almost the same level of importance as U.S. interests in Europe and the Far East.[25] Others maintained that the Gulf was more important than Europe, since the "loss" of the Gulf would inevitably peel Western Europe away from its alliance with the United States.[26]

The oil price boom that began with the OPEC embargo and price increases of 1973 had transformed the region into an important element of the emerging transnational economic system. Saudi Arabia, for example, had become a key participant in the International Monetary Fund, the World Bank, and the International Finance Corporation, ranking in influence just behind the leading Western industrialized countries and Japan. Most of the cash generated by sales of OPEC oil, however, was deposited in U.S. dollar accounts in Western Europe. This practice kept the dollar strong and contributed to the tremendous expansion of the transnational financial system in the 1970s.[27]

The coup d'ètat in Ethiopia in 1974, which replaced a longstanding U.S. client regime with a radical Revolutionary Council, was the first sign that the Nixon Doctrine could not ensure U.S. hegemony in the region. The regime's turn toward the Soviet Union in 1977, and the subsequent war with Somalia in the Ogaden confirmed the Pentagon's worst fears as Soviet advisors and Cuban troops joined the fighting.

The turning point, however, was the Iranian revolution, which deposed the Shah, in early 1979. Iran had been the world's largest purchaser of U.S. arms and a model client under the Nixon Doctrine, yet the Shah was toppled by a largely nonviolent mass uprising of the Iranian people. In his place was a coalition of Islamic clerics and leftists who competed with one another in denouncing the United States. The hostage crisis of 1979-81 fueled calls in the United States for revenge, and helped build a domestic constituency for a U.S. military buildup in the Middle East.

The Soviet invasion of Afghanistan in December 1979 added to the sense of panic in Washington's national security circles. For 25 years after the Soviet withdrawal from northern Iran in 1946 and the proclamation of the Truman Doctrine in 1947, there had been no direct U.S.-Soviet confrontation in Southwest Asia. U.S. planners felt they had successfully contained the Soviets. According to then national security adviser Zbigniew Brzezinski, "for the first time since the inception of the American-Soviet conflict [the USSR in 1979] crossed the lines that emerged at the conclusion of World War II. The third front was thus joined."[28] President Carter responded to the perceived crisis by unveiling the Carter Doctrine, in which he warned that the "United States would use any means necessary, including military force," to protect its vital interests in the Gulf.[29] While the "Soviet threat" was highlighted in public, U.S. analysts saw these threats coming from three main sources: attacks on U.S. allies by hostile regional nations, such as South Yemen, Iran, or Iraq; internal instability caused by factionalism, ideology, religion, or modernization; and political coercion or direct attack by the Soviet Union.[30]

Soon after the fall of the Shah, the United States supplied North Yemen, then under attack by rebels backed by South Yemen, with $300 million worth of F-5 fighter bombers, tanks, and armored personnel carriers. The weapons were paid for by Saudi Arabia and transported to Sana'a via Saudi bases. Hundreds of U.S. military personnel participated in this operation in Saudi Arabia.[31]

A more difficult problem was how to counter the perceived Soviet threat to the Gulf. This would require a major engagement of U.S. military forces halfway around the world, in a region lacking major U.S. military bases. "In addition," wrote Brzezinski later, "unlike its defense of Western Europe and Japan, the American engagement had to be undertaken here in support of governments that were not democratic and whose long-term stability was dubious." The United States even planned to defend Iran against a Soviet invasion, though Iran's government and much of its population remained extremely hostile to the United States.[32]

The Pentagon developed what it called the Zagros Mountains strategy, whereby U.S. forces rushed to the region would invade Iran and seize strategic mountain passes. While they harassed and delayed Soviet forces in northern Iran, other units would erect defenses in southern Iran to prevent the Soviets from reaching the oil fields of the Gulf.[33]

This strategy called for a rapid expansion of U.S. capabilities in the region, including military bases. Previously, periods of tension in the Gulf had prompted the United States to deploy aircraft carrier battle groups to the Arabian Sea. To deter a possible Soviet invasion, however, the Pentagon felt that a deployment of land-based airpower and ground troops was needed. This would be a stronger sign of the United States' political commitment to defend its interests, and it would provide more effective means of attacking Soviet forces in Iran or providing air cover over the Gulf itself.[34]

The search for military bases was on. In April 1980, the Carter Administration signed agreements with Oman and Kenya to provide the United States with access to military bases in exchange for military aid; a third agreement was signed with Somalia four months later.[35] The bases in Oman provided a good staging ground for action in the Gulf, but Kenya and Somalia were both too far away to be useful for anything but support facilities. Despite these deficiencies, the Adminstration signed the basing agreements to get something quickly; according to some observers, this had a political payoff, showing U.S. resolve in the face of the Soviet threat.[36]

Regional Contraints and New Approaches

The Carter Administration, however, found a cooler reception in the rest of the region, particularly in the Gulf Arab countries. When the United States raised the idea of a formal basing agreement with Saudi Arabia, the Saudis refused to discuss it. The problem, according to a top Defense Department official, was that "they did not see the threat in the same terms as we did."[37]

This should not have come as much of a surprise. Ever since the 1973 oil embargo, plans had circulated in the United States for a U.S. invasion of Gulf oil fields. President Ford had threatened in 1974 to use U.S. military forces if needed to "break an embargo or fashion reasonable prices."[38] The Rapid Deployment Force developed by the Carter Administration seemed inadequate to repel a Soviet attack on the Gulf, but many felt it would be an ideal force to seize oil facilities. The Gulf Arab regimes were thus suspicious of U.S. intentions, and in 1980 rebuffed the Carter Administration's envoys seeking military basing agreements.[39]

Even if they could be reassured on this point, moreover, the Arab states saw the principal military threat to the region coming not from the Soviet Union, but from Israel, the United States' chief regional ally. Many Arab leaders looked askance at U.S. attempts to draw them into a military alliance that might include Israel. Others might have been receptive to closer military cooperation with the United States, but feared that working too closely with Israel's patron would undermine their political legitimacy at home.

This points up the key divergence in the perspectives of the United States and the Arab Gulf states. While the Carter Administration was gearing up for a confrontation with the Soviets, most of the monarchs in the Arab Gulf states felt that the primary threat to their thrones was internal. To them, Iran seemed a more likely model than Afghanistan for their downfall. Given the experiences of most Middle East countries under Ottoman and British rule, Arab regimes have been extremely sensitive about being seen as pawns of the United States. The introduction of U.S. combat forces would, they feared, strengthen opposition movements, particularly Islamic fundamentalist groups that condemn the monarchies for their ties to the West.

This contradiction was intensified when Ronald Reagan took office. The Reagan Administration "repackaged" the Carter Doctrine with two new concepts: a "global perspective" which subsumed U.S. policy toward the Gulf within a strategic policy emphasizing superpower conflict and the Soviet threat, and a proposal for establishing a "strategic consensus" which would unite Israel and the pro-Western Arab regimes in an anti-Soviet alliance. This approach was immediately rejected by the Arab regimes, who could not publicly set aside the Arab-Israeli conflict and their own national interests.[40]

Privately, Gulf monarchs were willing to cooperate with the United States. In 1980, Saudi Crown Prince Fahd had told a visiting U.S. delegation headed by Brzezinski that he was "very supportive of the American plan to maintain a permanent military force" in the Middle East. While aiding the U.S. effort (forming a pro-Western alliance, the Gulf Cooperation Council, for example), Saudi King Khaled tried to appease anti-U.S. sentiment in his country, particularly from pious Muslims, by declaring at a 1981 Islamic summit conference: "Security comes from placing our confidence in God and in ourselves." At the same conference, the Saudi foreign minister described Western military bases, especially U.S. bases, as "lightning rods," provoking the Soviets into obtaining equivalent rights in the region.[41]

The unwillingness of the Saudi royal family to publicly embrace U.S. military planning for the region was perhaps prompted by memories of the demonstrations that had broken out in Saudi Arabia after the June 1967 Arab-Israeli war. Angry crowds had protested U.S. support for Israel, the Saudi regime's refusal to cut off oil to "imperialist" countries, and repression in Saudi Arabia. The U.S. airbase at Dhahran had been turned over to the Saudis in 1962, but the U.S. presence there was still substantial, and it was a target of protest.[42]

No doubt the sensitivities of the Saudi royal family to anti-U.S. sentiment in their country had also been heightened by the uprising in the Grand Mosque in Mecca in 1979. They were determined not to provoke the domestic opposition by allowing the United States to re-establish military bases on Saudi territory.

The drive to establish U.S. military bases in the region met other obstacles, too. Many in the Pentagon felt that pursuing a strategy of forward deployment similar to that in Europe or East Asia was militarily unwise and politically unfeasible. Developing peace-time bases in the Middle East would be expensive and commit a large fraction of U.S. ready forces. Even if the money could be appropriated, the Defense Department cautioned, "we cannot afford to tie down too many of our assets in one theater."[43]

These constraints suggested an alternative to U.S. security planners. There was a middle ground—between establishing major U.S. military bases in the Gulf and tolerating glaring strategic vulnerability—which could build cooperative alliances without inciting anti-Western sentiment.[44] "We went for a major change in the normal American way of doing things in Southwest Asia," a Defense Department offical later wrote. "We went for facilities, not bases."[45]

Taking the concept of the Rapid Deployment Force to its logical conclusion, the Pentagon developed a strategy for intervention in the Middle East which does not rely on large permanent U.S. military bases in the region. Except for several naval units, it does not rely upon the forward deployment of any U.S. forces during peace-time. Instead, the strategy has called for the rapid insertion of U.S. combat forces into the Middle East directly from bases in the United States.

This new strategy, however, demanded firm political agreements with friendly regimes to allow the United States access to their own military bases in times of crisis.[46] The model was provided by U.S. agreements with Saudi Arabia. In 1979, a Congressional study had judged that while the United States had no bases "in the strictest sense" in Saudi Arabia, it had access to Saudi facilities that served most U.S. needs. "The Department of Defense," the study frankly stated, "would probably consider them bases if the Soviets enjoyed the same rights in lieu of the United States."[47]

U.S. Air Force technicians working at a base in Saudi Arabia, as they prepared air-to-air missiles to be carried by F-15 fighters. Pool Photo via Reuters.

The Pentagon's new strategy envisioned a massive U.S. program to upgrade, expand, and improve military bases in Middle East countries in exchange for U.S. access rights. Its plans required technical, logistical, and security support from the "host nations." It also called for a variety of improvements in U.S. military capabilities, particularly the stockpiling of U.S. weapons, equipment, and supplies in the region, expansion of sealift and airlift capabilities, and the development of highly mobile, heavily armed combat forces.[48] All of these were to become priorities for the Reagan Administration's regional diplomacy and its Defense Department budget requests.[49]

Building the Infrastructure for Intervention

The Reagan Administration's military buildup placed a high priority on the development of "power projection forces" for intervention in the Third World. The Pentagon's program emphasized rapid growth of the Navy, expansion of "special operations forces" such as the Army's Green Berets and the Navy's SEALS, and the creation of new, highly mobile, heavily armed "light infantry divisions." While these forces can be used in many areas around the world, the Bush Administration's response to Iraq's invasion of Kuwait demonstrated that they have particular relevance for use in the Middle

East, where U.S. intervention relies heavily on seapower and mobile land forces.[50]

An important element of the U.S. military buildup of the 1980s was a program of enhancements which radically transformed the Rapid Deployment Force (RDF). Originally planned as a small "fire-fighting" unit for third world hot spots, the RDF ballooned into a major interventionary army, comprising roughly one-fourth of all active-duty Army and Marine Corps divisions, Navy aircraft carrier battle groups, and Air Force tactical fighter wings.[51]

Analysts who had judged that the RDF was designed principally for action in the Middle East were proven correct when on January 1, 1983, the RDF was officially transformed into the U.S. Central Command (CENTCOM), with responsibility for all U.S. military activities in the region stretching between Egypt, Kenya, and Pakistan. The creation of CENTCOM, the first new regional command in 35 years, institutionalized an important shift in the United States' strategic posture, placing the Middle East on the same level within the military hierarchy as Europe and East Asia.[52] Consistent with the need to maintain a low profile in the Middle East, Central Command headquarters were established at MacDill Air Force Base in Tampa, Florida. As with the Rapid Deployment Force, CENTCOM was created by assigning existing military forces to its command.[53] To get these forces to the Middle East, the Pentagon invested heavily in improvements in its sealift and airlift capabilities.[54]

CENTCOM's strategy for intervention in the Middle East required the "pre-positioning" of weapons, ammunition, equipment, fuel, and other supplies. Most of this was stockpiled at military bases in the region (see below), but some was placed on container ships, allowing greater operational flexibility. In 1985 and 1986, 13 maritime prepositioning ships were deployed around the world. One squadron of five ships is based at Diego Garcia, along with the 7th Marine Brigade, replacing smaller ships deployed to Diego Garcia in 1979.[55] As a result of the Reagan Administration's efforts, U.S. airlift capabilities increased by 80 percent between 1980 and 1990, sealift capabilities increased by 110 percent, and materiel prepositioning increased by 150 percent.[56] These improvements proved to be crucial to the rapid deployment of U.S. troops and materiel to the Gulf in August 1990.

The key to CENTCOM's strategy, however, was obtaining military base access agreements with a number of regimes in the Middle East, and with states that could provide logistical links from the United States, Europe, and East Asia. Despite the Reagan Administration's best efforts, however, formal access agreements have been signed only with Turkey, Oman, Kenya, Somalia, Morocco, and Portugal.[57] With other countries, the United States has informal understandings or, in some cases, secret arrangements. These are less reliable for planning purposes than formal access agreements, but they represent a concession to regional political sensibilities.[58] Following the Iraqi invasion of Kuwait, the United States relied on facilities in virtually all of these countries to support the deployment of forces to the Gulf.

Oman

The development of military bases in Oman, strategically located near the Strait of Hormuz, is perhaps the most important part of the U.S. buildup. Over $255 million has been spent on a massive construction program since 1980. Three Omani airbases—Thumrait, Sib, and Masirah—serve as staging areas for the U.S. Air Force deployment; tactical squadrons based in Oman are within range of most of the Gulf.[59]

The United States had had access to Masirah during and after World War II when it was a British RAF base, and Sultan Qaboos had allowed this arrangement to continue after the British withdrawal. Throughout the 1970s, the United States used Masirah for Orion PC-3 surveillance flights.[60] After U.S. forces used Oman as a staging ground for the failed 1980 Iranian hostage rescue mission, Sultan Qaboos threatened to revoke access.[61] His history of cooperation with the British and the United States, however, together with Oman's financial needs and its perceptions of vulnerability to external threats, apparently overruled this temporary dispute, and the Sultan signed a formal access agreement later that year.

When the United States began threatening Iran at the start of the tanker war in the Gulf in 1984, Sultan Qaboos began to be less enthusiastic about his emerging relationship with the United States. "The United States cannot expect an automatic hand from Oman in an intervention to stop Iran from blocking off the Strait of Hormuz," he said, unless it had the backing of all other Arab states in the Gulf area.[62]

Oman adopted a tougher stance in negotiations the following year to renew the access agreement with CENTCOM.[63] "Oman thought we felt that we had the unilateral right to do anything," remarked a Pentagon official, "and we probably thought we did, too."[64] The Omanis wanted it clearly stated in the treaty that Oman would have to approve U.S. use of its military bases in a contingency. They were also uncomfortable about war materiel being transported in and out of the country without their knowledge. The agreement was renewed, after the United States agreed to supply Oman with flight lists of goods being moved to and from the bases.[65]

At the base on Masirah Island, the U.S. Air Force has built an 800-foot pier, storage tanks containing 189,000 barrels of aircraft fuel and lubricants, a communications center, and an aircraft instrument landing system. At Sib, storage tanks for another 126,000 barrels of fuel and lubricants have been "built into the ground, [with] reinforced concrete walls, base slabs and roof, lined with steel plate." A command and control center and a tactical communications center are also located on the base, along with a liquid-oxygen plant to manufacture jet fuel. Most of the construction, however, has been at Thumrait, in Oman's southern province of Dhofar. Here, the Air Force has built its main ammunition storage facilities and additional stockpiles of fuel and lubricants. Sites prepared in the mid-1980s for a "tent city" at Thumrait have been used to shelter U.S. forces in the Gulf.[66]

Egypt

Before his assassination in 1981, Egypt's President Anwar Sadat sought to establish Egypt as the United States' main military ally in the region. He offered the United States full access to Egyptian military bases at Ras Banas, Qena, and Cairo West, but to avoid provoking domestic opposition he refused to sign a treaty.[67]

Ras Banas, a naval and air force base on the Red Sea originally built by the Soviet Union, was given a high priority for use as a storehouse and staging ground for the Rapid Deployment Force. It is strategically located in a remote area in Egypt directly opposite Saudi Arabia's oil terminal at Yanbu. Qena and Cairo West are primarily transit facilities; the latter was used as a staging area for the aborted raid on Tehran during the 1980 hostage crisis. All three bases have been used to ferry U.S. troops and supplies to Saudi Arabia. In addition, ships of the U.S. 6th Fleet in the Mediterranean have made port calls at Alexandria, and in the first months of the U.S.-Iraq confrontation in 1990, other ships in the Red Sea may have used the base at Ras Banas.

The United States has spent $55 million improving these bases, in spite of a dispute with Egypt over the use of local contractors which has delayed work.[68] The U.S. Congress balked at appropriating funds for base improvements in the absence of a formal access treaty, and by 1985 ambitious plans for joint development of the Ras Banas base were scrapped, at least temporarily.[69]

In addition, the United States has reportedly established a secret air base in Egypt, with 100 Air Force personnel and $70 million in prepositioned military supplies that can be used for AWACs and the support of fighter squadrons "in certain contingencies." News leaks in 1983 did not identify the location of the base, but a Pentagon official said it was "in the middle of nowhere," making it "a very good base for secret operations." The base was upgraded with Air Force operational funds rather than military construction money to keep the base secret from congressional oversight committees.[70]

Military bases in the Sinai Peninsula offer another option for Pentagon planners. Eight hundred U.S. troops are stationed in Sinai as part of a 3,000-strong Multinational Force of Observers monitoring compliance with the Egyptian-Israeli peace treaty. The first troops sent to Sinai came from the 82nd Airborne Division, the backbone of the RDF, and other battalions of the 82nd Airborne have been rotated through Sinai in six-month intervals. Pentagon officials have said they assume that any U.S. units serving with the multinational force would be available in an emergency for operations outside Sinai.[71]

Saudi Arabia and Other Gulf States

In 1981, Marine General P.X. Kelley, commander of the RDF, told Congress that "the strategic and geopolitical significance of Saudi Arabia is quite likely second to no other nation on the face of the earth in its importance to the future well-being of the free world." Hyperbole aside, it is widely acknowledged that Saudi Arabia holds the key to attaining U.S. military objectives in the Gulf. General Kelley continued: "If the United States is to deploy meaningful combat power to that part of the world under any scenario…it is absolutely essential that we have free and willing—and I emphasize those two words, free and willing—access to Saudi land bases, Saudi ports, Saudi host nation support, and a considerable labor pool from the Saudis."[72]

The deployment of U.S. and allied troops to Saudi Arabia in August 1990 followed this script quite closely. U.S. air and ground forces were deployed at several Saudi military bases, principally Dhahran, in the oil-producing Eastern Province, and Hafar al-Batan near the Kuwaiti border, with administrative headquarters in Riyadh. U.S. warships and supply transports docked at Saudi ports on both coasts. The Saudi military was placed on a war footing, and the civilian sector provided a wide range of support services.

U.S. access to Saudi bases is particularly important not only because of the country's key location, but also because its extensive network of military bases has been built to U.S. specifications under the supervision of the U.S. Army Corps of Engineers and private U.S. contractors. Since the mid-1970s, Saudi Arabia has engaged in an enormous military construction program, building four "military cities" (al-Hasa, Qasim, King Khaled, and Asad), other major bases at Khamis al-Mushayt, Tabuk, and Sharura along the country's borders, and naval bases at Jubail and Dammam on the Gulf and Jeddah on the Red Sea.[73]

These facilities are far larger than Saudi Arabia's own defense forces can use. They have been "overbuilt" specifically for use by U.S. forces. This explains how Saudi military facilities could have absorbed the rapid deployment of more than 300,000 U.S. ground troops and more than 500 aircraft in the months that followed Iraq's August 1990 invasion of Kuwait. When the first U.S. troops arrived in Saudi Arabia, stockpiles of weapons, ammunition, spare parts, and other materiel were already there for their use, prepositioned on the bases since 1981. Air-conditioned barracks housed U.S. Air Force personnel, and hangars and repair facilities serviced U.S. warplanes. The size of the U.S. deployment, however, outstripped even the overbuilt bases, and a number of temporary facilities were erected, including several in forward positions near the Kuwaiti border.

Because of the British military presence in Bahrain before 1971, it has well-developed military facilities, including a large airfield and a naval base. The U.S. Navy's Middle East Force was formerly homeported at this base. It still uses it on a regular basis.[74] In 1987, as Iran stepped up its attack on oil exports from the Arab Gulf states, Qatar allowed the United States to construct storage facilities for medical supplies, lubricants, and a large amount of jet fuel.[75]

A squadron of U.S. F-16's was deployed to airbases in Qatar in August 1990, along with several British Jaguars. Additional warplanes were sent to Bahrain. A squadron of U.S. cargo planes is based in Abu Dhabi, in the United Arab Republic.

Israel

Israel's inclusion in early plans for the Rapid Deployment Force made sense from a military perspective, and the Begin government offered the United States "unquestioned facility access."[76]

Analysts argued that U.S. access to bases in Israel would rest upon the close long-term relationship between the two countries, not a temporary alignment of an unstable regime. The size of Israel's military bases and the sophistication of its equipment mean that Israel would be able to receive and support large numbers of U.S. forces. Its air defense and anti-terrorist network offers protection, and specially equipped F-15's can fly from bases in Israel to the Gulf.[77]

The Reagan Administration's desire to forge a "strategic consensus" temporarily overruled Carter Administration decisions not to establish RDF related bases in Israel for fear of alienating Arab states. Within weeks of taking office in January 1981, the Reagan Administration was discussing a plan to preposition aircraft, tanks, ammunition, and other U.S. equipment in Israel, to be maintained by the Israeli Defense Forces.[78] Later in 1981, the United States and Israel signed a Memorandum of Understanding establishing the outlines of "strategic cooperation" between the two countries. Israel offered to fly cover for U.S. transports carrying RDF units to the Middle East, to stockpile tanks for U.S. use, and to service 150 or more advanced fighter jets stationed by the United States in Israel. In return, the United States agreed to finance expanded production of Israel's Merkava tank, and to share intelligence from U.S. satellite photos.[79]

The Reagan Administration was quickly made aware of the sensitivities of its Arab allies toward Israeli participation in RDF planning. The Memorandum of Understanding, therefore, was kept vague on the issue of military base access, mentioning only the potential for "access to maintenance facilities and other infrastructures."[80]

Nevertheless, military cooperation between the United States and Israel has flourished since the early 1980s. Under the Reagan Administration, Israel became a strategic asset not only in the Middle East, but globally, as the Iran-contra affair clearly demonstrated. U.S. and Israeli intelligence services work closely together in the Middle East and around the world. Israeli military contractors are developing important elements of the Strategic Defense Initiative ("Star Wars") system. U.S. warships in the Mediterranean have made numerous high-profile port calls to Haifa, and U.S. warplanes use bombing ranges in the Negev Desert. In 1989, the Pentagon revived plans for prepositioning $100 million of U.S. weapons in Israel. The political sensitivities of the United States' Arab allies, however, have continued to place restraints on the Pentagon's desire for facilities in Israel. U.S.-Israeli military cooperation, therefore, has usually been cast in light of larger U.S. security interests, particularly the East-West conflict. George Bush, campaigning for president in 1988, described Israel's role succinctly:

> By virtue of its military capability and the values and political objectives it shares with the U.S., Israel buttresses the [Western] alliance in its most vulnerable area—the southern region of NATO and the Eastern Mediterranean. Continued security and economic assistance to Israel and expansion of existing elements of strategic cooperation, including joint exercises, pre-positioning of combat equipment, spare parts and ammunition, intelligence-sharing and contingency planning will serve to strengthen American military power and influence in the Eastern Mediterranean.[81]

In the initial stages of the Gulf crisis in 1990, however, Israel proved to be a liability, not an asset, to the Western alliance. As the Bush Administration labored to build an Arab coalition against Iraq, it repeatedly urged Israeli leaders to keep a low profile. Any sign of "strategic cooperation" between the United States and Israel, it was feared, would alienate the Egyptians, Moroccans, and Syrians, who had deployed troops alongside U.S. forces, as well as the Saudis themselves. Israel's formidable military power, and its convenient location between Europe and the Gulf, could not be used by the United States in this time of crisis.

Support Bases

Further from the Gulf, the United States has established a string of support bases for transit and refueling, transports, resupply of naval forces, maintenance of equipment, storage of fuel and supplies, and communications links. The most important of these bases is Diego Garcia. Throughout the 1980s, the base was continually expanded and improved. Runways were lengthened, more harbor improvements were made, and more maintenance facilities and ammunition storage depots were constructed. Between 1980 and 1986, $660 million was spent for prepositioned Air Force and Navy equipment, providing 30 days of war stocks for CENTCOM forces.[82] Supplies loaded from Diego Garcia were among the first to reach the Gulf in August 1990.

Other bases were developed in Somalia, Berbera and Mogadishu, primarily to support the U.S. fleet in the Indian Ocean and Orion PC-3 aircraft on anti-submarine patrols. Since 1980, the U.S. Navy has spent $54 million improving runways at both bases, and extending a quay at Berbera. In Kenya, the Navy has spent $58 million improving the airfield at Mombasa and dredging the harbor to accommodate aircraft carriers.[83]

At Sidi Slimane in Morocco, the United States has spent $30 million improving airfields and storage facilities for fuel and lubricants, and more construction is planned.[84] At Lajes Air Force Base in Portugal's Azores islands, the United States has built storage tanks for 3.4 million barrels of fuel and lubricants, improved the runway, built a new control tower and installed a new air traffic control system. Housing facilities were constructed for personnel to be stationed there during contingency operations.[85]

U.S. access to Lajes is particularly important. During the 1973 Middle East War, the United States made extensive use of Lajes Air Force Base to resupply Israel, after NATO allies had denied the United States use of airfields in Europe. Although Portugal is a member of NATO, separate bilateral agreements cover Lajes, and it was the only unrestricted facility available for the operation.[86]

Before the 1990 U.S. intervention in the Gulf, 250 U.S. military aircraft used Lajes each month, en route between the United States and destinations in Europe, the Middle East, and Africa. This number rises substantially when military exercises are conducted by U.S. forces in Europe or the Middle East, and peaked during the deployment of U.S. forces to the Gulf in 1990. To service this traffic, 1,800 U.S. military personnel are stationed at Lajes, along with 1,900 dependents, 1,600 Portuguese workers, and Portuguese military forces.[87]

In addition to these bases which serve the U.S. Central Command, several other U.S. military bases provide important support for U.S. military operations in the Middle East. When the United States attacked Libya in April 1986, for example, F-111 fighter-bombers took off from airfields in Great Britain.[88] NATO airbases in Greece and Italy, and U.S. airbases in Spain, offer key facilities for refueling and resupply for U.S. forces en route to the Middle East. The bases in Spain played a leading role in the deployment of U.S. forces to the Gulf in 1990, while naval bases in Morocco, Portugal, and Spain support the U.S. 6th Fleet in the Mediterranean. Further to the east, U.S. bases in the Philippines, and naval anchorages in Singapore and Sri Lanka, support the fleet in the Indian Ocean.[89]

This complex network of military bases and facilities, along with U.S. capabilities for rapid deployment and "power projection," has created a vast infrastructure for U.S. intervention in the Middle East. Funds appropriated by Congress for Fiscal Year 1986 represented the completion of all major Pentagon requirements for bases in the region.[90] By negotiating access agreements with host countries, carrying out a crash program of military base construction and improvements, prepositioning weapons and other war materiel, and developing rapid deployment capabilities, the Pentagon overcame the limitations on its capabilities that were evident in its response to the Iranian revolution and the Soviet invasion of Afghanistan. When Iraq's invasion of Kuwait in August 1990 touched off a major international crisis, the Pentagon was ready for war.

Toward a Regional Security Strategy

Even as the United States was building this network of military bases throughout the Middle East, however, the strategic justification for them was changing. As one observer noted in 1986, "everyone has concluded that the Soviets are not going to invade Iran."[91] The Soviets had met stiff resistance from Islamic insurgents in Afghanistan and showed no intention of preparing a drive toward the Gulf oil fields. Moreover, the outbreak of war between Iran and Iraq in September 1980 refocused attention on regional threats to U.S. interests in the Middle East.

During the 1980s, U.S. strategic planning for the Gulf emphasized the "Iranian threat" to the Western-oriented Arab states. Theories of a global terror network focused attention of Libya, Syria, South Yemen, and radical Palestinian groups. Security planning, therefore, began to consider ways to counter these threats to U.S. allies. In addition, the United States became increasingly concerned in the 1980s with the possibility that radical Islamic groups, or other dissidents, would destabilize U.S.-backed regimes in the area. The assassination of Egyptian president Anwar Sadat in 1981 and the Iranian-backed subversion in Kuwait in 1983-85 raised fears that the real threat came from within.

As a result, the United States has since 1979 developed a multi-faceted strategy for protecting U.S. interests in the region against regional and internal threats. This approach draws heavily upon the relatively new strategic doctrine of low-intensity conflict (LIC), which seeks to confront a variety of political, economic, and military threats.[92]

In order to bolster friendly regimes against internal opposition, the United States has developed extensive programs of military aid and training. Two-thirds of all U.S. military aid is directed to the Middle East, and major military training programs are in operation in all Middle East countries which grant the United States access to military bases.[93]

The United States has also made major efforts to build up the capabilities of friendly regimes to counter military threats from other states in the region. The formation of the Gulf Cooperation Council in 1981 has led to increased military cooperation between the Gulf Arab states and the construction, with extensive U.S. involvement, of the most advanced integrated air defense system outside NATO and the Warsaw Pact.[94] In 1983, the GCC announced the formation of a Gulf Rapid Deployment Force (with troops from Saudi Arabia, the United Arab Emirates, Kuwait, and Oman) to confront local low-intensity threats.[95] The United States also developed a plan to train and equip, with funds from the Pentagon's secret "black budget," a Jordanian RDF of 8,500 troops to protect friendly regimes in the Gulf against internal opposition "without introducing U.S. troops in areas where they might cause political embarrassment."[96] These plans were deferred, but not abandoned, in 1984, in the face of Israeli opposition. In addition, the United States has armed and trained the Egyptian armed forces to play a role in a regional security strategy. A decade of annual training exercises alongside U.S. troops, code-named "Bright Star" and "Gallant Eagle," paved the way for the deployment of Egyptian forces to Saudi Arabia in late 1990.

When these methods have failed to contain internal or regional threats, U.S. forces have been used to prop up or defend U.S. allies. The Carter Administration, for example, used bases in Saudi Arabia to rush arms to North Yemen in 1979. Airborne Warning and Control (AWAC) planes deployed during the Yemen crisis returned to Saudi bases after U.S. hostages were taken in Tehran later that year, and again after the Iran-Iraq War erupted in 1980. The United States sent AWACs to Egypt at least twice in the early 1980s in response to tensions with Libya, and sent two AWACs, F-15 fighter escorts, and support personnel to bases in Sudan in 1983 as a show of force against Libyan-backed rebels in Chad.[97] The Marines deployed to Beirut in 1982 received logistical support from U.S. bases in Turkey, Greece, and Italy, and the U.S. attack on Libya in 1986 involved a variety of forces based in Great Britain, southern Europe, and Egypt. The U.S. Navy's clashes with Iranian forces in the Gulf in 1987-88 were supported by U.S. facilities in Bahrain, Saudi Arabia, Oman, and Diego Garcia. As we have seen, nearly all of these facilities were used to support the deployment of U.S. troops confronting Iraq in 1990.

Thus, while a supposed "Soviet threat" spurred the construction of U.S. military bases in the Middle East, the bases have more often been used to confront other adversaries in the region. Whether or not a genuine Soviet threat to Gulf oil fields ever existed, the Pentagon successfully used fears of Soviet expansionism in the early 1980s to enhance U.S. capabilities for intervention in the Middle East. In any case, radical shifts in Soviet foreign policy and dramatic developments within the Soviet Union have spelled the end of the "Soviet threat." U.S. facilities in the region, however, like other relics of the Reagan-era military buildup, have remained in place as East-West tensions have diminished. They constitute a powerful asset for the exercise of U.S. military power in the emerging "new world order."

African Connections

For reasons of geography, Middle East contingency plans are closely tied to plans for U.S. intervention in Africa. Several African countries (Morocco, Egypt, Somalia, Kenya) provide bases for the U.S. Central Command to transport troops and equipment to the Middle East. Yet when they are linked to other U.S. bases in sub-Saharan Africa, Central Command bases can also be used to project U.S. military force into the African continent.

The Pentagon has developed a strategy for intervention in Africa, as in the Middle East, calling for rapid deployment of troops from bases in the United States and Europe to "host country" bases. Not surprisingly, it has met the same political obstacles it confronted in the Arab states. The announcement of the 1980 U.S. basing agreement with Kenya, for example, sparked major student protests in the country, and may have contributed to an attempted coup in August 1982 by the Kenyan Air Force.[98]

Intervention plans in Africa thus rely on access agreements to bases in friendly countries in the region, and keeping the visible U.S. military presence and the affront to national sovereignty to a minimum. "The United States," wrote Secretary of Defense Weinberger in 1984, "must maintain and, as required, expand access and transit rights in pro-Western African states for the deployment of U.S. forces to Africa, the South Atlantic and contiguous areas; and work to deny or reverse similar access and transit rights to the Soviets."[99]

Essential to these plans are transit bases in Morocco, Liberia, and on islands in the Atlantic Ocean. The extensive network of bases in Morocco was used to ferry troops and equipment to suppress uprisings in Shaba Province in Zaire in the late 1970s, and most recently in the supply of weapons and equipment to UNITA forces in Angola.[100] In Liberia the United States gained access to Monrovia International Airport for Central Command refueling stops,[101] and the Navy continues to make port calls at a naval base it built there in 1944.[102]

In the Atlantic, the buildup of U.S. military facilities in the Azores and Madeira was, according to senior Pentagon officials, a response to the Soviet air and naval presence in Angola. A NATO program in the Madeira group is aimed at establishing a "viable forward support base" that can project military force more than 1,000 miles to the south, below NATO's normal limit of operations at the Tropic of Cancer. A 1987 NATO military exercise involved reacting to a simulated threat from Angola.[103] The British military base on Ascension Island in the South Atlantic is also available to U.S. forces on their way to Africa.

The most important forward base in Africa, however, is Kamina air base in southern Zaire. A former Belgian Air Force base in mineral-rich Shaba Province, Kamina has two 10,000-foot runways—long enough for the largest U.S. transport planes. The United States used the base in 1964 to drop Belgian paratroopers battling leftist rebels in Stanleyville (now Kisangani). In 1977 and 1978, the United States used Kamina again to airlift French, Belgian, and Moroccan troops to help the Zairois Army recapture the important mining city of Kolwezi from leftist rebels.[104]

In 1987, the Reagan Administration moved to negotiate a formal access agreement with Zaire so that the United States could begin turning Kamina into "a major U.S. facility for central and southern Africa." It set aside $2 million in Fiscal Year 1987 for construction at Kamina, mainly for repairs to runways, aprons, and the lighting system. The Pentagon has said Kamina could be used for emergency evacuations of U.S. personnel in southern Africa. It has also pointed out the base's usefulness in suppressing internal uprisings (as in 1977-78 in Shaba Province). Yet Kamina has been used in recent years primarily as the major base for the CIA's supply of weapons and equipment to the right-wing UNITA rebels in Angola.[105] Its remote location and unsurpassed facilities make it perfect for this mission.

As in the Middle East, the United States has developed in Africa a multifaceted plan for military influence in the region. It includes military aid for friendly regimes (Morocco, Somalia, and Zaire top the list) and training by Special Forces teams (in Liberia, Morocco, Somalia, Tunisia, and Zaire) to suppress internal opposition.[106] To counter regional threats where U.S. forces are not needed or not appropriate, the United States has developed the interventionary capability of the Moroccan and Egyptian armed forces, and it has cooperated with and encouraged French intervention in Chad and other African countries. Finally, as in the Middle East, facilities developed by the United States allow it to project its own forces into the region when necessary.

Conclusions

It appears that the Iraqi invasion of Kuwait and the mobilization of U.S. military forces in the Gulf may be the defining events for international relations in the 1990s. As the Berlin Crisis of 1948 helped set the terms for the Cold War, the Gulf crisis may define the landscape of the post-Cold War era. As this chapter is written, a shooting war has not yet broken out, though all signs point in that direction. Even if war is avoided, however, the consequences of the U.S.-Iraqi confrontation will transform the region and affect the entire world.

The crisis has firmly established a renewed role for the United States as the world's police officer, even if its allies must now pay the bills. For the first time in 45 years, the "Soviet threat" cannot be invoked by the West; as the East-West conflict recedes into history, the North-South conflict has emerged into sharper focus. The first major crisis of the post-Cold War era portends a world where rich countries unite against regional powers in the Third World, in an increasingly dangerous struggle over global resources.

It is no accident that these momentous changes should be set in motion by a crisis in the Middle East. In few other places is the contrast between rich and poor so great, the competition for control of resources so fierce, and the capability for warfare so frightening. U.S. strategy in the Middle East suggests the outlines for a new U.S. role in the post-Cold War world.

The strategy developed and maintained by the United States since 1979 to protect its interests in the Middle East calls for a division of responsibilities between the United States and its allies in the region. With extensive assistance from the United States, friendly regimes are responsible for maintaining internal security and responding to low-level regional threats. Direct U.S. military intervention, made possible by access agreements to military bases in the region, has protected these regimes from larger regional threats.

In some ways, this division of responsibilities echoes the symbiosis between U.S. and British strategies in the region from 1945 to 1970, when

British forces and their local allies preserved internal security, and U.S. forces focused on the strategic conflict with the Soviet Union.[107]

While this is an imperfect analogy, it highlights the neocolonial character of U.S. military strategy in the Middle East. In order to advance its strategic, political, and economic interests, the United States, like Britain before it, has forged close ties with unpopular and undemocratic regimes in the region. Further, to maintain this cooperative relationship the United States has helped these regimes suppress domestic opposition and expressions of self-determination. When these regimes are threatened, the United States has stood ready to defend them with U.S. lives.

Saudi Arabia, the key to U.S. strategy in the Gulf, provides a good example of the regimes entrusted to protect "U.S. interests" in the Middle East.[108] Political opposition to the royal family and to monarchical rule is forbidden. No political parties are allowed, and no disagreement with the regime's policies may be published in the press, broadcast, or disseminated in any form. Trade-union organization is illegal, and severe prison penalties are imposed on any worker who organizes or participates in a strike or any other form of collective industrial action. When joining the United Nations in 1945, the regime refused to sign the Universal Declaration of Human Rights on the grounds that the Koran covers all that is necessary. Civil liberties are nonexistent, and overt political activity is rewarded by imprisonment without trial.

This is the regime to which U.S. presidents have pledged their support since 1943. This is the political system that hundreds of thousands of U.S. troops have been sent to preserve. While the Iraqi regime of Saddam Hussein is no better in its respect for human rights, and in many ways has been far worse, U.S. intervention in the Gulf can in no way be seen as a defense of democracy or human rights. It is, rather, a defense of the Saudi royal family, of the other Gulf Sheikhdoms, and of their allegiance to the Western economic system.

All of the other members states in the Gulf Cooperation Council are absolute monarchies, with similar restrictions on civil liberties and human rights. Kuwait, the only GCC member to establish an elected parliament, suspended it by royal decree in 1986. Opposition political parties boycotted the Kuwaiti elections in the spring of 1990, charging they were not democratic. All of the Gulf states are chauvinist, ethnically based societies which deny citizenship to the millions of foreign workers who have migrated to the Gulf, and even to the children of immigrants born within their borders.

In its lack of respect for human rights, Somalia has one of the world's worst human-rights records. Israel, often touted as the only democracy in the Middle East, has adopted extreme measures to suppress the Palestinian people's quest for self-determination. The Moroccan regime severely limits political rights at home and has mounted an extensive counterinsurgency campaign, with U.S. weapons and advisers, against Polisario forces in the Western Sahara.

The regimes in the Middle East aligned with the United States are similar to "friendly" regimes in other parts of the Third World. Yet, because the United States has relatively few formal basing agreements with countries in the Middle East, access to military bases relies heavily on informal arrangements and promises by regional leaders. This makes preservation of the political status quo even more important for U.S. military strategy in the region.

The fact that even cooperative Arab rulers had, until August 1990, refused to grant formal military basing rights to the United States attests to the strength of popular opposition in the Middle East to the U.S. role in the region. The Pentagon's strategy of rapid deployment and contingency access to bases had been developed in part to mute this popular opposition. It has succeeded to the extent that there were practically no large U.S. bases, as there are in Western Europe and Asia, on which popular discontent and popular demands could be focused. The exception, Diego Garcia, seems to prove the rule; 25 years after Britain separated the Chagos Archipelago from Mauritius and deported the entire population, the government of Mauritius is still trying to regain control.

The Gulf crisis in 1990 is the first international crisis in 45 years in which U.S. military intervention could not be rationalized as a defense of democracy or as a response to a Soviet threat. Most people in the United States see it as a conflict over oil. The deployment of U.S. troops to the Gulf, and the regional security strategy upon which it relies, however, are not meant to protect U.S. or Western *access* to Gulf oil supplies. While oil facilities are notoriously vulnerable to sabotage and military assault, they are very difficult to protect militarily. (The long-term security of Western oil supplies would be better served by reducing tensions in the Middle East, not by injecting more force into an already highly militarized region.) Rather, U.S. intervention is fundamentally an attempt to preserve U.S. *control* over the region's oil by maintaining Saudi power in the region and within OPEC. This is one reason why reasonable proposals to develop safe and renewable energy resources have aroused little interest in U.S. halls of power. The issue is not energy itself, but the political and economic power which derives from control of energy resources.

Militarily, the deployment of U.S. forces to the Gulf in 1990 was at the same time the culmination of a decade of planning and development, and an important turning point. The military strategy originally developed to counter the alleged "Soviet threat" to the Gulf had been transformed through the 1980s into a regional strategy for low-intensity conflict—even as the United States developed its capabilities for meeting a medium-intensity threat from Iran. The scale of the new "Iraqi threat," however, set new wheels in motion. A U.S. military spokesperson familiar with the Gulf complained in September 1990 that all the high-intensity and medium-intensity people in the military have taken over from the low-intensity specialists.[109]

As U.S. forces dug in for a long stay in Saudi Arabia, the basic premise of U.S. strategic planning for the Gulf—that allied forces could address most internal and regional threats to their security—had not been abandoned. U.S. officials still maintained that "we will want to insure that our friends in the area have the means to deter aggression and defend themselves, making it less necessary to send U.S. men and women to help them."[110] It was easy to see, however, that U.S. officials had become increasingly concerned with developing U.S. capabilities for direct intervention in high-intensity conflicts. For the first time in several years, U.S. officials began, in late 1990, to speak publicly about the need for a permanent U.S. military presence on the ground in Saudi Arabia. Secretary of State James A. Baker III's proposal for a new regional security structure for the Middle East, modeled after NATO, revived memories of the Baghdad Pact and its successor, CENTO.

The Pentagon's long years of planning for direct U.S. military intervention in a serious "contingency" in the Gulf has achieved its goals. Now that the United States has a major military presence in the region, however, a new set of problems has emerged. As this book goes to press, it is too early to provide answers, but several of the questions are self-evident:

- Will the crisis with Iraq be settled quickly—with or without war—allowing the United States to withdraw its forces from the Gulf and revert to its low-profile basing posture?

- If so, will U.S. capabilities for intervention receive more public scrutiny in the future?

- If not, how long will the United States be able to maintain the political support at home and abroad for a continued military presence?

- How long will it be able to pay the bills, or convince its allies to pay them?

- Will the United States abandon its strategy of relying on access agreements and rapid deployment, in favor of a permanent U.S. military presence in the Gulf?

- Will the long-term presence of U.S. forces in the Gulf create resentment in the Arab states? Will this resentment turn to active opposition, destabilizing U.S. allies?

- How will the tension between two important U.S. objectives— close U.S. involvement with Arab regimes and U.S. strategic cooperation with Israel—be resolved?

- Will domestic U.S. opposition to U.S. intervention in the Gulf focus only on bringing the troops home, or will it address the issues of military bases, rapid deployment capabilities and regional security arrangements?

Further, the ability of the United States to launch a major military operation in the Gulf, a region where it has few formal military bases, suggests that massive intervention is possible in other regions of the Third World. The Defense Department has admitted that there are many locations where we might need to project force, not only in Southwest Asia and the Middle East, but also in Africa, Central America, South America, the Caribbean, and elsewhere. As the Soviet Union's military threat to the West diminishes, U.S. strategic planners will focus more attention on threats to U.S. interests arising from the Third World. The reduction of Soviet support for its clients and allies in many parts of the Third World has already altered regional balances of power, presenting new opportunities for U.S. interventions. As threats to U.S. interests (or perceptions of such threats) arise in Africa, South America, or South Asia, the Pentagon is unlikely to launch an effort to build large NATO-style military bases in these regions. It seems more likely that the United States will adapt the strategy that has proven so successful in the Middle East, and instead develop the military bases of friendly countries in exchange for access agreements.

In addition, as large U.S. military bases in Western Europe and East Asia become harder to sustain because of political and economic pressures, the Pentagon may choose to shift to a basing arrangement similar to that used in the Middle East, as an alternative to complete withdrawal. Greater control over U.S. military bases might be given to the Philippine government, for example, in exchange for an agreement granting access to U.S. forces.

It may be tempting for opponents of U.S. foreign military bases to accept this shift as a compromise which would improve conditions in host countries. This would be a dangerous compromise. While some of the most onerous effects of U.S. bases on host countries may be reduced by such arrangements, the fundamental effects will remain the same. As the experience of the Middle East demonstrates, a U.S. military strategy relying on access agreements to military bases can promote regional militarization, increase dependency on the United States, prop up undemocratic regimes, and suppress self-determination, while maintaining U.S. capabilities for massive direct military intervention.

Notes

1. Henceforth, the term "Middle East" will be used to refer to this entire region, stretching from Morocco to Pakistan, and Somalia to Turkey.

2. Report of Military Construction Subcommittee of House Appropriations Committee, cited in James A. Russell, "U.S. Lays Groundwork in the Persian Gulf," *Defense Week,* 22 September 1986, 1.

3. Ibid, 1.

4. Paolo E. Coletta, ed., *United States Navy and Marine Corps Bases, Overseas* (Westport, CT: Greenwood Press, 1985), 225-240.

5. The strategic location of Morocco, however, led to a permanent U.S. presence.

6. Peterson, *Defending Arabia* (New York: St. Martin's Press, 1986), 55, 58-59.

7. Most oil concessions in the region were held by European oil companies, except for Saudi Arabia, where U.S. companies had established a monopoly before the war. A subtheme of U.S. policy during the post-war period was to expand the influence of U.S.-based oil companies at the expense of their European rivals.

8. Lawrence Freedman, *Atlas of Global Strategy* (New York: Facts on File, 1985), map, 52-53.

9. Konrad Ege, "U.S. Bases in Saudi Arabia," *CounterSpy,* May-July 1981, 34.

10. Helen Lackner, *A House Built on Sand: A Political Economy of Saudi Arabia* (London: Ithaca Press, 1978), 37.

11. Ibid, 91.

12. *Defense Monitor,* April 1974, 3; Coletta, 98.

13. Admiral John McCain, former Pacific Commander-in-Chief, cited in *Defense Monitor,* April 1974, 2.

14. Michael Vlahos, "Force from the Sea: A Modest Proposal," in William J. Olson, ed., *U.S. Strategic Interests in the Gulf Region* (Boulder: Praeger/Westview Press, 1987), 194.

15. Coletta, 97-99.

16. *Defense Monitor,* April 1974; Coletta, 99.

17. Coletta, 99.

18. Ibid.

19. Freedman, 62-63.

20. While access to Berbera was lost when Somalia switched allegiances to the U.S. in 1978, the Soviets gained additional facilities in the Dahlak Archipelago, off the Red Sea coast of Eritrea. See Coletta, 98.

21. Coletta, 100.

22. David A. Andelman, "Navy Rushes to Complete Work on First U.S. Indian Ocean Base," *New York Times,* 7 April 1977, A1.

23. Coletta, 99-100.

24. Andelman, 8.

25. Christopher J. Bowie, *Concepts of Operations and USAF Planning for Southwest Asia* (Santa Monica: Rand, September 1984), 1.

26. Robert W. Tucker, "The Purposes of American Power," *Foreign Affairs,* Winter 1980-81, 248-257.

27. Howard M. Wachtel, *The Money Mandarins* (New York: Pantheon, 1986), 105-106.

28. Zbigniew Brzezinski, *Game Plan: How to Conduct the U.S.-Soviet Contest* (New York: Atlantic Monthly Press, 1986), 49-50.

29. *Washington Post,* 24 January 1980.

30. The threat of a politically motivated oil embargo, which worried many U.S. planners after 1973, now appeared rather small. See Bowie, 1.

31. Ege, 36.

32. Brzezinski, 51-52.

33. Charles A. Kupchan, *The Persian Gulf and the West: The Dilemmas of Security* (Boston: Allen and Unwin, 1987), 156.

34. Bowie, 3 bis.

35. Kupchan, 129.

36. Kupchan, 130.

37. Robert Komer, former undersecretary of defense for policy in the Carter Administration, cited in James A. Russell, "U.S. Lays Groundwork in the Persian Gulf," *Defense Week*, 22 September 1986, 8-9.

38. John M. Collins, and Clyde R. Mark, "Petroleum Imports from the Persian Gulf: Use of U.S. Armed Forces to Ensure Supplies," *Congressional Research Service Issue Brief*, #IB79046, 1979, 13.

39. Kupchan, 130-131.

40. Kupchan, 138-139.

41. David B. Ottaway, "Saudi Arabia and Its Arab Neighbors Plan Gulf Security Council," *Washington Post*, 27 February 1981, A25.

42. "Struggle, oppression and counter-revolution in Saudi Arabia," 6-7, cited in Lackner, 102-103.

43. Department of Defense, *FY 1981 Annual Report*, 118, cited in Bowie, 13.

44. Kupchan, 126-127.

45. Russell, 8.

46. Bowie, 1.

47. "United States Foreign Policy Objectives and Overseas Military Installations," Congressional Research Service Report prepared for U.S. Senate Committee on Foreign Relations, April 1979, 114, cited in Ege, 36.

48. Bowie, 1-3.

49. Department of Defense, *FY 1982 Annual Report*, 33, cited in Bowie, 14.

50. Stephen D. Goose, "Low-Intensity Warfare: The Warriors and Their Weapons," in Michael T. Klare and Peter Kornbluh, eds., *Low Intensity Warfare* (New York: Pantheon, 1988), 105.

51. Ibid.

52. Kupchan, 142-143.

53. Ibid., 106.

54. Ibid., 107-108.

55. Ibid., 106-107.

56. Ibid., 105.

57. See Chapter 8 for a description of U.S. basing agreements in Turkey.

58. Russell, 8.

59. Ibid.

60. Alvin J. Cottrell and Thomas H. Moorer, *U.S. Overseas Bases: Problems of Projecting American Military Power Abroad* (Beverly Hills, CA: Sage, 1977), 31.

61. Kupchan, 130.

62. *Foreign Broadcast Information Service*, 16 March 1984.

63. J. E. Peterson, "The GCC and Regional Security," in John A. Sandwick, ed., *The Gulf Cooperation Council: Moderation and Stability in an Interdependent World* (Boulder: Preager/Westview Press/American-Arab Affairs Council, 1987), 186 bis.

64. Unnamed Pentagon official, cited in Russell, 8.

65. Russell, 8-9.

66. Ibid.

67. Kupchan, 143-144; Daniel Volman, "Africa's Rising Status in America's Defence Policy," *Journal of Modern African Studies*, 22, I, 1984, 147.

68. Wayne Biddle, "House Panel Cuts Money for Bases," *New York Times*, 17 May 1984.

69. David B. Ottaway, "Egypt's Mood Turns Against Close U.S. Ties," *Washington Post*, 30 January 1985, A14; Kupchan, 151.

70. David B. Ottaway, "Egypt's Mood," A14; Walter Pincus and Fred Hiatt, "U.S. Has Secret Base With 100 Men in Egypt," *Washington Post,* 23 June 1983.

71. Robert S. Dudney, "Where Forgotten GI's Guard Sinai Peace," *U.S. News & World Report,* 29 August 1983, 26-28; Drew Middleton, "U.S. Sinai Unit: Ready for Other Flash Points," *New York Times,* 28 February 1982, 13. In 1986, top Egyptian civilian and military officials reportedly discussed leasing to the United States the Israeli-built Eytam and Etzion airbases in the Sinai, using the base rental fees to offset Egypt's military aid debt, but this has not occurred. *Defense and Foreign Affairs Weekly,* 26 May-1 June, 1986, 1.

72. Testimony before U.S. Senate Armed Services Committee on proposed sale of AWACs, September 1981, cited in Kupchan, 128.

73. Peterson, "GCC," 178-180.

74. Peterson, "GCC," 193.

75. Youssef M. Ibrahim, "U.S. Quietly Gets Gulf States' Aid Against Iranians," *New York Times,* 10 October 1987, A1.

76. House Foreign Affairs Committee, "U.S. Security Interests in the Persian Gulf," 1981, 75.

77. Kupchan, 135-136.

78. These stockpiles, according to the plan, would be ready for use by U.S. forces in the Gulf, and "in times of special emergency," they would be put at the disposal of Israel. This was hailed in Israel as "a revolutionary concept in the history of the military aid relations" between Israel and the United States. Gid'on Samet, "U.S. Considering Idea of Stationing Equipment," *Ha'aretz,* 25 February 1981, 1, translated from Hebrew by FBIS, 25 February 1981.

79. Drew Middleton, "Israelis Press Military Accord With U.S.," *New York Times,* 9 October 1981.

80. "Text of U.S.-Israel Agreement," *New York Times,* 1 December 1981.

81. *Near East Report,* 30 April 1990, 82.

82. Russell, 8-9. The atoll has been so heavily militarized that one congressional aide joked, "We're waiting for it to sink," (off-the-record conversation with Center for Defense Information staff).

83. Ibid.; Wayne Biddle, "House Panel Cuts Money for Bases," *New York Times,* 17 May 1984.

84. Russell, 9.

85. Russell, 8-9.

86. Cottrell and Moorer, 12-14.

87. David Fouquet, "U.S., NATO Build Up Bases in Azores, Madeira," *Washington Post,* 30 April 1990, 33.

88. At the same time, reports were circulating in the Portuguese press that units of the U.S. Central Command might be stationed at Beja Air Base on the Portuguese mainland. See Fouquet, 33.

89. Freedman, 22-23.

90. Report of Military Construction Subcommittee of House Appropriations Committee, cited in Russell, 1.

91. Thomas McNaugher, Brookings Institution, cited in Russell, 9.

92. Klare and Kornbluh, 55-56. According to Klare and Kornbluh, U.S. military operations in the region have followed quite closely five of the six specific "mission categories" identified as part of low-intensity conflicts:

1) foreign internal defense, or counterinsurgency: actions taken by the U.S. government to assist a friendly governnment resisting insurgency threats (Chad, Morocco, Somalia);

2) "proinsurgency": sponsorship and support of anti-communist insurgencies (Afghanistan, Ethiopia);

3) peace-time contingency operations: short-term military activities (rescue missions, show-of-force operations, punitive strikes) in support of U.S. foreign policy objectives (Lebanon, Libya, Iran);

4) terrorism counteraction: defensive and offensive measures taken by U.S. armed forces to prevent or counter international terrorism (Lebanon, Libya, Iran, Palestinian groups, Syria);

5) peacekeeping operations: use of U.S. forces (usually under international auspices) to police cease-fire agreements or to establish a buffer between hostile armies (Lebanon, Sinai);

Interestingly, U.S. forces in the Middle East have not been used for the sixth mission, antidrug operations, even though the region produces a great deal of illegal narcotics.

93. Iran under the Shah was the largest cash purchaser of U.S. arms and military equipment in the 1970s, a role ceded to Saudi Arabia in the 1980s.

94. Peterson, "GCC," 176.

95. Kupchan, 151.

96. Fred Hiatt, "U.S. Pilots Would Fly Planes in Jordanian Deployment Force," *Washington Post,* 22 October 1983, A19.

97. David B. Ottaway, "Egypt's Mood Turns Against Close U.S. Ties," *Washington Post,* 30 January 1985, A14; Bernard Gwertzman, "US Is Withdrawing Aircraft It Sent to Help Chad," *New York Times,* 24 August 1983, 9.

98. Volman, 151.

99. Caspar Weinberger, *Defense Guidance, 1985-1989,* cited in Volman, 144.

100. "King Hassan's American Card," *The Middle East,* September 1982.

101. Daniel Volman, "Walk Covertly and Carry a Stinger," *New African,* March 1987.

102. Coletta, 213.

103. Fouquet, 33.

104. David B. Ottaway, "Defense Dept. Seeks to Renovate Base in Zaire," *Washington Post,* 21 February 1987, A12; David B. Ottaway, "U.S. Joining Zaire Exercise," *Washington Post,* 18 April 1987.

105. "Reports of CIA Sending Arms to Angola Rebels via Zaire," *San Francisco Chronicle,* 2 February 1987. The United States has also reportedly used bases in Sudan to support covert operations in Chad and Ethiopia. See Goose, 96.

106. Goose, 84.

107. The importance of regional threats in the present equation reflects to a large degree the impact of an unrestrained arms race in the region, which has turned small nations into formidable military powers.

108. Lackner, 89.

109. From a conversation with Eva Gold, a staff member of the American Friends Service Committee, 27 September 1990.

110. "Excerpts from Baker Testimony on U.S. and Gulf," *New York Times,* 5 September 1990, A14.

Part V: Central America

Chapter 14

Honduras

Basing for Intervention

Eva Gold

In the 1980s, Honduras became a staging area for U.S. military operations in Central America. The U.S. military presence was rapidly built up, serving three clear purposes: to provide a credible threat of invasion of Nicaragua; to facilitate intelligence and logistical support for the *contras* and the Salvadoran military; and to ensure that Honduras would remain a reliable ally, preventing a Honduran insurgency from taking hold. The U.S. government saw Honduras as a stable, strategic partner that could serve as a buffer between revolutionary Nicaragua and the insurgencies in El Salvador and Guatemala. Honduras had long been dominated by the United States, and the Honduran government had cooperated with U.S. military ventures in the past.

The United States has regularly carried out military exercises in the Caribbean and Latin America from bases in Panama, Puerto Rico, and Cuba (Guantánamo Bay). Most U.S. troops sent to Honduras were deployed there for short periods of time, so the bases in the United States, Panama, and Puerto Rico remained their "home" bases. U.S. military installations in Panama provided logistical support. Throughout this period, the U.S. military presence in Honduras was described as a "temporary" response to threats in the region.

Honduras, historically a U.S. ally, was the focus of intense U.S. attention for only a decade. The U.S. interest was defined by the assignment to Honduras of a central role in its strategy to combat perceived threats to U.S. "national security." Despite the fact that official U.S. policy in the 1980s was to "shield" and "nurture" the new Honduran democracy, U.S. policy stood squarely behind Honduras' most anti-democratic element—the Honduran security forces. Any obstacle to this alliance was forcefully opposed. The need for equitable development in one of the poorest countries in the Western hemisphere was a nearly irrelevant consideration in the formation of U.S. policy.

During the 1980s, U.S. "low-intensity" conflict doctrine was evolving. Honduras provided an excellent site for U.S. experimentation with this new brand of war-making, which was low-cost, non-controversial and—most important—resulted in minimal loss of U.S. lives. To the detriment of Honduras, U.S. interest in their country was defined by its usefulness in the U.S.-Central American war. The elected civilian government of Honduras was too weak and too tied to the interests of the local military forces to demand more.

Historical Background

The basic U.S. relationship with Latin America was set in 1823 with the Monroe Doctrine. The United States then declared that the Western hemisphere must be "protected from" further territorial claims by European powers. Early U.S. interest in Central America centered on commercial development. By the mid-1800s, the United States was exploring construction of a canal to connect the Atlantic and Pacific oceans; Honduras, Nicaragua, and Panama were all considered possible locations.

Mining companies were among the first commercial interests to gain a foothold in Honduras. By 1900, Rosario Mining, a joint U.S.-Honduras venture, controlled nearly half of all Honduran exports.[1] The banana industry was established at the same time. United Fruit and Standard Fruit quickly displaced local producers, buying up tracts of valuable farm land. As their economic power increased, these companies diversified into banking, fishing, and other commercial and industrial sectors, gaining control over more and more of the Honduran economy. Their economic base contributed to their role as power brokers not only in local affairs, but in shaping national policy as well; Honduras became the quintessential "Banana Republic." Citing defense of these commercial interests, the United States intervened in Honduras on at least eight occasions between 1900 and World War II, sending U.S. troops or otherwise staging a show of force.[2]

At the end of World War II, the U.S. Army opened its School of the Americas in Panama. The U.S. military wanted to indoctrinate the Latin American officer corps with U.S. ideas on military strategy and objectives. Nearly 3,000 Honduran officers and cadets had attended classes there by the time it closed in 1986; more have received training since then at the Army's relocated school at Fort Benning, Georgia.

The United States first used Honduras as a base for intervention in 1954. The U.S. military used Honduran territory for training the "rebels" who were to lead an anti-communist coup against the democratically elected Arbenz government in Guatemala. The Honduran military also served as a conduit for U.S. arms to the rebels.[3]

After the Cuban revolution in 1959, the United States began using Honduras in its efforts to destabilize post-revolutionary Cuba; Honduras permitted the United States to establish a radio station on Swan Island to broadcast anti-revolutionary propaganda. In 1962, the United States began a program of joint U.S.-Honduran military exercises. Among the first of these was "Operation Brotherhood," a simulation of the defense of the primary Honduran airport against foreign attack, presumably by Cuba.[4] At this time, the U.S. military began stressing preparations for domestic counter-insurgency warfare in its training of Central American militaries.

Throughout the 1960s and 1970s, however, Nicaragua and its National Guard were more important to U.S. strategy in Central America than Honduras and its military. Not until the Somoza dictatorship in Nicaragua was under siege in the late 1970s did the United States take a more active interest in Honduras. Between 1978 and 1980, Honduras received $127.9 million in U.S. assistance, more than any other Central American country during this period.[5]

U.S. policy makers wanted more from Honduras than a replacement for Somoza's National Guard. They needed a military base from which to direct their regional strategy against the Nicaraguan revolution and the Salvadoran insurgency, and a local military leadership that would bring other regional militaries into line in support of U.S. policy in the region. The legal foundation for the U.S. presence was the Bilateral Military Assistance Agreement of 1954. This was signed when the United States was using Honduras as a base to topple the Arbenz government in neighboring Guatemala. This bilateral agreement complemented the pre-existing Inter-American Treaty of Reciprocal Assistance (Río Treaty), which calls for all American states to aid one another in the event of an external threat. The 1954 agreement stated: "Each Government will make or continue to make available to the other...such equipment, materials, services, or other military assistance as the Government furnishing such assistance may authorize and in accordance with such terms and conditions as may be agreed."[6] Protocols to the original agreement added in the 1980s made more explicit the terms for the U.S. presence in Honduras.

When Honduras held its first presidential elections in 18 years in 1981, the press characterized the victory of the Liberal Party as a popular rejection of military rule. The United States ostentatiously supported the Honduran elections, promising economic and military aid if they were clean. Rather than strengthening civilian government and democracy, however, the elections proved to be another step in the direction of greater militarization. Shortly after his inauguration, President Roberto Suazo Cordova appointed hard-line anti-communist Gustavo Alvarez Martinez as Commander-in-Chief of the armed forces. Together with the U.S. ambassador to Honduras, John D. Negroponte, General Alvarez and President Suazo proceeded to make Honduras a major line of defense against the new "communist" threats in Central America. Soon after the elections, talk of Honduran "neutrality" in the regional conflicts and efforts to promote regional peace came to a halt.

The U.S. Military Presence and 'Low-Intensity Conflict'

General Paul Gorman, Commander-in-Chief of the U.S. Southern Command (SOUTHCOM) from 1983 to 1986, designed a program of joint U.S.-Honduran military exercises to serve as a cover for the rapid U.S. military buildup. Using Pentagon funds free from congressional scrutiny, Gorman initiated "exercises" which involved the construction and improvement of airfields, roads, port facilities, radar stations, barracks, and other troop facilities. Several airstrips were upgraded to accommodate large U.S. transport planes and sophisticated fighter aircraft. When Senator James Sasser (D-TN) returned from a trip to Honduras in the winter of 1984, he called the buildup "substantial" and "beyond what could reasonably be expected or justified as necessary for the conduct of war games alone."[7]

The facilities were described to the public as "temporary" structures for military exercises. Only after the U.S. presence in Honduras had been firmly established did the Pentagon openly describe its long-term plans. In 1986, the Department of Defense presented Congress with a funding request for a five-year military construction program in Central America. The lion's share was for Soto Cano (previously Palmerola), the principal air base in Honduras, and for airstrips to be used by remotely piloted intelligence drones.[8] John R. Galvin, Commander-in-Chief of SOUTHCOM, acknowledged congressional concern about the "indefinite temporary U.S. presence" in Honduras. "It may take two years or five years or more," he told a House subcommittee.[9] Nominally, all U.S. facilities in Honduras were under Honduran control, even Soto Cano, where 1,100 U.S. troops outnumbered Hondurans two to one.[10]

Joint Task Force Bravo, a joint Army-Navy-Air Force command, was established at Soto Cano to coordinate U.S. operations. In 1984, an intelligence unit was deployed to Soto Cano to fly missions over El Salvador and Nicaragua. Additional reconnaissance missions flew out of San Lorenzo, a base near the borders of El Salvador and Nicaragua. Aguacate, an "improved" airstrip in the department of Olancho, was used by the CIA for delivery of

U.S. air strip in Honduras. Photo courtesy of Eva Gold.

supplies to the *contras*. (After a congressional cutoff of CIA funds for assistance to the *contras*, Aguacate became much less important, but supplies were run from Swan Island).[11]

In the early 1980s, the U.S. military established a regional military training academy (CREM) at Trujillo on the Honduran Atlantic coast. In a little over one year, some 4,000 Salvadorans, 3,000 Hondurans, and some Costa Ricans were trained there.[12] The school was shut down in September 1984, because of objections from some Honduran military leaders. They wanted to stop the training of Salvadorans in Honduras because of a brief but humiliating 1969 war between the two countries and the failure to resolve border issues which lay at the root of that conflict. Following the closing of the CREM in 1984, the Pentagon moved to create military training schools in individual countries. The Honduran Army Center for Military Training (CAME) opened in the fall of 1988.

According to the Honduran Documentation Center (Centro de Documentación de Honduras), based in Tegucigalpa, 60,000 U.S. active-duty National Guard and reserve troops were deployed to Honduras in a nearly unbroken sequence of 52 military exercises between 1981 and the end of 1986. In 1987 and the first months of 1988, another 25 exercises took place.[13] This program of U.S. military exercises continues into the present. Since 1983, the number of U.S. troops in Honduras at any one time has ranged from 1,000-6,000.[14] In addition to military construction, these troops practice military maneuvers, engage in "civic action," and train the Honduran military.

In 1982, U.S. troops assisted the Honduran military on a counter-insurgency mission against approximately 96 guerillas; U.S. advisors were implicated in the interrogation, torture, and death of an American priest traveling with the group.[15] In 1985 and 1986, U.S. troops ferried Honduran troops to the border of Nicaragua in preparation for an alleged Nicaraguan invasion. Both incidents were largely manufactured by U.S. policy makers and pressed on a reluctant Honduran government.

U.S. military actions in Honduras are consistent with the U.S. strategy of "low-intensity conflict" (LIC). LIC includes counter-insurgency, pro-insurgency, anti-terrorist strikes, anti-drug actions, hostage rescue, and other military actions short of conventional warfare. These are the types of conflict military strategists anticipate in the coming decades, particularly in the Third World. The 1988 report of the Department of Defense's Regional Conflict Working Group, entitled "Supporting U.S. Strategy for Third World Conflict" rules out direct U.S. combat in LIC situations, while supporting activities similar to those in Honduras:

> The United States should not commit its forces to combat in the Third World unless it can do so decisively, swiftly, and with discrimination…But overall, our strategy should emphasize using U.S. forces to complement U.S. security assistance, exploiting their potential for helping friendly forces engaged in low-intensity conflict with training, intelligence, communications, transportation, construction, medicine, logistics, and management.[16]

A key element of the LIC strategy for Central America in the 1980s was the circumventing of Congress. Concerned about public opposition to U.S. military intervention in third world countries, the Pentagon wanted to limit public and congressional scrutiny of U.S. military support for the *contras* and the Salvadoran military. They wanted to minimize direct U.S. combat involvement and hide the fact that the United States was conducting a protracted regional war. During military exercises, U.S. troops rotated through Honduras while their home bases remained in the United States, Panama, or Puerto Rico. In this way the issue of permanent foreign deployments was sidestepped.

In addition, many of the operations supporting U.S. troops in Honduras were performed from the home base. In Honduras, an Army communications unit arrived in 1984 with over 500 personnel and almost 100 motor vehicles, some quite large and heavy. After a brief trial, the CINC (commander-in-chief) sent the unit back to CONUS (Continental United States) with a directive that it be reconfigured into forward and rear echelons, the latter to remain in CONUS, linked to the former by satellite radio channels. Upon re-deployment, the unit's presence in Honduras was reduced to about

10 percent of what it had been, and it performed its mission better than before. The unit's CONUS echelon—at its home stations—operated at the same operational pace as the forward echelon, and training, productivity, and readiness advanced day-by-day just as it might have with the whole organization overseas.[17]

These military exercises exposed large numbers of U.S. troops to third world conditions and gave them practice in the type of action they might be called on to perform if direct U.S. military intervention became necessary. One aspect of the exercises was the "civic-action" programs in which U.S. troops delivered food and educational supplies, dug wells, built housing, and delivered medical services in rural areas. The civic-action program exploited the Honduran need for humanitarian assistance in order to achieve U.S. political and military objectives.

Medical military civic-actions (MCAs) provided U.S. troops with an entree to the remote Honduran countryside. Beginning in 1983, medical civic-action programs (medcaps) originating from Soto Cano visited rural villages several times each week. U.S. soldiers learned a lot about the geography and social structure of rural Honduras, as well as about medical needs. For each medical civic action, a village leader was identified and sites for a helicopter landing pad and a temporary clinic located. Troops practiced the logistics of moving medical teams with their equipment and communications gear. At the clinics, a rough census of the population was made.[18]

According to a military study of civic action in Honduras, the primary purpose of the medical MCA program was to make "the U.S. military presence as palatable as possible to the Honduran people."[19] Other goals of the program included enhancement of the image of the Honduran military and government, improvement of U.S. war-fighting capabilities, and improved local health conditions. It was also found that U.S. soldiers felt good about their experiences on MCAs. In the newspaper of Joint Task Force Bravo, Sergeant Greg Allen described caring for rural Hondurans: "Many of the people of Honduras suffered from health problems that could affect soldiers, so what better way to train medical personnel than to have them help people who otherwise would not have medical services made available to them." The troops worked hard, ending up tired, hot, and sweaty, but "most sensed the satisfaction of helping people who have never had help...."[20]

The medical MCA program in Honduras continued to grow. By 1987, military medical teams were assigned for one-and-a-half years to Honduras, working for six months in each of three rural provinces. Each team remained in rural villages for several days at a time in order to provide longer-term medical care than the previous incidental MCAs.[21] According to one knowledgeable source, an Army brigade of 30 medics was attending 33 communities in the province of Yoro in 1988.[22] This change was made to overcome resentment bred by one-shot visits to areas with little or no access to medical facilities. The shift also was based upon the perceived need to sustain a longer-term U.S. military presence in Honduras. In the words of one official: "The Americans had to do something to lessen the negative impact of placing so many foreign troops, even temporarily, within the borders of a sovereign nation."[23] Despite the desperate need for a comprehensive health-care system in the Honduran countryside, there is little evidence to suggest that the medical civic-action programs were designed to respond to this need.

The U.S. military buildup in Honduras was originally supposed to bolster a region-wide anti-Sandinista military front which the Reagan Administration had hoped to create. In the event of a major U.S. military invasion of Nicaragua, such a force could provide troops from the region and facilitate early withdrawal of most U.S. forces. This could then have been cited as proof of support from regional allies for U.S. military action, as was done in the case of the U.S.-led invasion of Grenada.[24]

Honduran Commander-in-Chief General Alvarez, eager to seize opportunities which would promote his stature as a regional military leader, invited the Guatemalan and Salvadoran militaries to participate with Honduras in U.S. war games. The Salvadorans engaged in a few small exercises, but cooperation between the two countries remained limited. Both the Salvadoran and Guatemalan militaries were more concerned with their own internal conflicts. The Salvadoran and Honduran militaries remained at odds over their unresolved border conflicts. The Guatemalan government, still resentful of U.S. condemnation of its human rights record, did not want to appear to support a U.S. plan. A later attempt to develop an inter-American intervention force disintegrated following the Falklands/Malvinas war.[25] As time passed, Honduras was left to carry the bulk of the burden of U.S. regional military policies and presence alone.

Military, Social, and Economic Impacts

"It is a characteristic of this decade that Honduras has always been seen as subordinate to other points of interest. We haven't been seen in terms of our own reality, but rather as a reflection of events in neighboring countries."[26] So observed Honduran journalist Manuel Torres.

The objectives of U.S. policy in Honduras have been dictated by perceived threats to U.S. national security interests in Central America, not by the needs of the Honduran people or government. Hondurans realized that the only way to advance their interests with the United States would be through "deals" allowing the U.S. military access to their territory. Hondurans also recognized that strong U.S. interest in Honduras would be limited by the duration of conflicts in neighboring Central American nations.[27]

During the trial of Oliver North, details of the U.S.-Honduras relationship were revealed. After Congress cut off military aid to the *contras* in 1985, the Reagan Administration provided "incentives" designed to elicit Honduran support for the *contra* army: promises of economic aid, delivery of military assistance, and expansion of the CIA's covert support to Honduran security forces. In response, Honduras quieted its demands for special U.S. aid as compensation for its vital role in support of the *contras*. The Reagan Administration thus prevented the Honduran government from exposing the U.S. role in continuation of the *contra* war despite congressional restrictions.[28]

As with other nations in which the United States has military bases, "rent" for use of Honduran territory was provided in the form of increased U.S. economic and military assistance. Between 1981 and 1986, annual U.S. assistance to Honduras quadrupled, from $37.5 million to $152 million. During that same period, U.S. military aid to Honduras increased from $8.9 million to $88.2 million. In subsequent years, as Congress reduced foreign aid appropriations, military aid to Honduras eventually dropped to $40 million.[29] After the electoral defeat of the Sandinistas in February 1990, U.S. military aid to Honduras sank to $20 million.

Honduras has always been disappointed with the levels of U.S. aid. In 1983, for example, the Honduran government proposed to the National Bi-partisan Commission on Central America that Washington provide $10 billion in aid over 12 years.[30] Though U.S. economic aid to Honduras between 1982 and 1988 totalled more than $700 million, mostly for economic stabilization, the Honduran economic crisis worsened and the nation became dependent on outside assistance.[31] Honduran journalist Manuel Torres explained the consequences of this dependency:

> Now that Honduras is going out of fashion in terms of U.S. assistance, the aid is being reduced. We are going to feel the shock of a drug addict in confronting this. In 1980 the per capita contribution of economic aid from the United States was about $47. By 1988 it had increased to a per capita rate of $67. Now there's going to be a dramatic decrease...So the next government will encounter a population with greater demands with even less possibility of meeting those demands.[32]

In Honduras, the United States strengthened the military during a period when official U.S. policy was to nurture civilian governments and democratic institutions. The Honduran armed forces had long depended on the United States as a source of weapons, ammunition, equipment, and training. By the mid-1980s, however, the United States was providing more than 50 percent of the Honduran military budget.[33] By 1987, Honduran military and para-military forces, which had increased from 14,200 to 23,700 during the previous six years,[34] were playing a central role in all spheres of government decision-making and required 20 to 30 percent of the national budget.[35] According to Manuel Torres:

> The second aspect of U.S. policy is the implant of the doctrine of national security...For Honduras, the doctrine of national security has meant a civilian government where nevertheless the seat of power has been in the hands of the very powerful military...The doctrine of national security aimed fundamentally to turn us into a counter-insurgency country. They created a clandestine structure of terror that still exists, with political disappearances, assassinations, and torture.[36]

Throughout the 1980s, Hondurans experienced increasing levels of political violence. While General Gustavo Alvarez Martinez was Commander-in-Chief of the Honduran armed forces, an estimated 112 people "disappeared," 93 extra-judicial killings were carried out, and 108 cases of torture were documented.[37] Battalion 3-16, a secret Army unit set up by Alvarez with U.S. assistance when he was in the intelligence branch was implicated in these disappearances, murders, and cases of torture.[38]

Toward the end of the decade, several cases of human rights violations in Honduras were brought before the Inter-American Court on Human Rights, a legal arm of the Organization of American States. In verdicts issued in 1988 and 1989, the Court held the Honduran government responsible for the forced disappearances of Manfredo Velasquez in 1981 and for the 1982 disappearance of Saul Godinez. The Court required Honduras to pay damages to the families of these particular victims and condemned the government for involvement in the disappearance of 100 to 150 people between 1981 and 1984.[39]

Although the number of human rights abuses decreased immediately after the coup overthrowing Alvarez, the numbers began to increase again in the second half of the decade. Witnesses in the trial of Honduras before the Inter-American Court on Human Rights were threatened, and two were killed. Torture of political prisoners was pervasive, while killing of common criminals by the security forces became a common solution to Honduras' mounting social problems. Human rights groups noted that political assassinations increased. Efforts by both domestic and international human rights groups to monitor and expose abuses were hampered by government and military opposition to investigations. Domestic human rights groups were systematically discredited, some international human rights monitors and journalists were expelled from the country, and some domestic journalists were threatened and intimidated.[40]

While repression was often directed at leaders of church, peasant, student, labor, and women's groups, an atmosphere of suspicion and distrust was created among the population at large as well. In September 1983, the government established the "Center for Emergency Information;" its telephone number was posted throughout Honduras and people were encouraged to report any "attitude which they considered suspicious and that concerned security."[41] The center was attached to the Public Security Forces (FUSEP) of the Honduran armed forces. The activities of the center dwindled after General Alvarez was ousted, but in 1988, Civil Defense Committees— groups of private citizens who denounced "unusual or suspicious" activities—resumed activities.[42]

The United States has been implicated in the abuse of human rights in Honduras. In its report "Honduras: Without a Will" the international human rights group America's Watch observed that the Reagan Administration ignored human rights abuses by the military out of consideration for the Honduran role in supporting the *contras*. The U.S. embassy actually supported a campaign to discredit Honduran human rights groups which criticized the military, especially CODEH (Committee for the Defense of Human Rights in Honduras) and its director, Ramon Custodio. Battalion 3-16, the military unit implicated in many murders and cases of torture, received training from U.S. advisors. According to several journalists, these advisors were aware of the Battalion's involvement in assassination and torture.[43] In 1985, the U.S. Congress approved a two-year waiver of the prohibition on aid to police forces in Honduras. Though the waiver was not renewed in 1987, Honduran security forces continued receiving U.S. aid through the Anti-Terrorism Assistance Fund and the Administration of Justice Program.

The presence of the *contra* army in Honduras provided many opportunities for graft. In 1986, the U.S. General Accounting Office disclosed that U.S. funds meant for purchase of supplies for the *contras* had been passed through a Honduran business into the hands of Honduran military officers.[44] Already predisposed to back the *contras* because of their ideological opposition to the Sandinistas, Honduran military leaders also had a financial interest in the continuation of the U.S.-backed *contra* war. As late as February 1988, when the *contra* presence was a topic of bitter internal debate, Honduran Commander-in-Chief Humberto Regalado wrote directly to House Majority Leader Jim Wright asking Congress to continue its support of the *contras*.[45]

The propensity for corruption within the Honduran military also made Honduras an ideal location for drug traders looking for trans-shipment points between Colombia and the United States. By the mid-1980s, U.S. officials and Honduran political leaders were aware that tons of cocaine were being shipped through Honduras to the United States. The *Los Angeles Times* quoted an unnamed State Department official as saying:

> We don't know the extent of the Honduran military's involvement in drugs, but our educated guess is that all of the senior officers have knowledge, many are involved…and they are all reaping the profits.[46]

The sudden increase in illicit drug activity in Honduras cannot be separated from the presence of the *contra* army and their U.S. backers. The export and sale of drugs appears to have provided *contra* leaders with weapons and supplies.[47] The United States turned a blind eye to the involvement of the Honduran military in the drug trade out of consideration for Honduran support for the *contras*.

In April 1988, members of the Honduran military handed over Juan Ramon Matta Ballasteros to U.S. authorities. Matta was a Honduran citizen wanted in the United States on drug-related charges. Observers speculated that the Honduran military allowed the United States to seize Matta because he was a private citizen, and because some officers feared Matta was becoming too powerful. At the same time, a handful of Honduran officers were exposed by the U.S. and Tegucigalpa press for involvement in drug trafficking, but their role in the drug trade has been ignored. As a U.S. congressional investigator explained, "the real contra-drug story is that we simply did not crack down on people that were doing us a favor." [48] The Drug Enforcement Agency and the Miami U.S. Attorney's office were ready to proceed against the Honduran military, but apparently the Pentagon and CIA resisted prosecution of their allies.[49]

While the involvement of Honduran officers in drug trafficking is hushed, the United States and Honduras have negotiated the installation of a radar facility on the Honduran Atlantic coast and an interdiction treaty which allows U.S. officials to board any commercial or private ship on the high seas carrying a Honduran flag which is suspected of carrying drugs. Such an apparently contradictory policy supports the conclusions of the Senate Foreign Relations subcommittee that foreign policy objectives often undercut efforts to fight the drug war.

Martha Sandoval Canales is a Honduran peasant who participated in an AFSC-sponsored speaking tour on the impact of U.S. military bases in foreign countries. She described another aspect of the corruption of Honduran life caused by the U.S. military presence:

If we try to see the women's angle, we may also see that the migration of women to the cities looking for better living conditions causes great problems. They are our sisters and daughters. When they do not find a job they may become prostitutes. They are exposed to infectious and contagious diseases. These women are shunned, especially in the case of those who suffer from AIDS. This situation contributes to the loss of moral and cultural values among our people. Some women believe that sleeping with a North American soldier is their ticket out of poverty or their chance to migrate to the United States. This is de-humanizing for our young women. For women who practice prostitution the impact is double. Not only is there fear of getting sick, but there is fear of being rejected by the community. In my country the number of women prostitutes is now enormous. But the people feel great contempt for them, and this is a great burden. Also, they are often left with many children and with no means of taking care of them.[50]

AIDS developed simultaneously with greatly increased prostitution in Honduras. The control of AIDS is made especially difficult by two factors: poor health conditions and governmental dependency on U.S. aid. According to investigators Tom Barry and Kent Norsworthy, the first known Honduran victim of AIDS died in May 1985. By the end of the 1980s, 248 cases of AIDS among Hondurans had been documented, though authorities estimated that 7,000 people probably carried the virus by then. [51] Many blame the introduction of AIDS to Honduras on U.S. troops and the increase in prostitution. The rapid spread of AIDS is a consequence of inadequate health care and lack of education. Martha Sandoval explained:

Because of its economic dependence on the United States, the government is limited not only in the way it acts, but also in the way it thinks. Its thoughts and actions must coincide with the thoughts and actions of the government of the United States. That enormous dependence! The government knows about AIDS and the sexual abuse of children in the area of Comayagua [near Soto Cano]. The government has to swallow this information, because to say anything means to be against the policy of the United States in the region.

Honduras is among the very poorest countries in the Western hemisphere. Tragically, the $1 billion in U.S. aid pumped into Honduras during the 1980s did little to improve the economic situation. In fact, poverty among Hondurans increased in the 1980s. According to Manuel Torres, just over half of the Honduran population lived in poverty in 1980, and of that group, 12 percent were living in extreme poverty. By 1988, 63 percent of Hondurans lived in poverty, and the number living in extreme poverty had increased three-fold.[52] Today, three out of every four Hondurans suffer from malnutrition to some extent, a direct consequence of the fact that 70 percent of the economically active population is under- or unemployed.[53]

Many Hondurans fear that the economic and social deterioration of the past decade will lead to civil unrest. In the summer of 1989, the industrial city of San Pedro Sula was shut down for several days by spontaneous demonstrations protesting a proposed increase in transportation fares. Demonstrations followed soon afterwards in Tegucigalpa. According to Honduran Labor Minister Guatama Fonseca:

> We'd be fooling ourselves if we said the future looked bright. Most of the *campesinos* are poor and illiterate. Our schools and universities are appalling, so we're not turning out qualified technicians. As bad as our production levels are now, they will undoubtedly decline even further...I have no doubt that the future of Honduras will be the same as that of Guatemala, El Salvador, and Nicaragua—that of great social upheaval and civil war.[54]

Future U.S.-Honduran Relations

U.S. policy in the 1980s was not designed to address the greatest threats to Honduras' future. U.S. aid militarized the country while increasing dependency and doing little to alleviate worsening poverty. Because of U.S. aid, Honduras had been able to postpone some of the harshest economic measures that other governments in the region were forced to implement—repeated currency devaluations, massive layoffs of public sector employees, and severe cutbacks in government services. But in 1989, newly elected Honduran president Rafael Leonardo Callejas inherited a bankrupt government and an economy plagued by foreign debt, fiscal deficits, depleted foreign currency reserves, and negligible new investment. In the context of shifting U.S. priorities, Washington cut total U.S. aid to Honduras from $132 million to $80 million in Fiscal Year 1990. One of Callejas's earliest decisions was to implement economic austerity measures. He publicly acknowledged that "perhaps this is a good time to remember that we cannot be so dependent on U.S. aid," and has identified himself as a staunch backer of Central American economic integration.[55] He is also emphasizing building stronger ties with the European Economic Community, Asia, and hemispheric neighbors Mexico and Venezuela. Even before his election, Honduras had signed its first trade agreement with the Soviet Union.[56]

U.S. policy, particularly the U.S.-backed *contra* war, had become increasingly controversial in Honduras in the latter part of the 1980s. Honduran human rights and student groups had protested the *contra* presence from the beginning. Peasants and coffee growers from El Paraíso, the province in which the majority of *contra* camps were located, later joined in.

When it became obvious that U.S. support for the *contras* was dwindling, even the Honduran military voiced concern. By the mid-1980s, Honduran labor, student, peasant, and women's groups were staging demonstrations against the *contra* and U.S. military presence. In the spring of 1988, the most militant of these protests took place.

In March 1988, 3,200 U.S. troops arrived in Honduras, uninvited, to repel a purported Nicaraguan invasion. A month later Ramon Matta was extradited to the United States despite the fact that no U.S.-Honduran extradition treaty exists. These two events, symbolic of flagrant U.S. disregard for Honduran sovereignty, led to a large public protest ending with the burning of the U.S. Embassy annex and cars parked in close vicinity. Although U.S. officials knew that this angry outburst did not represent the official Honduran position or even widespread Honduran public opinion, they recognized the danger of a growing and militant opposition to U.S. policy and presence. In the short term, the Reagan Administration tried to buy time by releasing $57.3 million for health-care projects, and agreeing to transfer twelve F-5E's, the most sophisticated aircraft in the region, to the Honduran Air Force.

U.S. soldiers were targets of protest too. A small Honduran guerilla movement claimed responsibility for some bombings and armed attacks against U.S. soldiers. Several dozen U.S. personnel were wounded or killed in such attacks by 1990.

Despite the 1987 Esquipulas II agreement, in which the five Central American presidents called for political—not military—solutions to the region's conflicts, the Reagan and Bush Administrations continued to resist all calls to demobilize the *contras*, keeping their primary camps in Honduras. U.S. backing for the *contras* changed only after the February 1990 electoral defeat of the Sandinistas in Nicaragua. Although U.S. aid to Honduras immediately decreased, U.S. operations at Soto Cano, where the United States had invested more than $40 million since 1983,[57] continued, as did the routing of U.S. military exercises.

By 1990, Honduran officials knew that their heyday was over. Washington's attention had turned to the new governments in Panama and Nicaragua and the search for a negotiated solution to the war in El Salvador which would fit U.S. policy interests. The outlook for substantial U.S. economic aid was made bleaker by the changes taking place in the Soviet Union and Eastern Europe. The rallying cry of "communist threat" was losing its potency, and Eastern European nations would now be getting a significant slice of a shrinking U.S.-aid pie. The Honduran government tried to bargain for more aid, but to no avail. For their part, they have postponed negotiations for Protocol III to the 1954 Bilateral Assistance Act, which is supposed to guarantee future access to Honduran military facilities, ports, and airstrips, and some Honduran leaders have threatened to develop Soto Cano as a commercial airfield. U.S. ambassador to Honduras, Crescensio Arcos, in arguing for continuation of the U.S. presence, claims U.S. GIs contribute $45 million to the Honduran economy annually.[58] There are many among the Honduran elite, as well, who would be uneasy with a U.S. pullout. In any case, given its legacy of dependence and history as a faithful U.S. regional ally, it is unlikely that Honduras would throw the United States out. It is equally unlikely that Washington will allow its military assets in Honduras to dissolve before the war in El Salvador is settled and while the situation in Nicaragua remains unstable.

Notes

1. Alison Acker, *Honduras: The Making of a Banana Republic* (Boston: South End Press, 1989), 59, cited in Antonio Murga Frassinetti, *Enclave y Sociedad en Honduras,* 43.

2. *Sojourners,* April 1982, 23.

3. Acker, 110-111.

4. Acker, 112.

5. Acker, 114, cited in U.S. Department of State Congressional Presentation, Security Assistance Programs 1981-1983, cited in Richard Alan White *The Morass* (Harper & Row: New York, 1984), 183.

6. See Agreement Between The United States of America and Honduras, Article I.

7. Congressional Record, 8 February 1984, cited in *From Banana Cases to Contra Bases, Chronology of U.S-Honduran Relations, January 1977 to July 1986,* Central America Historical Institute, October 1986.

8. James P. Wootten, "Honduras: U.S. Military Activities," Foreign Affairs and National Defense Division, Congressional Research Service, 11 February 1987, 2, 5. San Lorenzo is identified as the airfield from which unmanned intelligence drones take off.

9. Statement of General John R. Galvin, U.S. Army Commander-in-Chief, U.S. Southern Command, before the House Appropriations Committee, Subcommittee on Military Construction, Caribbean Basin Construction Program, 12 March 1986, 7.

10. Wilson Ring, "U.S.-Honduras Military Pact Rouses Ire," *The Christian Science Monitor,* 16 September 1988.

11. *El Heraldo,* 15 July 1988, from *Miami Herald,* cited in *Honduras Update* (unpublished summaries of Honduran newsclips), September 1988; *The Situation of Human Rights in Honduras, 1987,* CODEH (Committee for the Defense of Human Rights in Honduras), 5.

12. Peter H. Stone, "The Special Forces in Covert Action," *The Nation,* 7-14 July 1984.

13. *Honduras: Fuerzas Armadas 1988 - Contra insurgencia interna y disuasion regional* (Mexico: Instituto de Investigaciones Socio-economicas de Honduras, 1988), 70-83.

14. This is an extrapolation from figures published by the Department of Defense in their annual reports, Worldwide Manpower Distribution by Geographic Area, and from news-clippings and Pentagon releases about deployments for military exercise programs.

15. George Black and Anne Nelson, "Mysterious Death of Fr. Carney," *The Nation,* 4-11 August 1984, and subsequent articles appearing in *The Nation.*

16. "Supporting U.S. Strategy for Third World Conflict," report by the Regional Conflict Working Group submitted to the Commission on Integrated Long-Term Strategy, Department of Defense, June 1988, 25.

17. Ibid., 44.

18. Eva Gold and Mary Day Kent, "The Ahuas Tara II Exercises," NARMIC/American Friends Service Committee, Philadelphia, PA, February 1984.

19. Bernard Eugene Harvey, Major, USAF, "U.S. Military Civic Action in Honduras, 1982-1985: Tactical Success, Strategic Uncertainty," Army-Air Force Center for Low-Intensity Conflict, October 1988, 2.

20. Ibid., 17.

21. Interview by Eva Gold of the U.S. Southern Command, Panama, February 1988.

22. *La Tribuna*, 15 June 1988, cited in *Honduras Update*, June 1988.

23. "U.S. Military Civic Action in Honduras," 36.

24. For background on coalition warfare, two documents are useful: "The Role of the U.S. Military, Caribbean Basin," Final Report, 26 October 1981; and "Non-NATO Contributions to Coalition Warfare," Final Report, 23 February 1981, both issued by the U.S. Army War College, Carlisle Barracks, PA.

25. Richard Lapper and James Painter, *Honduras: State for Sale* (London: Latin America Bureau, 1985), 84.

26. Honduran journalist Manuel Torres at a peace conference held in Honduras as reported in *Zeta Magazine*, March 1990, 24.

27. An observation made numerous times by Mark B. Rosenberg, in his unpublished papers, "Narcos and Politicos," 7; "Toward a Redefinition of U.S.-Honduran Relations: Alternatives and Options," 3.

28. "Key Parts of 1985 Honduras Deal Carried Out," *Washington Post*, 2 May 1989; North trial transcripts.

29. Congressional Presentation for Security Assistance Programs, Fiscal Year 1981 and Fiscal Year 1986.

30. Peter McCormich, "Hondurans Want More from U.S.," *Philadelphia Inquirer*, 25 December 1983.

31. "Toward a Redefinition of U.S.-Honduran Relations," 8. As an indication of the scale of U.S. assistance relative to the Honduran economy, Rosenberg points out that the dollar volume of U.S. economic assistance (including Economic Support funds for stabilization) in 1985 was greater than the income generated by coffee, Honduras' second most important export. He also states that leading Honduran bankers acknowledge that U.S. economic assistance has become critical to the Honduran economy.

32. *Zeta Magazine*, March 1990, 24.

33. Ernesto Paz, "The Foreign Policy and National Security of Honduras," in Mark B. Rosenberg and Philip L. Shepherd, eds., *Honduras Confronts Its Future, Contending Perspectives on Critical Issues* (Boulder, CO: Lynn Rienner Publishers, Inc., 1986), 185.

34. *The Military Balance, 1981-1982* (London: The International Institute for Strategic Studies, 1981), 97; Ibid., 1988-89, 198.

35. "Toward a Redefinition of U.S.-Honduran Relations," 2.

36. *Zeta Magazine*, March 1990, 24.

37. Ivan Santiago G., "Honduras: Despite Military Investigation, Repression, Disappearances Continue" (Lima: Latinamerica Press, 12 September 1985).

38. Acker, 123.

39. "Honduras under Jose Azcona" (Lima: Latinamerica Press, 9 March 1989).

40. CODEH (Committee for the Defense of Human Rights in Honduras), *Human Rights in Honduras, Special Report, 1988*, 2; Americas Watch report, "Honduras: Without the Will."

41. Lapper and Painter, 94.

42. *Human Rights in Honduras, Special Report, 1988*, 6.

43. James LeMoyne, "CIA Accused of Tolerating Killing in Honduras," *New York Times*, 14 February 1986; Dennis Volman, "Killing of Honduran Army Officer Linked to Testimony on U.S.," *Christian Science Monitor*, 19 November 1985.

44. Government Accounting Office, Congressional Testimony, 11 June 1986, cited in *From Banana Cases to Contra Bases*.

45. *Human Rights in Honduras, Special Report, 1988*, 5.

46. Mort Rosenblum, "Hidden Agendas," *Vanity Fair*, March 1990.

47. See Bill McAllister, "From Shriner to Smuggler," *Washington Post*, 8 April 1988; Patrick Tracey, "Pilots, Guns and Money," *City Paper* (Philadelphia), 8-15 April 1988, No. 191.

48. *New York Times,* 14 April 1989.

49. Rosenblum.

50. Interview with the author.

51. Barry and Norsworthy, *Honduras: A Country Guide* (Albuquerque: The Inter-Hemisphere Education Resource Center, 1990), 78.

52. *Zeta Magazine,* March 1990.

53. Barry and Norsworthy, 50.

54. Barry and Norsworthy, 59.

55. Council on Hemispheric Affairs, "Honduras Opposes U.S. Presence," *Washington Report on the Hemisphere,* Vol. 10, No. 20, 11 July 1990.

56. Inforpress Centroamericana, "Encouraging Trade With The Soviets," Central America Report, Vol. XVI, No. 33, 25 August 1989.

57. Inforpress Centroamericano, "Honduras—'Blue broom' strikes government workers," *Central America Report,* Vol. XVII, No. 7, 23 February 1990.

58. "Honduras Opposes U.S. Presence."

Chapter 15

Panama

Protecting the United States' Backyard

Mary Day Kent

Bases in Central America are part of a larger structure of U.S. control over the region, and they must be seen in this context. They seem relatively small and insignificant when compared to the mammoth structures of the major bases in Germany or the Philippines. But it is impossible to overstate the impact of the U.S. military presence in Central America on involuntary "host" societies.

The dramatic December 1989 U.S. invasion of Panama is the most recent and explicit example of this control and of the role that regional bases play. "Operation Just Cause," as the military labeled its invasion, offered the military an opportunity to test many of the lessons from Vietnam, Grenada, and the numerous operations conducted in Central America over the past decade. Although the invasion and defeat of the Panamanian Defense Forces (PDF) were accomplished in less than 24 hours, it was the previous two years of economic and political pressure that made possible what *New York Times* columnist William Safire called the "quick application of overwhelming strength." The other key element was the existence of what analyst Harry Summers described as "major logistical support in place." The role played by the U.S. bases in Panama was spelled out less euphemistically in a report in the *Army Times:* "Hostile assault wasn't needed in Panama where U.S. troops already had airfields at Howard Air Force base, logistic support, a division-size force in place, and a command and control network."[1] Without the infrastructure of U.S. bases, it has been estimated that at least 40 additional daily flights would have been required to assure the presence of sufficient troops, weapons, and supplies needed for the invasion.

U.S. soldier on guard duty following the December 1989 invasion of Panama.
Photo courtesy of Fred Bronkema.

While the invasion demonstrated the convenience and utility of the bases in Panama, it also revealed the military's vision of its needs and priorities for the 1990s. In the first five hours of the invasion more than 7,000 troops parachuted into Panama from U.S. bases. The United States took 10 times as long to insert the same number into Grenada in 1983. Another new element for the 1990s was the inclusion of Drug Enforcement Administration officers in the first wave of the invasion.

Despite these new elements, including the testing of the Stealth aircraft, Apache attack helicopters, bulletproof vests, and new food rations, the essence of the operation was a return to the direct, overt, and unilateral U.S. intervention not seen in the region for several decades. Unlike the Grenada invasion, which involved the Eastern Caribbean states as participants and endorsers, the invasion of Panama was consistently opposed and condemned throughout Latin America and around the world. The headline that appeared in the *New York Times* the morning after the invasion, "Bush's Presidential Rite of Passage," made the political motives painfully clear.

Structures of Intervention

Although U.S. military intervention is, or has been, a major factor in the histories and lives of all Central American nations, Panama and Honduras are the only Central American countries in which U.S. military bases are currently located. The bases in Honduras are a development of the 1980s, and they played a crucial role in the Reagan Administration's counter-insurgency war strategy. The U.S. military establishment in Panama is by far the largest in the Western Hemisphere outside of U.S. territories, dating from the military's role in building the Panama Canal in the early 1900s. Panama is the site of the U.S. Southern Command (SOUTHCOM), one of the four regional commands worldwide. SOUTHCOM is responsible for the coordination of military operations and training programs throughout Central and South America. Through the Southern Command, military aid, training, and operations are organized for all of Latin America south of Mexico. Through SOUTHCOM, military exercises, short-term missions of state National Guard units, intelligence and monitoring efforts, as well as logistics and supply services are woven together into an integrated force for intervention.

In 1988, U.S. troops in Panama numbered approximately 11,000. In addition, a detachment of 1,000 "security" troops was dispatched to Panama in March 1988, as tensions mounted between the United States and the *de facto* military government of Panama led by Manuel Antonio Noriega. At the height of the post-invasion U.S. occupation there were 24,000 troops, but by May 1990 the number had fallen to the pre-invasion level. There are an additional 50,000 people in Panama who are either civilian employees of the U.S. military or who are civilian dependents of the military. Between 1983 and 1987, 28,000 U.S. National Guard personnel were also dispatched to Panama for brief periods of training and military exercises, averaging 5,000 per year.[2] This, in a country whose population is only a little more than two million.

Since the signing of the Panama Canal Treaty in 1977, the strips on either side of the Canal have been officially recognized as "Panama" instead of being known as the "Canal Zone." However, this area, roughly five miles wide and 50 miles long, remains the location of one of the world's greatest concentrations of U.S. military forces. In addition to the Canal—and the housing, administration, ports, and support facilities associated with the Canal—this narrow strip across the Isthmus of Panama contains 11 distinct "major" installations and another 12 "U.S. military facilities." Under the terms of the Canal Treaty, these installations are divided into "Defense Sites" (essentially bases under total U.S. control until the expiration of the Canal Treaty in 1999) and "areas of military coordination" (facilities that the treaty authorized and which are the joint security responsibility of the two countries).

The most important of the defense sites are: Quarry Heights, the location of the SOUTHCOM offices; Fort Clayton, headquarters for the U.S. Army components of SOUTHCOM, including the 193rd Infantry Brigade, the

Cartographic School of the Defense Mapping Agency, and the U.S. Army's tropical testing center; Fort Kobbe; Howard Air Force Base, often cited by the military as "the only U.S. controlled jet-capable air base in Central and South America"; Fort Amador; Rodman Naval Station, location of the U.S. Navy Small Craft Instruction and Technical Training School; Albrook Air Force Station, site of the Inter-American Air Forces Academy; Fort Sherman, with the U.S. Army Jungle Operations Training Center; Fort William Davis; and the Galeta Island Naval Security station. The base that used to be known as Fort Gulick, the former site of the U.S. Army School of the Americas, is now called Fuerte Espinar and is jointly coordinated with Panama.[3]

The principal functions of this constellation of bases are command and coordination of U.S. forces in Latin America, intelligence gathering and monitoring, promotion of close working relations with Latin American militaries, and the defense of the Panama Canal. In the Southern Command's own literature, defense of the Canal is listed first, but in reality this is the least significant of the functions and the one requiring the smallest proportion of personnel and resources. Ironically, the canal was closed for 24 hours at the beginning of the 1989 invasion—an unprecedented event for the international waterway which had functioned without interruption since 1914. It was not closed by any of the potential threats often cited by Washington, but by the United States itself, in the name of protection and neutrality.

Panama: The Fifth Frontier

In the late-twentieth-century debate over how the United States should structure its relations with the rest of the world, Panama has retained its significance as a symbol, long after its actual military importance for the United States has diminished. Former SOUTHCOM commander General Fred F. Woerner observed that his command represented only 0.1 percent of the United States' 1987 military budget.[4] His predecessor at SOUTHCOM, General Paul Gorman, has maintained that he recommended that the Southern Command be relocated to the U.S. mainland as early as 1983.[5] Retired Admiral Gene LaRocque, in his 1988 proposal for restructuring U.S. bases toward defense and away from intervention, recommended eliminating U.S. bases in Panama and replacing them with rapid deployment forces based at sea or on the U.S. mainland.[6] Yet the vision of Panama expressed by the Heritage Foundation as "America's Gibraltar" and as "a military asset of immeasurable importance to the U.S." remains dominant in the United States.[7]

The comparison with Gibraltar conjures up both the historic, geo-strategic importance of the location and Panama's legacy of imperial culture. The motivation for building the Panama Canal is generally credited to the Navy's experience in 1898, when the battleship Oregon required 68 days to travel from San Francisco to Cuba, around Cape Horn at the tip of South America, to join the fighting of the Spanish-American War. During World War II the value of the Canal to the U.S. war effort was dramatic, allowing the Navy to fight effectively in two oceans. Retired Major General David S. Parker estimated that "the Canal paid for itself several times over" in World War II.[8] During the war years, commercial traffic passing through the Canal dropped to one-quarter of its normal level, but the number of U.S. military or government ship transits rose by more than five times the pre-war level. The number of U.S. military forces in the Canal Zone peaked at 69,000 in 1943.

Today, many U.S. politicians and much of the U.S. public retain an image of the Canal and the surrounding military bases that was fixed in 1945. During World War II the United States obtained consent from the Panamanian government to use Panamanian land, waters, and air rights beyond the Canal Zone—extending into all of Panama's territory. Between 1942 and 1948, the United States operated as many as 130 distinct military sites in Panamanian territory outside the Canal Zone, ranging from large air bases to dozens of small sites for searchlights. At the end of the war, the U.S. negotiated an agreement that expanded still further its use and access to Panama, an agreement that was massively rejected in a spontaneous uprising of the Panamanian people.

The post-war period marked other changes. New aircraft carriers were too wide to pass through the locks of the Panama Canal. This was an implicit recognition of new military realities in the nuclear age. The role of the U.S. presence in Panama shifted from global reach to regional intervention, and the bases became sites for research and training. In 1987 only 32 U.S. Navy ships transited the Canal.[9]

Although the post-war mission of U.S. forces in Panama has emphasized counter-insurgency warfare and hemispheric control, the controversy that developed around the Carter Administration's negotiation of a new canal treaty revealed that the U.S. public and politicians still cling to old perceptions. Opposition to the canal treaties was a key plank in Reagan's campaign against Carter. The proposed Latin America policy drafted for the Reagan campaign in 1980 by the right-wing "Committee of Santa Fe" held firmly to the belief that "politics changes: geography doesn't," and advocated turning the canal over to the Inter-American Defense Board to defend the hemisphere against the Soviet naval presence in Cuba and the Caribbean. Eight years later, the conservative Heritage Foundation was issuing special reports raising alarm over the risks to U.S. security from instability in Panama, calling the canal "vital" to U.S. trade and defense, and claiming that the Southern Command was a "strategic forward command area" essential to U.S. defense.[10]

The Defense Department, however, has appeared to accept the impending transfer of U.S. bases to Panama in 1999, as agreed in the Carter-Torrijos Canal treaties of 1977. In 1984 one of the primary military training centers in Panama, the U.S. Army's School of the Americas, was closed and moved to Fort Benning, Georgia. Retired Major General David Parker, a former governor of the Canal Zone, reported that "to the surprise of many critics of the move, [the school] reportedly performs much better in its new location, due to improved facilities and environment."[11] In December 1988 the Defense Department officially announced its plans for a "phased withdrawal" from Panama throughout the 1990s to be completed by the Treaty deadline of noon on December 31, 1999.

Unless there is a clear shift in U.S. military policy, the missions currently carried out by U.S. forces in Panama will be terminated, moved, or transferred to the Panamanian Defense Forces. There have, however, been proposals to maintain some of the bases under a rental agreement with Panama—comparable to lease arrangements in other countries. Many officials in Panama shared General Noriega's belief that the primary motive behind the 1989 invasion was to reassert control over the Panamanian Defense Forces so that future agreements on base rights could be negotiated with a cooperative and reliable Panamanian counterpart.

A Platform for Intervention

The Canal Zone literally divides the country in two and makes travel from one side to the other impossible without passing through U.S. military checkpoints. With the changes brought about by the 1977 treaty, some of the fences along the former Zone border have come down, and the line is less conspicuous, but the number of crossing points remains extremely limited, and all are monitored and easily controlled by the U.S. military. This structure contributed to the speed and completeness of establishing U.S. control at the time of the invasion.

The location of the Canal and the Canal Zone has meant that the U.S. blocks what would otherwise have been the expansion of Panama's capital city. The communications towers of the SOUTHCOM headquarters on Quarry Heights loom over the center of Panama City as a constant reminder of the U.S. military presence.

The actual border, as it cuts through the city, is a street that has been the site of countless U.S.-Panamanian confrontations over the years. One side of the street is a busy urban shopping area that also contains the country's most elite and politicized public high school. Behind these buildings lie streets of densely packed slum housing. This is the location of El Chorillo, the poor neighborhood that was almost totally demolished during the 1989 invasion. The other side of the street marks the beginning of the former Canal Zone area: unoccupied, undeveloped, clean, and green.

The various names given to this street over the years tell the story. Known for most of the century as Fourth of July Avenue, the name was changed by the U.S. Canal Zone authorities to John F. Kennedy Avenue shortly after Kennedy's assassination in 1963. This change was almost immediately followed by one of the most serious confrontations between Panamanian students and U.S. soldiers, the so-called flag riots of 1964 in which at least 22 young Panamanians died. The Avenue next to the former Zone is now known in Panama as the "Avenue of the Martyrs," while it continues to be "JFK Avenue" to the North Americans on the other side of the street. The Avenue may be symbolic, but well before the invasion it was a grating reminder to Panamanians of the long history of U.S. domination of their country.

The first treaty covering construction and U.S. control of the Panama Canal and Zone, after President Theodore Roosevelt engineered Panama's separation from Colombia in 1903, called for the United States to have powers in the Zone "as if it were sovereign." Additional rights were spelled out for the United States to establish the standards of sanitation and public order in Panama and to act with force when the U.S. deemed it necessary to maintain these standards. This has left an ambivalent legacy which did provide Panama City with clean water, sewage systems, electric power and malaria control, courtesy of the United States, at generally higher standards than most Central American cities. The negative side was that these benefits came with total control exercised by the United States. Panamanians became physically and psychologically dependent on U.S. goodwill for water, electricity, and other essential services. Until the early 1960s, Panamanians were regularly subjected to clouds of insecticide sprayed from Canal Zone trucks that drove through Panama's streets on malaria control missions. For many years the only television in the country was the armed forces station, and the armed forces radio filled the airwaves with U.S. top 40 hits. To this day, Panama does not have its own currency.

When the United States first began construction of the Canal, almost everything necessary for the enterprise had to be imported, from complex heavy equipment to the household supplies needed for daily life. The majority of the workers on the Canal were also "imported," from the United States, Europe, and the Caribbean. The U.S. Army Corps of Engineers supervised the construction project and, along with the indisputable achievement of the Canal itself, also instituted an elaborate system of worker hierarchy based on race and national origin. According to this system, regarded at the time as a model of administrative accomplishment, the jobs, pay, housing, food, and recreational opportunities for each category of worker were meticulously allocated along racial lines. The fundamental division was between the "Gold" workers and the "Silver" workers, along with the finer distinctions, such as between white North American workers and their "lower ranking" Spanish or Italian counterparts. This creative euphemism for what was essentially the same as the Jim Crow system of the U.S. South transported to Panama, established "Gold" and "Silver" schools, restrooms, railroad cars, drinking fountains, and the pay lines where the workers collected their respective "gold" and "silver" wages. The "Gold and Silver" system continued until after World War II and was only abolished with President Truman's 1948 order to desegregate the U.S. Armed Forces.

At the same time that the United States brought modern institutional racism to Panama, it also brought thousands of Black workers from the British colonies of the Caribbean. When the Canal was finished in 1913, many of these workers stayed on either as Canal Zone or base employees, or in the Republic of Panama itself. Their presence heightened tensions around differences of race, language, and perceptions of competing loyalties. English-speaking, Protestant, West Indian Blacks were confronted by discrimination in the Canal Zone and resentment and distrust in Spanish-speaking, Catholic Panama.

Direct U.S. military intervention into the internal affairs of Panama has been frequent since 1903. U.S. troops occupied the province of Chiriqui between 1918 and 1920 to control disturbances and post-electoral agitation. In 1925 the Marines attacked impoverished Panamanians engaged in a rent protest against slum landlords in downtown Panama City; they then remained in control of the entire capital for several days. In 1941 Washington organized the coup that overthrew elected President Arnulfo Arias, a popular nationalist politician sympathetic to Germany. He was replaced by a leader willing to allow the enormous World War II expansion of U.S. bases. The 1950s and 1960s witnessed cycles of popular protest against the U.S. presence, with the U.S. military taking action to suppress it. Popular protest peaked in 1959 and again during the flag riots of 1964. These last two protests led the United States to renegotiate the Canal Treaty's terms, a lengthy process that was begun by President Johnson in 1965.

Another form of intervention has been the use of the Canal Zone as a back door into Panamanian politics—the hiding place or source of support for politicians favored by the U.S. who would otherwise have faced defeat or exile. In this tradition, the 1989 invasion-related swearing-in ceremonies for the Endara government were held under U.S. guard at Albrook Air Force Base. Even Panamanians staunchly opposed to General Noriega regarded this blatant U.S. sponsorship as a serious handicap for the Endara government in its efforts to gain international credibility and domestic support.

The impact of official, U.S. military intervention has been aggravated in Panama by the presence of U.S. civilian employees in the Canal Zone. Often referred to as "Zonians," these civilians are in many cases second- or third-generation residents in the Canal Zone. Many have roots in the segregationist traditions of the U.S. South. Some of the most irritating and arrogant U.S. behavior in Panama has come from these civilians and their dependents—rather than from the U.S. military.

Another level of frustration for Panamanians has been Panama's role as "host" country for a long list of U.S. interventionary activities elsewhere in the Third World. These actions include most of the roles of the Southern Command: coordination, intelligence, training, and provision of supplies. Bases in Panama were used to train U.S. troops for jungle warfare during the Vietnam War and to support the U.S. invasion of Grenada in 1983.

These interventionist missions were highly visible throughout Central America after the Nicaraguan revolution in 1979. As a center of coordination, the Southern Command served as the focal point for decisions about military advisors and training teams for all the Central American countries except Nicaragua. It has been the site for special military exercises and National Guard rotations in the region and for training courses for the armies of other Central American nations. Specific requests for weapons and supplies for Central America's armies, to be presented to Washington, have been compiled and designed on U.S. bases in Panama. These operations are supported by information provided by the most sophisticated intelligence gathering installations south of the U.S. border. The other major role played by SOUTHCOM facilities in Panama is logistical support. As the Iran-*contra* revelations illustrated, Panama played a crucial role as the supply point for U.S. weapons to *contras* in Honduras and to the Salvadoran military. General Noriega deeply offended public opinion in Panama when he allowed the United States to conduct a *contra* training exercise in Panama in 1985.

More Than a Canal

For military planners in Washington, the bases in Panama are convenient for carrying out operations that could, if necessary, be based elsewhere in the United States or Central America. For Panamanians, however, the U.S. presence has been the central determining (and deforming) experience in their nation's history. The central theme of Panamanian history is the struggle to assert a separate and independent identity that places Panama's interests first. From Panama's U.S.-engineered independence in 1903 until the signing of the Carter-Torrijos Canal Treaty in 1977, the Canal was the defining issue of Panamanian politics. Throughout decades of tension with the United States over the U.S. presence and control of the Canal and the Canal Zone, the issues important to each side have been fundamentally different. The United States has focussed on the concepts of property, investment, and security. Meanwhile, the Panamanians have raised the banners of sovereignty, dignity, peace, and justice.

The conflict between Washington and General Noriega also revealed basic differences in perception. The North American perception of the problem was framed in terms of drugs, financial corruption, and U.S. military security. The Panamanian perspective, whether pro- or anti-Noriega, emphasized the Canal treaty, democracy, and human rights as the key issues. The irony was that Noriega and his military were the inevitable result of past U.S. policies and interventions. More Panamanian military forces have been trained by the United States than those of any other nation. Noriega himself is acknowledged to have been on the CIA payroll for years. The 1984 Panamanian elections, the first after 18 years of military rule, were crudely manipulated by Noriega to "elect" his chosen civilian candidate, Nicolas Arditto Barletta. The U.S. acquiesced in 1984 and undoubtedly gave Noriega the impression that similar fraud in 1989 would also go unchallenged.

The events following the May 1989 Panamanian elections illustrated key features of the U.S. military presence in Panama, as well as limits to U.S. power. The bases, strategically located in the center of the country and only minutes from downtown Panama City and Panamanian military installations, facilitated a series of pre-invasion actions between May and October 1989. These operations were designed to instigate a military coup and, at the very least, demonstrated the enormous ability of the United States to intervene at will in Panama. U.S. troops occupied the Panamanian National Legislature. U.S. tanks and troops surrounded Panamanian government and military buildings. Marines were lowered from helicopters to the U.S. Embassy in the heart of the capital city. There were frequent parades of tanks and armored cars through the capital and other parts of Panama. These operations would have been inconceivable in almost any other sovereign country. Panama responded with its own forms of petty harassment and with several attacks on individual U.S. personnel. It became clear that Washington's message had been received in Panama City in October, when an unsuccessful coup—undermined by confused support from Washington and U.S. troops in Panama—was attempted from within the Panamanian Defense Force.

In the 1970s, when the Treaty negotiations were underway, Panamanians began looking toward the future, when control of the Canal would finally be theirs. Then they would confront the legacy of U.S.-sponsored militarization, the challenge of creating a truly neutral means of operating the Canal, and the need to find other and more diverse sources of economic development than dependence on Canal tolls and the income received from purchases of the U.S. military forces and employees. The Canal generates about 8 percent of the Panamanian Gross Domestic Product (GDP) and is one of the largest sources of employment for the nation, providing 7,000 jobs for Panamanians, at a time when Panamanian unemployment is on the order of 40 percent.[12] Another 5,500 Panamanians are employed directly by the U.S. military. SOUTHCOM calculated in 1986 that the total of U.S. expenditures in Panama (Canal tolls, Canal administration, and U.S. bases—including local spending by civilian employees) was $577 million, a figure which appeared to demonstrate that 12 percent of the national economy is directly dependent on the United States.

The events of 1989, however, demonstrate that the health of the Panamanian economy is not first among the United States' interests in the country. In July 1989 the U.S. military removed 6,400 troops and their dependents from Panama onto U.S. bases or back to the United States. While these actions were designed to protect these people and to increase the pressure on General Noriega, they also deepened the economic crisis confronting Panama's private sector. Then came the invasion, the economic costs of which have yet to be fully calculated. Estimates are that the invasion resulted in between $1.5 and $2 billion of damage, including the direct destruction of the attack and the looting that followed. Promised U.S. aid to rebuild the economy remains just that—*promised* aid.

The other primary sources of income for the country are also deeply dependent on the United States: export of bananas, provision of flags of convenience for shipping, registry of "paper companies," import-export business through the Colon Free Trade Zone, and an oil pipeline that transports Alaskan oil. The illegal drug trade is also largely oriented to the U.S. market, but it is not easy to quantify. The U.S. Chamber of Commerce in Panama estimates that at least half of Panama's private sector business is U.S.-related.[13]

The 1988-89 preliminaries to the U.S. invasion, while failing to depose General Noriega, did provide a striking example of the economic devastation that even "low-intensity" war could wreak on Panama's economy. Economists estimated that the gross domestic product (GDP) for 1988 fell 21 percent because of two non-economic causes: the local political conflict and the U.S. economic sanctions. The effects of the economic crisis surpass the impact of any Panamanian natural disaster in recent decades. Ten years of strong economic growth will be required to restore Panama to its 1987 economic level.[14]

The 1989 tensions and invasion reflect the central paradox of the U.S.-Panama relationship at the end of the twentieth century: the U.S. presence has provided the "secure" conditions necessary for the growth of Panama's economy of international service, while the United States is also the principal cause of the potent mix of nationalism, militarism, and frustrated aspirations that undermine the stability of that relationship.

Facing the Twenty-first Century

When the 1977 Carter-Torrijos Canal Treaties were signed, General Torrijos introduced a note of grim reality into his speech before the glittering diplomatic assembly at the Organization of American States. Acknowledging the success of the negotiations and the long and difficult process that shaped the new agreement, Torrijos remarked that "This treaty...does not enjoy the approval of all our people, because the 23 years agreed upon as a transition period are 8,395 days, because during this time there will still be military bases which may make our country a strategic reprisal target, and because we are agreeing to a treaty of neutrality which places us under the protective umbrella of the Pentagon. This pact could, if it is not administered judiciously by future generations, become an instrument of permanent intervention."[15]

The element of the Treaty that causes the greatest concern among Panamanians is the "DeConcini Amendment" (named for the Democratic Senator from Arizona), which seems to undermine the Panamanian sovereignty regained in other portions of the Treaty. Although the Treaty clearly specifies that the United States must leave all the military bases in Panama by the end of 1999, the DeConcini Amendment reserves for the United States the unilateral and perpetual right to intervene in Panama if the neutrality, security, or functioning of the Canal were to be threatened. The Amendment also raises the possibility of new negotiations to create or to continue U.S. military "defense sites." Another feature of the Amendment spells out the right of U.S. or Panamanian warships to receive accelerated and even preferential passage through the Canal if either country claims this is necessary.

The general belief in Panama is that the transfer of the Canal is irrevocable, and that the United States has no right to select or to judge the government in power when the Canal returns to Panamanian control and the bases are closed. There is, however, a growing sense of urgency about the need to prepare for the day when Panama will be in charge. Panama lacks any strong tradition of "civil service." There is, thus, a realistic fear that in the future, Canal employees will be vulnerable to pressure if the politics of Panama continue to be run by military force—even if that force is no longer the "narco-dictatorship" that many people considered the Noriega government to be. Deep cynicism remains about U.S. efforts to cleanse and restructure the Panama Defense Force, with many fearing that after the initial purge of pro-Noriega officers, the vast majority who served in the old PDF will return to perpetuate old-style corruption and the exercise of arbitrary power.

In addition to fears that the United States will use pressure to gain continued access to military bases in Panama, another important issue of considerable concern remains: the possible construction of a new sea-level canal. Although the 1977 Treaty describes this as a bilateral issue between Panama and the United States, with exclusive rights already conceded to the United States, the economic and geological factors involved in the construction of a new canal are currently being studied by a tri-national committee which includes Panamanian, U.S., and Japanese participants. This committee is due to present its report on prospects for the construction of a new canal in 1991.

With the possibility of a new Canal, the issues of international law that the United States has long ignored take on new importance. One of these issues was raised by General Torrijos in his OAS speech. Panama is a hostage to U.S. nuclear-warfare policy and to its great power ambitions. This not only carries the potential risk of making Panama a target in a nuclear exchange, but also places Panama in the position of non-compliance with the Treaty of Tlatelolco, the Latin American nuclear-free-zone treaty. As with other bases around the world, the United States refuses to reveal whether or not nuclear weapons are stored in Panama, and it refuses to confirm or deny the presence of nuclear weapons on Navy ships sailing through the Canal. Panama is in a position similar to that of Puerto Rico, another signatory of the Tlatelolco Treaty, which is also unable to control U.S. actions in its territory that violate the treaty.

For years, Panamanian legal scholars have emphasized aspects of international law affected by the U.S. military presence and by U.S. control of the Canal, with particular attention to the many ways that the United States has violated Panama's neutrality. As Panama looks forward to assuming greater control over the Canal, Panamanians from across the political spectrum are presenting serious proposals to make the Canal a truly neutral operation. They see this as an idealistic goal and as a practical necessity. One surprising popular and positive outcome of the 1989 U.S. invasion was that the concept of a neutral Panama, with a security force comparable to that of

Costa Rica, has become a topic of serious consideration within Panama and internationally. Should these two possibilities be implemented, they would require a fundamental shift of U.S. policy. The Southern Command would have to be relocated, and U.S. bases would have to be closed. Genuine democracy in Panama would be the only way to achieve a neutral and civilian-controlled future for Panama.

A neutral and demilitarized Panama would offer some tribute and consolation for the loss of life and for the suffering endured by the Panamanian people through the past decades of U.S. intervention and colonialism.

Notes

1. *Army Times,* 15 January 1990.

2. U.S. General Accounting Office, "Central America-U.S. National Guard Activities," report to Rep. Richard A. Gephardt, July 1988 (GAO #U.S.AID- 88-195).

3. United States Southern Command, "Fact Sheet," February 1987. Issued by Public Affairs Office, Quarry Heights, Panama.

4. General Fred F. Woerner, "U.S. Southern Command: Shield of Democracy in Latin America," 23, *Defense 87,* November-December.

5. *New York Times,* 9 February 1988.

6. Admiral Gene LaRocque, "What Should We Defend? A New Military Strategy for the United States," *The Defense Monitor,* Vol. XVII, #4, 1988.

7. Michael Wilson, "Washington's Nine-Point Agenda for the Panama Problem," Heritage Foundation Backgrounder, 12 February 1988.

8. Maj. General David S. Parker, Ret., "The Panama Canal Is no Longer Crucial to U.S. Security," *Armed Forces Journal International,* 56, December 1987.

9. Wilson, 7.

10. Bruce Weinrod and Michael Wilson, "The U.S. Challenge in Panama," Backgrounder Update, Heritage Foundation, 29 February 1988, 2.

11. Parker, 58.

12. Charlotte Elton, "Serving Foreigners," *NACLA Report on the Americas,* July-August 1988, 28.

13. Ibid., 29.

14. Silvio Hernandez, Excelsior, 15 February 1989, translated and reprinted in *Central America Newspak,* Issue #79.

15. General Omar Torrijos, speech to the Organization of American States, quoted by Tom Barry and Deb Preusch, *The Central America Fact Book 1986,* 301.

Part VI: Conclusion

Chapter 16

Economic Alternatives for the U.S. Bases in the Philippines

Eduardo Gonzalez

When Philippine President Corazon Aquino said that, with the sweeping changes in Eastern Europe, it was time to consider alternative uses for the U.S. military bases in the Philippines, few would have argued with her.[1] The end of the Cold War has undermined the rationale for continued U.S. military power projection, placing intense pressure on the United States to introduce plans for significant reductions in troop strength and the conversion of bases and military-related industries.

U.S. military policy is at a critical juncture. The U.S. national security elite seek to reinforce U.S. dominance at a time when the United States no longer possesses unlimited financial resources to do so. Clark Air Base and Subic Naval Base, the crown jewels of U.S. military operations in the Pacific, are not insulated from this policy crisis. U.S. Congressional cost-cutting moves, and growing Filipino demands for political self-determination, are leading to calls for the closure of the bases, with some in the United States calling for the relocation of the bases to other Pacific or Asian nations. At this writing, the debate between U.S. and Philippine elites over the future of the installations is focused on compromises which would allow the retention of the bases. With the Philippine elite committed to negotiating a new bases access treaty with the United States, retaining access to Clark and Subic has been made easier.

In this light, Aquino's call for economic conversion rings hollow, as the only sticking points that appear to remain are how much money or rent the Philippine government will receive in return, and what limited reductions in U.S. forces can be arranged to contain nationalist sentiment in the country. At the same time, Aquino's statement also suggests how deeply the vision of positive "alternative uses" has crept into the debate over the bases. Today, as the battle for the hearts and minds of Filipinos rages, there is growing interest in economic conversion among policy makers, legislators, ordinary Filipinos—and business entrepreneurs. Indeed, the private sector has developed an impressive array of conversion studies, all indicating that alternative uses of the base lands would yield immense economic benefits for the Philippines.

Since the private sector often prefers a low-key approach, their studies have long lacked dramatic immediacy. In the late 1980s, however, two powerful tendencies combined to change that. First, the anti-bases movement grafted the conversion idea onto its platform and began critiquing the emerging conversion proposals. Second, economic conversion started attracting a constituency in government strong enough to force the Aquino administration to begin undertaking its own alternative-use study through the National Economic and Development Authority, its planning arm. The Philippine Senate also got into the act, facilitating the establishment of a legislative-executive council to study the conversion of the base lands. Today, peace coalitions in the Philippines, with the support of some government officials, are the most active conversion proponents.

The growing appeal of economic conversion, with its vision of positive alternatives to U.S. bases, has placed the United States in an awkward position, which has responded to the shifting dynamic by attempting to stall the momentum of the debate and to redirect it toward a narrow focus on the dire economic consequences of a bases withdrawal. A USIA propaganda offensive has been designed to stress the economic payoff of the bases. In September 1989, as part of that campaign, U.S. Ambassador Nicholas Platt claimed that the bases contribute about 7 percent of the country's GNP. He was emphatic that "You can't just rip that out in a year without having a disastrous effect on the economy...It doesn't make sense to think in terms of simply shutting down your eighth largest partner."[2]

The Economics of the Bases: Benefits and Burdens

Proponents of U.S. bases have always argued that the bases pump money into the Philippine economy and are a primary source of jobs. According to this view, their removal would trigger economic dislocation and massive unemployment. The two biggest military installations in the country, Clark Air Base and Subic Naval Base, inject about $1.4 million a day into the Philippine economy.[3] A University of the Philippines study indicates that the total economic benefits of the bases amount to just over 2 percent of the GNP.[4]

For the broad majority of Filipinos, the payoff from the bases is not what has been advertised. The bulk of base spending consists of consumption expenditures that do not contribute to the capital investment necessary for economic development. The bases actually employ less than 1 percent of the country's non-agricultural work force.[5] Taking advantage of cheap labor, as in the case of the ship workers at Subic Bay, is a dubious economic contribution. Despite comparable skills, Filipino base employees receive only one-tenth the pay of their U.S. counterparts. They receive a fourth of what Japanese base workers are paid and half of what the Korean base workers earn.

In addition, some of the social consequences that must be attributed to the bases in varying degrees, including prostitution, insurgency, risk of nuclear accidents, the spread of AIDS, and environmental neglect are what economists call "negative externalities"—costs that are borne by society at large as a result of the bases. Policy makers' failure to incorporate these costs into the equation overstates the economic benefits of the bases and underestimates their real costs.

Olongapo and Angeles: Dependence and Unbalanced Development

To be sure, the bases are quite important in shaping the local economies of communities in which they are located. Any economic dislocation, in the event of the withdrawal of the bases, is more likely to occur in base-dependent communities. Yet Clark and Subic have proven to be the wrong stimulus to the growth of economic activity in their host regions. Olongapo, the city neighboring Subic, offers a classic example of unbalanced development. There is little by way of manufacturing, or even of small-scale enterprises. Instead, entertainment, domestic services, and real estate (catering to the housing needs of base personnel) overwhelm Olongapo's economic landscape. Entertainers and housemaids account for over 90 percent of the city's labor force. So dependent has the city become on its entertainment industry, that Mayor Richard Gordon has organized demonstrations of prostitutes at the Subic gate to win media and popular support for the retention of the bases.

Olongapo is almost totally dependent upon continuing infusions of U.S. dollars for economic health, and this has been costly in terms of missed opportunities for more independent growth. For decades, the presence of the bases made it easy for Olongapo officials to look the other way, instead of generating alternative economic investments that would have allowed the city to grow and diversify on its own. Perhaps more important, by permanently monopolizing the labor force of highly skilled ship workers within the area Subic makes a valuable work force unavailable to other capital investment opportunities.

In a similar vein, Clark Air Field provides an important economic lifeline to its host community, Angeles City. Entertainment bars and recreation halls line the main roads leading to Clark. Yet Angeles differs from Subic in an important way. Angeles has a diversified and competitive economy, and is less dependent economically on Clark. Entertainment bars comprise a smaller proportion of the city's business establishments, over 70 percent of which involve machine repair, dress-making, furniture, leather crafts, and trading.[6] None of these relate directly to the bases. Its diversified economy would make it easier for Angeles to absorb the dislocating effects of the loss of Clark. The Angeles Chamber of Commerce, a powerful and dynamic group of businessmen in the city, opposes the closing of Clark. Because of Angeles' broad economic base, the organization is less fearful about the future of Angeles without the base.[7]

A diversified economy also serves as insurance against a growing trend toward the self-containment of the bases. In recent years, with increased attacks on U.S. forces based in the Philippines, base authorities have accelerated the provision of on-base housing. This has created a temporary housing construction boom and an excess supply of off-base housing. As a result of this glut in the local housing market, the house-leasing and hotel industries in the area have fallen on difficult times. Yet the business community is confident that the city can absorb the shock. Self-containment, ironically, could provide the push that would permit the city to seek alternative investments, like handicraft and furniture export—a move that makes economic sense not only for the region but for the whole country.

The bases are, in the final analysis, an economic burden. This should be good news to Filipino planners. It lessens the costs of transition to a base-less economy. It also points the way toward economic conversion as the least painful way of overcoming the human costs of the continued presence of the bases. For the anti-bases movement, this news is a tool to keep the bases debate from being held hostage to the economic argument. Opposing the bases does not have to mean opposing growth and development.

Civilian Reuse of Clark and Subic Bay

A mild surprise in the 1988 agreement between U.S. Secretary of State Shultz and Philippine Foreign Minister Manglapus, was the concession won by the Philippine government that all capital improvements would be left in place in the event of a U.S. pullout.[8] These are economic prizes that any corporation would covet. Any sensible conversion plan would seek to transform the base facilities to serve a civilian economy in a fashion similar to their present use. With minimal modifications and minimal retooling, these facilities could be put to civilian use, yielding immediate economic returns. Subic Naval Base could become a major international or regional seaport. Clark Air Base could become an international aviation complex. After all, each base boasts immense resources.[9]

Subic, probably one of the best ports anywhere in the world, is deep enough to bring huge ships right up to the dock, and is thus ideal for international shipping. Three wharves can accommodate 25 ships at any one time. Cranes can work 20 containers per hour. There are dry docks, ship repair facilities, air strips, and storage areas. Subic Bay itself is a self-contained city, with two large hospitals, residences, shopping malls, recreational centers, machine shops, a generating plant capable of supplying energy to a population of 100,000, roads, sewage facilities, etc. The U.S. Navy estimates that these facilities have an aggregate value of $1.18 billion.

Lloyd Dumas, one of the leading authorities on economic conversion in the United States, suggested during a 1986 visit to the Philippines that a Philippine deep-water fishing fleet could be maintained and repaired with Subic Bay as its homeport. The port facility could also serve as a transshipment plant for the fish.[10] At present, the Philippines, with an archipelagic coastline longer than that of the United States, imports fish from Japanese trawlers fishing in Philippine waters. The José Diokno Foundation suggests, in addition, that Subic could become the hub for industries that build land vehicles, small boats, bicycles, utensils, hand tools, and pre-fabricated housing materials.[11]

Converting Subic into a commercial port would also address more immediate needs. A University of Philippines study suggests that if the current rate of economic growth in the Philippines continues into the early 1990s, a larger volume of international trade would make conversion of the Subic facility an economic and commercial necessity. Thailand's experience, the study notes, indicates that an acute shortage of port, storage, and cargo-handling facilities could limit further economic expansion after years of continuous growth.[12]

Clark has a similar infrastructure, but with an emphasis on aviation facilities. A two-mile runway could accommodate the largest commercial aircraft. Its fuel storage capacity is equal to that of the JFK airport in New York City. In all, the Clark facilities have an estimated value of $972 million. A 43-mile oil pipeline also connects Subic and Clark. The most discussed conversion possibility for Angeles is moving the Ninoy Aquino National Airport from Manila to Clark. This would bolster Angeles' economy and decrease the population pressures on Manila, which are straining the city's infrastructure to the breaking point.

Even without the withdrawal of the bases, some conversion is possible. A base conversion plan prepared by Leonardo Mariano for the Congressional Economic Planning Service, widely known as the Mariano proposal, calls for a mixed-use development plan in converted base lands. At the core of this plan is an export processing zone and an integrated corporate farm. A commercial complex and an upscale international retirement zone are also high-profile features of the Mariano proposal. This project would obviously have broad appeal in the private sector, but it is typical of proposals that have a bias toward an enclave economy, "insulated from the larger economy and sustained largely by foreign capital inflows"—with limited benefits for the ordinary citizen.[13]

Equally ambitious, in terms of the kind of infrastructure it requires, is the idea of the Olongapo Freeport—an economic proposal to convert Olongapo into a Hong Kong-style freeport to cushion the sudden impact of the loss of Subic and to provide an extra source of income for city residents. Few would disagree with the objectives of this scheme, but as a critic observes, "in this age of import liberalization, the world is not in want of freeports."[14]

Yet another plan is the agro-industrial estate alternative. It envisions an industrial estate concentrating on light manufacturing industries that require little capital and that are designed to meet the needs of the local market. A similar but more modest conversion plan is a "people's agro-industrial complex," proposed by a retired army general. The proposal calls for livestock and crop production, but the centerpiece is a 2,000-ton alcohol processing plant. The proposal is not new; it was a plank in the ill-fated Kilusang Kabuhayan at Kaunlaran (the "basic needs" movement) platform— a propaganda campaign of the Marcos regime. Yet, given a new lease on life, this project might work if an effective and inexpensive way of converting sugar cane into high grade alcohol on a small-to-medium scale can be successfully introduced.

Lloyd Dumas' report, referred to earlier, notes that projects along the lines of the agro-industrial estate alternative could solve a number of problems simultaneously: "The additional market for sugar cane, a major crop in serious depression in the Philippines, could be developed. A reduction in oil imports could result with use of alcohol as an energy resource. Finally, [productive or income-generating] activity could be carried on at converted facilities at Clark and Subic Bay... Clark is in the middle of a productive agricultural area where the sugar cane could be pumped to Subic through the pipeline for transit."[15]

These conversion schemes can be implemented in the converted base lands without closing the bases. It can thus be said that they are irrelevant to the bases question, because they leave the facilities untouched. However, conversion projects like the agro-industrial estate have the potential of diversifying the local economy, reversing the pattern of slow growth, increasing income and productivity, and building a stable economic base less dependent on the bases. That would be a significant beginning.

The Tasks Ahead

The technical tasks facing conversion advocates and planners in the Philippines are enormous but not insurmountable. First, conversion research must be focused where it matters most—the base facilities. It is also necessary to conduct detailed market research, keeping local, national, regional, and international markets in mind. Producing profitable civilian products that need only few plant readjustments and minimum retraining are the best possible alternatives.[16] Subic obviously must continue to be a shipping and ship repair facility, and Clark should be maintained as an aviation complex, although other products could evolve in both cities as they deepen and diversify their economies.

Second, the "regional location fit" of any conversion plan should be considered seriously. The government has done a sound job by incorporating the base facilities in its "new town development" proposal. Often mistaken for the government's conversion plan, this is a regional development blueprint. The "new town" idea is designed to avoid "linear development" along major routes and highways, and to prevent the tendency toward chaotic land use patterns on prime agricultural lands. The key strategy under the new town concept is to regroup the Clark-Subic area, a region the size of Delaware, into three interactive zones: 1) an industrial-urban-commercial-residential zone; 2) a food bowl zone; and 3) a green zone.

The developed areas of Angeles would serve as an alternative metropolis to Manila. It would be the nucleus of the new town, offering urban services, light industries, and commerce. To spur growth, this new metropolitan area would require both a major airport and a major seaport. This is where Clark and Subic come into the picture. Undeveloped base lands, including the Crow Valley Weapons Range, would be used primarily for food production. Forest lands would be the core of the green zone, ensuring the area's ecological stability.[17]

Many agree that "the new town concept" provides a solid framework, consistent with sound regional development policies. Once this program is in place, it could serve as a powerful means for dealing with the conversion of Clark and Subic over the long term. There are worries, however, about planning and coordination. Thus far the government has shown little capacity for effective implementation and management. The plan's attempt to introduce a green zone theoretically provides for sustainable development, but it is not clearly articulated.

Third, groups who will be threatened by economic dislocation arising from the withdrawal of bases must be identified and offered economic adjustment assistance. Vulnerable groups include base workers, women in the entertainment business, food producers serving the bases, and the housing industry. A successful implementation of the conversion plan for Subic and Clark would require, at the very least, the reorientation of the bases' civilian workers to the demands of the commercial market. As Dumas argues, "subsidizing conversion of the work force gives the (facility) ready-to-go civilian oriented employees."[18] Because of the workers' marketable skills, a conversion scheme which draws on existing facilities as the starting point would have a higher chance of success.

The Federation of Filipino Civilian Employees Associations, the labor union at Clark and Subic, whose pro-bases stand comes as no surprise, has good reason to favor minimum disruption in the event of withdrawal of the bases.[19] They believe that shipping and ship repair in Subic, and aircraft repair and maintenance in Clark are the logical reuse activities that would keep the skilled work force in place, probably with better pay and benefits. Many base workers say they would be tempted to follow the bases wherever they might be relocated in the Pacific.[20] Although this event would cushion the impact of a massive layoff, it runs counter to the broader aim of securing a base-free Pacific.

If a partial dislocation cannot be avoided, a host of worker assistance programs must be in place by the time the bases are closed. One type focuses on unemployment benefits, or direct cash transfers to replace earnings lost due to layoffs. It can be argued that to be fair, people who shoulder the costs of economic adjustment through loss of their jobs must be compensated.[21] However, this would be expensive and obviously unappealing to the government, given its scarce and overextended resources. More enforceable worker support schemes come under the label of "positive adjustment programs": job search assistance, retraining for other types of jobs, and relocation assistance. These measures reduce the amount of time individuals spend away from active work.[22] In practice, both substantial direct aid to workers and positive adjustment programs are likely to be essential.

Local industries caught in the transition from a base economy to a peace-oriented economy may need to rely on direct financial incentives, such as tax credits, grants, and loans. This would be true of the house leasing industry. Handicraft manufacturers and food producers, on the other hand, may need assistance to find a new market niche.

Easily the most vulnerable, because they are the least prepared to enter the formal labor market, are the women entertainers (hostesses and prostituted women). In sheer number, they are also the largest group. Even under current conditions, their work is seasonal and unpredictable, because of the cyclical nature of aircraft and ship arrivals. Many are migrants from poor regions, which means that out-migration would likely take place during the base closing.[23] Assistance might come in the form of cash for actual moving expenses and relocation. Those women who choose to remain, however, should be offered vocational counseling and training for marketable skills.[24] Starting grants should be made available for those with plans of opening small business shops. Cooperative ventures which allow the women to pool their resources should also be supported.

Lessons from the U.S. Conversion Experience

Conversion advocates awed by the enormous effort involved in conversion should be heartened by the successful conversion attempts within the United States. Base closings and contract cuts initiated by the Pentagon occur in response to policy shifts in the deployment of troops and weapons nationwide, as well as for reasons of economy, efficiency, and politics. A survey compiled by the Pentagon's Office of Economic Adjustment showed that, nationwide, impacted communities successfully converted 100 U.S. bases between the years 1961 and 1986.[25] The number of new jobs generated (138,138) far surpassed the loss of jobs (93,424). The numbers speak for themselves: conversion efforts created 12 new colleges and 33 vocational-technical schools or community colleges with 53,744 students, 75 industrial and office parks, and 42 airports.

Local communities have been primarily responsible for the successful conversion effort. As the survey notes, "They are the real heroes in the adjustment process." This is not to say that securing community initiative was easy. In the same way that workers in Angeles and Olongapo are resisting the closure of Clark and Subic, impacted communities in the United States receive news of base closings with apprehension, and usually enter a stage of intense lobbying to forestall the closing, rather than immediately embark on a positive recovery action. Once representatives of various sectors in the community "get their act together," the conversion process begins. Community redevelopment councils take over, representing labor unions, professionals, planners, and local and state representatives. The conversion body is empowered to develop and implement the conversion plan, and is able to take advantage of federal and state incentives, such as tax breaks and direct grants. The Office of Economic Adjustment often provides technical and financial assistance. The Colorado-based Social and Economic Analysis Corporation, which is doing a comprehensive survey of 100 impacted communities, notes a point that should be instructive for the conversion of Clark and Subic: the inclusion of an airport or shipping facilities can accelerate development.[26] Social and economic conditions vary among base communities, but the key to a successful conversion is a set of constants: community empowerment, mobilization of community resources, and government policy initiatives.

Non-negotiable Points

In the Philippines, conversion advocates agree that regardless of how a conversion coalition is organized, and whatever conversion scheme is adopted, a set of basic guiding principles is important. The following are recommended:

- Vulnerable groups should receive prompt support during the transition and they should receive priority in the distribution of benefits from the economic conversion. Base workers, women entertainers, and tribal communities should be first on the list of the conversion coalition members.

- Conversion must be an empowering mechanism within the community among workers, women's groups, farmers, tribal communities, the private sector, and local government officials.

- While oversight of the conversion process must remain national in nature, conversion management must be a broad coalition effort. This is the surest way to guarantee that the economic conversion is appropriate to the social needs of each community.

- Economic conversion should promote a sustainable and equitable development, placing emphasis on the balance between short-term social and economic needs and the long-term goals of diversified and humane development and the preservation of the environment. The conversion should favor the interests of the majority, who are poor.

- Economic conversion should be subordinate to the political goal of dismantling the bases and establishing a nuclear-free Pacific. A conversion plan that leaves base workers unprotected in the arrangement actually assists the United States in relocating the bases to other Pacific nations by providing a readily available work force. Both of these dangers must be resisted.

Notes

1. *San Francisco Chronicle,* 10 January 1990.

2. Quoted in University of the Philippines (UP) Research Team, "Towards Economic Alternatives for the Baselands: A Preliminary Study" (Quezon City: University of the Philippines, 1989), 44.

3. Or, equivalently, $507 million annually.

4. The actual figures are 1.92 percent of the 1985 GNP and 2.29 percent of the 1987 GNP. See UP Research Team, "Towards Economic Alternatives."

5. Boone Schirmer, et al., "U.S. Bases in the Philippines: In Whose Interest?," *Third World Reports* (Cambridge: Third World Reports, 1989), 21.

6. UP Research Team.

7. Ibid.

8. Schirmer, et al., 22.

9. See UP Research Team, "Conversion of US Bases in the Philippines: Report on Trip of Dr. Lloyd Jeffrey Dumas" (Quezon City: University of the Philippines, 1986), 71.

10. Ibid.

11. Schirmer, et al., 22.

12. UP Research Team, 15.

13. Ibid.

14. Ma. Fe Luisa Warque, "Some Alternative Plans," *NASSA News,* September-October 1989, 7.

15. UP Research Team

16. Suzanne Gordon and Dave McFadden, "Introduction," in Suzanne Gordon and Dave McFadden, eds., *Economic Conversion: Revitalizing America's Economy* (Cambridge, MA: Ballinger, 1984), xv.

17. Warque, 8; UP Research Team, 23-26.

18. Lloyd J. Dumas, "Making Peace Possible: The Legislative Approach to Economic Conversion," in Gordon and McFadden, eds., 78.

19. UP Research Team, 71.

20. Ibid.

21. Jane Kulik and Charles Fairchild, "Worker Assistance and Placement Experience," in John Lynch, ed., *Economic Adjustment and Conversion of Defense Industries* (Boulder: Westview Press, 1987), 191.

22. Ibid.

23. UP Research Team, 73.

24. Ibid.

25. *Office of Economic Adjustment, 1961-1985: 25 Years of Civilian Reuse* (Washington D.C.: Department of Defense, 1986).

26. See Richard C. Williams, "Military Cuts: Disaster or Boon?," *Blueprint for Social Justice,* November 1989, 3.

Chapter 17

New Directions for U.S. Policy

Bruce Birchard

> Military power in today's world is incompatible with freedom,
> incapable of providing security, and ineffective in dealing with evil.
>
> *—Speak Truth to Power, 1955*

The American Friends Service Committee is a pacifist organization, committed to general and complete disarmament and an end to all military forces and military violence. AFSC's position is based on the historic testimony of the Religious Society of Friends (Quakers), which was first formulated by Friends in 1660 in a letter to King Charles II of England:

> We utterly deny all outward wars and strife and fightings with outward weapons, for any end or under any pretence whatsoever, and we do certainly know, and so testify to the world, that the spirit of Christ, which leads us into all Truth, will never move us to fight and war against any man with outward weapons, neither for the kingdom of Christ, nor for the kingdoms of this world.

For more than three centuries, Friends have retained this testimony, maintaining in season and out, in good times and bad, that the deliberate killing of human beings can never be justified. While our pacifist commitment is based upon religious belief, it is also our experience that militarism and war sow seeds of hatred and are ultimately self-defeating. True peace can only be built on a foundation of justice and cannot be gained by military force. This is our starting point as we attempt to identify a path away from the barren military policies described in this book and toward a more hopeful future.

It is currently fashionable in the United States to assert that "we won the Cold War." With the demise of communist economic and political systems, we are told that the capitalist system and its military forces have triumphed. The "four pillars"[1] of post-war U.S. foreign policy seem vindicated: Deterrence has "worked." The Soviet Union has been "contained." Third world governments that have chosen socialist systems have felt the impact of military intervention, CIA destabilization, and economic pressures. A liberal capitalist international economic order, working in U.S. and allied interests, has effectively controlled resources, markets, and domestic capital and has assured inexpensive labor in much of the world.

What is the cost of this "success" to ourselves and to others? Here at home, maintaining the national security state has exacted a heavy toll. So much of our financial, human, and technological resources have been squandered on building the weapons and forces of death that the compelling needs of our country and its people have gone unmet. The number of Americans living below the poverty line has vastly increased. Urban decay, homelessness, unemployment, poor medical care, and a failing educational system have created a climate of despair in which drug-dealing and crime flourish. Pollution of the air we breathe, toxic wastes, and contamination of our lakes and rivers threaten ecological disaster, even as the deterioration of our highways and bridges, our mass transit systems, our water and sewer systems weaken our economic infrastructure. The life expectancy of African-American men in Harlem is lower than that of men in Bangladesh. The infant mortality rate for the United States is higher than that of Taiwan. Our functional illiteracy rate of 20 percent is 40 times higher than Japan's one half of one percent. And everywhere, it is people of color who suffer in dispro-portionate numbers, exposing the blight of racism which so egregiously plagues our society and cries out for redress.

Nor has the quality of U.S. democracy escaped the impacts of militari-zation and intervention. McCarthyism scarred the nation in the 1950s. Severe repression of the civil rights, Black power and anti-war movements by the FBI and police marked the 1960s and 1970s. The Iran-*contra* affair and illegal surveillance of activist groups opposed to U.S. policies in Central America undermined democratic freedoms in the 1980s. An almost paranoid preoc-cupation with "national security" led in these decades to excessive secrecy, manipulation of the media, and suppression of dissent. In too many ways, the demands of "national security" have been designed to protect the advantages held by U.S. elites and have driven us toward the image of what we supposedly oppose.

The focus of this book has been on one particular manifestation of this search for security through the amassing of great military power: the global network of foreign military bases and installations. We have traced the role of the bases in preparations for war and in U.S. military intervention in the affairs of other countries, as well as their impacts upon host nations and peoples. These bases have been an integral part of the U.S. government's determination to project its power worldwide, to make credible our threat to initiate nuclear war to protect U.S. "vital interests," to keep recalcitrant nations in line, to influence the foreign and domestic policies of other nations, and to protect U.S. corporate interests.

If the virus of violence has infected our country, an epidemic of violence has plagued many other lands. Since the end of World War II, the world has been convulsed by violence on a staggering, horrifying scale. Vietnam. Afghanistan. Korea. India. Pakistan. Bangladesh. Indonesia. The Philippines. Sri Lanka. Cambodia. Tibet. Syria. Egypt. Iraq. Iran. Israel and the occupied territories. Lebanon. Kuwait. Biafra. Angola. Mozambique. Ethiopia. Somalia. The Sudan. Argentina. Chile. El Salvador. Guatemala. Nicaragua. The list goes on and on, almost entirely in the Third World. The killing, maiming, torture, and "disappearances" have all been rationalized by a theology of national security which justifies any means in the pursuit of "security" for the nation-state. Nations have developed—and used—weapons of unprecedented lethality and destructive power, and in the process, the distinction between combatant and non-combatant in war has largely been eliminated.

Though the United States and the Soviet Union have inflicted much of the violence upon the rest of the world, both directly and indirectly, the capacity of many third world governments to wreak massive violence upon one another and upon their own peoples has also grown. At least 18 nations outside of Europe, North America, Japan, Australia, and New Zealand now possess some combination of modern military aircraft, tanks or armored vehicles, artillery, missiles, and ships, either by virtue of large-scale imports or development of a domestic military-industrial infrastructure. Several of these nations have nuclear weapons or the capacity to produce them quickly. Many more have chemical weapons and missiles, or the capacity to produce them. Most are nations which have been involved in regional power struggles and/or military combat during the past two decades. The U.S.-Soviet arms race is thus being replicated in many parts of the Third World, where the likelihood of war is much higher than it ever was in Europe. Arms sales and technology transfers from developed countries contribute to these regional arms races and increase the danger of war—as recent events in the Middle East have demonstrated.[2]

The Need for a New Approach to Real Security

The urgent need for a new approach to real security is clear. The only major military threat to the United States is the threat of nuclear attack. Continuation of the nuclear arms race and the policies of "nuclear deterrence" and "flexible response" increase rather than decrease the likelihood of nuclear war. They do so by giving potential enemies more reason to fear a U.S. nuclear attack in a severe crisis, which in turn would provide the only rational defensive reason for that enemy to consider launching a nuclear attack on the United States. The only defensive circumstances under which such a desperate attack might be contemplated by rational political leaders would be during a major crisis in which a nuclear attack on one's own military forces or country seemed likely. In this situation, it might appear advantageous to launch the first strike in the desperate hope of limiting the damage to one's own nation.

To lessen the probability of another nation making such a first strike against the United States in a crisis, U.S. leaders should undertake to reduce the threat perceptions of potential enemies. As the United Nations' Palme Commission and, more recently, Soviet President Gorbachev have stressed, nations must use diplomatic and political means to reduce the nuclear threat. Adding more accurate and destructive weapons is counter-productive. Legitimate national security cannot be secured at the expense of another nation. There can only be an increase or decrease in the "common security" of the world community of nations and people.[3]

Continuation of the nuclear arms race also endangers U.S. security by encouraging proliferation of nuclear weapons. As long as the nuclear powers insist upon keeping (and threatening to use) their nuclear arsenals, other countries will feel entitled to do the same. Nuclear weapons appear to be the price of admission to the club of the really powerful. The current nuclear powers have no special right to these weapons of mass destruction. They have no more "moral authority" than other nations. Moreover, the materials and technologies needed for development and production of nuclear warheads are more easily obtained as long as some nations are producing them. According to the U.S. Commission on Integrated Long-Term Strategy, "forty or more countries in Europe, Asia, the Middle East and elsewhere will have the technical wherewithal to build [nuclear] arsenals" within approximately 10 to 15 years.[4]

Beyond ending the nuclear arms race, the United States needs to develop broad new policies toward the Third World. Continuation of current policies of military and CIA intervention is unconscionable and leads to growing resentment of the United States by large populations in many affected countries. Recent government documents indicate that no significant change in the overall direction of U.S. policies toward the Third World is contemplated. In a landmark report done for the U.S. Secretary of Defense and the President's National Security Advisor entitled *Discriminate Deterrence,* The Commission on Integrated Long-Term Strategy stressed that, "In the past forty years all the wars in which the United States has been involved have occurred in the Third World." The report continues:

> Many of our problems in the Third World are centered on what is now called "low intensity conflict." The term refers to insurgencies, organized terrorism, paramilitary crime, sabotage, and other forms of violence... To defend its interests properly in the Third World, the United States will have to take low intensity conflict much more seriously. It is a form of warfare in which "the enemy" is more or less omnipresent and unlikely ever to surrender.[5]

The commission praised U.S. support for "the saving of democracy in El Salvador" as a positive example of low intensity conflict, citing "American technology [which] gave the Salvadoran government a new tactical intelligence capability" plus assistance with weapons systems and training as important types of U.S. aid. It went on to observe that this type of conflict must be fought by "diplomats, information specialists, agricultural chemists, bankers and economists, hydrologists, criminologists, meteorologists, and scores of other professionals," as well as by the U.S. military.

With the electoral defeat of the Sandinistas in Nicaragua in the spring of 1990, the Bush administration claimed victory in another "low-intensity conflict." Though the U.S.-supported *contra* army was never able to defeat the Sandinista government militarily, the human, economic and spiritual costs of the war to the Nicaraguan people finally made them "say uncle." With a surrogate army and economic strangulation, Washington convinced enough Nicaraguans to vote out the Sandinistas in order to increase the likelihood that Washington would end the *contra* war and provide economic aid.

The continuing, U.S.-supported counter-insurgency war in the Philippines provides another example of a "low-intensity conflict." President Corazon Aquino has called for a "Total War Policy" against the relatively small communist New People's Army. This has meant massive military sweeps of rural areas, the arming of thousands of local paramilitary groups, and tacit support for vigilante groups and death squads. In 1989, such military and paramilitary actions in the small island of Negros alone caused the deaths of approximately 700 people. Of these victims, more than 300 were children, most of whom died of malnutrition and starvation while trying to survive as refugees from the fighting. This conflict, like those in Central America, Angola, Mozambique, and Cambodia, may be "low-intensity" for the U.S. government, but not for the victims.

While the United States still has enormous military bases and forces in Europe, the history of the post-war period shows that the violence of war has been almost totally confined to third world countries. The record of U.S.

military intervention in the Third World and the development of strategies for "low-intensity conflicts" in third world nations suggests a strong racist bias in U.S. military policy. The fact that so many people in the United States have readily supported the *contra* war (as long as U.S. troops were not at risk), the bombing of Libya, the invasions of Grenada and Panama, and U.S. support for UNITA's brutal war against the government and people of Angola indicates that U.S. public opinion is also strongly tinged with racism. Public sentiment for "nuking Khomeini" and "reducing Iraq to a parking lot" is only the most extreme form of such racist jingoism.

In terms of the specific topic of this book, it is clear that resentment of the United States is being fostered in many nations by its military bases, troops, and weapons. Maria Socorro Diokno, a Filipina woman who participated in a 1989 speaking tour of the United States organized by the AFSC, expressed this resentment well:

> For almost ninety years, my people have suffered under…your government's continuing domination over all aspects of our life. Since your military troops landed in the Philippines in 1898, my country has been caught in the web of the international race for world superiority and domination. We have become the unwilling victims of the…rivalry between the larger powers of the world.[6]

As the final editing of this book was completed, the United States had sent more than 400,000 U.S. military forces to the Persian Gulf and to previously prepared military bases in response to the Iraqi invasion of Kuwait. War seems imminent. Even if this introduction of large U.S. forces into the region does not lead to a major war in the Middle East, it appears likely that it will increase Arab resentment of the United States and may lead to the destabilization of the Gulf monarchies which the U.S. claims to be defending.

Surveying this world scene, observing the unconscionable price that militarism and violence have exacted over the past four decades, and troubled by the failures of the U.S. government to lead in new directions in the context of a drastically changed world, the AFSC sees an urgent need for new approaches to peace-making. In the remainder of this chapter, we present ideas about alternative approaches and policies and assess prospects for change. We believe there is now real promise for moving the world closer to true peace with justice.

Positive Policies for Real Security

What policies could the United States adopt to provide for our security without threatening the security or well-being of other peoples and nations?

One of the most urgent changes is for our nation to respect the right of self-determination of all countries, and to support just and equitable economic development for the world's peoples. Policies of military intervention and economic domination do not win friends and are not in our long-term national interest. We reap what we sow, including repression, violence, and war. We should free ourselves of the illusion that our government is "defending democracy in the Third World" and recognize that it has pursued the interests of U.S. political, military, and business elites in Central and South America, the Caribbean, the Middle East, Africa, Asia, and the Pacific. In the process, the United States has waged major wars (Indochina and Korea), engaged in direct military intervention (recently including Lebanon, Grenada, Libya, Panama, and the Persian Gulf), engineered the overthrow of elected governments through covert, CIA-supported coups (Guatemala, Chile), organized or supported "proxy wars" (the *contras* against the Sandinista government of Nicaragua, South Africans and UNITA against the Marxist government of Angola, the Khmer Rouge against the government of Cambodia), and supported repressive dictatorships (including the Somozas in Nicaragua, the military junta in Chile, Ferdinand Marcos in the Philippines, and Mobutu Sese Seko in Zaire). This is not a record of which a great nation can be proud.

As this book has made clear, the global network of foreign U.S. military bases and facilities has facilitated these interventionist adventures. Our bases have been used for direct military intervention, for "containment" of the Soviet Union, for demonstrating and applying political and military power, and for preparing for nuclear and conventional war. For the United States, withdrawal from all foreign bases will come only when the commitment to global democracy and self-determination replaces the commitment to global empire.

The AFSC believes that no government should station troops or weapons in foreign countries. All the troops—U.S., Soviet, British, French, Indian, South African, Iraqi—should "go home." All foreign bases should be closed. The United States and other countries that have maintained troops in other countries should provide financial and other support, as requested, to help with efforts by host nations and communities to convert former foreign bases to productive civilian uses.

The global infrastructure for nuclear and "conventional" war should be dismantled, including the hundreds of small facilities for command, control, communications, and intelligence (C3I) located abroad. The one exception we would make, and it should be temporary, is those few installations involved in the monitoring necessary for verification of treaties, the detection of troop movements, and other aspects of "confidence building." These functions should be assumed by an international body under the United Nations as soon as possible.

The world community of nations needs to develop a standard of respect for the right to self-determination of all nations. No country should commit violent acts of intervention. This policy, which finds support in the history and national values of the United States, is also stated in the Charter of the United Nations. Appropriate sanctions should be developed to deal with governments that do not abide by this standard. The firm response of the United Nations and most governments in organizing an economic blockade of Iraq (which should not include essential foods and medicines) and instituting other diplomatic and economic sanctions is a generally positive case in point.

We stress the need for disarmament and note that the Strategic Arms Reductions Treaty (START) will neither halt nor reverse the arms race. START will accomplish some reductions from the current stockpile, but both sides will probably have more nuclear warheads after START than they did when negotiations began on this treaty in 1982. START will do little to prevent the United States and the Soviet Union from proceeding with the development and deployment of a new generation of nuclear weapons.

Because of its interest in developing new, "modernized" nuclear weapons, the Bush Administration refuses to halt its nuclear weapons testing program. A first step toward a new nuclear weapons policy would be for the United States to respond positively to Moscow's long-standing offer to halt all nuclear weapons tests, which they did unilaterally for an 18-month period in 1985 and 1986. After this initial step, the U.S. government should stop the production and deployment of new nuclear weapons and reduce its stockpiles, eventually to zero.

The United States should seek to negotiate, complete, or strengthen a range of treaties to eliminate all nuclear weapons and other weapons of mass destruction, reduce military forces and conventional weapons, and decrease the opportunities and incentives for proliferation of the technologies of mass destruction. In addition to a Comprehensive Test Ban Treaty, these should include treaties on all strategic, intermediate-range, and tactical nuclear weapons, chemical weapons, treaties which would drastically reduce—and eventually eliminate—foreign conventional military forces in Europe and Korea, as well as nuclear-free zone treaties and regional demilitarization agreements. The Anti-Ballistic Missile and Non-Proliferation Treaties should be strengthened.

One lesson from the arms control efforts of the late 1980s is that breakthroughs are much more likely to be made through unilateral initiatives than through the slow process of negotiations. This was dramatically demonstrated by the unilateral Soviet initiatives in the latter 1980s to reduce conventional and nuclear forces in Eastern Europe and Asia. These reductions fundamentally altered the long stalemated East-West security equation and made less militarized systems of security possible in both Europe and Asia. Treaties are needed to finalize and make legally binding the steps that governments are willing to take, but they take so long to complete that the pace of arms development and production outstrips them. We should urge our own government to take unilateral steps for disarmament and reductions in military forces as a way of reciprocating Soviet steps and in order to encourage further ones.

As one such initiative, the United States should reduce its military forces far below the levels announced by the Bush administration in early 1990. As these reductions are carried out, military forces and weapons should be confined to the United States. As an interim step on the road to general and complete disarmament, we advocate the restructuring of residual forces and weapon systems at a strictly defensive level and posture. The United States should give up its capacity to attack or intervene in the affairs of other nations. During this interim period, U.S. forces should only be sufficient to deter or repel an actual military attack on the territory of the United States. Given the natural protection afforded the United States by its size, economic power and geographical position, required force levels would clearly be modest.[7]

Such changes in military policies would likely be acceptable to the Soviet Union. As noted in Chapter 3, "The Rise and Decline of the Second Superpower," most have been proposed by President Gorbachev and other Soviet leaders. Despite the enormous changes in the Soviet Union and in the U.S.-Soviet relationship, however, the Bush Administration and the Department of Defense have been slow to initiate major changes in U.S. military policies and forces. They persist in their "old thinking." As described by Paul Walker in Chapter 2, "Military Power Projection Abroad," U.S. military planners continue to develop new refinements on the old strategies to project U.S. power and protect privileged economic positions. In its 1990 publication, "National Security Strategy of the United States," the Bush Administration repeated its commitment to the policies of nuclear deterrence and "flexible response" (i.e., the possibility of responding to conventional attack with a nuclear counterattack). This report reiterates the need for "forward defense" with "significant American military forces in Europe, in Asia and the Pacific, and at sea," and for "force projection"—"the means to move [U.S.-based military forces] to reinforce our units forward-deployed or to project power into areas where we have no permanent presence."[8]

This kind of thinking has to change, and it must begin with a redefinition of our relationship with the Soviet Union. This process urgently needs to be expedited, because it is the key to other necessary global restructuring. It would open the way to strengthening democractically controlled international institutions at the regional and global levels, including the United Nations and its associated agencies. The world needs more institutions that are supra-national, yet accountable through democratic structures to the world's people. Ways need to be devised for power within these institutions to be shared fairly without crippling their ability to act.

There is a particular need for improving capabilities for international conflict resolution and mediation. In 1985, the United States refused to respect a World Court decision that condemned its government for the mining of a Nicaraguan harbor and ordered Washington to pay reparations to Managua. The Reagan Administration insisted that the Court had no jurisdiction in such a case. Instead of responding to the World Court with arrogant disrespect, the U.S. government should abide by its decisions and seek to strengthen it.

Instead of playing "world policeman," our government should seek to cooperate with other nations to address regional conflicts and injustice. In many cases, regional efforts to deal with conflicts are most appropriate. The efforts by Central American governments to wind down the conflicts in Central America through the Contadora process and the Arias plan provide a good example of such regional initiatives. Unfortunately, the Reagan Administration did everything it could to undermine these efforts in order to continue supporting the *contra* war which brutalized people in Honduras and Costa Rica as well as killing and wounding tens of thousands of Nicaraguans.

Another promising approach to regional conflicts is the use of United Nations peace-keeping forces. They have played important roles in ending or limiting wars in Africa, the Middle East, and Asia, even though the approval of both sides to a conflict has generally been required before they could be introduced, which is clearly a limiting factor. The one occasion in which this provision of the UN charter was abused was in the creation of a "UN force" to fight in Korea, a force made up primarily of U.S. and South Korean troops and commanded by U.S. generals. Otherwise, UN peace-keeping forces have been used with considerable success to monitor and, in some cases, enforce agreements between previously warring parties. This is another interim step on the path to a disarmed world.

Ultimately, as steps are taken toward general and complete disarmament, the United States and other nations should develop means of civilian-based defense which do not involve armed forces at all. Instances of nonviolent defense against both invading forces and internal coups or tyrants abound, some successful, some unsuccessful. But no nation has set about systematically preparing for a nonviolent defense of its people and its institutions. A number of valuable studies have explored this possibility, and they offer persuasive evidence that, given the necessary will, civilian-based defense could effectively supplant military forces for truly defensive purposes.[9] Such a defensive system has the additional advantage of being difficult to use in an offensive manner.

Disarmament will create some problems, and they need to be anticipated. If, for example, the United States proceeds with plans to cut military forces and close some military bases, there will be serious economic consequences. In the long run, we believe most of the economic effects of such a policy shift will be positive as resources and people are redirected toward socially useful ends. However, it will be important to plan the transition phase so as not to make military personnel and workers bear the economic brunt of these policy changes. Many men and women who work in military industries and in the armed forces themselves will lose their jobs. Though many studies indicate that communities can generate more employment in civilian services and industries than most military industries do, there is a "lag time" between the ending of military jobs and the creation of civilian jobs.

To prepare for dislocations during such transition periods, the AFSC has long urged our government to initiate and support a process of economic conversion and job retraining for military personnel and workers in military-related industries. At the national level, this should involve preparation of broad economic development policies which focus on certain production and service industries, plus support for mandated local planning processes and benefits for temporarily unemployed or underemployed workers. At the local level, all communities with military bases and/or military industries should establish economic conversion boards and initiate conversion planning. This is a sounder and more constructive approach to a real problem than the standard effort to mobilize local politicians to "save" a military facility which the Pentagon wants to close. The entire conversion process should be democratically controlled, involving local, state, and national governments as well as corporate management and organized labor. These steps should be initiated now, as a number of domestic U.S. military bases and military-related industries are already closing or cutting back, and the number of men and women in uniform is decreasing.[10]

The emphasis in conversion planning should be on meeting the needs of working people and their communities. As noted earlier, the real threats to the security of most Americans are internal: unemployment, poverty, homelessness, poor health care, environmental degradation, the failure of our educational system, a weakened industrial base, and a deteriorating economic infrastructure. These problems are in desperate need of being addressed. They need more than a "peace dividend," the morsels left over after the Pentagon cuts back on some ships, planes, and troops. We need a restructuring of the U.S. political and economic system which guarantees a much stronger response to the real security needs of our people while pursuing foreign policies which contribute to freedom, peace, and security for people abroad.

Prospects for Change

Is it utopian to believe that such an unprecedented change in U.S. policies can occur? No—because we are living in unprecedented times. We stand at an historic moment of great possibility. Never has there been such an opportunity to break with a bitter past. The Cold War between East and West is over. The Soviet Union, pressed by its own intractable economic problems, has led the way with unilateral reductions of its military forces in Europe, Asia, and much of the Third World. The U.S.S.R. has withdrawn its forces from Afghanistan and pressured Vietnam to withdraw its troops from Cambodia. As described in the chapter on "Soviet Foreign Policy and Foreign Military Bases," Soviet leaders want to structure a smaller military force in a manner which lowers the threat perceptions of other nations, notably in Europe and Asia. Moscow has given up its Eastern European empire. In the face of enormous economic problems, strong nationalist currents and rising unrest within most of the Soviet republics, Soviet leaders are trying to stave off dissolution of the nation itself into quasi-autonomous or independent states.

We have also witnessed an unprecedented growth in the use of primarily nonviolent tactics in successful revolutions against oppressive regimes. In Eastern Europe, in Chile, in Korea, in the Philippines, in South Africa, in Panama, and in China, citizens have taken to the streets to demand fundamental changes and overthrow despotic governments. The global medium of television now brings these protests into the living rooms of the affected nation and of the world, inspiring protesters in other parts of the same country and arousing the sympathy of millions of people in other lands. The pressures have frequently risen to the point that tyrannies either have collapsed or have had to resort to desperate, violent acts of repression, the latter generally resulting in strong condemnation by other governments and peoples.

These striking developments are accompanied by increasing worldwide awareness that security in our interdependent world is more a function of economic strength than of military power, and that no national economy is isolated from economic conditions or actions in other nations. The declining utility of massive military power is widely recognized, spurred by the

Filipino anti-bases activists lead participants of the 1983 international conference against U.S. bases in the Philippines to the U.S. embassy in a demonstration against all foreign military bases. Photo courtesy of Maria Socorro Diokno.

spectacle of the massively armed superpowers sitting on the sidelines as the cataclysmic events in Eastern Europe, the reunification of Germany, and the economic integration of much of Western Europe proceeded apace.

There is a rising tide of public opinion against militarism in many countries around the world. Resistance to foreign military bases and forces is growing. In Eastern and Western Europe, in the Philippines, in Korea, in Japan, in Honduras and in many other nations, masses of people, if not always their leaders, are pressing foreign troops to leave.

Filipinos have been resisting U.S. military domination since the United States seized the Philippines in 1898. In 1990, as negotiations between the U.S. and Philippine governments over a new Military Bases Agreement got underway, tens of thousands of Filipinos protested. Twelve of the 23 members of the Philippine Senate signed a statement opposing renewal of the bases agreement. Opposition to the bases grew and broadened. Many protesters were beaten or arrested for taking part in demonstrations. Some organizers may be imprisoned for years for their political activity, and several have been killed. As this book goes to press, it appears that their efforts may be at least partially successful, for in negotiations the government of the Philippines has told the United States government that it must prepare to give up Subic Naval Base and Clark Air Base.

Filipinos are not alone in resisting foreign military bases and weapons. Throughout the 1980s, opposition to nuclear weapons and military intervention led to organized resistance against foreign bases, military exercises, and port calls by nuclear-capable ships. The women of Greenham Common, who encamped for years outside the gates of a U.S. cruise missile base in Britain, are stirring examples of commitment to an anti-bases struggle. They and millions of other activists helped to focus popular opposition to new U.S. and Soviet nuclear missiles deployed in Europe in the early 1980s. Their protests contributed to the political climate which made the INF Treaty and removal of all U.S. and Soviet intermediate-range nuclear weapons from Europe possible. In 1990, continued anti-nuclear sentiment in Germany, coupled with the historic changes in Eastern Europe, forced the United States to cancel plans to deploy a new generation of land-based, short-range nuclear missiles in that country.

In the Federal Republic of Germany, local people and some local governments have protested the damage to their farms, their towns and their environment by U.S. military forces stationed there. One German woman who joined an AFSC-sponsored speaking tour of the United States gave eloquent voice to the feeling of resentment sparked by the foreign U.S. military presence:

> The Hunsruck is our home. Generations before us worked these fields with their hands. We love the woods, the meadows and the deep valleys leading to the Mosel and Rhine rivers. We want our children to grow up and enjoy this place too. But when we look closely, we realize that we are living between bombs, missiles and tanks...In many cases, our land has been taken from us to be used by the military...Our roads are filled with military vehicles...Low-flying jets from more than ten nations constantly roar overhead...You take a walk, and, after a few hundred yards, you run into a fence with a sign: NO TRESPASSING. USE OF DEADLY FORCE AUTHORIZED.[11]

Tens of thousands of Germans have protested and resisted the continued foreign military presence in their country. In one area of the Federal Republic of Germany, long plagued by U.S. jets engaged in low-level flight training, people put up weather balloons on several hundred feet of wire and warned pilots not to fly over their towns!

One of the most valiant struggles against U.S. militarism has been waged by people of Belau in the Pacific. The 15,000 people of this tiny island nation, which has been dominated by the United States since the end of World War II, have been forced to vote seven times on a "Compact of Free Association" with the United States. Through the terms of the Compact, the United States has demanded the right to store or transit nuclear weapons

Blockade of the Cruise Missile Station Hasselbach/Wueschheim. Photo courtesy of Wolfgang Bartels.

through Belauan territory and to take over precious land for military use. In return, Belau would end its status as a Trust Territory of the United Nations and achieve nominal "independence." The seven votes have been forced on the people because enough Belauans have opposed the Compact each time to prevent its approval. Opponents of the Compact have been attacked by pro-Compact Belauans and had their houses firebombed; one elderly man was shot and killed. However, Belauans opposed to the Compact have continued to prevail in each referendum, and the United States is temporarily stalemated.

In 1985, popular anti-nuclear pressure in New Zealand encouraged the government of Prime Minister David Lange to enforce a ban on nuclear-armed vessels by requiring all ships that wished to enter New Zealand's waters to confirm that they did not carry nuclear weapons. U.S. leaders were furious, refusing to rescind the Navy's "neither confirm nor deny" policy, and forced New Zealand out of the ANZUS alliance. Neither this nor U.S. efforts to undermine New Zealand's economy sufficed to change the policy. Popular support for this policy has been so strong that even the conservative party now supports the ban. As a result, the U.S. Navy continues to be denied access rights. Activists from many Pacific nations, coming particularly from communities of indigenous peoples in the region, have initiated a campaign for a

"Nuclear Free and Independent Pacific" which aims to rid the Pacific of U.S., French, and Soviet nuclear weapons and completely end the domination of the region by foreign powers.

In the United States, citizens' movements in Boston and San Francisco have been successful in opposing Navy plans to "homeport" nuclear-capable ships in their harbors. Citizens of New York and New Jersey protested the homeport plan for Staten Island for seven years before newly elected Mayor David Dinkins called for a halt to all construction in 1990, and this homeport could be scrapped also. Other citizens' campaigns have exposed grievous safety violations in nuclear weapons plants; several have been forced to shut down as a result. Demands for major cuts in military spending have contributed to these cutbacks. Military budget cuts and the cry in Congress for greater "burdensharing" by U.S. allies in Europe and the Pacific have also limited the Pentagon's ability to "buy off" nations which host U.S. bases with promises of huge amounts of military and economic aid.

This is significant because Washington is or will soon be negotiating with several countries (the Philippines, Oman, Kenya, Morocco, Turkey, and Portugal) to renew military basing agreements. The United States may also seek to extend indefinitely its massive military presence in the Persian Gulf. Pressures for major changes in U.S. military policies have been created by the end of the Cold War, the birth of a new political, military, and economic order in Europe and the Soviet Union, the rise of Europe, Japan, and other regional powers, the increasing importance of economic over military power, and the serious strains within the U.S. economy. With public pressure against U.S. bases growing in many nations, we have an important opportunity to dismantle this worldwide network of military control and to get U.S. troops out of other countries.

While the brunt of this struggle is likely to be born by people in the nations which host U.S. bases and facilities, there is much to be done at home as well. We must resist attempts by national security elites to define and carry out new missions for our armed forces. With the Soviet Union no longer qualifying as "The Enemy," these leaders are eagerly casting about for new enemies to serve as justification for continuing the huge military-industrial complex. Recalcitrant third world countries are inviting targets for further intervention through "low-intensity conflicts." Attempts to militarize the "drug war" and introduce U.S. military "advisers" and hired mercenaries into Peru and other Andean nations are already underway. As this book goes to press, however, it is the situation in the Persian Gulf which is most alarming. The United States was finally able to win permission from Saudi Arabia to deploy ground forces in the region in response to the Iraqi invasion and occupation of Kuwait. War could erupt at any time. We believe that U.S. forces should be withdrawn and replaced by a much smaller United Nations peace-keeping force; Iraq, of course, should withdraw from Kuwait as well.

Enough is enough. All have paid a terrible price for the past decades of war and violence. But there is hope for a better future. The world is changing, and public opinion in the United States is changing with it. Many people have turned against the profligate military spending of the Reagan years and appear ready to accept a major shift in the use of our resources to meet human and domestic needs. The time to act is now, to move in radical new directions that offer a promise of life, not death, that knit communities together rather than tear them apart, that preserve the creation rather than destroying it.

Notes

1. Richard Barnet, "Four Pillars," *The New Yorker,* 17 November 1987.

2. Michael Klare, "Wars in the 1990's: Growing Firepower in the Third World," *The Bulletin of the Atomic Scientists,* May 1990, 9-13.

3. The Independent Commission on Disarmament and Security Issues, Olof Palme, chair, *Common Security: A Blueprint for Survival* (New York: Simon and Schuster, 1982).

4. *Discriminate Deterrence,* Report of The Commission on Integrated Long-Term Strategy (Washington, D.C.: U.S. Government Printing Office, 1988), 10.

5. Ibid., 14.

6. Maria Socorro Diokno, letter written for AFSC's "Voices of Hope and Anger" speaking tour, April 1989.

7. The Institute for Defense and Disarmament Studies, 2001 Beacon Street, Brookline, Massachusetts, 02146, publishes excellent materials on non-offensive defense. See also Harry B. Hollins, Averill L. Powers and Mark Sommer, *The Conquest of War* (Boulder, CO: Westview Press, 1989).

8. National Security Strategy of the United States, The White House, 1990, 23.

9. See American Friends Service Committee, *In Place of War* (New York: Grossman Publishers, 1967); Anders Boserup and Andrew Mack, *War Without Weapons: Non-Violence in National Defense* (New York: Schocken, 1975); Adam Roberts, ed., *Civilian Resistance as a National Defense* (Harrisburg, PA: Stackpole Books, 1968); Gene Sharp, *Making Europe Unconquerable: The Potential of Civilian-Based Deterrence and Defense* (New York: Ballinger, 1985).

10. The Center for Economic Conversion, 222C View St., Mountain View, California, 94041, promotes planning for conversion of U.S. military bases and industries. Seymour Melman and Lloyd Dumas have both published important books and articles on this subject which are accessible to the non-specialist reader. They have both been involved in establishing The National Commission for Economic Conversion and Disarmament, P.O. Box 15025, Washington, DC, 20003, which prepares materials on conversion.

11. Lilo Klug, letter written for AFSC's "Voices of Hope and Anger" speaking tour, April 1989.

About the Contributors

Mariano Aguirre is Coordinator of the Centro de Investigacion para la Paz (CIP), Madrid, and fellow of the Transnational Institute, Amsterdam.

Walden Bello is a senior analyst specializing in Pacific and Philippine affairs at the Institute for Food and Development Policy. He has co-authored *American Lake: The Nuclear Peril in the Pacific*, *U.S.-Sponsored Low-Intensity Conflict in the Philippines*, and *Development Debacle: The World Bank in the Philippines*.

Bruce Birchard is national coordinator of the Disarmament Program of the American Friends Service Committee. He has worked for peace and justice organizations since 1974 and has published many articles on peace issues. He is a member of the Religious Society of Friends (Quakers) and has served since 1984 on the National Board of what is now Sane/Freeze: Campaign for Global Security.

Aurora Camacho de Schmidt is a Mexican citizen who resides in the United States and works as a staff writer for the American Friends Service Committee.

Yarrow Cleaves serves on the Peace Commission for the city of Cambridge, Massachusetts and is involved with the Interhelp Network. She works on developing international links to support grassroots resistance to U.S. foreign bases.

Ben Cramer is a journalist based in Paris.

Denis F. Doyon is national coordinator of the American Friends Service Committee's Middle East Peace Education Program.

Cynthia Enloe is the author of *Bananas, Beaches & Bases: Making Feminist Sense of International Politics*, and *Does Khaki Become You? The Militarization of Women's Lives*. She is the head of the Government Department at Clark University.

Joseph Gerson is the Peace Education Secretary of the American Friends Service Committee in New England. He edited *The Deadly Connection: Nuclear War & U.S. Intervention,* and led the campaign to prevent the transformation of Boston Harbor into a homeport for the Battleship Iowa Task Force. He has worked closely with justice and peace activists in the Middle East, Europe, and the Asia/Pacific region.

Eva Gold is an American Friends Service Committee staff member who has studied and written about U.S. policy in Central America throughout the 1980s. She has made numerous trips to the region.

Eduardo Gonzalez served as an economic writer for the American Friends Service Committee. He has a Ph.D in public policy from the Wharton School of the University of Pennsylvania. In the early 1980s, he was a student activist in the Philippines and editor of the *Philippine Collegian.*

Diana Johnstone has served as the European editor of *In These Times* and took leave to work for the Greens in the European Parliament. She is the author of *The Politics of Euromissiles.*

Mary Day Kent lived in Panama in the early 1960s and attended Balboa Junior High School in the Canal Zone. She has since lived and worked in many other Latin American countries. She is the coordinator for the International Classroom of the University Museum of Archeology and Anthropology at the University of Pennsylvania.

Laura Simich worked with Mobilization for Survival, helping to organize opposition to the homeporting of the Battleship Iowa Task Force and its nuclear weapons in New York City.

Paul Walker is a national security analyst and co-director of the Institute for Peace and International Security in Cambridge, Massachusetts.

Christine Wing was co-coordinator of the American Friends Service Committee's National Disarmament program from 1984 to 1989. She is currently a doctoral candidate at Princeton University.

Bibliography

Arkin, William, and Richard Fieldhouse. *Nuclear Battlefields: Global Links in the Arms Race.* (Cambridge, MA: Ballinger, 1985).

Ball, Desmond. *A Suitable Piece of Real Estate: American Installations in Australia.* (Sidney, Australia: Des Ball, Hale & Iremonger, 1980).

Bamford, James. *The Puzzle Palace.* (Boston, MA: Houghton Mifflin, 1982).

Barnett, Richard J. *The Alliance: America-Europe-Japan: Makers of the Postwar World.* (New York: Simon and Schuster, 1983).

Campbell, Duncan, and Michael Joseph. *The Unsinkable Aircraft Carrier: American Military Power in Britain.* (London, 1984).

The Center for Defense Information. *The Global Network of United States Military Bases.* (Washington, D.C. , 1989).

CND. *Over Here: U.S. Military Bases in Britain.* (London, forthcoming).

Coletta, Paolo E., ed. *United States Navy and Marine Corps Bases Overseas.* (Westport, CT: Greenwood Press, 1985).

Cottrell, Alvin J., and Thomas H. Moorer. *U.S. Overseas Bases: Problems of Projecting American Military Power Abroad.* (Washington, D.C.: Georgetown University, Center for Strategic and International Studies, 1977).

Danielsson, Bengt, and Marie-Thérèse Danielsson. *Poisoned Reign: French Nuclear Colonialism in the Pacific.* (Penguin Books, 1986).

Duke, Simon. *U.S. Defence Bases in the United Kingdom: A Matter for Joint Decision?* (London: Macmillan, 1987).

Duke, Simon. *United States Military Forces and Installations in Europe.* (London: Oxford University Press, 1989).

Enloe, Cynthia. *Bananas, Beaches & Bases: Making Feminist Sense of International Politics.* (Berkeley: University of California Press, 1989).

Enloe, Cynthia. *Does Khaki Become You? The Militarization of Women's Lives.* (Boston: South End Press, 1983).

Gerson, Joseph, ed. *The Deadly Connection: Nuclear War & U.S. Intervention.* (Philadelphia, PA: New Society Publishers, 1986).

Greene, Fred. *Stresses in U.S.-Japanese Security Relations.* (Washington, D.C.: The Brookings Institution, 1975).

Harkavy, Robert E. *Bases Abroad: The Global Foreign Military Presence.* (London: Oxford University Press, 1989).

Harkavy, Robert E. *Great Power Competition for Overseas Bases: The Geopolitics of Access Diplomacy.* (New York: Pergamon Press, 1982).

Hayes, Peter, Lyuba Zarsky, and Walden Bello. *American Lake: Nuclear Peril in the Pacific.* (New York: Penguin Books, 1986).

Kupchan, Charles A. *The Persian Gulf and the West: The Dilemmas of Security.* (Boston, MA: Allen and Unwin, 1987).

Olsen, Edward A. *U.S.-Japan Strategic Reciprocity: A Neo-Internationalist View.* (Stanford, CA: Hoover Institute Press, 1985).

Schirmer, Daniel B. *Republic or Empire: American Resistance to the Philippine War.* (Cambridge, MA: Schenkman Books, 1972).

Simbulan, Roland G. *The Bases of Our Insecurity.* (Manila: BALAI Fellowship, Inc., 1985).

Spaven, Malcom. *Fortress Scotland: A Guide to the Military Presence.* (London: Pluto Press, 1983).

Sullivan, John, and Roberta Foss, eds. *Two Koreas—One Future?* (Lanham, MD: University Press of America, 1987).

Szulc, Tad. *The Bombs of Palomares.* (New York: Viking Press, 1967).

Thompson, E.P. *Mad Dogs: The U.S. Raids on Libya.* (London: Pluto Press, 1986).

U.S. House of Representatives. *Interim Report of the Defense Burdensharing Panel of the Committee on Armed Services., One Hundredth Congress, Second Session. August 1988.*

Williams, William Appleman. *The Tragedy of American Diplomacy.* (New York: Delta Books, 1951).

INDEX

About South End Press

South End Press is a nonprofit, collectively run book publisher with over 150 titles in print. Since our founding in 1977, we have tried to meet the needs of readers who are exploring, or are already committed to, the politics of radical social change.

Our goal is to publish books that encourage critical thinking and constructive action on the key political, cultural, social, economic, and ecological issues shaping life in the United States and in the world. In this way, we hope to give expression to a wide diversity of democratic social movements and to provide an alternative to the products of corporate publishing.

If you would like a free catalog of South End Press books or information about our membership program—which offers two free books and a 40% discount on all titles—please write us at South End Press, 116 Saint Botolph Street, Boston, MA 02115.

Other titles of interest from South End Press:

The U.S. Invasion of Panama: The Truth Behind 'Operation Just Cause'
Prepared by the Independent Commission of Inquiry on the U.S. Invasion of Panama

Freedom Under Fire: U.S. Civil Liberties in Times of War
Michael Linfield, with an introduction by Ramsey Clark

Walking to the Edge: Essays of Resistance
Margaret Randall

The Praetorian Guard: The U.S. in the New International Security State
John Stockwell